OUT IN INNER SPACE

OUT IN INNER SPACE

A Psychoanalyst Explores the New Therapies

BY DR. STEPHEN A. APPELBAUM

1979

Anchor Press/Doubleday, Garden City, New York

Library of Congress Cataloging in Publication Data

Appelbaum, Stephen A
Out in inner space.

Includes index.
1. Psychotherapy. 2. Group relations training.
I. Title.
RC480.A66 158
ISBN: 0-385-14478-4
Library of Congress Catalog Card Number: 78-69651

PRINTED IN THE UNITED STATES OF AMERICA

Acknowledgments

Among her other attributes, my wife, Dr. Ann Appelbaum, is a marvelous editor: linguistically skilled, clear-thinking, and knowledgeable. She polished, and sometimes reshaped, my writing and thinking in this book, as she has with many other publications of mine and others. This time, she not only edited but herself lived through many of the experiences described. She participated in some of the experiments firsthand, and in all of them through accommodating to the demands they posed on what used to be our less hectic, more predictable life.

Toward the beginning of my twenty-one years at The Menninger Foundation, Dr. Martin Mayman, who was responsible for my going there in the first place, mentioned how difficult it was to find a colleague able and willing to edit one's work seriously. I was to remember this remark with poignancy when he edited this book in an early draft, giving me all the benefit of his brilliance, perceptiveness, and friendship.

To enter Dr. Karl Menninger's office is to wade through an ever-changing tangle of books, all of which he seems to have read. One of the drafts of this book fell under his critical scanning eye; it and I emerged enriched by the experience, as is usual when Doctor Karl gives a manuscript the benefit of his editing and wisdom.

Dr. Roy Menninger encouraged this study along before I even knew that it was to be a study, let alone a book, and supported it until help came in the form of The Spencer Foundation. That help was organized and administered by Dr. Phillip Woollcott, the then director of the Department of Education at The Menninger Foundation.

Jacqueline Onassis was the first person outside my professional circle to read this manuscript, when it was about half written. With staunch aid, advice, and warm encouragement, she helped me bring it to completion and publication.

Others who have critically and helpfully read parts of the manuscript are Drs. Meredith Titus-Maxfield, Fred Shectman, and Sydney Smith.

A note of gratitude also to those members of the alternative therapies who graciously welcomed this alien visitor, and educated him.

Contents

Introduction, by George Leonard ix

PART ONE New World A-comin'

1 *California, Etc., Here I Come* 3
2 *A String of Perls* 36
3 *The Human Potential Movement* 44
4 *A Tale of Two Worlds* 55
5 *The Meeting Game* 76
6 *More Than Skin Deep* 110
7 *The Twain Shall Meet* 124
8 *And a Potential for Criticism* 136

PART TWO What Is That Below Your Head?

9 *Bodies Beautiful, and Healthy—Massage, Rolfing, Patterning* 145
10 *Use What You Have, Correctly—the Alexander Technique* 169
11 *One Part Interpretation, One Part Energy Release—Bioenergetics* 178

PART THREE Fast Mood Chains

12 *Latin for "It Is"*—Est 195
13 *From Laredo to the Planet with Betterment—Silva Mind Control* 238

PART FOUR Go East, Young Robot

14 *Climbing the Himalaya in Chicago—Yoga* 267
15 *The Electric Razor's Edge—Transcendental Meditation* 289

PART FIVE Dusting off the New Medicine

16 *Medicine Without Medicine—Alternative Medicine* 307
17 *The Will to Have Cancer and What to Do About It* 334
18 *Further Afield with Cancer—Diet and Other Alternatives* 373
19 *Are You Being Taken by What You Take In?* 401

PART SIX Passing Through Customs

20 *What to Do? What to Do?—Conclusions and Beginnings* 417
21 *A Station Stop Named Ending* 469

Epilogue 473

Appendix 475

Index 511

Introduction
by George Leonard

All through the fall of 1964, I crisscrossed the United States interviewing psychologists, psychiatrists, philosophers, brain researchers—anyone I could think of who might offer me expert opinion on the limits of human potential. At Harvard I talked with B. F. Skinner, for seven non-stop hours, about people and pigeons and incredible feats of learning. Not long after that, I found myself dodging a mouthful of sea water propelled at John Lilly by a discontented dolphin at his institute in Coral Gables, Florida. Dr. Lilly hadn't succeeded in talking with his dolphins but had plenty to say to me about the glories of human consciousness. I spent several days at an experimental elementary school at the University of Washington in Seattle, where Sidney Bijou and his colleagues were coaxing remarkable behavior even from those children classified as "autistic." At UCLA's Brain Research Institute, Ross Adey showed me evidence of previously unknown waves deep within the brain that suggested practically infinite human creative capacity. Farther south, at the Western Behavioral Sciences Institute, in La Jolla, I talked at length with Carl Rogers, whose belief in the indomitable human capacity for positive growth was creating a revolution in psychotherapy. My experts were a diverse lot. They often differed with one another on method and theory. But on one thing they were all agreed: the average human being uses only a tiny fraction of his or her real abilities.

I was on the trail of what I hoped would be the biggest and most important story of my career at *Look* magazine. I could see it running in two successive issues, maybe three, and I had no doubts about what it would be called. The title was, simply, "The Human Potential."

As was the custom at *Look* in those days, I had been given practically unlimited time and resources to do the job. My travels continued; I kept count of the number of interviews. By February of 1965, I had completed thirty-seven, and it seemed about time to give my Air Travel Card a rest and get down to the typewriter in earnest. But it was the unplanned, thirty-eighth interview, the very last one, that was to have a decisive effect on my life and in some small way help shape the movement about which this book is written.

By that time, several people had mentioned a rather mysterious young man named Michael Murphy, who ran a seemingly unclassifiable institute on the wild Big Sur coast of central California. I was told that Murphy, like the hero of Maugham's *The Razor's Edge*, had gone to India seeking enlightenment, had lived for eighteen months at the Aurobindo Ashram in Pondicherry, and had continued meditating eight to ten hours a day after his return to the United States. The institute, named Esalen for the coast Indian tribe that once had inhabited the site, was supposedly a forum for new ideas, especially those that combined the wisdom of East and West. I heard that Esalen's first brochure flew under the title of a series of 1961 lectures by Aldous Huxley: "Human Potentialities."

Despite the seeming convergence of purpose and even terminology ("human potential" was not a common term in those days), I didn't seek a meeting with Murphy; his operation seemed too problematical. Anyway, I already had more interviews than I could handle. Then, one day, I went to see a San Francisco brain researcher, a woman whose judgment I trusted, to check facts on the central nervous system. She read some of my notes and preliminary drafts, looked up at me with eyes sparkling, and told me quite firmly that I *had* to meet Mike Murphy with no further delay. "He's in town today, and it just happens he's having dinner at my house—and you're coming too; period."

The dinner was magical. Murphy's knowledge of Eastern philosophy was encyclopedic, and he talked about it as if it were a delicious tale of suspense and adventure. He had a strong sense of history and a compelling vision of the future. Nor was Murphy the kind of guru-seeker you can sometimes spot by the vague look in their eyes and the smug tilt of their chins. This seeker was on a decidedly American *sadhana*. You could easily see him in a warm-up suit, never in a flowing white robe. "In addition to his other gifts," Calvin Tomkins was to write in a 1976 *New Yorker* profile, "Murphy is endowed with a warm, responsive nature, extravagant good looks, and a wild Irish charm."

After dinner, we drove to my house and continued talking for hours. The meeting of minds, of visions, was extraordinary, with each of us bringing just what was needed in the way of background knowledge to dovetail with that of the other. While Murphy had been studying Eastern philosophy and humanistic psychology, I had been studying social and political movements in the United States: changes in family life and sexual patterns, educational reform, the rise of political extremism, the problems of the inner city and, more than anything else, the explosive problems and the hopeful portents around the matter of race.

We met at a vivid moment in the nation's history. Lyndon Johnson, hot off a landslide victory over Barry Goldwater, was pushing an idealistic civil rights bill and an ambitious War on Poverty. John Kennedy was dead, but the nightmare of future assassinations was unimaginable. Vietnam was still distant. Watergate was only a word. And all across the nation, there was the ferment of hope, of changed consciousness. Social movements proliferated: sexual liberation, the Free Speech Movement out of Berkeley, a new awareness of the rights of Chicanos and American Indians.

Standing over all of this like a beacon was the civil rights movement led by Martin Luther King, Jr. As a native Southerner, I knew how deep and wide the roots of racial prejudice reached. We southern whites were segregated, not just from our black brothers and sisters but from the national and international community, from the riches of our own Western culture, from intimacy with members of our own race, from our own bodies, our own selves. I saw Martin Luther King as working for whites as well as blacks, for my friends, my family, for me. If King and his lieutenants could pull this off, could somehow change the American heart and mind, then what would not be possible?

In the spirit of those times, it was natural to think in terms of "movements." Just as the civil rights movement would break down the barriers between the races, and thus other barriers, a human potential movement would help break down the barriers between mind and body, between Eastern wisdom and Western action, between individual and society, and thus between the limited self and the potential self. I don't think we used the term "human potential" in conjunction with the word "movement" during our first meeting, but it began popping up—casually, half humorously—very soon in the many meetings that followed.

Murphy and I quickly became close friends, then colleagues. On any given weekend during the two years that followed our first meeting, you might find me and my wife at Esalen or Mike Murphy (who was then unmarried) at our house at San Francisco. I became a member of the Esalen board, then a vice-president, serving without pay and also donating my time for the seminars on social and educational reform that I led. We planned a long-term Esalen residential program. We met with others to explore ideas and theories of the human potential; it was inevitable, we thought, that the techniques and insights of this new movement would be applied to the larger society—in education, race relations, city planning, politics, counseling, health care, and the like.

As the pace quickened, we thought up lists of scholars to ask to Esalen. Murphy fired off enthusiastic invitations to various eminent persons; almost to a person, they accepted. During the fall of 1965, for example, Esalen seminars were led by Rollo May, Bishop James A. Pike, Alan Watts, Gardner Murphy, Carl Rogers, Maurice Friedman, B. F. Skinner, Frank Barron, Virginia Satir, J. B. Rhine, and S. I. Hayakawa, among others.

It was a heady time. Will Schutz and Fritz Perls came to live at Esalen. New methods proliferated. The Esalen lodge became a carnival of innovation; you had to talk without taking a breath to have your idea heard above the general clamor. In 1967, the institute opened a branch in San Francisco to take on urban problems. I joined forces with the distinguished black psychiatrist Price Cobbs to lead marathon interracial confrontations. Mike Murphy moved to the city. Best yet—oh, glorious, golden days of grace!—all this happened pretty much out of the public eye.

Then came the media—the television and radio reports, the magazine articles, the books—and we were faced with the contradictions, the paradoxes, and the heartaches that inevitably accompany any serious challenge to cultural homeostasis. In the fall of 1967, a fairly objective article about Esalen appeared in the Education section of *Time*, and there was a UPI feature pegged on Esalen's move to San Francisco. But it remained for a remarkable piece of writing in the December 31, 1967, issue of the New York *Times Sunday Magazine* to open the floodgates.

I had learned by then that much of the publishing world used a very simple method of certification and reality testing: Until something appeared in the New York *Times*, you couldn't be sure it was real. When something appeared in a *favorable* light in the *Times*, you could bet it was not only real but worthy of further coverage. I knew of *Look* writers who schemed to have the *Times* report on marginal subjects that they wanted to get into *Look*. The *Times* clipping (ipse dixit) would be attached to their subsequent story queries to the editorial board.

So here we had "Joy Is the Prize," by Leo Litwak, telling of the author's personal experience in a five-day Will Schutz encounter group and speculating on the Esalen vision. The article had the requisite air of initial skepticism and closing irony but was generally positive. Not only that, it just happened to be one of the best magazine articles ever written, cited by expert panels on journalistic excellence, anthologized more than a dozen times. Within days of its publication, as the new year of 1968 began, editors all over New York were being bombarded with queries about doing a story, a show, a book on this strange place on the California coast and the "movement" that it portended.

Observing the media blitz of 1968–70 from afar, cynics might have been tempted to speculate that Esalen had a very busy if not very wise press agent. If so, they would have been quite mistaken. The Esalen policy on media coverage has been consistent from the beginning: Never absolutely refuse coverage; the workings of a free society require the free flow of information. When the reporters do come, be candid and co-operative. Always, however, discourage coverage, delay it, consider every day without it blessed and happy.

The trouble is, so much reporting consists of playing variations on familiar themes, finding old categories in which to fit new material. But here was something that refused categorization. Should an Esalen piece appear in the Education section? Or should it be in Religion, Behavior, Medicine, Life Style? Actually, Esalen has appeared in all these sections of our major news magazines, and has failed to fit comfortably in any of them.

Some reporters made an honest effort to understand Esalen and the human potential movement on its own terms. But even here they labored under a misconception. Since the *Times* article happened to have been about an encounter group, reporters continued for years to assume that human potential and encounter were synonymous. The fact is that encounter groups have made up only about 15 per cent of Esalen's programs.

Other reporters, as might have been expected, masked their bewilderment with cynicism. Then there was the opposite extreme: those who were entirely swept away. The true believers, writing without perspective or a dialectical sense, helped create false expectations that led to eventual disillusionment.

What was wanting was a firm place on which to stand, a strong yet not rigid viewpoint from which to gain perspective on developments that have the power to threaten, to seduce, or simply to unsettle. Which brings us at last (with thanks for your patience) to the present volume, the subject of this introduction.

But first, one piece of unfinished business: My article on the human potential—it grew to more than twenty thousand words—never ran in *Look*. It was "too long, too theoretical." Blocked off from that channel of expression, it spread out in many other directions. Had the article simply been published in the ordinary course of things, I cannot imagine that my own life would have been so decisively changed.

It is ironic that the most complete, most informative and well-balanced book ever to be written about the supposedly anti-Freudian human potential movement is the work of a psychoanalyst, a dedicated Freudian. The book examines the therapeutic value of techniques developed in a movement whose leaders frequently disavow therapeutic intent.

Stephen A. Appelbaum is truly an Odysseus. His journey takes him through stranger psychic and physical adventures than any purely geographical travel could provide; he moves from one dizzying and exposed outlook to another. Nor is Appelbaum a mere voyeur. When a volunteer is called for to take the gestalt "hot seat," to strip down to his shorts and submit to an Alexander demonstration, to be wired for biofeedback, to take a crash course in autogenic training, to be manipulated (and injured) by a bioenergetic practitioner, to be Rolfed, structurally patterned, massaged, or acupunctured, it is Appelbaum's hand that shoots up.

This psychoanalyst possesses not only the adventurous spirit of Odysseus but also the patience of Job. All in the line of duty, he goes through *est,* then volunteers to assist during an *est* training at Leavenworth Federal Penitentiary. From there, he proceeds to Silva Mind Control training, during which he temporarily becomes a psychic. He carries his sleeping bag to a yoga retreat to spend fourteen-hour days in meditation and other difficult Eastern practices. He brings fruit, flowers, and money to a TM practitioner and gets his mantra. In several cases, after putting his body and spirit on the line for one "alternative therapy" or another, he completes the cycle by making a formal address or writing a scholarly paper for the therapy in question.

Appelbaum is touched, moved, shaken by what he experiences. He is intellectually stimulated. His own analytical work is influenced. *Yet he never loses his bearings.* He remains true to his training. He continues to "feel loyalty to the system of thought and profession that have nourished and rewarded me." Because Appelbaum has a firm place on which to stand, we do too. We find that we can share his experiences without reservation. We learn that we can trust his judgment as to what is excessive and what is fundamental, what is silly and what is profound, what might prove dangerous and what might be the salvation of our culture in the diverse practices and theories that have come to be lumped under the term "human potential movement."

There have been previous books on the subject, notably Rasa Gustaitis' *Turning On* (1969), Jane Howard's *Please Touch* (1970), and the encyclopedic 1975 Book of the Month Club choice *Powers of Mind,* by Adam Smith. Despite the authors' obvious good intentions, these books have always left me feeling somewhat dissatisfied. I've always wondered why writers on this particular subject have considered it necessary to force their language, to crack wise, to make up new terms—as if their readers will desert them unless presented with something unbearably novel, clever, or cute in every other sentence. Jane Howard, for example, can find a term such as "Bod Biz" (meaning "body business," I guess), then use it at a rate of several times per page, noting various "Bod Biz persons" and discussing the "hagiography of Bod Biz." The net result of the hyped-up language is to distance the writer—and thus the reader—from the material written about.

Out of the purpose comes the product. Howard, a staff writer for *Life* magazine at the time, tells us that she picked this particular topic for a book "not because of any infatuation with the 'behavioral sciences' but, rather, because the movement is a curiosity." Rasa Gustaitis, a free lance, informs us that "in the spring of 1967 it was time for another trip. So I looked for a writing assignment that would take me out of New York and to some scenic spot for a couple of the hot months. Nothing interesting came to mind until I heard of Esalen Institute in California." The case of Adam Smith (nom de plume for the humorous and insightful economic analyst Jerry Goodman) is somewhat more complex, but he tells us that he originally planned simply to take time off from his busy schedule to do some research on health, figuring to return unscathed to full membership in the business community.

In all three cases, the material ended up affecting the writer at a deeper level than might have been anticipated. Still, it must be said that they all embarked on their projects with no purpose really more fundamental than "to write a book." As for point of view, Howard and Gustaitis approached the subject with the hard-eyed, value-free curiosity of the professional magazine writer, and Jerry Goodman with the wise-guy Wall Street persona of his "Adam

Smith." Not even the most coruscating wordplay can make up for such inadequacies of purpose and viewpoint.

The use of hyped-up language in writing about the human potential movement seems to have become a convention, and even Appelbaum isn't entirely immune; the convention creeps into his chapter and section titles ("Fast Mood Chain," "The Electric Razor's Edge"). But don't despair; that's the end of it. Appelbaum gets right down to his purpose, which is to experience, understand, and evaluate the practices that have emerged from the human potential movement. During most of his odyssey, Appelbaum was on assignment for The Menninger Foundation, of Topeka, Kansas, where he had worked since 1957 and at which he held several senior posts. He reported directly to Roy Menninger, president of the foundation, who wanted to know what was to be learned from the alternative therapies. We are fortunate that Appelbaum decided to transform the findings of a professional investigation into a more popular form.

We are also fortunate, I think, that this report originated in the American Midwest, rather than on one of the coasts. There is a wide misconception, fostered by magazines and television networks, that the human potential movement is concentrated almost entirely in California, with a few outposts on the East Coast. Actually, the movement is a nationwide phenomenon, with great strength in the Midwest and Southwest. It is to those regions, in fact, that I now most often travel (from California) to present my own energy-awareness work. Stephen A. Appelbaum ventures forth to the East and the West, but his home is the American heartland, and you might be surprised to learn what is going on in Lincoln, Nebraska, and Kansas City and Dallas and Laredo.

What I have learned is that the average high school

counselor in Iowa knows more about the aims of the human potential movement and the uses of its techniques than does the average New York editor. The latter apparently can be taken in by one faddish article that makes this movement the scapegoat for the self-indulgence that is actually necessary for the survival of our present misguided economic system. The best of the human potential theorists are actually dedicated to the transformation of this system into something more humane and less devoted to selfish consumerism.

There are undoubtedly some people who participate in human potential activities for purely selfish reasons, but in my experience their number is relatively small. When several hundred Iowa high school counselors attend sessions on energy awareness and gestalt, it is not to satisfy some self-indulgent whim. They are there to improve their counseling.

The midwestern roots of this volume might also serve to remind us how very American the human potential movement is, despite its sometimes exotic trappings. The columnist and historian Max Lerner has proposed a compelling genealogy that takes it directly back to the Founding Fathers. In its optimism and pragmatism, its holism and transpersonal concern, its belief in human potential, this movement bears a clear family resemblance to the Jeffersonian circle. It is American, too, in its diversity, its swift and sprawling growth, its lack of elegance and polish.

Looking out on the vast landscape of what has come to be called the human potential movement, as a matter of fact, Mike Murphy and I have sometimes wished we could retire the term. We strongly disagree with certain extreme statements offered as human potential doctrine. We are appalled by the practices of some organizations that fly the human potential flag. We'd feel more comfortable if the whole thing had turned out to be a bit neater, more respectable.

We also realize that real change doesn't work that way. Any significant transformation attracts an embarrassing fringe element and draws the fire of the established order. Any true reform involves confusion and discomfort. It's probably a small price to pay for what has been achieved.

Enough time has passed for us to realize that the human potential movement is not merely a fad, nor is it the creation of any one organization or special interest group. It has arisen, rather, as an adaptive response to the challenges now facing this most advanced of the advanced industrial nations. Nor would the disappearance of Esalen or *est* or Rolfing or gestalt or energy awareness prevent the long-term unfoldment of the historical trend from which the movement emerged.

Suffice it to list some of the behavioral and moral implications of what might be called the human potential world view: a sense of *communitas* along with the acceptance of increased personal responsibility; a de-emphasis on competing and winning, along with a re-emphasis on participating and experiencing; a move from aggression, toward gentleness and enjoyment, from dominance of nature to blending with nature, from exponential growth in production and consumption to a more moderate, more ecological standard of living, along with a more equitable distribution of goods and services; a further move toward a holistic approach to all of life, toward the realization of human potential in body, mind, and spirit. We might note that the adventures offered and the life style implied here do not involve the burning of great amounts of fuel, the depletion of natural resources, the pollution of the biosphere, or the exploitation of nature and other people.

If these opinions of mine are only partially true, it is a

matter of some importance that we be well informed on the subject. If we need information, we need perspective even more. Here at last we have found an informant who can help us make sense out of what previously has only bewildered: a dedicated Freudian who, like Freud himself, is also delightfully open-minded, speculative, and even adventurous. Being in good hands, we may proceed.

PART ONE

New World A-comin'

1

California, Etc., Here I Come

For me at least, the airlines are missing a good bet. They advertise their food, which is rotten, their on-time schedules, which are only sporadically met, their comfort, which for my six-foot-one-inch frame is laughable. They ought to advertise instead what a wonderful place airplanes are to commune with one's self—no telephones, mail, appointment calendar; for me, what I have left behind and where I am going temporarily seem not to exist. The steady hum of the engines (often aided by pressure in the ears) feels like a protective blanket, insulating me against other interferences. Up in "outer space" I find ideal circumstances for exploring inner space.

In October 1973, on a flight from Topeka, Kansas, to Los Angeles, California, I had reason enough to be contemplative. To begin with, I asked myself what I was doing there. I was a clinical psychologist and psychoanalyst on the staff of The Menninger Foundation, a Middle Westerner by choice and middle-aged somewhat contrary to choice. I was by training and inclination orthodox in my espousal of psychoanalytic theory, conscientious about applying the rule book of scientific research, materialistic in my philosophy, and a little smug about how right I was with respect to all these matters. And yet there I was winging to Lotus Land to attend a convention on behavior modification, with a couple of days of side trips scheduled in order to look into a few of those funny therapies touted by their adherents as being "alternative" to conventional psychiatry and psychology.

I began to answer my question as to what a nice guy like me was doing on the way to places like that by recalling the mailed flyer announcing the behavior modification convention in Los Angeles and my curiosity about that increasingly popular method of therapy not formally practiced at The Menninger Foundation. But countless other such announcements had passed through my mailbox without causing anything more than a grumble about junk mail. I considered also the role of Dr. Roy Menninger, president of The Menninger Foundation, son of the late Dr. Will Menninger and nephew of Dr. Karl Menninger, who along with *their* father (Dr. Charles Frederick Menninger) were founders of The Menninger Foundation. Through the years, this world-famous center for psychiatric treatment, education, and research has welcomed bearers of news from the world outside smallish Topeka, in the rural center of the country, from Aldous Huxley to Ludwig von Bertalanffy, from Karl Pribram to Margaret Mead. Carrying on a family tradition, Doctor Roy had low-keyedly let it be known to the staff that he was interested in new ideas and experimentation with them. As things turned out he was to arrange financial support for my explorations for a couple of years, until they became supported by the Spencer Foundation, as administered by the Department of Education of The Menninger Foundation. Then he continued to support me emotionally. But at the time of that first plane flight the initiative was mine; I had only a vague impression that Roy would at least approve of what I was doing. I had a matching vague impression that many of my colleagues might not approve, indeed might begin to wonder about me. The Menninger Foundation's innovations have been mostly within the context of traditional psychiatry and psychology, notably psychoanalytic ego psychology. It was just that tradition which had drawn me there in the first place. Other activities at the Foundation—some research projects, training programs, consulting services—existed in a somewhat anomalous position: officially there, geographically there, but not exactly "there" in the sense of being identified with the kind of work for which the Foundation was most famous. While things have changed somewhat, partly as a result of the work reported in this book, for the most part this state of affairs continues. Traditional clinical activities are at the core of the Foundation's work; a creative tension sometimes exists between those activities and departures from them, and sometimes they just run parallel.

One can get a lot of help and sustenance from his colleagues when he is clearly and unequivocally identified with their activities, and I was the comfortable recipient of such support from my psychoanalytic and psychological brethren. I wondered uneasily how any activities outside the mainstream would be received, but as it turned out, such fears were for the most part groundless. Each year, I am invited to teach courses in the alternative therapies at the Menninger School of Psychiatry and the Topeka Institute for Psychoanalysis. The course taught at the latter is possibly the only such formal course taught in any psychoanalytic institute in the world. At the time of that airplane flight my worry had only in part to do with the reality of my colleagues' opinions; rather, it was an expression of my own concern about the breaking of established patterns, my trepidation at setting off into the unknown, not only an unknown of the foreign outer world but the sensed unknown effects of the journey on my inner experience and my way of life.

So a candid answer to the question of what I was doing there had to include an assessment of myself, just as it does now to help the reader estimate how much of what I report observing may have been idiosyncratically colored by the observer.

In October 1973 I was head of psychology in the C. F. Menninger Memorial Hospital, practicing child and adult psychoanalysis and psychotherapy, supervising and teaching psychological testing and psychotherapy, an instructor in the Menninger School of Psychiatry and in the Topeka Institute for Psychoanalysis. I had published several dozens of articles, was finishing a book researching change through psychotherapy, and had been a speaker and teacher at a number of institutions and conventions in this country and abroad. I had been working at The Menninger Foundation for sixteen years, not too much longer than many people feel is just about right to feel accepted according to the local high standards. These external honors and activities were matched by an internal sense of capability. Like a jazz musician who can improvise in any key or a shortstop who can field anything hit near him, I felt comfortable plying my trade—comfortable though not entirely complacent or casual; scientists are forever poised on the edge of an abyss of ignorance, for knowledge, after all, is infinite. But I could at least have toiled in my own vineyard, accepting and building upon relatively stable and unchallenged assumptions and premises about the psychiatric, psychological, and existential nature of man, secure of that place in the passing parade.

And maybe the prospect of playing out the string in unchallenged comfort was part of the trouble. My astrologically informed friends, met in my travels through the human potential movement, in which astrology has a lively following, tell me that as a Sagittarius I am inclined toward restless travels. A friend who believes in reincarnation, another frequent belief in alternative therapy circles, told me that in my past life as an aristocrat just before the French Revolution I was quite a gadabout, a rake constantly on the move. Be that as it may, I do seem to be one of those people who require constant challenge, who can hardly finish one task before going on to the next, for whom events quickly become commonplace, thus necessitating something promisingly new. Intellectually, also, each new finding or observation almost simultaneously raises new questions. Such a trait makes for good research and poor leisure.

People who require constant challenges may be viewed as intrepid and creative pioneers, which is something of a romantic idealization, but certainly a nice way to view oneself. I suppose in the work reported here I am something of a pioneer, since, as far as I know, no other psychoanalyst has made a study like this one—in which he experienced, as well as learned about, a variety of alternative approaches. Or such people can be viewed as being driven by neurotic engines, a metaphor which, when applied to me, is not entirely unfair. The line between inclinations that can be labeled "neurotic" and those that can be esteemed as adaptive, autonomous, or sublimatory is often hard to discern.

In 1973, to a greater extent than before, I was admitting to awareness various criticisms of my ways of working, some generated by others, some by myself, as I observed the vicissitudes of the interaction between lives and psychoanalytic diagnosis and treatment. I asked myself whether I thought psychotherapy a hundred years from now would be exactly as it is now. If so, I could quit investigating and just try to perfect my skills. If I could not confidently assume that it would be, then I could not simply ply my trade in comfort without trying to contribute to change and improvement. Unless one is either an inveterate rebel or blessed with a remarkable sense of security, one tends to mute criticisms while struggling for internal and external acceptance. One tends, moreover, in the early goings of a therapeutic career to be so taken with hopes and evidences of success as to not be able to give proper due to such clinical work and theoretical understanding as may fall short. But the bearer of the nose once pressed against the plate-glass window can better examine the merchandise after getting inside.

A cliché in the descriptions of conventional psychotherapists who have joined the counterculture and practice alternative therapies is that they are white-bearded satyrs who have seen the error of their ways and discovered Joy and Wisdom. Some of my colleagues have tried to fit me into this stereotype, convinced that this is the only available role once one has stopped devoting oneself exclusively and rigidly to those ways of working and thinking in which one has been trained.

Rather than being disillusioned and hostile to psychoanalytic thinking, I continue to find the validity of psychoanalytic concepts confirmed in daily experience with my patients, my friends, and myself. And, unobjective as it may be, I feel loyalty to the system of thought and profession that have nourished and rewarded me. But such considerations do not diminish the scope of my conclusion that psychoanalysis, and the procedures derived from it, may not yet have achieved the utmost in theoretical elegance or therapeutic efficiency; or that psychoanalytic thinking exhausts the ways of improving our personal lot or our conception of ourselves and the universe.

Some aspects of my personality that encouraged and influenced this study include: 1) a soft-headed, speculative bent and 2) a hard-headed, critical bent. With respect to the first, I still believe in magic, I still imagine that someone has "the answer," I still nourish limitless untrammeled hopes, I still thrill to those speculative leaps that unite the apparently diverse and arch on into the unknown. In this study I relied on those characteristics to help me to be open to ideas and experiences that clashed with my previous experiences and beliefs.

Yet at some point openness becomes gullibility. I was helped to step back, I hope at least in the nick of time, from gullibility to responsibility by the other side of myself. For I also believe that much thinking is merely disguised wish, that logic is a thing of beauty and a joy forever, and that one of the great designs of all time is the pattern constructed from empirical observations connected by inferences and hypotheses, on up through succeeding levels of increasingly abstract theory. At those times when I fail to work at being open-minded, I have a low tolerance for fuzzy thinking, poor logic, and pie in the sky. I ordinarily tend to be skeptical, if not cynical. I believe that things are almost always more complex and problematical than they may at first appear, and that in science, as in life in general, much is promised and little is delivered.

When, in my airborne cocoon, I was not listening for existential echoes, I was trying to prepare myself for what lay ahead—except that I knew precious little about what that might be, about behavior modification or the "side trips." Almost by chance, I had included in my itinerary what was to become my first encounter with the human potential movement. As I was preparing for the trip, an ex-patient of the Center for Feeling Therapy had presented himself for an examination at The Menninger Foundation, and I became curious about the experiences he described. I learned that the center was an offshoot of Arthur Janov's primal therapy, which I knew about mainly through reading unflattering reviews of his books. I called an old friend in Los Angeles for suggestions as to whom I might see to acquaint myself with the new therapies, and that is how my itinerary came to be.

I had experienced my first culture shock in the course of phone calls for appointments with the people my friend had suggested. There was a nonprofessional attitude on the other end of the line, sometimes a bit suspicious, a bit bewildered, unimpressed if not oblivious of The Menninger Foundation, yet laid over with instant sweet friendliness. I was immediately "Steve," which struck me as odd, since I am on "Stephen" terms with myself even at the best of internal times. I was neither to hear the title "Doctor" nor to see a tie (other than my own) during the rest of the professional encounters on this trip, except an occasional one at the behavior modification convention—and behavior therapy is outside the human potential movement.

This informal friendliness should have been comfortable and reassuring, and at times it was; yet it was also unsettling; I wasn't used to it; there seemed no rules to follow, and so how could I know whether what I was doing was right or wrong? (Human potential people would chortle at that one; they would say there are no rights and wrongs in human encounters, and social regulations are simply means of maintaining distance, stifling spontaneity.) I did not know that point of view at the time; mostly I knew the creepy feeling that I was entering a never-never land.

I had tried to prepare myself by reading material from

the Center for Feeling Therapy, Janov's *The Primal Scream*,[1] several articles on psychosynthesis, a couple of texts on behavior modification, and a brochure description of the activities of Esalen, the seminal California camping ground of the human potential movement. The reading was a bit slow, as I kept interrupting it by making huge X marks and exclamation points and penning sarcastic questions and what I thought were trenchant observations. I made a list of issues to discuss with the primal therapy people, finishing it, almost literally, as I stepped from the plane. I remember being particularly surprised in the readings by the emphasis on bodily stimulation, whether by touch, breathing, dance, or swimming, and also by the extreme measures taken to generate feelings. I was less surprised than incensed at the way psychoanalysis was taken to task, based usually on a lack of understanding of what psychoanalysis was about in the first place. Yet I was already becoming beguiled by a whole culture and way of thinking different from my own, finding it hard simply to dismiss it, wondering how it came to be, what sustained it, what it could accomplish, and what it might offer to me as practitioner and person.

Introduction (Mine) to Gestalt Therapy

Eating plastic eggs Benedict in a plastic Ramada Inn in plastic Los Angeles helped lead me to expect that I was to learn about a plastic therapy named gestalt therapy. Gary Yontef, bearded and in sports clothes (these, he said, were his dress-up clothes), immediately realized that we had to start with the ABC's of gestalt therapy. The key word was "awareness," by which Gary* meant a sharply observed and

* A treatise could be, and probably will be, written about the ways people address and refer to one another. In the human potential movement,

experienced understanding of the present moment. To bring about such awareness, gestalt therapists used a variety of techniques, unkindly called by some, gimmicks. These included attention to tone of voice, posture, habits, and muscular tensions. The patient may be consciously involved with what to him are important issues, but he gives away underlying attitudes and feelings in these mannerisms. He may announce that he is going to kill himself, said Gary, to which the therapist might react by calling attention to his fiddling with his ear. Gary considered breathing exercises another especially useful way to expand consciousness, and consequent awareness. He was intent on discriminating gestalt awareness from simply expressing one's feelings, as in encounter group therapy. Evidently the patient was to learn, not just experience. Yet, in the bit of role playing that we fell into, I used what turned out to be a dirty word: "Why?" A "why" question points toward causes, whose articulation lends itself to scientific formulation at a remove from experience and behavior. By contrast, a "how" question focuses attention on observable events, the processes of behavior, what actually occurs in non-inferential terms. The gestalt goal of awareness itself includes large elements of "why," but the tone and direction of gestalt investigation avoids intellectualization, according to Gary. An insight by any other name is an insight, I thought, or was it?

I learned that gestalt work is done individually and in groups. When done individually in offices, it shares some of the structure and rules of conventional psychotherapy.

---

people are invariably called by their first names. In my daily life my decisions as to how to address and refer to people are influenced by age, respect, length of time known, and other, more subtle nuances of relationships. I shall do the same in this book. Inconsistent as it may be, such varied usage will reflect my experience of the person and the context in which the means of address occurs.

In groups, the dynamics and processes of groups, often attended to in traditional group therapy, are for the most part ignored. Rather, people who are "ready" work individually with the therapist, while the rest of the members serve as props, a kind of Greek chorus, offering reactions to what they have observed. Gestalt therapy is seen as a never-ending process for patient and for therapist, there being a continuing need for at least refresher experiences.

Arranged by Gary, my next appointment took place on the well-pillowed floor of the home of a gestalt group leader, Bob Martin. Some eight members drifted in, some taking coffee, some introducing themselves to me. I soon learned that I was astride some kind of borderline between being an observer and a participant. I was introduced to the group as a visitor. One person immediately commented on my being dressed in a way that reminded her of her life in New York. Although I told her that I was from Kansas, she continued to identify me as coming from the East Coast. At one point she seemed a bit apologetic about that, so I told her that she was right in her impression that I was at the moment uptight and buttoned-down, even apart from my clothes.

After some chitchat, one woman said that she felt like "working," and took a place opposite the therapist on the floor, the so-called "hot seat." The therapist first worked with her facial expression, at one point butting heads with her to illustrate her tendency to oppose him. For example, when he asked her to make a simple direct statement about each person in the room, she thought she could not do it. When he shifted to another task, she then tried to go back to the previous task. In this context there was a bit of loose talk by therapist and patient about "castration." When the therapist commented on her eyes, they filled with tears. She cried more and more as she related her feelings to the loss of her father. She described her relationship with him in eloquent, idyllic terms. She said how much she missed her father, how bleak life had been when he died leaving her to fend for herself, and she was tired of looking after herself. The therapist invited her to touch hands, first one, then both, upon which she fell into his arms, crying even more piteously as she talked further about her lost father. Finally, she said that she had come to the end of her work for the day. Each of the members then offered their reactions to patient and therapist.

When invited to comment, I said that as an outsider I felt a little awkward commenting on such a moving experience. I did think, however, that it was only half an experience, in that the angry part of the relationship was absent. (I was taking my cues from the seemingly flippant talk about castration and the demonstrated oppositionalism, which I did not think sufficiently came to grips with the angry feelings that seemed to me out of awareness.) I was interrupted by the therapist saying that he thought I was being "analytic," explaining things rather than offering my feelings. He was right. He might also have added that I was cheeky, and that it is poor technique to interpret impulse (anger) without a therapeutic alliance and a sense of the defenses. I then said that my feelings were those of "dismay" and "sadness." I was troubled that she might go on suffering with this lost relationship until she had better learned to hate. In a later, private discussion with the therapist he said that he knew about her anger but considered it background, rather than foreground, and expected it to come out in its own time in bits and pieces. I told him I thought it was ready to be moved along right now and that I was afraid that her sadness was serving to defend against its emergence. We left it at that.

At the beginning of the second of the two hours, the

leader asked someone to act as therapist in his stead, but all seemed reluctant. Finally, one person was encouraged to do so on the proviso that she would act as a bad therapist and someone would act as a bad patient. A great deal of merriment then ensued as each of them said and did what, in gestalt terms, would be the wrong thing. Martin used this exercise to demonstrate that nothing in principle was necessarily good or bad, it all depended upon the situation. Then he was able to help the acting therapist see how she had been responding throughout her life to rules and regulations that were inhibiting her. With the acknowledgment of this, she, too, began to cry.

One reason for this particular exercise, I later found out, was that this was a training group, composed of some therapists licensed by the state, some working for a certificate in the local gestalt institute, along with some just attending for therapeutic benefit to themselves.

As I sat observing them, and at the same time observing myself, I learned, or was experientially reminded, of some aspects of my personality. I believe Bob was correct in calling attention to my slipping from feeling to explaining, and as a result I was put in better touch with my sadness and dismay. I was also put in better touch with my envy of his being in charge of the group and of this patient's well-being. I was made aware of my worry and guilt at possibly having, with my remarks, acted upon my envy to the detriment of the patient. I was relieved that she seemed thoughtful rather than distressed and afterward said she was glad I had commented, and liked my face. (Such remarks, offered freely between human potential people, come across less as seductions than as reflecting openness and candor.)

This first gestalt experience of mine was moving and provocative. I could have gotten so caught up in what I considered technical errors as to have dismissed the rest, and I was tempted to do so. But I could not quite explain away the fact that in a short time people had cried what looked like deeply felt tears, made available to themselves important aspects of their past and present lives, and seemed to believe that they were embarked on a therapeutic path. For me, something clearly important was going on, and I wanted very much to pursue its meaning and possible usefulness. My plans began to take shape, to have a central purpose. I was not to be a curious onlooker at a sideshow; rather, I felt I had to learn about these new approaches at some depth, experience them as part of that learning, compare and contrast them with conventional psychotherapy, and throughout try to evaluate their usefulness. A firsthand study no longer seemed optional.

Feel, Damn You, Feel!—
Primal Therapy and Variations on the Theme

There may have been something in my reading of Arthur Janov's books and the telephone arrangements to visit his primal therapy institute which caused me to make several wrong turns on the way there. I did enjoy, however, my first look at the sign on the building, as I usually do when I first see signs on buildings or names on doors representing people or institutions about which I had previously only read or heard. It probably has something to do with the feeling of dreams coming true, fantasies becoming reality. Anyway, when I entered, I noticed a few glum faces and heard a whimper or two. I later learned that if I had come a bit earlier, before most of the patients had left for their formal sessions, I would have heard a great deal of open, uninhibited crying, even in the waiting rooms.

I soon found myself sitting in a low chair, with Leslie on

a higher one to my right, and Bernie on a higher one to my left. I think we were in Janov's office, to judge from the diplomas impressed on plastic, and a dramatic poster-size picture of him next to the elaborately carved desk. I remember noting that among the carvings were lions' heads. The walls were cushioned, in keeping with what I learned was the necessity for soundproofed rooms so as not to inhibit the bloodcurdlingly loud screams from the depths of the soul, the famous "primal scream."

In response to a what-do-I-want-to-know question, I turned to the notes I had made on the plane and began to ask some questions. Leslie interrupted saying that he wanted to know more about me, what did I want, what was I here for? Evidently they were suspicious that I wanted to be a patient or to bootleg knowledge of primal therapy and become a therapist without being trained by them, or maybe I was just a hostile critic looking for ammunition. All of this despite my letter following up our phone conversation and my *curriculum vitae*, which were right there on the desk. I suppose that when one asserts, as Janov does, that he has "the only cure for neurosis," one can expect enmity, envy, and thievery. But a little benefit of the doubt backed up by a little testing of reality seemed to me to be in order. I also thought that Janov might have at least popped in and said hello, but he was not to be in evidence. As I was to do many times in the succeeding years, I had to try to prevent feelings generated by my interactions with the new therapies from solely determining my evaluations of these therapies. Here, then, is an abstract of primal theory, a theory and therapy that ought to be evaluated in its own right.

All of us carry around great Pain (always printed with a capital "P") which dates from the early years of our life, when parents and society would not let us freely acknowledge our real feelings. We built up a number of false selves that sealed off those feelings and led to symptoms—bodily symptoms, symptoms of feeling empty, compulsive attempts to make up for the loss of feeling, and symptoms that characterize our emotionally isolated society. How we *function* in such a crazy, feelingless world gives no indication of our sickness. How, when, or if we *feel* tells all.

Primal therapists help the patient to go back into the past and lance the boil of dammed-up feelings, the catharsis of which is alleged to be curative (with credit given to Janet, Breuer, and Freud). The procedure begins with a stimulus-deprivation experience. The patient stays in a hotel for a couple of days, without television, reading, people, or other stimulants. Then, for three weeks, for as many consecutive hours as are necessary or as the patient can take, he is helped to reclaim his feelings and their associated memories. The therapist has only this one patient, and is supposed to be on call for him as needed; he never has to interrupt an hour just when the patient is on the way to the discovery of feelings.

A "primal" is something like an LSD flashback, the person being assaulted by memories, feelings, and associated tears from the past. Quite literally the treatment is designed to get tears to flow like pus from a boil; pasts evidently comprise mostly misery. People have major primals, usually during the treatment, and may be "tripped off" to have at least minor ones at any given moment during the treatment and afterward. Following the initial three weeks of individual work, the patient continues for up to eight months in groups of fellow primal patients. This "therapeutic community" provides an atmosphere in which the person can continue to cry and experience primals among sympathetic others. The specific techniques of the therapy are simplicity itself, the therapist mainly pointing the patient toward the past, toward his feelings, toward his Pain, unrelentingly attempting to destroy the false selves, the defenses, which would otherwise inhibit the fullest possible emotional expression of these traumas. Such traumas include birth itself, which primal therapists claim to recover more or less regularly as a memory, especially those births whose complications made them exceptionally traumatic. The array of possibilities for relationships between the patient and therapist is unattended to, if not discouraged; the direction is exclusively to the past Pain. The elegance of secondary-process language, even dreams and symbolism of all kinds, are usually considered as defensive activity against primal experience.

Having worked through his defensive barriers, a primal patient is highly susceptible to all stimulation. For example, he may eschew completely or cut down on alcohol, drugs, coffee, work, or sex whenever these are used for defensive purposes. Small amounts of these provide the same amount of stimulation as larger amounts did previously.

Primal therapists assert, and adduce research that purportedly proves, that pulse rates, temperature, and blood pressure are lowered through primal therapy. These changes occur particularly when the primal experience is at its height, and may continue for some time after the treatment. Since primal therapy was developed only a few years ago, no one can know how long its effects may last. A two-to-three-degree drop in temperature, a twenty-beat-lower pulse rate, and substantially lowered blood pressure become the new norms for the person. Primal therapists suggest that their patients will live longer, and are quite convinced that they get rid of bodily disease through this treatment. Furthermore, not only do autonomic changes occur, as manifested in a better complexion, a better look in the eye, and a better posture and walk, but structural changes occur as well. For example, hands and feet and breasts are said to grow; patients report that they now have to shop for larger-size gloves, shoes, and brassieres. When I was not incredulous at such claims, I was impressed by them. If true, such a treatment was indeed one to be reckoned with. I was shortly to hear that the claims were exaggerated though not necessarily untrue.

Primal therapists consider encounter therapy experiences to be far from adequate, being restricted to the present and of too little intensity. They criticize those approaches which attempt to help the person find more than he ordinarily has within him, to achieve higher degrees of creativity and sublimeness, to say nothing of mystical changes. Rather, they say that we are only what we are; we can achieve no more than to release ourselves in feelings and tears. But if we do that we will have achieved a definitive cure, "the only cure for neurosis." The only cure does not come cheap. A six-to-eight-week course of primal therapy at the time costs sixty-five hundred dollars, or approximately seventy-five dollars per hour.

At Janov's center I was not allowed to view primal sessions, because it was said that my presence might interfere with the therapy. Sometime later, in Topeka, Kansas, of all places, I met some ex-primal patients who afforded me a firsthand look at (at least mini-primal) experiences. Sounds of the human voice as delivered by such patients become vehicles of anguish on the order of Medean climaxes. The unearthly groans, screams, and shouts during primals were totally out of keeping with the character and deportment of these people when they are not having a primal. Opportunities for such emotive experiences are considered so therapeutic that some ex-primal patients build soundproof cubicles in their homes, where they can regularly treat themselves by way of expressing primal feeling. Ordinarily, they have another person who has undergone primal therapy there to assist them. They believe that unless one has gone through primal therapy oneself one cannot fully understand the depth of the experience and thus be empathically supportive.

As Janov acknowledges, Freud, along with Breuer, started it all when he discovered that people could overcome their symptoms by expressing the feeling connected with a forgotten past event. But, according to Janov, Freud simply failed to exploit fully the curative powers of abreaction and catharsis. His interest in exploring the contents of the unconscious, in learning meanings, and in establishing a new psychology led his treatment away from the expression of feeling and into the verbalization of causes accompanied by little or no feelings, according to Janov. Janov has gone back to Freud's therapeutic beginnings, but to the *n*th degree.

But meaning and feeling are not mutually exclusive. Even Janov's primals include meaning; his patients regularly discover the circumstances of early life that produced their primal Pain. Discoveries of meaning in psychoanalysis have all along been understood as being most helpful when suffused with emotion. Janov would likely reply that intensity of feeling achieved in primal therapy is so great as to be almost qualitatively different from that ordinarily achieved in psychoanalysis. Could it be, I wondered, that the comparatively limited range of emotion in psychoanalysis is indeed putting limits to its curative, even exploratory effectiveness.

I wonder, too, if Otto Rank was not on the right track when he tried to exploit and implement Freud's insights into the importance of birth in the development of personality. How many intractable symptoms, for example, resist therapeutic efforts because these efforts fail to come to grips with birth or intrauterine events, which are dealt with only by way of derivatives from later years?

The stimulus deprivation and relentless pressure to experience feelings could plausibly push some people into psychosis, especially those who are precariously close to it at the beginning of therapy. Janov selects his patients according to their letters about themselves, and in this way probably avoids working with many flagrantly disturbed people. But finer diagnostic screening would likely eliminate less obvious risks.

Janov seems to be arguing for a kind of new, supersonic dimension of feeling in therapeutic work, and his claims of change are commensurate. His is either a colossal achievement or the work of a colossal mountebank, whether an intentional or a misguided one. In principle it ought not be too difficult to establish which is true. To Janov's credit, he has a research laboratory and works in conjunction with scientists from UCLA and elsewhere in order to prove his claims objectively. Nonetheless, he goes a lonely way. As the possessor of "the only cure," he holds himself aloof from the human potential movement as well as the psychoanalytic mainstream. He has abrasively alienated others who could contribute to the explorations of his work. He leaves us, or at least he left me, titillated by possibilities and promises but feeling that he was elusive. It is bad enough that as a scientific community, we are often reluctant to pursue, fairly and objectively, the unconventional and innovative. With Janov we seem confronted, also, with a reluctant dragon.

Feeling Therapy

Feeling therapy is a breakaway camp from the primal therapy of Janov. Having read three long pieces of work about it in advance, I was prepared for thoughtful people with a formal scientific bent, and was not disappointed. While I had to struggle toward objectivity with my irritation at Janov's group, I had to struggle not to be persuaded unobjectively in favor of the work of Joseph Hart and Richard Corriere. We began our relationship with a long, animated lunch-time discussion in one of those Beverly Hills palaces of gastronomy. The actor Cliff Robertson had lunch nearby, and we noticed that he forgot his sunglasses and had to return for them. In the parking lot, Joseph Hart discovered that he had left *his* sunglasses. Whatever that may have meant, it led to a discussion of the psychopathologies of everyday life, which was much like Freud's although the language was different. We agreed that it would be fruitful to compare systematically their theory and Freudian theory, translating each into a common language in order to pinpoint actual rather than merely semantic differences.

These men had broken with the primal therapy group partly because of ethical issues. The primal therapists with whom I had just previously talked had in fact been their therapists. These therapists were available to them as needed during the three intensive weeks, they claimed, but not afterward, as promised. Further, these feeling therapists thought that the generalizations and claims made by the primal therapists were in excess of the research findings. They were convinced that abreaction was not enough and had to be followed by further processes. In pursuing these processes, their therapists are hyperalert to the mismatch of behavior and feeling. They encourage the patient to recognize in himself feelings and attitudes that he tries to avoid through seeing them in others. They take the patient back into the past for expression of his true, dammed-up feelings, and then force these true feelings to be integrated with present activities. They are likely to do such things as telling a patient who is siphoning off his interest, energy, commitment, and feeling through watching television to get rid of his television set before he can return to therapy. They believe that primal experiences themselves can serve as defenses against integrating feeling experiences of the past into the present, that many patients have primals in order to please the therapist rather than as actual abreaction of memories. Between the genuine feeling and its blockage, imposed by the culture, is an emptiness, a lag. They look for such lags in everyday behaviors that are reactions to unexpressed feelings about just-previous events. The leaving of sunglasses, they thought, represented an emptiness, a blankness, a lag, an indication that some feeling on the parts of Robertson and Hart had been blocked. Did they, I wondered, think they had discovered repression?

Feeling therapists share with primal therapy a similar structure: stimulus deprivation, three-week intensive individual work, and nine to twelve months of group meetings. They may add years of further work, describing their work as both intensive and long-term. Feeling therapists say they actually *do* make themselves available to the patients as needed, yet at the time charged only twenty-five hundred dollars, which works out to be around twenty-five dollars per hour.

They had observed the same physiological changes as the primal therapy people had, but were more restrained in their assertion of the degree of these changes and how long they would last. They were aware of the need for continued and better research, which they claimed they were doing.

The feeling therapists not only believe that it takes a person who has gone through feeling therapy to understand one of their patients fully, but society must be redesigned to accommodate the different point of view of people imbued with feeling therapy. They opt for a subculture organized according to the understanding that feeling is primary and expression of it necessary; in effect, culture as a "therapeutic community." The therapists live in such a subculture as well. Their recent book on dreams includes a description of one.[2] For them, the line between therapist and patient is vague. Constant treatment seems to go on between designated patient and designated therapist, as well as in informal, *ad hoc* combinations that may vary from moment to moment.

In talking with a local psychotherapist, I was told that there is a general impression in Los Angeles that post-primal and post-feeling therapy patients are rather sluggish. This observation was meant to be critical, and the criticism may be justified. Yet such behavior does correspond to the goal put forth by the primal and the feeling therapists, of reducing frantic and compulsive activities. If that observation is accurate, it seems to me a remarkable demonstration of power, for good or evil, that such patients have changed enough to have gotten themselves this reputation. Now from the depth to the height.

Psychosynthesis—High on the Higher Self

One summer when I was an undergraduate, I journeyed across country to take a crash course at UCLA, in the Westwood section of Los Angeles, in order to fulfill a foreign-language requirement. In my early twenties I took another crash course, this one on how to have an identity crisis (What to Do with Your Life, I), also in Los Angeles, at first in what used to be known generically as Hollywood and later at the self-same UCLA, in Westwood. And here

I was again, tooling up Wilshire Boulevard toward Westwood with, I was beginning to suspect, another crash course on my hands, if not another identity crisis. How remarkable, then, that after ten minutes or so of discussion with the man who was to acquaint me with psychosynthesis, Robert Gerard, we discovered that we had been classmates at UCLA twenty years before. I remembered him as the one student who never got less than an A in any subject, and as being friendly though somehow secretive. It turned out that he had been practicing yoga professionally. His secretiveness reflected his double life, which he thought, probably wisely at the time, he had to keep secret from the academic authorities.

I summarized for him what I had gathered from my readings to see whether we were talking about the same thing: Psychosynthesis is not simply a psychology or simply a philosophy, but an attempt to bring about a new way of living. For example, it offers ideas about child-rearing practices and formal education. Its goal is to create a new person, and with such a new person, a new society. It specifies three levels of consciousness: one corresponding more or less to the psychoanalytic view of the id, the lower conscious; the middle conscious is much like the commonsense view of consciousness; and there is a superconscious, which is the repository of the inspirational, creative, and sublime. Psychosynthesis techniques are designed to help people achieve the higher self of the superconscious. People consistently underestimate themselves by not maximizing the superconscious, often not recognizing that it is there at all. Guilt feelings stem from the individual's not fully maximizing his potential. Psychosynthesis techniques include the keeping of diaries, mental reviews of the day's events, reminding oneself to think about serenity and to put one's body into postures of serenity, continually questioning oneself as to who one is, all of this with an accent on the positive and the power of will.

Gerard was particularly enthusiastic about the usefulness of "guided imagery." One way guided imagery is done is by the therapist's suggesting a scene, for example a meadow, and then having the patient imaginatively elaborate the scene. Symbolically the patient would put obstacles in his own path, for example imagining a wall, which would be translated by the therapist as a resistance. The therapist would encourage him on to further elaborations and would try to pierce the resistances, or the therapist might simply ask the patient to let an image come to mind. When one suggests that the patient think of something that goes downward—a tunnel, a hole, or subway steps—what ordinarily follows is from a "lower" impulse. By contrast, thinking of something that goes up results in altruistic feelings and other high and refined transmutations of the lower consciousness, including, ultimately, mystical experiences. Because imagery is closer to primary thought and words than words, deep and meaningful experiences are said to emerge.

Perhaps I was influenced by my memory of Gerard as often beating me in the UCLA competition for grades, perhaps I was dazed into submission by the rapid fire of new points of view on that trip. At any rate I was then more tolerant of psychosynthesis than I was to be a year later, when I attended an all-day psychosynthesis institute in Estes Park, Colorado. There I found psychosynthesis to be an airy discipline, glibly throwing around words that seem to have referents only in other words. Some key concepts described there:

Self—This is the "center of pure consciousness," "aliveness." While the rest of the world is ephemeral, and thoughts and feelings are changeable, the Self is continuous.

Will—Will was more or less defined as conscious intention, and exercises were taught that were designed to aid one to become conscious of one's capacity to will happenings.

Transpersonal Sense—This means to be in touch with altruistic love, to be enlightened, to have harmony with a power higher than oneself, to experience ecstasy, well-being, and creativity.

Trying to test the apparent reality of what seemed to me to be the wool-headed innocence of this material, I tried to draw out one of the other participants. She bridled at any critical implication, apparently satisfied if not delighted at all that she was hearing and experiencing. I later saw her on the arm of the leader of the discussion, a slim and darkly handsome Italian. So much for science. I took the scene as a symbolic illustration of the ubiquitous danger of subjectivity, prejudice, and longing interfering with judgment. I include my subjectivity, prejudice, and longing of one sort or another. Sanctimonious vagueness, which is characteristic of psychosynthesis, is especially hard for me to tolerate. So maybe that is why I never could quite get the hang of the psychosynthetic quest for Higher Self. Maybe Robert Gerard didn't either, or at least he apparently thought that he could improve on it. I learned from a recent brochure that he has formulated his own approach, called "Integral Psychology." Maybe he is still a top student.

Behavior Modification—the Not Quite Human Potential

Now to behavior modification, the original reason for making this California trip and the accidental stimulus of all that followed. While the boundaries around the human potential movement are rather vague, with approaches like primal therapy and feeling therapy somewhat in and somewhat out, there is no doubt that behavior modification is out. Indeed, along with psychoanalysis, it is a bête noire of that movement. Even more than psychoanalysis, it is identified as inhumane; and rather than expanding potential, behavior modifiers are said to reduce people to a collection of responses programmed by others. Nonetheless, from the point of view of a psychoanalyst, it is an alternative therapy, one with a dazzling rise in popularity in the past decade.

Members of the Fifth Annual Southern California Conference on Behavior Modification, sponsored by California State University, all seemed to live in Orange County, most within hailing distance of San Clemente. By contrast with the dashiki-and-love-bead gestalt set and the faintly luxurious sports clothes of primal therapists, "behavior mods," as they are sometimes called, were hardly mod but certainly behaved themselves. While the primal therapists and gestalt people were free and easy with their bodies, the behavior modification people kept their distance, not unfriendly, just in place and clean. A spareness permeated the atmosphere. The sandwiches were dry, the coffee weak, the fire laws governing the number of people admitted to a lecture hall were scrupulously observed, and one had to present a badge for admittance. An antipsychiatric and especially antipsychoanalytic attitude found its way into many jokes, gibes, and caricatures. Among the books in the display area, along with such (to me) esoteric items as *Toilet Training for the Mentally Retarded*, was a generous selection of anti-Freudian volumes.

By reading the texts of Wolpe and Lazarus and asking several fellow participants, I received a brief course in the theory of behavior modification.

Behavior is learned and instilled in the brain and autonomic connections, an idea not unlike the sensorimotor theories of psychoanalytic ego psychology. Behaviors are maintained by a fear of unpleasant consequences or by the expectation of pleasant ones. In classical conditioning the experimenter or therapist sees to it that wanted behaviors become associated with pleasantness and that unwanted behaviors become associated with unpleasantness. In instrumental or operative conditioning the person himself acts on the environment, his act resulting in reward or punishment.

The major therapeutic techniques are desensitization and assertion training. In desensitization the person begins by achieving an anxiety level of zero, often with muscle-relaxation techniques. Against this base line are posed a hierarchy of anxiety-provoking thoughts based on degrees of closeness to the feared situation. With regular practice the patient is able mentally to get closer and closer to the feared situation with less and less anxiety until finally he exposes himself to it in real life.

In assertion training the patients are encouraged to stand up for themselves, to develop a good concept of themselves, and once convinced of their self-worth find it easy, for example, to approach a stranger, to return goods to a store, and to turn down requests for charity. (Behavior modification proponents are not against giving to charity on principle, they just believe one should be free to say no if that is one's decision.) Such situations and the training for them were demonstrated in a three-hour workshop that included a good deal of role playing, along with emphasis on a firm handshake, direct eye contact, upright posture, and strong voice quality. Calm and forceful standing up for one's rights was contrasted with simple aggressiveness, which fails to take the other person into consideration. Some people and some how-to-do-it manuals fail to make that distinction, thereby encouraging crass demandingness.

While behavior modification theory is sparse and the techniques few, individual variations, the adroit arrangement of cues in particular situations, and the constructions of hierarchies of anxiety are extensive and ingenious. In one study five Big Men on Campus were put in a group with the patient, who until then had behaved as a born loser. A panel of professors observed their discussion and pressed a button turning on a green light when relevant, forceful comments were made, and a button turning on a red light when irrelevant, weak comments were made. The experiment was rigged so that the born loser got many more green lights, presumably began thinking of himself differently, and by the end of the experiment was earning the green lights through his changed behavior. I could not restrain the image of a psychoanalytic couch rigged up like a pinball machine all set to explode upon the achievement of insight.

The major symptoms to which behavior modification is addressed seemed to be overeating, smoking, and phobias. While it is true that the laws of learning are general laws, much was made of the need for careful individual diagnosis in the selecting of cues, the establishment of hierarchies, and other diagnostic procedures.

When an assessment of the cues preceding a rape revealed that the rapist did not know how to seduce a woman, he was taught to do so. A woman being treated for obesity was sent to the beautician, taught how to dress, involved in weight-watching, and had dates arranged, at first with overweight males. Members of a singles group had regular practice in dating other members and learning what things about themselves were objectionable to others. Alcoholics were given Antabuse, with the understanding that if they did not appear for their Antabuse at the police station they were to be jailed for a week for each such offense. David Fisher, apparently a stand-up comedian as well as a behavior therapist, said, in his keynote address, that behavior modification methods are not so good but the alternatives are terrible. He described how he was called in as a consultant to the California Prison System, particularly around the question of how to prevent homosexual behavior in prisons. He told the authorities that he could solve their problem of homosexuality in prisons, but in order to do so he would need some girls. The result was conjugal meetings.

I admire the premium that the behavioral modification people put on problem solving. Pursuant to this they insist upon specific enunciation of problems and complaints, painstaking examination of the key situations and the cues in them contributing to unwanted behavior, impatience with platitudes, generalities, and obscurities. The end point of the procedure for them is the result, preferably one that can be measured. Explanations are no substitute for results, and they are reluctant to repeat the same procedures without evidence of success.

Much of behavior modification strikes me as oversimplified and narrow-minded, applicable to some but not much of the human condition. But can conventional therapists say that the behavior modifiers' attitudes of objectivity, precision of language, and problem-solving tension could not be helpful, perhaps as a correction for occasional relative inattention to the facts of beginnings, middles, ends, and goals of long, expensive procedures? Would not their brisk, results-oriented point of view sometimes lead to change of techniques, therapists, structural arrangements, to a recognition of the necessity to terminate or to find fresh, clearer reasons to continue? Probably it would. But therapists would have to be wise enough to discriminate between a genuine need for change and a resistance better dealt with by pursuing its analysis with patience and respect for the patients' dread, just then, of knowledge and change.

The process and effects of learning are so ubiquitous that we may tend to overlook them. Upon a moment's reflection one is able to think of many of his conditioned habits and automatisms. For example, when driving an unfamiliar car, a person attempts to hit the horn where it would be on a car familiar to him, although he had noted how the horn worked when he first got into the car. The person writing a forty-dollar check for theater tickets reinforces his memory of the date of the performance, while his unreinforced guest to the performance may need to be reminded. We reinforce what and how much people tell us by being accepting, with smiles and nods and by not interrupting, or with compliments and adulation; and we negatively condition people by beating them in arguments and implying that we are looking for bad things when we question their motives. These kinds of events go on in our daily relationships, and there is hardly any reason to question that they occur in psychological treatment as well. Psychoanalytic psychotherapists try to be neutral, not taking sides with urges, conscience, society, not giving advice or imposing their own solutions. Yet in the heightened anxiety and susceptibility of psychotherapy the patient, with strong motives to learn what the therapist considers a good patient and a bad patient, may attune himself to all manner of cues inadvertently supplied by the therapist. Recognizing the implicit behavior modifications they practice should help therapists in thinking through the processes of change and realizing fully how they come about.

If one wants to remove symptoms or if for whatever reason removal of symptoms is the sole aim of the treatment, then behavior therapy might well be worth trying. It is inexpensive of time and money, and in and of itself not harmful. The often cited danger of behavioral therapy is that whatever was causing a symptom will find another, and perhaps even more destructive, way of expressing itself. But this so-called "symptom substitution" is not as common and inevitable as some conventional psychotherapists claim. Certainly it is not as simple a matter as one clear symptom always popping up in the wake of overcoming another.

A more subtle danger of behavior therapy is to encourage the person to think of himself solely in terms of symptoms, in effect as a machine to a greater extent than as a person. Many people come to conventional psychotherapy with a symptom, and in the course of overcoming that symptom remake their whole selves, develop a different view of themselves and the world around them, not only overcoming what has been injurious but developing heretofore undreamed of insights and capabilities. Is the removal of a single symptom so valuable as to justify foregoing more extensive personal growth? Sometimes it is; oftentimes it is not.

The flight back never quite made it; I was never to return to my starting point. On the way back from California, again in my airborne musing tank, I tried to draw some conclusions. In the past four days I had been in contact with whole cultures that were as imbued with their beliefs and confident of their activities as I had been with mine. I had been subjected to a barrage of antipsychoanalytic criticisms, most of which I could dismiss as uninformed but some of which zeroed in on questions that I had raised for myself. I had observed techniques that seemed to be powerful as ways of producing beneficial change. Moreover, I was struck with the possibility that none of the approaches by themselves might be the last word, but perhaps acquaintance with all of them would yield a more effective and better-reasoned therapy than any one of them could claim to be by itself. Hardly anyone, I realized, was in a good position to explore that possibility, and maybe I could at least make a beginning.

Gestalt therapy seemed to me intuitively to be a likely starting point; I later learned that it had been the starting point for many recent searchers for beneficial human change.

2

A String of Perls

JUST AS PSYCHOANALYTIC theory and practice are central to conventional dynamic psychiatry and psychology, gestalt theory and practices are central to the human potential movement. Thumbing through an ecumenical catalogue of human potential activities, such as the catalogues Esalen puts out detailing its scheduled meetings, one often sees a practitioner of, say, yoga, massage, or biofeedback identifying himself as trained in gestalt therapy and as amalgamating gestalt practices with his main intervention. Even when unacknowledged, this usually is the way it is, for several reasons. Gestalt therapy has some slight prestigious linkage with academic psychology. It was sired by Fritz Perls. His writings, his personal magnetism, and the movies made of him at work made gestalt therapy popular and influential. Originally trained in the theater, Perls's giftedness on stage contributed to his being an effective educator; people flocked to hear and see him. He was a dominant figure in residence at Esalen while that organization was serving as a clearinghouse for the emerging human potential ideas. Not much passed through Esalen without being influenced to some extent by Fritz and his gestalt therapy. (Founder or no, he, too, is customarily called by his first name.)

Occasional debates occur about how centrally creative of the work Fritz Perls was, though no one doubts his being its chief popularizer. There are those who claim that the writer and social critic Paul Goodman and Perls's wife, Laura, did at least as much as Fritz in developing gestalt therapy. Laura Perls told me about that, along with what conventional society would consider "confidences," in about the first fifteen minutes of our meeting. How we got together reveals something of the quality of human-potential life.

A year after my first brush with gestalt therapy, I had come again to Los Angeles to be in a gestalt therapy workshop led by her so I was set to see her as the person who would be my therapist. Upon entering the elevator of a Ramada Inn, I saw a woman discussing with a bellhop some kind of problem about getting the key to her room to work. She had a German accent and looked as if she were in her mid sixties though there was much about her that seemed younger. I briefly thought that perhaps this was Laura Perls, but I reminded myself that, when going somewhere, for instance to a ball game, one is inclined to think that everyone seen on the bus or on the street is involved in that enterprise. At any rate, it was not my style to breach boundaries between people without the usual introductions or other ritual contacts. I thought no more of it until I saw the woman the next morning in the coffee shop. Again I had the same thought, and again I took a table near but separate from her. She, however, called over to ask me if I was Dr. Appelbaum, so I joined her. She could have known or guessed who I was with a little prior information, powers of observation, and maybe guesswork.

Human potential people would be satisfied to say that she and I were not fated to meet the night before but were meant to meet the next morning. The reasons might be unfolded as time went on, or perhaps never would be known, but nonetheless were there. Ram Dass, in *The Only Dance There Is,*[1] tells of meeting the man he was seeking, among India's millions, the man having made elaborate plans based on the supposition that the two would, somehow, meet at that time and place without prearrangement.

Be that as it may, my encounter with Laura Perls turned out to be a most enjoyable and educational event. In the style of people in the human potential movement, she was open and candid about the history and inception of gestalt psychotherapy as entwined in the lives of Fritz Perls and herself. She told of Fritz's interest in and study of the theater, their acquaintanceship with the gestalt academic psychologists Köhler and Koffka, and how these purist scientists would be amazed, if not appalled, at how the name of their discipline was now used, based upon only a tangential understanding and application of their principles. She told also of herself and Fritz's maintaining separate residences, in different parts of the country, coming together as needs and circumstances dictated. One could infer that one or both of them suffered from unconscious disturbances that made it impossible for them to live together in the commonly accepted style of man and wife. With effective psychoanalysis, they might have overcome such difficulties. Or they may have simply been living out a point of view that pervades the human potential movement: People ought to work out their own destiny, including how much effort they want to put into solving neurotic conflicts, recognizing that not all neurotic conflicts are solvable at a cost worth the gain, if solvable at all. Instead of continued attempts to change themselves, to fit into the Procrustean bed of society's conventions or psychiatry's criteria for "mental health," they decide on styles of life that fit with the way they are, and concentrate on exploiting and enjoying the life they have chosen. This is not a small issue. It is at the cutting edge of such decisions as whether a person should have psychological treatment, what kind of treatment that should be, what goals are appropriate to it, and when it should end. The ferment generated by the human potential movement has sharpened such issues for all psychotherapists.

Not only does one not submit, in the human potential movement, to social conventions, one does not submit to anything else; in principle, everything is within our power to change. Laura Perls does not submit to the aging process. As she gulped a handful of vitamin pills, she told me that without them she does not have the energy that is available to her when she takes them. While she looks at least ten years younger than her probable age, she acts a generation younger. As I was to learn in the next two days of the workshop, she, like other gestalt therapists, is indefatigable. They work open-endedly with respect to time, far into the night, and they stay working with individuals until something has been "worked through." It makes no sense to gestalt therapists to end at fifty minutes if the client is in the midst of a piece of work or to extend a session beyond a few minutes if the patient is not willing and able "to work" at the time.

My attempts to draw her out as to the theoretical implications of her way of working met with no success. Like many human potential therapists, she was not interested in abstract, disciplined, scientific appraisal. All that seemed to matter to her was the immediate reality, action and interaction, guided, as it turned out, by a remarkable intuitive capacity.

A psychoanalytic therapist might, to a greater or lesser extent depending upon the nature of the patient and the goals of the treatment, keep himself relatively unknown to the patient in order that the patient might put onto him his idiosyncratic perceptions and then learn from them. By contrast, Laura Perls was willing to enter into an immediate relationship with her "patients," as with our encounter in the coffee shop. Bemused by the contrasts between what therapy would probably be with Laura Perls, and therapy as I had conceived of it up to then, I found it acceptable, as well as pleasant, to have breakfast with my weekend therapist and to share a cab with her to the workshop.

Once there I felt insufficiently disheveled, insufficiently limber to sit on the floor (*de rigueur*), insufficiently free immediately to try to get to know the group of people who knew each other but not me. In order to deal with my feelings of insufficiency, I did my splendid-isolation number. I sat with my knees drawn up, and encircled them with my arms. I almost corporeally retreated into my head, the part that I felt confident was sufficient and would allow me to rise a safe distance above my surroundings. In what seemed to me a frightening rush of disloyalty, my new "friend," Laura Perls, began the meeting by calling attention to my physical posture. I felt caught between trying to maintain composure in front of what I was convinced at the time were ten pairs of unfriendly eyes and trying to become aware of my bodily posture and the purpose of adopting it.

Let us, mercifully, shift to another vignette of gestalt therapy, which took place a week later, at Esalen.

Esalen is the Vienna of the human potential movement, a choice spot on one of the world's most beautiful seacoasts, an Eden cliff above the Pacific Ocean and below the

Big Sur mountains. Here Esalen gathers to itself thousands of pilgrims to be healed, to learn, to teach. With gestalt therapy as its backbone, it is home for an array of counter-culture activities and ideas: physical and mental therapies, meditations, athletics, dance, art, and alternative medicine. I had come for a week called "Experiencing Esalen," which was to provide a sampler of diverse local activities. The major share of the week was spent in what were essentially gestalt therapy groups, supplemented by some dance and exercise therapy, various kinds of massage, group nude bathing in hot spring water, optional acupuncture, and optional "Rolfing."

To leave one's accustomed surroundings and way of life and to enter a wilderness and a novel way of life is in itself an invitation and opportunity to alter one's consciousness. Added to these nonspecific elements are activities designed to do the same. The result is a gradual but impressive opening of self to self, an enhanced receptivity to feelings and ideas ordinarily kept out of awareness, a readiness for experience.

Several days into the week, I awoke vaguely out of sorts, a crashing mountain storm paralleling my inner experience. Through the chill sea air and wind, I made my way to breakfast, the splashing, unstable muddiness underfoot matching my sense of self. I stopped in at the infirmary to make an appointment with the resident physician, Hector Prestera, for an acupuncture session. As it happened, he had time for me right then. I mentioned a few minor complaints but suggested that I could best use a treatment for general neurosis. He claimed to have made a number of diagnostic observations during our brief talk, and I was to read in his book published later how he makes diagnoses on the basis of bodily configurations. At any rate, he believed he knew where to place the needles for maximum effect. I cannot say that I felt any effect at all, then or later, beyond the enjoyment of satisfying my curiosity and marveling that I could be stuck with an array of needles without feeling pain.

A bit late for the gestalt therapy meeting, at which the use of dreams was to be central, I hurried across the slippery terrain and, coming down an incline, crashed to the ground hard against sharp rocks bordering the muddy pathway. Scratched and bleeding from these wounds, fresh from having needles stuck in me, and remembering the night before, when someone had gratuitously revealed a personal problem to me with an implicit plea for help, I was reminded of a "Jesus Christ" identity fragment unearthed during my psychoanalysis. Stigmata and all, I went on to the gestalt therapy meeting, sober and reflective, sure that if ever I was ready "to work," it was now.

I volunteered to take the "hot seat," to seek awareness with the therapist. (Others in the circle can seek awareness through introspection, applying to themselves the thoughts and feelings enunciated by the therapist and patient.)

We had earlier been asked to think of a dream, and now I was asked to tell that dream. Included in it was a scene in which my mother was on a stage with a klieg light playing down upon her. Rather than asking me what a klieg light brought to mind (as I might have done in my role as psychoanalyst), the therapist asked me to *be* a klieg light. As a klieg light, I bathed her in color, warmed the scene, defined her for others, made her performance possible. In short I self-evoked a sense of doing things for my mother, and elaborated upon this scene a whole way of life, a need to help her, look after her, cure her. Roles are reversed, the son becomes a god shining down on her, he is expected to perform miracles. Through further associations, stemming from the dream, I uncovered some of the genetic antecedents of this situation through the recognition of my mother's relationship to her father. For many years the doted-upon only child of an indulgent father, she learned to expect excessive care and adulation from men. Throughout her life she was to try to live out the flouncily dressed, adored young lady taken by father, sporting a gold-headed cane, to the city's best restaurants. I as her first child and son was the inheritor of this tradition. The family joke, about my trying to hold a chair at the table for her to sit on when I was too small to move it, became intelligible and sad. A helping profession was, for me, a natural; the trick was not to have to bleed at it.

In this session I covered a lot of intellectual and emotional ground in a short time. Neither I nor gestalt therapists would claim that such an experience as I had would necessarily happen to the average expectable participant. I had, after all, been psychoanalyzed previously and already had a context of understanding in which this dream could be placed. Furthermore, my consciousness—or defenses—had been considerably softened by the cumulative influences and travail of the week, to say nothing of that morning's acupuncture and bloody "accident." Nonetheless, as clearly as I can separate the many factors, I do believe that this way of working with dreams was in this instance effective. The experience of the Jesus-identity fragment, this aspect of my relationship to my mother and her relationship to her father as antecedent of my experience of her, all were for me now in living color. Insight had been extended and enlivened.*

* See the Appendix for an extended comparison of psychoanalysis and gestalt therapy.

3

The Human Potential Movement

I HAD A tiger by the tail, or it had me. What had started out as an exploration of new therapies had now become an exploration of a new culture, a new philosophy, a new way of life. For the new therapies were inextricably entwined with the human potential movement and the counterculture. Moreover, there were strident voices within the human potential movement claiming that a therapist cannot work effectively unless his therapy *is* an outgrowth of his culture, his way of life, ultimately of himself. Did that mean, I wondered, that in order to practice or even to understand the new therapies successfully I would have to live differently? And how different was different? Would I have to change my politics, the way I wore my hair, my friends, colleagues, family?

At the very least it was clear that I would have to better understand the counterculture. Thus, my study of therapies was expanded to include social roles, mores, values. I learned about these from books, observing behavior during meetings such as are described throughout this book, and through my own experiences living in the counterculture.

According to the counterculture there is, and needs to be, a new world a-comin'. Here, in the shadow of extinction, we have perhaps just enough time to recognize the errors of Western society, and save ourselves. Unless we stop destroying our natural environment, we may extinguish ourselves through disease or lack of natural resources. Unless we practice good nutrition, we may drown ourselves in a sea of Coca Cola. Unless we stop worshiping machines, our skills may atrophy through lack of exercise of human values as we become more machine than man. By our dress, language, and morals ye shall know us; we are dropouts from the formalistic, overideational, possession-driven culture; soldiers in the vanguard of a new world a-comin'.

That is the credo. The counterculture was an expression of the turbulent sixties, much of its intensity fueled by the fury over the undeclared war in Viet Nam. Its jerry-built theory was pieced together from the ideas of such people as Kurt Goldstein, Aldous Huxley, David Riesman, Arthur Koestler, Gordon Allport, Rollo May, and Abraham Maslow as these were melded with Eastern philosophy into a set of assumptions about the nature of human beings and how they should live.

A case can be made that a major architect of the counterculture was Martin Luther King. He offered a conception of equality among men which was at odds with the prevailing views in the United States at that time. He asserted that there was to be a new era. No longer would the emperor be presumed to wear clothes; in a democracy there ought to be democracy. He dared to hope, and to translate hope into action, against what to many at the time seemed hopeless odds. In the chaotic sixties, King's movement was paralleled, probably interstimulated and reciprocally influenced, by radical youth groups, draft resisters, and free-speechers. These groups were inflamed by the festering sore of Viet Nam and the threat of being drafted or otherwise coerced into supporting what many people considered to be an awful cause. The stage for all this fear and dissatisfaction had been set by the previous decades' cold war and the threat of nuclear annihilation. For many people it all became simply intolerable.

Mrs. Park's march to the front of the bus was soon to be repeated in practically all of our institutions. Other ethnic groups and women and psychiatric patients and students demanded, fought for, and increasingly got their say, founded upon what they considered to be the inherent right and dignity of the individual. They asserted humaneness as against the impersonality of organizations. They argued for and showed by example the individual's potential for expressing himself, for taking responsibility, for having an effect. Hardly an organization exists which has not recently experienced a pressure toward such equalization as an expression of the idea that there is value to be found and nurtured in every person.

Martin Luther King chose to help the individual by way of social action; his was a rather authoritatively led movement of the poor and disadvantaged. The human potential movement is a middle-class expression of the counterculture, a movement that relies less on authoritative leadership than on education and the provision of opportunity, less on social action than on individual change. The counterculture objective is to help its citizens change ideas about themselves and others and how life should be lived, to promote a "new consciousness." With such a new consciousness people will be able to overcome their political, economic, educational, and social difficulties, to find new ways to get along as a society, to work productively, to establish the right conditions for optimal learning, and to enjoy life. So it is said.

"Human potential movement" is a loose, informal term that refers to a wide variety of activities, all resting on the belief that there is more to most of us than meets the eye, that we have much unrealized potential. It further rests on the assumption that individual change can be brought about through self-help. Primarily one merely needs to be open to the possibilities of change, to be educated about some of these possibilities, to experiment with them, and to be determined to have them make a difference. Practically any activity or interest can be entered into under the aegis of human potential beliefs: sports, dance, nutrition, astrology, graphology, meditation, mysticism—and psychotherapy.

Ironically some human potential adherents use the word "therapy," as in "alternative therapy" or "new therapy" or "women's therapy." The word causes or should cause them theoretical dismay. Dismay should arise because "therapy" implies that there is something wrong with a person, which requires treatment. Human potential people believe, instead, that we all function below our potential and may want to improve the quality of our lives without needing to justify such efforts by declaring ourselves "sick." Even though some of the human potential activities resemble conventional therapy—in the qualifications of their practitioners, their structure, their legal and social sanctions—"patients" are called "clients" or "students" or "the person I work with."

Certainly all people, not just sick ones, might attempt to improve their lives, and among these attempts can be included psychotherapy. Much is wrong with the words and underlying concepts of "sick," "well," "normal," and "abnormal," as adopted from conventional medicine, and there is much wrong with the subject-object mode, also adopted from conventional medicine, of a doctor doing something to a passive patient. And there is much about the way human potential therapies are conducted that makes the line between therapist and patient vague. Nonetheless, I shall be referring to those who occupy the patient role in the new therapies as patients. I do so out of the convenience that this is how I refer to the people with whom I work, and with the belief that it is possible to use the term for practical reasons without falling prey to its inappropriate and harmful connotations.

"Conventional psychotherapy" is only a slightly less ambiguous term than new or alternative therapy. It, too, can refer to a wide variety and mixture of theories and activities, from psychoanalysis to counseling. Unless otherwise specified, I use it to refer to so-called dynamic psychotherapy, a set of activities guided by Freud's understanding of personality, the prototypical form of which is psychoanalysis.

While the activities under the umbrella of the human potential movement are diverse, they do permit the following generalizations: As we have noted, human potential activities are separate from conventional therapy in that they rest on the belief that people are fine as they are, but could be better. The office or institutional format of conventional therapy is often rejected by human potential practitioners. They choose to meet instead for extended periods, at irregular intervals, at retreats, public meeting rooms, or in forests. Human potential therapy borrows heavily from the wisdom of the ancients, particularly Eastern religions and philosophies. Human potential practitioners emphasize the here-and-now as against what they consider rummaging around in a past that cannot be altered. They esteem feelings over ideas; in their view man has put aside his basic nature in favor of the abstract, cognitive approach to life fostered by parents, school, and other agents of society. Human-potential adherents emphasize the importance of the body, its balance and grace, the full exploitation of its capacity for action and pleasure, and its use as a means of feeling better emotionally. They distrust traditional scientific method and disciplined thinking and writing out of a fear that these will promote an intellectualization of processes whose main intent and value is experiential and emotional.

The rise in human potential activities in a little over a decade has been phenomenal. Many cities now have some kind of human potential center where young people in particular come to meet, organize, and participate in the various activities. Nowadays if you or a member of your family needs psychiatric help or simply feels that life should be better than it is, you have a wider range of putative therapies to choose from than ever before. Lest you lack information or require encouragement, you need but flip the pages of a popular magazine, turn on the television set, go to the movies, or stop by the bookseller's. The human potential movement is a growth industry.

Why did the counterculture funnel so much of itself into the relatively parochial pursuit of therapy? One reason is that its Eastern-religion forebears include health with the teaching of ways of life. Another is that its ideas serve as self-justifications for the emotional disturbances of its proponents. ("There is no such thing as psychological illness.") Still another reason is that we have come to see conventional psychotherapy as a secular religion, so a new secular religion has to replace the old therapy as well. Conventional therapy became seen as coercive, unjust, conservative, and in need of replacement just as were big business, big government, big labor, big education, big social stratification—as an elite and dangerous establishment.

How ironic! Only a few short years ago, psychoanalysis was seen as the egalitarian "left," the cutting edge of a psychological rebellion against the organicists in psychiatry, and as a humanist force in conventional culture. Now it is seen as an orthodoxy characterized by subject-object duality, misguided as to the nature of humankind if not its outright exploiter, as an arm of the state used to brainwash, punish, and control. Not only that, but even with the best will in the world psychoanalysts and psychoanalytically inspired psychotherapists are alleged not to help their patients—too much emphasis on ideas and too little on feelings, too little responsibility and credit given the patient, too much concern with the past as compared to the present, too much adjustment to a culture that is itself unhealthy.

Moreover, conventional psychotherapy rests on the assumption that all that is required is work on the mind, that with the mind in order the patient will learn about, select, and embark on any other self-help interests and activities that might be useful. In the new therapies, by contrast, work with the mind may be emphasized to a greater or lesser extent, but in any instance it is likely to be accompanied by other self-help opportunities, particularly those that focus on the body and the "spirit." And if the human potential therapist himself does not provide these opportunities, the human potential culture in which he functions will.

More than a little sophistry is mixed in with the wisdom of some of these ideas. Conventional therapists are gradually freeing themselves of the doctor-patient, sick-well dualities, beginning to consider that what they do is as much education as medicine. Increasingly they recognize that traditional ideas and labels for sickness fail to represent the malaise of the human condition, and that anyone has the right to get help to improve his lot without being designated as sick. By the same token, sagacious human potential observers increasingly recognize that people are not impervious to the slings and arrows implicated in traditional psychopathological syndromes. Some people really are sick by conventional criteria, and they may require therapeutic activities that at least temporarily contradict some aspects of human potential philosophy, by degree if nothing else.

Astrology, meditation, psychotherapy, bodily manipulation, exercise, massage, nutrition, control of involuntary physiological states, psychic phenomena, and reincarnation —all these and more are comprised in the human potential movement. Surely there is an emotional wellspring that brings together such diverse activities and their adherents, people who could, in principle, carry on their work independently. Can we find one word to express succinctly what unites the planks of the human potential platform? Yes, we can; the word is "hope." The human potential movement is distinguished not only by dissatisfactions with self and society, but by hope. Its members do not go quietly into the night of misery, emptiness, and institutionalized cruelty to man and his environment. Rather, they rage against these with their cornucopia of interests and explorations, ineffably optimistic that they can make a difference. Borne by such hope, they greet new and daring adventures in self-help with enthusiasm; the sky is the limit. By contrast with conventional psychotherapy's reductionism, which sucks events up into its established way of thinking, the human potential therapist offers expansionism, an open invitation to new ways of thinking.

Hope comes in many shapes and sizes. It can be found in psychotic delusions of grandeur (perhaps as God or Napoleon, I could like myself or get my way better). It is palpable in the moist eyes searching the altar. It radiates from the muscles of those who chop down trees to build a new society, from Walden to hippie communes. It rides the shoulders of the person who drops a coin into a fortune-telling machine. It may be that hope, or the wish for hope (which is a kind of hope) burns brightest in the darkest night of the soul: the natural habitat of hope may be at the brink of despair.

Is the new consciousness (and the assertion of the new culture which follows from it) just another spasm of hope, another in a series of panaceas that come and go or degenerate into institutions and rituals? Perhaps it is just a manifestation of a society that goes in for fads whether they be finned automobiles or streamlined hope packages. Is human-potential hope nothing more than the elaborated and rationalized childhood fantasy that somewhere, somehow, someone will make it well, all the way from the skinned knee to death itself? Hope soothes us: "It will get better." Surely there must be a portion of fashion and make-believe in human potential hope. That is not, however, what it is all about, according to its theorists. Rather, hope stems from the almost religious conviction that most humans barely scratch the surface of their potential. They live behind the bars of their limitations, without realizing that they have the power to escape.

Is there no such hope in conventional therapy? Human potential people argue that hope in conventional psychotherapy is suffocated by an artificially assumed neutrality and a limited view of reality. Karl Menninger, as a spokesman for traditional psychotherapy yet with the maverick, ebullient instincts of a human potential person, has written of hope as being neglected by psychiatry.[1] But hope is required to bring a patient into the office and sustain him through the vicissitudes of conventional treatment. Is hope any the less for its being inexplicit, or for its being examined rather than unquestioningly asserted, for the hopes to require proof of the pudding? Does not hope for the impossible in the long run encourage increased despair and disappointment? In answer, human potential people would point to the four-minute mile, which generations of runners could not achieve because it seemed to be beyond the capability of man. When it was finally achieved, it became commonplace for the mile to be run in less than four minutes. To human potential people, grim psychopathological thinking and dubious prognoses are merely affirmations of the insuperable four-minute mile which lead to self-fulfilling prophecies of failure instead of propelling us forward on the wings of hope.

I found these views to be heady stuff indeed. And it was not only the seductiveness of unlimited hope, the promise of joy, the fascination of the novel. Human potential ideas sandpapered my conscience, that voice which reminded me of the immorality of living in affluence in a poverty-stricken world. It inflamed my latent suspicion that we must be doing something fundamentally wrong to have created the monstrosity of the nuclear age and the sad statistics of suicide, alcoholism, disease, and divorce even as we live in chromium splendor. I found it difficult to move between the two worlds; I struggled with entry and re-entry as I went from my traditional activities to my explorations of the human potential movement and back again.

About a year into my study I encountered a book, *The Only Dance There Is*, by Ram Dass, which set forth many of the same problems I was being forced to wrestle with, and enunciated the solutions being propounded by the author as a spokesman of the human potential movement. As I sought to assimilate and accommodate the welter of new ideas that were bombarding me, I found that Ram Dass, another psychologist, had made a journey similar in some ways to the one I had embarked upon, but had worked out an accommodation between two worlds that was quite different from mine. At a time when I was struggling to construct a bridge between two worlds for myself, I experienced Ram Dass as moving too fast for me in a direction toward which I was then only groping. Little by little I was able to ease into his somewhat fey style, and get on tolerant, if not friendly, terms with his ideas. The dialogues, debates, and dialectics found in the review of Ram Dass's book that follows are extrapolations from those which took place within me as I was writing it.*

* Much of the following material is drawn from my introduction to the 1975 hard-cover edition of *The Only Dance There Is*.

4

A Tale of Two Worlds

Ram Dass has lived in two worlds. As Richard Alpert he grew up in a wealthy, establishment family, was educated in and became a member of the educational establishment, and as a social scientist and psychotherapist worked in the scientific and clinical establishments. As Ram Dass, inspired by the change in consciousness he experienced from ingesting psychedelic drugs over three hundred times, he has searched in the wisdom of the East for enlightenment and has alternated his searches in India with proselytizing in the Western world. Richard Alpert, or Ram Dass, the man, can be understood with the aid of psychiatric constructs and from the perspective of social expectations; but Ram Dass is a metaphor as much as a man. As such, he must be experienced and evaluated in terms of our civilization and ourselves. For Ram Dass has made concrete the dissatisfactions and yearnings of all of us, the timeless fantasy that a radically different way of life could be found beyond the dimensions of time and space. So our wish-driven imagination created and responded to the myths of the gods on Mount Olympus, *Gulliver's Travels*, and *2001: A Space Odyssey.*

No one is satisfied with the way things are, not even the most complacent defenders of the *status quo.* The latter give themselves away by their strident, automatic identification of change as rebellion, or by the pale surface of self which is all that is left of their capacity for profundity and feeling. Ram Dass rings the bell on and for us. Break out, he says; your awareness is choked, your limits are illusory.[1] Life, the only dance there is, is capable of infinite variations. Even our dreamers have barely begun to dream of them all.

We live in the best of times and the worst of times. We can put people on the moon, but they may then have no habitable earth to come back to. We can communicate instantaneously to practically everywhere, but what we send is destructive make-believe. We have devices for the saving of labor, but the energy saved is used to intensify our pointless, killing pace or is inverted into depression. We can extend life expectancy and lower infant mortality rates, but we cannot feed, clothe, or house the consequent expanding populations or even guarantee them air to breathe. We have achieved the highest standard of living of all time, for a few of us, while to the rest of us this achievement is a mockery. And if one examines closely how this "highest standard" is lived, then one learns why he dreads seeing the gray look beneath the tanned faces of the successful. Even Richard Cory put a bullet through his head.

It may be that every age considers itself to be the best of times and the worst of times. There is reason to believe, however, that Western man will no longer put up with life as usual, that the breaking point has been reached, that the alternatives between extinction and fundamental change are finally, irrevocably upon us.

As Ram Dass says, technology (of all things) has brought us to this revelation. What used to preoccupy us through decades or a lifetime because of its unavailability is now dumped into our childish laps. Landing on the moon and the full repertoire of sex activities turn out to be limited achievements, and we crave something more or different. Like Artie Shaw, who captured the awakening self-realization and the depression that follow precocious success in the title of his book *The Trouble with Cinderella*,[2] we find out, perhaps in time to do something about it, that we have been greyhounds chasing rabbits. This well-kept secret, which previously died with its owner covered with chagrin, now becomes known to increasing numbers of people who still have vigor and years. One of these is Ram Dass.

Ram Dass says that we live wrong, that we have traded our birthright for the tyranny and plastic of civilization. To reclaim this birthright we must look civilization straight in the eye, question each of its assumptions, and search for the answers to these questions deep within ourselves. George Leonard, another prophet of what he calls the coming "transformation," describes us as suffering with "the cherished gift of Civilization," which, while making possible our technology and productivity, "limits us, separates us from the simplest pleasures, makes us miserable in our own skins."

Here are some of the discontents, challenges, and consequent horizons that are cited by Leonard, and others. They are represented by Ram Dass the metaphor and explicated by Ram Dass the man.

> We live in the future, and miss the present.
> We separate ourselves from others, and so fragment ourselves.
> We declare people and objects distinct from one another, and in so doing we become indistinct.
> We stop up our bodies, and choke our souls.
> We strain some of our senses, and miss sensation.

We open up the outer world, while closing ourselves off from it.

We believe we are taking in as much information as we can, while in fact we are preventing much information from becoming conscious to us.

We assume that matter, time, and space are discrete and fixed entities, even though relativity physics and quantum mechanics have provided a basis for challenging this assumption.

We esteem a narrow band of consciousness while derogating "altered" states of consciousness, thus limiting ourselves as we limit our perceptions.

We assume that because matter appears solid to a narrow frequency of wave length it is inherently solid, although outside this band of frequencies it tends toward transparency and permeability.

We are convinced that the physical body is limited by its skin, despite the many reports of "out-of-body experiences" and despite science's having shown us the impossibility of assigning physical positions to subatomic particles.

We assume that our capacity to explain all human phenomena and reduce them to psychiatric and psychological constructs is a declaration of the one and only reality, rather than a useful perspective which is not designed to offer a position with respect to other possible realities.

Let us examine Ram Dass according to these and other topics, somewhat in the manner in which he organizes the thoughts in his book.

"Consciousness" for the prize fighter and the man on the street is when you are upright and awake, and unconsciousness is when you are horizontal and out cold. In psychology, consciousness refers to the waking state in which one is alert, perceives and thinks objectively, and has energies fully deployed for a specifiable task. While this formulation does not include a dimension of joy or happiness, in Western society there is an implication that this state of mind breeds efficiency and productivity and is, or should be, experienced as pleasant. We value the doer as against the dreamer. Most people seem to flog themselves toward this kind of consciousness, struggling against fatigue and depression. The tired businessman is ubiquitous.

Deviations from this kind of consciousness are called altered states of consciousness. A mild form of hyperconsciousness may be found in such excessively vigilant attitudes as are useful in battle, and exaggerated in paranoia. For the most part, however, the phrase altered states of consciousness refers less to hypervigilance than to a lowering of vigilance (at least vigilance in relation to the conventions of reality). It refers to a loosening of the processes of mind and the controls over emotion, a tendency toward emotional warmth, subjectivity, passivity, openness to other than day-to-day experiences, toward merging rather than separateness. More or less controlled alterations in consciousness are available through hypnosis, orgasm, and the arts, and can be induced by a variety of drugs. Exaggeration and lack of control in this direction lead to psychosis. Because our environments are geared toward encouraging an alert, productive, conventional standard of consciousness, an alteration in consciousness can be brought about simply by removing people from these environments. This was the wisdom in the family doctor's recommendation, when two aspirin failed, to take a vacation. In short, for Western man, consciousness is being wide-awake and, therefore, able to get the job done in no-nonsense, realistic terms. It is the apex toward which we strive, which, while allowing for the eccentricities of art and the group-shared night on the town, views with varying degrees of suspicion if not outright hostility the less-awake, the ethereal, the soft-headed.

Ram Dass reverses this formulation. Conventional ways of thinking, feeling, and behaving are, to him, expressions of unconsciousness. To be conscious is to be aware of and in touch with all human potentialities. Perception, for example, is not founded upon or limited to the five senses. Rather, there are ways of knowing that might be called, for want of a better word, "mystical." These can become available to any of us if we achieve the state of consciousness that allows them. Thinking need not be limited to the objective, rational, and linear. Time and space can be condensed: past, present, and future are available all at once, as is what is here and what is there. Thus, one can communicate with another person as if he were here although he may be miles away, and one can experience in the here-and-now either the past or the future. Neither thought nor language need follow the laws of conventional logic, the grammar of the mind. These laws are constraints on the capabilities of mind and expressiveness.

Ram Dass escapes the infinite regress of determinism (learning about and overcoming trends in personality that determine behavior is itself determined) by suggesting surrender to a greater law than determinism, a law that transcends cause and effect and has its own lawfulness, as unlawful as that may appear to be.

To be fully conscious is to overcome the separation of subject and object; one is, rather than does; one finds identity with everybody and with everything. Ram Dass says that one does not follow the Ten Commandments; one becomes the Ten Commandments.

Though Ram Dass does not use the term, much of his description of the fully conscious mind conforms to the characteristics of primary process, Freud's name for the mind of the dreamer and the psychotic. In this system, instead of conventional grammar there are condensation, displacement, paradoxes, and opposites. It follows that Ram Dass would say that the dreamer and the psychotic are more conscious than is the ordinary citizen in his waking life. Ram Dass is tolerant and indulgent toward psychosis and sometimes seems to equate psychosis with wisdom. But an altered state of consciousness alone does not produce wisdom; the wise man does.

Implicit in Ram Dass's conception of consciousness are the practically unlimited potentialities of people. No longer held back by conventional thought, which results in the constraints of time, space, and physics, people can, as Ram Dass says, move mountains.

Such a reverse conception of consciousness was enunciated by the psychoanalyst Lawrence Kubie in his conception of normality as that hypothetical condition in which all contents of the mind are released from repression and become fully conscious. In this somewhat puckish excursion by Kubie, abnormality was defined by an absence of awareness. Sanity is achieved by becoming fully aware of what is being defended against.

Ram Dass describes the range of consciousness, from emptiest to fullest, as marked by planes, or energy centers, called chakras, running from the base of the spine to the top of the head. Ideally, psychic energy flows freely from one plane to another. In fact, Western man lives in the first three chakras (those having to do with survival, sex, and power); he may have glimmerings of the fourth (beginning of mysticism), and is oblivious to the other, transcendental ones (those having to do with the energy and cell organization of the universe, the basic laws of the universe, transcending the body and finally merging into the oceanic). In the fashion of hydraulics, and as in the psychosexual libido model of Freud, energy may be caught or fixated, with consequent concentration at one or another level. In principle these fixations or blocks can be worked through so that the energy can continue upward, or be sent to any plane of consciousness in order to be available for the tasks to which that plane of consciousness is best suited. The same scheme is used by such descendants of Wilhelm Reich as the bioenergeticists. These workers take a radically literal attitude toward the chakra formulation and have designed exercises whose specific purpose is to dissolve the blocks that restrict the flow of energy.

Locked into our limited levels of consciousness, we do not even know what we are missing, says Ram Dass. He found out what we are missing through taking LSD. He now says that should not be necessary. An expansion of consciousness is available to anybody, and he cites as examples the Eastern individuals, whom he has observed, who defy Western man's expectations and predictions through such capacities as telepathy, clairvoyance, the enduring of pain, and remaining healthy on two glasses of milk a day and two hours of sleep a night.

The call is clarion-clear: If we would but expand our consciousness, we would think, feel, behave, and live differently and better, and discover infinite capacities now dormant within us. Our frontiers lie not in outer space but in finding inner space for such growth.

"Melodrama" is Ram Dass's charming word for our furrowed-brow, relentless *involvement* with objects, be these people, interests, or our own thoughts, feelings, and reactions. His use of melodrama is best defined by contrast with his recommended position of detachment, his version of the Buddha's teaching. Detachment is an ephemeral mid-point between being hysterically serious and remotely distant. Such a position provides a vantage point that makes possible a sense of irony and of alertness to paradox. It defends us from the traumatic and cataclysmic. Since, as the Buddha says, all decisions are both right and wrong, we neither need to strain to be right nor be crushed at being wrong. Ram Dass: "I can only do what I do because the minute I'm concerned I'm caught," and, "the minute I'm caught I can only catch you." In another example of detachment, he says that he has not given up being a Western scientist but he has given up the attachment to being a Western scientist. In that attachment he might suffer should his research design be criticized, might connive and sweat for recognition, and might compromise his capacity to think. Standing aside from such melodrama, he can use what he wants of Western science, free of such entrapments.

In literary criticism "melodrama" can be used as a put-down, as indicative of an artistically inferior production. In expanded consciousness, where there is no such thing as put-down, melodrama is simply what takes place in another kind of consciousness. In psychiatry one may be tempted to assess detachment as evidence either of narcissism, in which attachment doesn't occur because the person doesn't care enough, or schizoidness, in which attachment is too frightening to be allowed. If Ram Dass were in the state of consciousness that would admit of a rejoinder, he would deny that either of these psychiatric statements is applicable. He might suggest instead that the reader himself experience Ram Dass's thoughts. Implicit in them are more warmth and connectedness than might be expected from a primarily narcissistic person, more courage and connectedness than might be expected from a schizoid one. Rather, his detachment feels avuncular; its soberness and realism are leavened by a kindly twinkle. He inspires one to believe that it might be possible, after all, to be more "there" if one is not there, more "serious" if not serious, more "attached" if unattached.

Ram Dass's ideas about detachment may bring to the mind of psychoanalysts "desirelessness" and "neutrality." Gestalt therapists and others in the human potential movement will translate these ideas into "doing one's own thing," taking responsibility for one's self. Indeed, the Gestalt Prayer conveys the same sense of attached detachment: I do my thing and you do yours. And if by chance we find each other, it's beautiful. If not, it can't be helped.

However, such words read better than they convey reality. Most human interactions, and particularly those designed explicitly or implicitly to help bring about beneficial change in another, are subject to attachments, to values and goals that may be extrinsic to the choices or needs of the participants, especially as these change during the process. There are attachments to technical roles and therapeutic interventions, attachments to conceptions of mental health, attachments to social institutions and to social desiderata such as marriage, children, occupation; and attachments to cultural values such as the taboos against cannibalism, incest, and murder. When attached to such values, we cannot fully analyze, evaluate, learn about, or contemplate them; we can only act in relation to them, bound by a circumscribed situational field. The "therapeutic alliance" between a patient and a psychotherapist may be constrained by the very mutuality of its goals. The agreement to attach one's self to these goals is entered into at one point but is non-negotiable over time as long as the attachment fails to permit re-evaluation of goals. How much better, Ram Dass would say, if we simply agreed to expand awareness, wherever that led. And if we stood across the room and watched ourselves expanding awareness, all would be well no matter what was revealed or what eventuality should come our way. It would perhaps be a bit funny as well.

A corollary of detachment is that he who governs least governs best, that there are in people inherent goodness, reparative capacities, untapped energy, and unexploited talent, which await only the freedom to appear. Another corollary is that to live wisely is to avoid the opposition inherent in a position of attachment. To be attached to one object is to be in opposition to another, and to be in opposition is to underline in the first place a subject-object conception of relationships. Detachment, instead, allows subject and object to merge, enhances the flexibility that allows alliance through oneness, identification with one's self and the other. As in the Japanese martial art *aikido*, if one "goes with" an apparently opposing force, then one adds one's own self to that force in a now shared direction, with the dual result of avoidance of conflict and the summated deployment of energy. Western theorists who declare conflict inevitable do so on the basis that opposition is a necessary way of life, as indeed it is if people have attachments. Detached from such melodrama, there is nothing to oppose.

Finally, detachment from the past and the future allows the fullest possible experience of the present. When a rose is a rose is a rose, there can truly be roseness. So long as we are attached to wanting, we are subject to suffering from ungratified wants and gratified wants that create their suffering through the realization that they may not be eternally gratified. The fantasied empty future spoils the present moment.

Ram Dass looks back and forth between his two worlds, often defining his new self in counterpoint to his professional-clinician self. He views the latter as a somewhat lamentable expression of Western man's limited consciousness, as caught in a cause-and-effect thicket, mired in its conceptions of how people should think, feel, and behave. As with so many participants in the human potential movement and other protagonists of the new consciousness, Ram Dass says that he has tried psychoanalysis and practiced psychoanalytically based psychotherapy and has found them wanting. He says that he was analyzed for five years, at the end of which his analyst told him that he was too sick to live in society. He cites as evidence for his technical expertise his having been a psychotherapist in a student health service for eight years. These are questionable credentials. Any analyst who would end five years of analysis with the remark that the patient was too sick to live in society has probably not conducted an analysis worthy of the name. And if he did not say those words, then the claim that he did is either a garden-variety misunderstanding or Ram Dass, if not too sick to live in society, was too "sick" in various ways to be adequately analyzed. If so, such an attempt should not have been made at all, to say nothing of letting it continue for five years.

As to his eight years as a psychotherapist in a student health service, such an experience is no guarantee of talent or training. An unfortunate fact of our time is that poorly trained and untalented people do all kinds of things purporting to be therapeutic, and do so under the imprimatur of glittering titles and institutional affiliations. Ram Dass mentions nothing about his work being supervised, which would be necessary for the adequate training of all young therapists, nor how much of the eight years was devoted to this work, nor what prior training he may have had for it, etc. Without for the moment taking substantive issue with any of his conclusions, on the basis of the evidence he presents he simply is in no position to inspire confidence that he was ever able to test adequately the procedures and results of psychoanalytic work. Indeed, his reporting of note-taking during the hours suggests just the opposite. The taking of notes during hours is found more often in *New Yorker* cartoons than in the offices of responsible psychoanalytic practitioners. It is just such an activity that does tend to separate therapist from patient, to shift the balance from feeling and experience to cognition and theory, complaints that Ram Dass levels at psychoanalytic therapy.

At the same time that Ram Dass fails to portray himself as an impartial investigator familiar with the phenomena he is judging, he nonetheless does raise trenchant issues with which psychoanalysts should deal.

Psychoanalysts may use their network of concepts and constructs to explain, or explain away, phenomena that can be dealt with in other ways. In principle, this does not have to be. Freud, for example, was seriously interested in the occult. And while all psychoanalysts understand that they may correctly adduce motives for an individual's belief in God, this says nothing about whether there is a God.

The clinical theory of psychoanalysis may handicap the quest for the widest and deepest experiential understanding of another. Any theory, like any lens, has inherent characteristics that establish boundaries and dimensions of observation. Thus, paradoxically, awareness may be limited at the same time that it is expanded. Yet some psychoanalysts behave as if there were no explanations other than psychoanalytic ones to account for human phenomena. They view with suspicion those observations that cannot be encompassed by psychoanalytic theory or that violate the principles of scientific materialism in general. Psychologists, too, look askance at their colleagues who, for example, consider the possibility of information being received from other than the five senses. The more the theory does account for, the more we are inclined to credit it with ultimate fidelity and veracity, and in so doing discount other points of view. The likelihood of this is increased as the culture at large and some individual practitioners become unduly impressed not only with the beneficial changes that psychoanalytic work brings about but with such trappings of success as prestige, power, and money. Success may breed complacency and parochialism.

The history of clinical psychology and psychoanalysis makes understandable some other emotions that lead to institutionalized parochialism. These professions were developed in an atmosphere of rigorous, hardheaded science, whose achievements reinforced its exclusive claim to knowledge and to the means of finding knowledge. In this atmosphere, such new disciplines as psychoanalysis and clinical psychology have had to struggle to be regarded as scientifically respectable. They tend, therefore, to be holier-than-thou in their devotion to the traditional values and concepts of the Western mind as expressed in the concepts of Western science.

Another prominent criticism of psychoanalysis based on the Eastern wisdom that Ram Dass explores and espouses is that psychoanalysts miss the full experience of the present through their preoccupation with the past. To some extent such a criticism is more properly leveled at an antiquated version of psychoanalysis in which the theoretical understanding of the importance of past events is acted upon in psychoanalytic technique in such a manner that the hours are spent primarily hunting through early memories for "traumas." More sophisticated practitioners work in ways that are consonant with the understanding that the past is repeated in the present, that the most useful interpretations are those which are experientially alive in the relationship between patient and therapist in the here-and-now. To what extent any individual analyst can extricate his work with patients from his theory about the importance of the past, or is personally evocative enough to suffuse the present with feeling, is an empirical rather than theoretical question. Both critics and defenders have insufficient evidence for making hard and fast generalizations about which analysts do what.

Western man tends to overlook the present by way of his cultural orientation toward future goals. He often postpones satisfactions until he has finished his education, until he has more money, until the children are grown, etc. To the extent that he pins his hopes for happiness on the acquisition of specific externals, he may overlook and indeed lose the talent for experiencing what could be available to him in any given moment, what could be borne in upon him by a full openness of his senses, rather than by being striven for. In gestalt therapy, anxiety is described as stage fright, an orientation toward the future designed to protect one from anticipated shame, and eventualities that are assumed to be dangerous, at the cost of overlooking the possibilities of the present. We cannot enjoy the ice-cream cone, Ram Dass writes, because the sense of its future ending infiltrates what otherwise would be a moment of full enjoyment. Anxiety, the wound stripe of civilization, is defined as the experience of worry over the future, which as a moment's introspection by any of us will demonstrate diminishes, if not eliminates, an appreciation of the present.

To the extent that any psychotherapy is tied, explicitly or implicitly, to future goals, it may encourage such a destructive orientation toward the present. Though the present may not be concretely overlooked, its full impact may be underemphasized, nuances of it blotted out, feelings drained.

Ram Dass criticizes psychoanalytic psychotherapy also for its alleged emphasis on cognition as compared to feeling. Ram Dass implies that psychoanalysts are engaged, in effect, in an obsessional defense against feeling, manipulating ideas and making discoveries of motives in part to counteract painful experience. This is what might be expected, some critics say, from people who have pursued advanced degrees in our educational system, with its premium placed on success, ideas, organization, precision, all of which often come at the expense of spontaneity and intensity of feeling. Cognition versus feeling is a hoary issue in psychoanalysis. It has long been recognized that the comprehensiveness and intricacy of the several psychoanalytic theories, the tendency toward formulating cause-and-effect relationships in the clinical theory, and the search for explanations may influence the practitioner in the direction of undue ratiocination. Psychoanalysts of an existential and poetic inclination, especially, have attempted to counteract such tendencies through focusing upon experience and feelings.

Ram Dass, however, along with many others these days, suggests that the range of feelings with which psychoanalysts work is greatly limited by psychoanalytic technique no matter how flexibly, spontaneously, or evocatively it is used. In their view, feelings remain locked in the body, throttled and cut off by tense muscles and shallow breathing, and can be made available only when the body and breathing are worked with directly. This may be done more or less independently of working psychologically, as in structural integration (or "Rolfing"), or combined with psychological analysis so that the feelings are related to people, events, and thoughts, as in primal scream therapy, gestalt therapy, and bioenergetics. The swift and intense generation of feelings in many of these therapies may arouse admiration and envy in a conventional dynamic psychotherapist, who usually labors long and hard with many of his patients before such outpourings begin to occur. Whether and how such intense feelings are ultimately useful to the patient, and whether such usefulness is enduring are questions whose answers remain elusive. But the challenge is posed by Ram Dass, and ought to be met.

Ram Dass raises again the accusation of reductionism in psychoanalysis. From his discussion one would assume that he has in mind the simplistic, though perhaps unfortunately prevalent, thinking that implies that when a motive or cause for behavior is adduced, it constitutes the only reason for this behavior. Ram Dass either has not heard of the prominent concept in psychoanalysis of overdetermination (multiple causes for any given psychological event) or he has observed conventional therapists who fail to keep it in mind in their discussions of clinical work. Ram Dass further seems to believe that conventional psychoanalysts think of people only as a collection of motivations, without capacities for selecting, discriminating, judging, and adapting. None of us is prepared to speak for any one psychoanalyst as to his practice and beliefs; the system and training are insufficiently agreed upon for that. In principle, however, this kind of reduction is more in the mind of the beholder than indigenous to psychoanalysis.

Ram Dass is on firmer ground when he speaks of reductionism as the narrowing of the range of behavioral observation that occurs by way of the constructs of psychoanalysis being credited as sufficiently comprehensive and plastic to explain practically any behavior. Backed up by the prestige of at least approximations of the scientific method, and further buttressed by the values of Western society, this alleged capacity of psychoanalytic theory can be used to rule out explanations of phenomena in other than "scientific" terms. Despite its long, turbulent adversary position with regard to Western society and its values, psychoanalysis is now being used by that society to buttress prevalent philosophical assumptions and beliefs. Western society may still not fully believe psychoanalytic explanations, but it takes comfort in the existence of a branch of science that purports to explain all human phenomena according to the rule book of Western science. Whether this encompassing explanation is reductionism or reality is ultimately an empirical question. Ram Dass believes he knows the answer. However that may be, he does us a service by raising the question.

Finally, Ram Dass warns us against our haste to eradicate depression with drugs or interpretation as if to feel depressed were merely pathological. Despair, he says, is an absolute prerequisite for growth, for movement to another plane of consciousness. Do not adjust, he says, but treasure your discontents, honor your despair. Another dizzying paradox: The conventional psychotherapeutic contract is sanctioned by society in a health-sickness context (and practiced as such by some people). According to this model, presenting problems are to be solved, symptoms are to be removed, life is to be made more comfortable. Yet, the pure psychoanalytic position fundamentally is to help the patient toward free choice without prior prejudices toward what those choices may be. From a "therapeutic" point of view, one may want to rid the patient of depression and anxiety. But from an existential point of view, psychoanalysis is in agreement with Ram Dass that a certain amount of discomfort makes progress possible. It can provide the impetus for sublimation, a concept that shares characteristics with what Ram Dass seems to be referring to in what he calls "more evolvement" as a result of depression. Implicitly both Ram Dass and psychoanalysts recognize the value of the capacity to bear depression.

According to Ram Dass, conventional language itself is a constraint on thought and feeling. Its linear structure is inadequate to convey the metasystemic patterns and experiences he is trying to delineate. He believes that the only form of language that can come close to communicating what he has in mind is poetry. He himself tries to solve the problem of speaking about the unspeakable by writing in a quasi-poetic, allusive style that includes moderately "free" associations and frequent swings between the terms of Western science, Eastern philosophy, and Esalen hip. Relax, he implies, just go with it, let it happen, let life *be* a waterfall for a while. You'll get it if you're open to it, and if you are not open, no amount of polished syntax will help. It is a good mood in which to read his book, and if you give him half a chance, Ram Dass will help you to achieve it.

So here it is, an invitation to the greening of the person, to listen to the sound of one hand clapping. Scientists and citizens, questers all, you have "got to make love with the unknown . . . risky though that woman may be because she's got a lot of weird foibles. And you've got to make love with her with the total faith that if your intent is pure, the thing will be O.K. The truth will out. You've got to risk it all to have it all."

In the early 1960s Ram Dass had to go to India to learn to think the thought he reports on here. A decade later his trip would have been unnecessary. Much of what he reports on, the conclusions he draws, his portents for the future are readily available in a variety of human potential and explicitly therapeutic techniques and philosophies. East has come West in varied forms. In part this is due to Ram Dass. His struggle to find a new world and the bridge that he has built between his two worlds is one on which many pilgrims now walk. His tale of two worlds is now on the front page.

At the end of his A *Tale of Two Cities,* Charles Dickens has Sydney Carton go to the guillotine secure in the belief he is doing a far, far better thing than he has ever done before. Masochistic, martyred, romantic as Carton may have been, none of these excludes still another perspective. He had finally found his values and the courage to act accordingly. He had emerged from the dissolute funk of meaninglessness, and organized his identity and purpose. Ram Dass may also be guillotined, or guillotine himself. But as a bearded, sheet-clad metaphor, bumping clumsily, yet with a certain grace, in the Aqua Velva, button-down world, he may have found salvation. As an expression of ourselves questing for transition, we need him, all the more as the machine age gives way to the man age, as our attention shifts from the production of the dance to the dancer, as we experiment with infinite variations on the only dance there is.

Not long after I finished the introduction, Ram Dass chanced to give a lecture at the nearby University of Kansas, and I introduced myself to him there. He knew nothing of a hard-cover edition being brought out, to say nothing of the fact that it was to include an introduction by me. All this seemed so Kafkaesque that when the book finally came out, I sent him a copy to make sure that at least he could learn what had happened to his book firsthand. I received in reply the following note, handwritten in neat, controlled script on polite, small-size note paper. Ram Dass seems to be in a play within a play.

> Stephen,
>
> Your introduction to *The Only Dance* is a delight. It literally took me hours to begin to appreciate your cleverness. And I still can't know what I have missed, not being fully cognizant of the current therapy dialogues.
>
> All of your criticisms are true enough. The psychoanalysis, theory, and practice that I am whipping is a dead horse, and I was using it more as a provocative example (or perhaps scapegoat) of Western mentalities than considering a serious dialogue.

> You must appreciate that since 1963, no even semireputable representative of the "Establishment" in either religion or science has taken me or my writings seriously enough to ever criticize them publicly. In view of this it may be understandable why my end of the dialogue has gotten outdated and definitely sloppy.
>
> I suspect that in the future, these communities, as reflected by people such as you, will wish to engage in dialogue. At that time perhaps I'll read up on current analytic thinking in order to honor the profession appropriately in any critiques.
>
> Thanks for the copy. My father was definitely impressed.
>
> Ram Dass

"My father was definitely impressed." Now, what does that mean? Since much has been written about Ram Dass, we can assume father was not "definitely impressed" simply by a number of printed pages being devoted to his son. He may have been impressed by a member of an establishment institution's taking his son seriously. Somewhat sad to say, Ram Dass seems to have been impressed by that himself. Father is characterized in the book as a wealthy conservative businessman, with morals and mores to match. He could have been impressed and relieved at any sign that the gulf between him and his son and the two worlds they represent might be narrowing, however slowly.

And why did Ram Dass choose to include his father's state of mind in the note to me? He had turned his back on the father of big houses, fast cars, private planes, had rejected his religion, mode of dress, speech patterns, and social role. Yet it takes only a sense of what it is like to be a father or a son to notice in his book the wish to unite father and son, to sense the hurt feelings of being ignored by father's establishment, and the wish that there could be a bridge between their two worlds. The inner world is played out wide-screen in social movements, styles of life, and choice of therapy. Metaphors piled upon metaphors.

5

The Meeting Game

IMMERSING MYSELF IN the human-potential waters from a diving board in Topeka, Kansas, was my research design, if such a sprawling, *ad hoc* campaign can be inflatedly named as such. The planning meetings were those introspective airplane rides. My one experimenter turned out to be reasonably reliable, though I occasionally worried about his endurance and mental stability. And since "subjects" were scattered over the globe, the collection of data involved a good deal of travel. I would make forays from Topeka on long weekends, during vacations, and take an occasional week away in order to conduct my "experiments."

In case you are wondering how it was possible to maintain a full schedule of treating patients and teaching while exploring other ways of working around the country, my patients rather acidly wondered the same, especially when I had to cancel their appointments. Other sources of occasional acid were my family, who at times kind of lost track of where I was, and myself, who at times plain resented not having time to curl up with a good book or watch a junky movie. So I had a combination of internal and external resistances, logistic problems, and other constraints helping decide what trips to take when.

There was no lack of opportunities. I regularly received notification of human potential meetings in the mail. This steady flow of brochures is an expression of the proselytizing enthusiasm of the movement. One need not go to Esalen, for Esalen in one form or another sooner or later will come to you, or at least to a nearby city, in the form of a human potential meeting. These meetings are chuck full of ideas and activities novel to conventional Western society, science, and academia. They are fun, a kind of theater where, often, big human potential names are featured in an atmosphere and with strategies designed as much for enjoyment as enlightenment. They help promote continued attention to change and the psychological good life. One may attend such a meeting now and again just to loosen up internally, to be reminded of human potential values, to increase awareness, or to expand consciousness. And they can be therapeutic; the activities designed to promote beneficial change may do so if that is what the participant intends. With so much to offer, with such a wide range of inducements, with national publicity and a new market, it is no surprise that the human potential meetings are popular, often oversubscribed. Following is a description of one such meeting. In part it is a condensation, including ideas and experiences from several meetings.

The New Dallas

Dallas's Texas School Book Depository loomed over the infamous "grassy knoll." A few blocks away, a weekend workshop convened which was entitled "Body-Mind-Spirit." It was an ironic juxtaposition. The John F. Kennedy Museum, situated within the arc of the bullets' trajectory, epitomized a bleeding, senseless way of life. The conference was dedicated to a new world's coming, what George Leonard, one of its leaders, calls "the transformation."

Most of what follows actually happened at the Dallas workshop. Some of it happened at other such meetings and is incorporated here.

Here are the workshop leaders:

George Leonard is a founder of the human potential movement, a major statement of which is included in his book *The Transformation.*[1] He was a senior editor of *Look* magazine for seventeen years before he transformed his own life into a study of bodily awareness and the oriental martial art *aikido,* in which he has a black belt. He also became a competitive runner. He is a continuing prolific author, lecturer, and conceptualizer of the inner man as related to the outer world. In his recent book, *The Ultimate Athlete,*[2] we learn that he was a flyer. By following the sounds in a hotel ballroom we come upon him as a pianist. As keynote speaker he set the tone for the weekend with the story of a man with a black belt in judo who asked that he be buried in his white belt so that he could go on learning. To learn, said Leonard, one must be willing to be a fool. Leonard's intellect, his literal and figurative stature, and his informal dignity made being foolish, letting one's hair down, and taking one's shoes off seem friendly, inviting things to do. All right, clowning and crawling on the way to walking, it would be. On the note of, "Heck, there's a transformation coming, let's get in on it," Leonard sent us into the weekend.

Will Schutz was an academically trained psychologist who became a chief spokesman of encounter group therapy and a man for all seasons in the human potential movement. As experiencer and practitioner, he seems to have overlooked nothing in the panoply of its activities: bodily interventions, psychological interventions, and the philosophical underpinnings of both. He is sharp-minded, sharp-tongued, and sharply funny. Distillations of his thinking are available in *Here Comes Everybody*[3] and *Joy*.[4] Typical of him was his first remark to the meeting, even before saying, "Hello": "You are totally responsible for whatever happens to you this weekend."

Ilana Rubenfeld is a charming proponent of body and mind as an integrated force for health and beneficial change. She is a teacher and board member of the American Center for the Alexander Technique, which is the training institute for the Alexander system of bodily interventions and manipulations, and she is a gestalt psychotherapist. A trained musician, she used to conduct symphony orchestras. Glittering in a rainbow of exotic jewelry and clothes, a magician who transforms bodies and minds (sometimes right on the spot), she seems at the same time the little girl next door.

Karl Pribram, in his white beard looking like a preoccupied Santa Claus, is a medical researcher on the brain whose work is available in many research papers and books. In recent years he has suggested the neurological bases for Freud's concepts, and at this meeting offered a neurological understanding of human potential concepts.

Betty Fuller, an actress-director-producer in theater, radio, and television, plays herself in the *cinéma vérité* film *Here Comes Everybody*, a record of an encounter group co-led by herself and Will Schutz. In the film that was shown at the meeting she bares her soul in a vivid and moving presentation, demonstrating an openness about oneself that is typical of many human potential people. In this meeting she led groups in bodily exercises and in the study of interpersonal relations.

Al Chung-Liang Huang, a literary collaborator of Alan Watts, is a master of *t'ai chi*, dance and theater, brush calligraphy, and other Asian fine and martial arts. His participation is both real and symbolic of the influence on the human potential movement of ancient oriental knowledge and practices. A slickly handsome one-time actor, his movements, his very walking are as close to a human being flying as one is likely to see.

You may have noticed how many of the workshop leaders have changed their careers. This is perhaps inevitable in an enterprise so new that one in his forties could not have settled upon it in adolescence and continued on uninterruptedly. Such career changes also may reflect the kind of personality drawn to the human potential way of life. The movement seems to attract people who have diverse interests, who are restless, questioning, and who dare to make changes. Or, such people could simply be malcontents, chronically dissatisfied rolling stones. To judge from their activities, writing, and bearing, if they are the latter, they are certainly not the sour and chronically complaining kind of malcontent; rather, theirs seems an incessantly questing, and implicitly optimistic, discontent.

Based largely on the remarks of Will Schutz, here are some general ideas and philosophical positions in the human potential movement. The activities of the movement can be categorized as interpersonal ones such as encounter groups, intrapsychic ones such as gestalt therapy, bodily interventions such as the Feldenkrais and Alexander techniques, and mystical ones such as are embodied in a variety of Eastern philosophies, for example reincarnation and mysticism. Whatever the mode of approach to existence, it takes place in a context of belief in limitlessness. By contrast, most of us live with a restricted level of awareness, a hedged-in consciousness, the limits of which are taken to be our physical, mental, and spiritual borders. When we expand awareness, we expand limits. Before the invention of the microscope, we were unable to see the germ world. With the invention of expanded consciousness, we see worlds of expanded possibilities. We are bounded neither by five senses nor the laws of physics. Or so says Will Schutz. Another wing of the movement wishes he were not so absolutist about it. These theorists concede at least some externally imposed and immutable restrictions on human potential.

That "truth" and "honesty" underlie beneficial interpersonal experiences, including conventional psychotherapy, is hardly news. But there is novelty in the way human potential people apply and understand these ideas and values. Truth is defined as what one experiences. This is by contrast to truth arrived at by the experimental method or deductively within systems of thought. The latter truths are dependent upon the assumptions and practices of the method or system. Thus, according to the scientific method, truth is what scientists believe is true because it conforms to the rules of the scientific method. Experiential truth is independent of such external agreement and is therefore unarguable. Reality in human potential terms is a construction of each individual, varying from moment to moment as he varies, perhaps matching that of others, perhaps not. Honesty is the truth, the experience of reality, that one person chooses to tell another. Rather than a moral value, it is operational; you tell it the way you see it, and that is being honest. In general, human potential people do tend to tell others more about their truth than most others do.

Selfishness is another idea that is ordinarily couched in implicitly moral terms, sometimes elaborated psychiatrically as "narcissism." In the human potential movement, selfishness is all there is, just as being true to oneself is all there is. One may do for another, one may try to be helpful to another, but only because one wants to for oneself. Altruism from this point of view is self-deceit, or, in the word of Will Schutz, "bullshit." (This may be as good a time as any other to take notice that, according to Fritz Perls's taxonomy there are three varieties of shit: 1] "chickenshit," as in cocktail-party chatter. (During the workshop we had an exercise in which we were enjoined to talk nothing but chickenshit, get it out of our systems, and perhaps notice how boring it was.) 2] "Bullshit" is intellectualized talk. 3] "Elephantshit" is highly intellectualized, metapsychological, metaphysical, philosophical talk. It follows that "nonshit" is telling the truth about one's experience.

"Awareness" is a simple word and idea but one whose implications are anything but simple. During the weekend we had several exercises in descriptive awareness, concentrating on how people looked and acted and forcing ourselves to describe them simply, in observational, rather than inferential or interpretive, terms. This may sound easy, but it is not for many of us, so imbued are we with interpreting, rather than merely registering. While interpreting adds meaning, it may also subtract some of what is there to be seen. Awareness, like consciousness, may be infinitely expandable and encompassing. In principle we can become aware cosmically and cellularly; new frontiers are there to be discovered behind our eyeballs.

If reality is defined by our experiences, and experiences change momentarily, then a life of reality takes place only in the here-and-now. According to human potential theorists, most of us tend to substitute the past for the here-and-now, by way of reverie or explanations of the present in anticipation of the future. Either way, we rob the present of experience, rob ourselves of ourselves. We do so, in part, out of cowardice, fear of what may happen right now spontaneously, or what we can make happen right now through making decisions and taking responsibility. Conventional culture conveys information from the distance of history or abstraction while practicing a taboo on the interpersonal and intrapsychic experiences of the students as these take place in the present. We teach children, as we have been taught, to live elsewhere, and so they miss out on where they are.

Will Schutz's grave announcement that all workshop participants were solely responsible for everything that happened to them raised the question as to whether he really meant "everything," and he did. Such adventitious circumstances as a fire in the hotel, irresistible impulses, and crippling inhibitions, the seeming laws of chance—all were to be included. As in yoga philosophy, if our consciousness is sufficiently evolved it transcends all other considerations. (You should be able to sense the imminence of a hotel fire and get space elsewhere.) Many of us are accustomed to blame other people or events external to ourselves for our plight, while others of us tend to blame parts of ourselves: our instincts or our bodies. In the human potential movement, people are the sole creators of their own destiny; they are as they choose to be. Group pressure, for example, does not cause people to behave in a certain way. Rather, people choose to behave in a certain way in response to group pressure. Even feelings experienced as spontaneous are chosen. We choose to feel happy or sad, excited or bored. Again, some human potential theorists would object that allowance has to be made for chance, coincidence, habit, while Schutz's left wing would have everything determined by the person himself.

I felt some chagrin at being reminded that I could not

blame my instincts, neuroses, unconscious, for what I did or failed to do. I felt some fear at what I might do or not do, since now, with free choice, my half-emancipated fantasy was that I might do almost anything. I was excited at the new possibilities I sensed might emerge, and was somehow relieved that any mistakes (whatever mistakes are) were to be my own. This is the sort of thing that contributes to the slightly dizzying reorganization of self I found to be typical of such meetings.

Radical self-responsibility opens a whole new approach to the practice of medicine. Rather than disease being caused by an external agent, as in the microbe theory, the person takes advantage of the external agent to bring about the result he chooses. As Louis Pasteur is said to have remarked on his deathbed, "The microbe is nothing; the surround is everything." Thus, cholesterol does not cause heart disease; a way of life uses cholesterol to cause heart disease. (It is alleged that some African tribes consume more cholesterol than do Americans but do not develop heart disease. Indeed, many Americans consume great amounts of cholesterol with no ill effect.) The "surveillance theory" of cancer suggests that most of us have cancer cells from time to time, but only a relatively few of us choose, at a particular juncture in life, to "have cancer," which we bring about by shutting down the immune system. Continuing questions in all diseases are why some people fall ill under certain conditions, while others, under apparently the same conditions, remain healthy; why the same treatment is effective with one person and ineffective for another though both persons seem to have the same disease.

Psychoanalysts and others have long and unmistakably demonstrated that choice, even execution, takes place outside the doer's awareness. Indeed, psychoanalysis arose from the observation that bodily symptoms were caused and could be alleviated by bringing to awareness the mental events that had led to the formation of the symptoms. So-called psychosomatic medicine was the next step in bridging the perennial philosophical, religious, and medical body-mind problem. Structural changes in the body, actual disease, could be influenced by thoughts and feelings out of awareness, and ameliorated by these thoughts and feelings coming into consciousness. Human potential people, particularly those strongly influenced by gestalt therapy, radically apply the principle that the organism always functions, or tries to function, as a whole. Thus, they see the body-mind dichotomy as misleading. Rather, all disease is an expression of the whole self, a final common path on which thoughts, feelings, inheritance, and physiology converge.

Schutz continues: All other things being equal, blocked expressiveness at the developmentally higher levels results in expressiveness at the lower levels, and a system of organs is chosen for that expression according to what has been blocked at a higher level. For example, the liver, one of whose functions is "to decide" what is toxic and what is not toxic, may develop hepatitis as a result of the person's difficulty deciding between what is good and what is bad for him in psychological terms. Heart disease may express a troubled love life. Leukemia and Hodgkin's disease may reflect a lack of human nourishment by way of their diminution of red-cell nourishment. Physicians should treat the patient, rather than the disease. Their "treating" would hark back to the original meaning of the word "doctor," which is "teacher." They would provide the conditions under which the patient would learn to make choices for health, rather than disease.

Such a point of view recognizes the truism that the body heals itself. A wound, for example, can be "treated," which means only that conditions are provided for healing. It is then up to the person to heal, which some people do quickly and well, and others do slowly and poorly or not at all. The human potential ideas about the body, health, and disease have found expression in a new medicine that is analogous to new psychotherapy. (New medicine is examined further in Part Five.)

Self-responsibility was applied by Schutz to a wide variety of fields. For example, from the point of view of individual choice as the determining factor in human behavior, the function of governments is simply to remove obstacles to citizens' self-determination. The implication for law is that there are no excuses for crimes. If we are free to choose life, then perhaps death is an unnecessary limitation. Schutz cited Jonas Salk as suggesting, on the basis of molecular biology, that nothing in the cell inheres toward death. Aging and extinction may be, like the four-minute mile, a function of our sense of limitation, a flagging in our will.

Will Schutz carries further this understanding of the subservience of the body to the essence of the person by suggesting that the essence lives on after leaving the body, and continues to choose, as in reincarnation. The essence chooses new parents, for example. It does this with respect to unsolved problems in the previous life, as, for example, a Nazi murderer choosing to be a thalidomide child in order to solve the problems of culpability.

Typical of the human potential way of life was an invitation for the evening that I chanced to hear. A woman was telling the man how she felt about their date, what her needs were, and how she would like to go about satisfying them. She then inquired what "space" he was in, where he was in his feelings and wishes at the moment. While such an invitation may seem little different from, "This is what

I would like to do tonight" and "What would you like to do tonight?" it is different in important respects. The emphasis, first of all, was on each other's experience at that moment. Nothing was taken for granted. The possibility was left open that either party would not like to do anything with the other, even though it was clear there had been a previous understanding that they would be together. This approach was also an invitation to introspection: What really was going on with each person? What really did he and she want? Self-experience was to determine the decision, not institutionalized forms or prior plans. This point of view was illustrated in one of the exercises we did in which we faced one another, then rocked back and forth, toward and away from each other, then opened and closed our eyes, alternately admitting and shutting off one another. All this was a way of recognizing that people may choose from moment to moment to be attached and to withdraw, that there are separate needs, which may come and go. The implicit wisdom is that relationships may be more fulfilling when freshly chosen than if the participants feel constrained always to be together. Paradoxically, the option of being separate might enhance being connected.

Some seventy-five people milled around in a smallish area of the ballroom without bumping into one another by using "soft eyes," a seeming out-of-focus approach to the world that apparently increased peripheral vision. Focused, "hard" eyes resulted in bumping into one another. Sending awareness to one's back seemed to result in having eyes in the back of one's head, a sense of what was behind. By sending awareness to one's "center," or *hara*, one could get a feeling of groundedness, solidity. By ignoring one another, touching one another gently, pushing one another jarringly, we became aware of these ways of using our bodies in relating ourselves to one another, and incidentally developed a sense of kinship with what before had been a motley and separate collection of strangers. Other exercises were designed to develop a sense that fields of energy were radiating from each other and could be increased through concentration. So we were not bounded by our skins, unconnected, coming together only through physical touch. Rather, we were sending and receiving fields of energy.

Awareness of the body could prevent injury to it and could program achievements into it. We were told of football players who played their games mentally in advance so that, when the actual game was played, they were better able to anticipate the moves of others and themselves.

We were shown ways of standing, walking, and sitting which, on inspection, either contributed to or detracted from the natural alignment and support of our bodies. We could curve our spine so that parts of the body were forced to accommodate weight inefficiently, creating obvious stress and strain, lock our knees so that we become "pushovers," tilt our pelvises, thereby dumping our viscera outward and forward and creating tension in the lower back, or rearrange ourselves so that weight and gravity would work in favor of less stress and strain and greater smoothness and efficiency. We became attuned to the submissiveness and self-derogation inherent in slumped shoulders or caved-in chests, the excessive assumption of responsibility involved in carrying the world on our shoulders by heightening and squaring them. (The role of the body in human potential thinking is further examined in Part Two.)

We demonstrated that, by applying a good deal of strength, we could lift our standing partners off the floor or bend their stiffly outstretched arms. But when our partners imagined that their legs were sending a beam of energy through the earth, we could no longer pick them up. And when their arms were sending out a beam of energy across the horizon, we could no longer bend these arms. We observed and demonstrated to ourselves also that we could no longer prevent our arms being bent once our partner had moved his hand up and down our body in ways that presumably involved the meridians of acupuncture. Two members of our group, who had independently studied some of these phenomena previously, demonstrated that they could weaken or strengthen one another's capacity to keep his arms out straight regardless of the amount of pressure applied, without touching or manipulating at all. It was done from a distance of some dozen feet simply through concentration. The laws of physics, the boundedness of senses and skins, the limitations of self, all seemed to fade away. Much in the atmosphere was the question, if these things are possible, then what is not possible?

Another way to concern oneself with the body was to attend to what was put into it. There seemed general agreement that our eating habits and the foods ordinarily available to us were injurious to health and welfare. Here and there, people had knapsacks with food they had brought with them. Even in restaurants herbal tea was produced from handbags in order to avoid coffee and ordinary tea; and sugar was, it seemed, unanimously considered a poison. Will Schutz and Betty Fuller had participated in "natural hygiene fasting," some forty days of existing solely on water. The principle is that if the body is let alone, not even occupied with digesting, it will rid itself of accumulated toxins, beginning with what it needs least, such as excess fat and disease. The concomitant disagreeable smells to the breath and urine and coating of the tongue all signal a leaving of toxins. When the toxins are gone, all becomes sweet and clear again. (Chapters 18 and 19 have more to say about nutrition.)

Moshe Feldenkrais is a seventy-plus-year-old Israeli who holds a Ph.D. in physics, has patents on machines he has invented, speaks twelve languages, and has a black belt in judo. He had developed a problem with one of his knees for which surgery was recommended, but with only a fifty-fifty chance of success. Not satisfied with these odds, he set about studying his knee, and then the rest of the body. In the process of curing himself he formulated principles and techniques to implement bodily health. In his view there are no such things as tightened, frozen, immobile, or awkwardly arranged muscles. These difficulties actually occur in the brain, which controls the muscles. Consequently, instead of training the body, one should allow the brain additional options, more information, so that it can experiment with and select the most helpful ways of using and controlling the body. Feldenkrais exercises, then, are ways of heightening the brain's awareness. For example, we worked for some forty minutes on relaxing one shoulder so that it could meet the floor, but needed only a few minutes to do the same thing with the other shoulder. The brain had already learned the muscular arrangements that facilitated what seemed at first an impossible bodily position.

F. S. Alexander was an Australian Shakespearean actor who lost his voice, and consequent livelihood. Unable to gain help from others with this problem, he began to study himself in a series of mirrors. He discovered that, prior to speaking, he was making involuntary inhibitory movements. This initial discovery led to the understanding that just about all of us misuse our body outside our awareness through making useless or harmful muscular contractions. The result is a misaligned, often unattractive, and stress-laden body. The Alexander technique is a direct muscular intervention which, gently but firmly, rearranges the muscles—their relationships to one another and to other parts of the body. These interventions are followed by exercises that encourage continued efficient use of the body in its ordinary tasks of sitting, standing, walking. There are only some fifty practitioners of the Alexander method in the United States, though it has a fairly long and illustrious tradition in England. About half of the Alexander practitioners in the United States are in New York City, many trained by Ilana Rubenfeld in a two-and-a-half-year program under the auspices of the Alexander Institute. (The Alexander technique will be explored in more detail in Part Two.)

Following demonstrations and practice by some seventy-five members of the workshop, Ilana selected one member of the group on whom to demonstrate the Alexander method of direct work on the body. This subject was a middle-aged woman who, despite the beauty of her face and figure, suffered intermittently with rheumatoid arthritis and had developed a thickening of her joints and restricted mobility. This discordance seemed echoed also in what one could tell of her personality, a seeming restriction and constriction behind which one sensed latent capacities for openness, freedom, and expressiveness. She lay down on a table, and after eying her diagnostically, Ilana began a series of gentle pushes, pulls, and probes of bodily parts. During the course of this work, the audience seemed somehow to participate in what Ilana described as an exchange of energy between practitioner and patient. Like a Greek chorus, they offered their attention and reacted to the experience taking place before them. In an electric moment, one was reminded that the body is in some disciplines referred to as a temple. When the subject got off the table, her smile illuminated the room. She said she felt loose and free, later discovered that she could hold a pencil, make reaching movements, and straighten her spine in ways that she could not just previously. As she walked through the room, she radiated at least one meaning of transformation. What only the most perceptive might have noticed previously was now there for all to see. She seemed to have become a queen.

All Alexander interventions are not as dramatic as this one. Ilana acknowledged that this was one of the most successful of her many demonstrations. My several Alexander treatments, to be described in Part Two, had not resulted in my appearing to become a king. Nonetheless, I did feel better after them, for whatever reason, and when I remember to remember, I exchange my slouch and shuffle for a healthier posture. The benefits derived from the Alexander technique include amelioration or cure of specific bodily ills, bringing ordinarily misused bodies into efficient juxtaposition with earth and gravity, and encouraging ways of using the body that contribute to continued physical, and possibly mental, health.

A beautiful and evocative entry into the unconscious was provided by an exercise led by Ilana in which a group of four people were asked to imagine a store, then to imagine buying something in that store, then to speak as the thing that they had bought. One participant, who despite her wedding ring, somehow previously had seemed to me to be unmarried, imagined herself to be a beautiful, expensive guitar, "who could make such lovely music if someone would only come along and play me." Another person, of apparent intellectual and aesthetic inclinations, imagined himself to be a sterling silver pin, designed in artistic ways with a blue stone serving as a beacon of light; then he added that despite his attractiveness and ability he wished that he were not simply an ornament, something for someone else to enjoy. This exercise demonstrated how quickly such a simple device could bring to awareness, in moving, poetic, and evocative terms, important wishes and characteristics of the personality.

Shortly after the Dallas meeting, I participated in a conversation in which an acquaintance said that he would like to give up his job and move to a sunny climate and raise roses, "but I can't." Fresh from a reminder of gestalt therapy techniques and attitudes, I suggested that "can't" is properly used only to refer to activities that are not within the repertoire of possible behaviors. The more felicitous verb was "won't." (I don't really talk that way, or at least not too often.) He at first insisted that "can't" was appropriate because it reflected his fear of taking the risk of such a change. With this admission it became clear that his decision not to change his life was more accurately described as "won't." In principle, he *could*, but he chose not to, for at least the reason he was aware of or gave, namely fear. In this recognition he had moved from the position of a person who felt trapped by external circumstances, without choice or option, and without considering at the moment his fear, to a person who had confronted himself with his fear, who recognized that he was fettered only by his timidity, that he was indeed a person with choices.

Also shortly after my return from Dallas, I resumed work on the flagging will to live of a psychotherapy patient who had recently been diagnosed as having cancer. Her role in what turned out to be my continuing work with cancer patients is related in Part Five. I had believed previously that disease is an expression of the person, that the will to health and life heavily determines the course of physical events. As a result of the weekend in Dallas, however, I believed these things more firmly. Belief, after all, is not all-or-nothing; it comes in all shapes, sizes, and degrees, and these vary from time to time. A believer is sometimes a true believer, and sometimes even truly believes. The depth and intensity of my convictions about my patient's power to reverse her cancer enabled me to increase my capacity to evoke the experience and reality of this power. I heard myself sound more convinced of what I had been convinced of before. Information brought back from such human potential workshops as that of Dallas tends to be available for evocative use because it is learned in an evocative context. It may not always be new to the mind, but even when old may have new spirit breathed into it.

This Dallas, of the seventies, turned out to be a far different Dallas from the one of November 1963. That spasm of senselessness was the excreta of a way of life. Absorbed with outer space, inner space had become filled with rot, and there was more to come. Some twelve years later, the worse for the wear of our times, our times welcomed this Dallas meeting and its harbinger of new and different times.

Even in Nebraska

During my stay at Esalen I chanced to meet a woman somewhere the other side of middle age who was imbued with enthusiasm for human potential ideas and wanted to do something to help others to share her enthusiasm. What she did was to see that traveling human potential meetings stopped in Lincoln, Nebraska. Through her efforts, this small city in the heart of traditional America became a beachhead for the dissemination of human potential ideas in the Midwest. Mankind's struggles and his hopes to improve his lot seem the same whether he gets to the hotel ballroom on a freeway or across the prairie, by plane or covered wagon. Well, not exactly covered wagon.

To get to Lincoln I merely had to drive 175 miles in an uncovered convertible. On rural roads cars, too, can become sanctums of contemplation—especially on the way back. At these times I would almost palpably rearrange my viscera, quiet my nervous system, slipknot my feelings—and try to subject the winging, group-shared ideas of the weekend to what felt to me then to be the landlocked knowledge of weekdays.

The Nebraska meeting of 1975, "Body, Mind, Spirit: Self-Unity," was peopled to a large extent by those who would constitute "The New Dallas." The ideas and activities were much the same. In particular it emphasized the heady, romantic, inspirational view of man put forward by Schutz, George Leonard, and others in Dallas: The "potential" in human potential meant, in effect, unlimited potential. Since we choose everything in our lives, there is no limit to the choices that we can make: be healthy rather than sick, live rather than die, be or not be where a ton of steel falls, and choose what kinds of parents we will have in our next reincarnation. We need not obey the limits of space and time, need not be constrained by getting information from the five senses. We can vary levels of consciousness, and in so doing discover otherwise dormant, unsuspected, virtually limitless power.

A year later, another human potential meeting, entitled "Forces of Life," was held at the same Lincoln, Nebraska, site according to the same general format and again billed as offering new ways of living. The self-selected participants came from the same geographical areas, and included the characteristically mixed bag of attendees at such meetings, predominantly students and mental health professionals. I had hesitated about going to this meeting, since I expected that it would simply be more of the same; but the chance of serendipity only a car ride away was decisive. As it turned out, the meeting was indeed instructive, but in unanticipated ways. The differences between the two Nebraska meetings reveal some of the dangers as well as the opportunities of the human potential movement.

There were the usual profusion of new and brightly refurbished, usually provocative ideas. Many of these came from Rollo May, who is often billed as an "existential psychoanalyst." It seems to me that there ought to be a hyphen between existential and psychoanalyst. Philosophy is one thing, analysis is another, and I am inclined to believe that one interferes with the other, however elucidating and valuable it may be in its own context. However, I tried to put aside such workaday considerations, the better to enjoy being in the presence of May's warm, profound, and darting mind. I especially appreciated his ideas about creativity; for example, that the artist, by definition, is the enemy of society. Rather than opting for safety, the acceptance of what is available as all that is possible, the artist plays with devils. He seeks to tame them, daring the unknown. To some of us he poses the threat of revelation and change, as he holds up a mirror in which the rest of us must confront ourselves.

Sam Keen, author and general man about human potential ideas, offered his view of development to and beyond the socially condoned. Development begins with a childhood stage marked by trust, receptivity, and femininity, in which the basic word is "yes." This period is followed by a rebel stage marked by separation, distrust, and masculinity, in which the basic word is "no." Then there is an adult stage characterized by moderation, adjustment, conformity, in which the basic words are "yes" and "no." In the adult stage one establishes oneself as worker, worrier, or helper, and fixes one's niche in the competitive rankings. However, those who live life to the fullest, who maximize their potential, go on to other stages. The "outlaw" stage is an assertion of the wish to decide for oneself, a recognition that otherwise one does not live one's own life but, rather, has it ordained for one. Instead of asking, "What should I do?" the outlaw asks, "Who am I?"—a stage of turmoil and risk. Those who work this stage through move beyond it to the stage of "lovers and/or fools." They recognize that the world does not simply comprise individuals but is a community, not a battlefield or merely a place of work but a kind of erogenous zone. God does, indeed, turn out to be love. To the lover, any life can be infinitely interesting, and all lives coalesce into a universal one. The "fool" views all this, as he participates in it, with a sense of irony, detached attachment, taking what comes, less solving and more accepting, making up the rules as he goes along.

Joan Halifax-Grof suggested further possibilities for learning what is on the other side of the mountain, for melting the boundaries between oneself and others and between oneself and the universe: In principle, any event that breaks up familiar patterns of body or mind carries with it the potentiality for new experience. Some kinds of sickness provide such experiences; the rhythms and functions of the body are broken up while, at the same time, people confront their mortality. Changes in electrical activity of the brain through one or another variety of meditation or self-hypnosis is an indicator of differential brain functioning in which various capacities can be expedited. Rapidly alternating light and dark stimuli seem to drive unaccustomed brain waves, as can be seen by changes in consciousness from flickering strobe lights and the seizures reported by people driving past a monotonously regular row of back-lit trees. Depriving a person of accustomed sensory stimuli induces a changed consciousness, as numerous experiments with isolation have demonstrated.

John Lilly, and others, use a salt-water tank for such purposes. Torture, beyond a certain point, becomes transcendent, as the flagellants seem to have known. Sleep deprivation and fasting are other ways of disorienting oneself in favor of new orientations. Still another way is hyperactivity, as can be seen, for example, in pentecostal church rituals. Changes in rhythms of breathing have a similar effect. Finally, psychedelic plants and such preparations as LSD afford the opportunity for experiences of mind largely unknown to conventional ranges of consciousness.

Over some twenty years, Stanley Grof has observed four thousand LSD sessions, given for experimental purposes, in conjunction with psychotherapy and as an aid to dying patients. Among the phenomena he has noted are experiences of birth and rebirth, of cosmic unity, of heaven, and of hell.

Such speculative and romantic ideas as these, skating along the brink of what is intellectually tolerable and experientially familiar, run the same danger that tragedy runs in the theater: one false step and the performance degenerates into comedy or farce. Danger—as well as opportunity—comes from ideas being presented informally rather than through the reading of papers; paper reading may be dull, but it is safe. Extemporaneous presentations require high quality to make the risk worthwhile. The participants in the Nebraska meeting of 1975 (and as duplicated by almost the same people in Dallas of 1976) were of uniformly high quality; they pulled it off. In Nebraska 1976, however, some of the presenters (those named here not included) were simplistic rather than simple, their comments were often indistinguishable from conversations over the backyard fence, swirls of jargon words doing their best at puffing up ideas. I wished, in embarrassment for them, that they at least had had available the traditional scientific forms of paper reading and formal discussions; they would then have had only limited opportunity to be held directly accountable by the audience and would have been able comfortably to escape into vague abstractions. That was a game I had seen successfully played (and played myself) in countless scientific forums. Instead, in keeping with human potential openness, at this meeting the audience had its vociferous, complaining say. As is usual with unstructured discussions in large groups, reason hung shakily on the ropes.

Another source of dissatisfaction, not previously in evidence at those human potential meetings I have attended, may have stemmed from the steady diet of lectures. In the typical Esalen roadshow, lectures and discussions are combined with work on the body, as in samples of Alexander and Feldenkrais exercises, and there are other experiential activities. The cumulative effect is to add to the excitement of new ideas the stimulation of interpersonal contact and an "open" body. By the end of such meetings people know each other and themselves in spontaneous, often novel, ways.

But what does it mean that ideas should be responded to so negatively because their presentation is less than glittering and is unaccompanied by priming the body and fun and games?

If good presentation is so important, how much was the persuasiveness of previous human potential figures a function of good theater rather than good reasoning? I wondered to what extent I and others were more bamboozled by the charming wit of, say, Will Schutz, than helpfully educated by his insights. Were we just washed along by waves of feeling, kindergartners persuaded that school was good by ice cream and cookies? Watch out for the media, I said to myself, if you wish to evaluate the message. With the poor presenters at this meeting, and in an atmosphere that was abstemious by usual human potential standards, the points of view threadbare of logic creaked and groaned, and the glitter was chintzy.

I wondered, too, about the effect on the group of a pulling back on the part of some of the speakers from the winging position asserted by Leonard, Schutz, and others at previous meetings. Just a year before, George Leonard had scoffed at the classical existential image of man being forever condemned to loneliness, bounded by his skin. And Leonard illustrated his point with exercises designed to show how energy radiates from people, just as Kirlian photography shows auras extending beyond the body's putative boundaries. Yet at this Nebraska meeting Rollo May talked about people's being fundamentally lonely, having within them a sanctum sanctorum, and struggling for love just to help overcome the numbness of having to be solitary. Will Schutz, as the spokesman for the human potential extending of unlimited hope, had told us in Dallas that all was in our power. We merely had to exercise choice and live according to the expectation that wishes can be made to come true. Yet here was Richard Farson saying that we do not solve problems, we simply experience dilemmas. Here was Sam Keen saying that, rather than using "potential" to refer to infinity, let us observe its etymological root, which is "power." But power need not refer to a force whose effect is as strong as there is energy to power it. It can refer to developmental power, the power of an acorn to become what it is to become, an oak tree, to fulfill in this way its potentiality. In other words, potential is limited by developmental patterns.

Frustration at the recognition of limitations on what to some seem to be unlimited possibilities was acted upon in one of the workshops, this one convened to study how to master life crises. Rather than supplying formulae for mastering life crises, in so many words, the presenters reflected the question back to the audience. The answering rage was, I think, only partly accounted for by the rather clumsy way the workshop was conducted. Rather, it seemed to me that the people had come many miles to this meeting partly through having been seduced into believing that at human potential meetings they would not only get the answers but that their potential would be portrayed as unlimited, their wildest hopes realizable. They seemed to have confused *their* supposedly unlimited potential with the supposedly unlimited potential of others to solve their problems.

But what of the tension involved in viewing people as having unlimited potential while at the same time stubbing one's toe on his limitations? How does one think about such an uneasy and seemingly conflictual position? And what are the limits, if any, of hope?

The easy way out is to reductionistically dismiss the hope aspect of the human potential movement simply as a romantic wish fulfillment, an expression of the child's belief that wish equals deed, that he or his parents can make anything possible. The interest in health, by the way of nutrition and body therapy, and in reincarnation, plausibly supports the idea that untrammeled hope is indeed fueled by the wish to defeat death. Yes, the sprawling, disorganized human potential movement does have its share of little old ladies in tennis shoes, mixed-up kids, and desperately aging adults. But apart from these stereotypes there is the inherent tension between hope and hopelessness, the need for sober examination of suppositions and practices that bring so many of us to a dead stop at unpalatable "reality," afraid to experiment imaginatively to create a new "reality." We live with limitations, but we don't have to like it. Believing in fantasies of perfection that can come true as in fairy tales or can be made to come true as in Horatio Alger may be to court despair and guilt. But, believing in our inadequacy, our helplessness, is to court failure, low self-esteem, and then more failure, in a never-ending circle. The easy way out is to say that one should just learn what one's realistic limitations are; that sounds seductively reasonable. But human-potential people would say that in the pursuit of reason most of us sell ourselves short. We make do with "adjustment," "adaptation," a kind of comfort that spares us the anxiety and work of recognizing our true potential. One can never know in advance what one's limitations are, or how far one's potential will carry one, so a "realistic" assessment is often a sellout.

We do know for sure, however, that potential requires potentiating, and that to give ourselves fully to maximizing our potential we need to be free of a priori barriers. I am not sure how much of what I say now comes from the human potential movement, is an extrapolation from psychoanalysis, or is just talk from the cracker barrel. But maybe instead of trying to control the riding of two horses going in opposite directions we should dismount. Isn't the point, after all, to make the most of what is now, on the way to whatever will be? Perhaps life is best lived as a moment-by-moment process, a series of means, rather than ends. The potential that we do have which *is* unlimited is to make the most of each instant. So why not enjoy the struggle, swing with the paradox that everything is possible but one can enjoy what is now, however short of the ultimate it is? Life is to be lived between now and then, between problem and solution, between beginning and end. Our human potential is for unlimited struggle, without either prior conditions or fixed end point. More than half the fun ought to be in getting there.

A Rocky Meeting of the Association for Humanistic Psychology

The central organization of the human potential movement is the Association for Humanistic Psychology (AHP). It publishes a scientific journal and a newsletter, and sponsors regional meetings and an annual national meeting. One such national meeting took place in 1975 at the Estes Park YMCA Camp, in the Rocky Mountains of Colorado. It is hard to imagine a less auspicious site. Liquor was not allowed, and as part of the registration procedure one had to subscribe to the ideals of Jesus Christ. Since the Association for Humanistic Psychology had its convention there, the personnel of that camp may never be the same. The little gray-haired ladies and the fresh-faced college students on the staff were amazed and appalled at the style of life, dress, and activities of the humanists. If drinking was not too much in evidence, it was because the participants were "smoking." The ideals of Jesus Christ ran a poor second to those of George Leonard, Rollo May, and the Buddha. At an early meeting, we were told by the organizers of the meeting to mind our behavior and not offend our hosts, so that we would be allowed to use the site for future conferences. A rabble-rousing member hoped that AHP would have its own meeting place and not have to submit to the standards of the YMCA or hotels; he wanted "complete freedom." To the credit of Rollo May, he said it was impossible to have complete freedom, that the association must always be in touch with the demands of the real world. He could think of nothing worse for the organization than an isolated meeting ground that encouraged the belief that it could go its own way independently of the rest of the world.

Whatever the outcome of that argument, Estes Park is unavailable for future meetings of the AHP. When the last van of the humanists had departed, the management of the YMCA camp sent a note to its regular residents apologizing for the conduct of the conference members and promising that the humanists would never again convene in Estes Park. Whether one considers this an indictment of the human potential movement or of the YMCA culture depends on where one stands. As usual, I stood, or was caught, in the middle. The compulsively disheveled, pot-smoking rebels for rebellion's sake, flaunting bad manners and worse logic encouraged me to try to protect this pristine wilderness setting and down-home gentility from such louts. And yet the bucolic "good citizens," mindlessly content to carry on an undeclared war in Viet Nam and hiding from any idea contrary to their own or that of their fathers and grandfathers, made me lust for fiery dissent.

A similar tension existed within the humanistic organization. Strong as Rollo May's voice was, it was still beleaguered by the emotional fervor that characterized the membership. At various times I was chillingly reminded of Hitler's speeches, in which slogans and oratory played upon the emotions of the audience in lieu of disinterested, objective attitudes and genuine attempts to solve the ostensible tasks of the group. Speakers at this meeting who used the right words—"the whole person," "transcendence," "actualizing," "love"—found an immediately receptive audience. Those who put a premium on thought, asked for examination of these slogans, talked of power, pragmatism, realism, were lucky not to be hissed. Like Nixon getting away with going to Russia, Rollo May, George Leonard, and Charles Hampden-Turner got away, barely, with talking the language of the "enemy," by examining without prejudice the nature and uses of power, calling for thoughtfulness, and kicking humanist sacred cows.

In the previous year, leading intellectuals of the human potential movement had conferred at government expense in order to hammer out theoretical issues relevant to humanism, and some of them reported those deliberations to this meeting. That such theoretical discussions were supposed to be antithetical to human potential values was not lost on some of the (literally) war-painted attendees. If the speakers had been lesser lights or worn three-piece suits, they might have been stoned.

Rollo May reminded this group, as he had the conferees, that the word "theory" comes from the Greek meaning "spectacle," a way of seeing. Rather than arguing about being subjective rather than objective, he thought that we should recognize that theory was needed as a matrix from which both the subjective and the objective spring. Brewster Smith, an academic psychologist, said that he was concerned about the human potential emphasis on the transcendental, which could be used as a way of avoiding problems of the nontranscendental human condition. Stanley Krippner (the then president of the AHP) called attention to how research contributions to the theory may be handicapped by the experimenter's belief influencing his results. For example, much humanistic research may be so influenced by the state of consciousness of both the examiner and the subject that it becomes a relevant but uncontrolled variable. Stanley Grof said that humanism should incorporate the findings of other disciplines in its theory.

In his keynote speech George Leonard examined the nature of power with respect to the human potential movement, and along the way suggested, as Wilhelm Reich had done in *The Sexual Revolution,*[5] decades earlier, that we might never have a new politics without a new sexuality.

Many political stands are taken for essentially sexual reasons, he said, for example the need to prove oneself masculine by pursuing wartime victories. Charles Hampden-Turner suggested that humanists have to care about theory in order to have one, that they have to be willing to look at all theories, not just their own; otherwise they would merely contribute to a Tower of Babel. Theory-building, according to him, created tension; it was lonely work, but necessary as an alternative to simply accepting what one or another fellow humanist opined.

Hampden-Turner's remarks at this conference crystallized for me the growing tension within the human potential movement between looseness and organization, idealism and realism, emotion and thought, self-sustaining speculation and ordered rationality; in short, the same differences that characterize its conflict with those outside the human potential boundaries. Perhaps the human potential movement will fall apart, with one fragment being the intellectual and rational one against which it defined itself in the first place. A more sanguine prediction, however, is that the human potential values will be maintained even though organized into an increasingly rational framework. Human potential leaders at this conference, gingerly making public declarations of the need for theory, seem to be betting that the line between harmful scientism and human potential values can be observed, thereby enriching both the values and their systematic status. If so, this meeting signaled a beginning rapprochement between conventional and new therapies, between culture and counterculture. The emergence of such a coherent point of view in the human potential movement may change the character of confrontations between conventional and new therapies from battles to opportunities, moving us toward as yet undiscovered positions embodying contributions from both. Perhaps even the Estes Park Y Camp may invite back a human potential convention that, in turn, will better behave itself.

On the way back from human potential meetings, and for a day or two afterward, I am usually a changed man. My family, my friends, my patients remark upon it, and I can feel it. Indeed, one of the frequent warnings offered to neophytes by human potential people is that they have to be careful when they return home. They have to remember that others have not shared their experiences and will be unprepared for their new insights, feelings, and ways of expressing themselves. Ordinarily we returnees ascribe our "high" to the ideas and activities of the meeting. Surely, we feel, the new ideas to which we have been exposed must be correct, since they have promoted these new, liberating feelings, have brought to our attention new ideas and methods for improving life—no matter that things simmer down after a few days. We still have the memory, we have glimpsed the promised land, and we have more meetings to look forward to. Without denigrating the content and activity of the meetings themselves, the emotional reaction and good opinion of such meetings can be understood in other ways as well. Underneath a group's manifest activities there is a whole different world.

I first studied groups systematically in the late fifties by participating in groups of eight to ten members that met "to study the psychology of groups," without directed leadership, agenda, or schedules of production or activities. Under such circumstances one can predict certain patterns and developments with absolute accuracy. One of these events is a blind, patriotic devotion to "the group," and at varying levels of genuineness an experience of togetherness and goodness among all the members. In some magical way the group and its members seem to become exalted, repositories of wisdom and kindness, and with a messianic mission.

I later attended a series of meetings with around fifty participants also designed to study the psychology of groups under varying conditions. These meetings went on for a week to two weeks, with most of the participants at some distance from their homes. Though the format, theory, and activities were often different from the small groups, the same events occurred. The emotional intensity of them was, if anything, increased by the meetings taking place twenty-four hours a day for four consecutive days, removed from the familiar people and activities that ordinarily anchor us in stable but limited internal and external environments. The pressure-cooker atmosphere of these experiences resulted in altered states of consciousness characterized by instant friendliness, powerful sexual and aggressive urges, and a sense of community and shared discovery. I and my colleagues characteristically left these meetings, too, exhilarated with the experience of newfound wisdom and rediscovered passions, light-footed with hope for a different and better existence. A commonly reported consequence of such heady experiences is for participants to attempt immediately to apply their new sense of self to their "back home" work and relationships, often to the consternation of those not yet so enlightened.

Another danger is for the participants to persuade themselves that the content and activities of the weekend were solely responsible for what happened. Under the sway of group phenomena practically anything that even has the look of being wise and therapeutic is salable. Moving, uplifting, educational, and inspirational as such meetings can be, indeed because they are, a cautionary note is required. While it is often nice and valuable to put aside for a weekend one's critical and evaluative capacities, if such weekends are to be more than temporary enjoyments, they require integration with the rest of one's faculties and perspectives. Otherwise the meeting game becomes the mating game, enjoyable but transitory eruptions of passion, fun to play, but of limited value to the greater game.

Does it seem that I speak from experience? It ought to. As I got into the rhythm of attending and returning from human-potential meetings, a few raps on the knuckles in the form of steely-eyed, challenging questions taught me how to return safely to home, friends, and colleagues: ask myself those steely-eyed questions first.

6

More Than Skin Deep

The emphasis of the human potential movement on the whole person, the unity of body and mind, puts it in an awkward position with regard to neurology and physiology. Few of its members are neurologists or physiologists; which in some respects may be an advantage. Unhampered by "the facts," they are thus helped to be free to speculate, to create imaginative hypotheses about the neurological and physiological substrate of behavior. The amount of neurology and physiology that I know is measurable only if one has a measure finely calibrated to pick up minute quantities, so I can hardly evaluate firsthand the validity of their speculations. But, then, I am not always aflame with desire for evaluations; like most Freudians, I appreciate the liberal use of metaphor as a means of creating order, conveying information, and as a holding action while new data are collected. A premature need for evaluation can shut down necessary further exploration. And sometimes the metaphor turns out to represent reality anyway. Freud, for example, to account for psychological phenomena, created an imaginative nervous system that is lately receiving corroboration on strictly neurological grounds. Now, with the borderland between mind and body only beginning to be understood, it seems to me to be an appropriate time for speculation.

The neurological icing on the human potential cake is perhaps best surveyed by reading regularly the *Brain-Mind Bulletin.* This four-page biweekly reports experiments and conferences relevant to human potential theorizing about the functioning of the mind in neurological and quasi-neurological contexts. For a while, there were few issues of the *Bulletin* that went by without some notice being taken of functions alleged to reside more in one half of the brain than the other. That may seem a fragment of esoterica and hardly relevant to the human potential movement, until one notices that the functions supposedly indigenous to each side correspond respectively to characteristics of the human potential world and the world against which it is arraigned.

In countless households over the land, one spouse likes the refrigerator neatly arranged, clothes in order, and the house clean. The other spouse likes things, or at least allows things, to be the reverse. According to the new wave of neurological thinking, such domestic travail is an expression of how the respective partners use their brains, one employing the left side of the brain, one employing the right. Much of our thought, whether it be literary, political, psychological, is governed by polarities or dualisms: classic/romantic, conservative/radical, reason/passion, love/hate, masculine/feminine, secular/sacred, introvert/extrovert, yin/yang, tough-minded/tender-minded, conscious/unconscious, science/religion, science/art, abstract/concrete, optimism/pessimism, left/right, specificity/mass action. Since everything that takes place in the mind involves something physical or physiological, however minute, perhaps dualisms are also represented in the body. Such is the reasoning, to some extent supported by neurological study, for the grand hypothesis of the neurological wing of the human potential movement, "the split-brain hypothesis."

According to this hypothesis, those qualities esteemed and employed by the new world a-comin' are in the right brain; the old-world characteristics are in the left brain. Here are some of the distinguishing characteristics of each (left-brain characteristic listed first): verbal/visual, linear/patterned, analytical/holistic, reality/dreams, rational/mystical, factual/emotional, obsessive/hysterical, conscious/unconscious, beta/alpha. (The last entry refers to brain waves, beta being associated with focused attention such as we use in performing our daily, mundane activities, while alpha waves predominate in less concentrated, more arcane activities.)

According to human potential theorists, in modern Western society our educational goals and methods implement our esteem for left-brain functioning. As a result, we continue to hone left-brain skills while allowing right-brain skills to atrophy. Just as we have valued "male" thinking over "female" thinking and lawyers over laborers, we minimize right-brain characteristics except when found in artists (whom we regard ambivalently). By retraining the right brain, thus redressing the balance, we may achieve a brain that can draw with equal facility from both of its sides. We would then have the ideal, the renaissance man, the person whose behaviors would be determined less by what he has most available in his brain than by what the particular task requires. Freud is an example of a person who was able to use well both sides of his brain; he was a scientist and an artist, a rigorous pragmatist and an unabashed speculator.

Psychoanalysis can be conceived of as helping patients to

shift from aspects of the right brain, namely unconscious symbolism, dreams, intuitive and emotional characteristics, to verbal understanding according to the rules of rational, conscious thought. At the same time, psychoanalysis provides the freedom to adopt a right-brain attitude, to be more emotionally responsive, more trusting of one's intuition, more creative.

Evidence in favor of the split-brain hypothesis is gathered through observing people's behavior after injury to one or the other side of the brain or surgery on those fibers connecting the two halves. Despite data collected in these ways, some neurologists maintain that the formulation is vastly oversimplified or outright untenable.

What does it mean that, with respect to the split-brain hypothesis, many human potential adherents put aside their anti-science attitude out of eagerness to press their cause with the aid of neurology? Does this behavior indict their usual anti-science attitude as just so much sour grapes, or is it a refreshing bit of pragmatism? Probably both. There are lots of indications in the human potential movement of the psychology of have-nots versus haves. Yet its members are not blindly antagonistic to knowledge; like anybody, they appreciate for personal and functional reasons corroboration of their ideas from other disciplines. It probably helps all of our (left-brain) Western minds to think that the new world a-comin' has nice, solid, synaptic underpinnings. Our faults, then, are not in the stars but in our lopsidedly developed cerebrum and thus perhaps amenable to retraining. Formal experiments in retraining are already underway. Perhaps psychotherapy has unwittingly been such an experiment all along, loosening up the excessively left-brained and tightening up the excessively right-brained, and thus making possible synchronous functioning.

Freud described instinct, his word for energy, as on the borderline between the mental and the physical. And so it has remained, dancing seductively between the two, persuading everybody to attend to it but not yet revealing its secret. Through the centuries, energy has remained baffling in systematic disciplines and has uncomfortably accrued to itself surplus meaning. But never before has it achieved such sprawling, protean use as it has in the human potential movement. Its effects there, for example, can immediately be observed just by listening to the casual conversation of a human potential adherent. Indeed, "energy" is in the forefront of the human potential assault on the English language, an all-purpose word whose inexplicit meanings often come to one drenched in sanctimonious goodness. I recently received a letter from a cultured, linguistically sensitive person which included the following well-wishing statement: "I send you my energies for your work." In a notice for a workshop on "balancing energy fields" are such statements as "committed to the continuation of the energies already developed here," "you are invited to come and experience the atmosphere and energy of the space," "the desert has its own powerful and majestic life energy. . . ."

That the human potential movement should be concerned with energy is hardly surprising. Few psychological, philosophical, or cultural traditions have not been. Rather, most have felt the need to postulate some kind of universal energy. Mesmer had his natural force, Bergson his *élan vital,* the Chinese call it *chi,* the Indians call it prana, the Russians call it bioplasm; for MacDougall it was hormic, for Wilhelm Reich it was orgone, and Freud named it libido.

In common usage, as well as in the human potential movement, energy is sometimes spoken of as a thing; thus, you *have* or do not *have* energy. In physics, however, energy is a force, a capacity to do work, a dynamic, more than a substance. In psychotherapy, energy may be both a thing and a capacity, depending on the practitioner's theory. At first Freud conceived of energy as being a thing. He named neuroses brought about by the damming up of such energy "actual neuroses," the "actual" meaning an actual substance. He later conceived of libido, or psychic energy, as a grand construct, a theoretical device with which to order and explain his observations, and probably not a substance.

In assuming that energy was a thing, Freud in his early days and Wilhelm Reich and others were continuing the tradition of the East. In Eastern religions, energy, as an assumed substance, determines at what level of consciousness and behavior we function. As energy moves up the alleged physiological pathways, new consciousness and behavior become available. One can move or concentrate his energy by the use of his mind, as in meditation and visualization, for the purpose of self-healing, among other things. Psychic healers claim to transmit their energy to others. Kirlian photographs (discussed below) show that the alleged energy is diminished in the healer while it is increased in the healed. When Rev. Rosalyn Bruyere, a psychic healer, touched me, I felt an intermittent burst, like a benevolent machine gun, which gave me the impression that she was moving her hand up and down rapidly. In fact her hand was perfectly still. She did this once during lunch when she was carrying on a casual conversation with me and others, once when I was a demonstration subject for her class on healing, and once in her Healing Light Center when, apparently, she healed my once arthritic finger.

The extreme position of energeticists is that all we are is energy, the so-called structures being congealed patterns of energy that are fixed and material only as pictures in our minds. Irving Oyle, a general practitioner who has become a leader in alternative medicine, puts it this way: "Along with heat and light the sun beams a flow of subatomic particles or waves to earth where the magnetic field attracts them. These particles constitute the solar wind. They radiate through us, traveling through the meridians of the fourth circulatory system. The human body is not something which is there all the time—it is being re-created from instant to instant by the vibration of these subatomic particles, which vibrate back and forth between energy and matter." In traditional oriental medicine and other ancient healing methods the essence of all things is a common energy, and so all things are as one, separateness reflecting only specialized patterns of this energy.

According to oriental medicine, energy travels through the body by way of pathways called meridians. These are analogous to other circulatory systems, indeed are sometimes called the fourth circulatory system (the other three being cerebrospinal, lymphatic, and blood). The streams of energy congregate at "points," where diagnostic and healing interventions are made.

In addition to deploying and concentrating energy with the mind, there are mechanical means of stimulating energy. Prominent among these interventions are acupuncture, the judicious insertion of needles. Acupuncture is said to be helpful for a wide variety of purposes, for example bronchial asthma, low back pain, toothache, stopping smoking and losing weight, many sports injuries, and to eliminate wrinkles, bags under the eyes, and other ravages of age, as is now allegedly done on a number of movie and television stars. That the effects of acupuncture are not the same as those of hypnosis or suggestion, which require some subject co-operation, is demonstrated by the use of acupuncture for veterinary anesthesia and treatment, in which presumably the animals are not mentally co-operating. Further, when needles were placed at some distance from the traditional points, in effect a placebo, the procedure is ineffective, suggesting that more than suggestion is involved. Sonopuncture is the stimulation, with high-frequency sound instead of needles, of the same areas as are used in acupuncture. Acupressure substitutes manual pressure for needles, sound, or heat. A Japanese acupressure massage is *shiatsu*.

I experienced acupressure during my first meeting at the East-West Foundation (see Part Five), when in addition to being diagnosed through visual surveillance, I was poked in a few spots and asked to tell whether these hurt. Several areas of my body did respond with a sort of burning pain that seemed disproportionate to the amount of pressure applied, as if something other than local trauma was involved. Some months later I had a full-scale *shiatsu* massage. When spots on my body allegedly representing internal organs, although anatomically far from those organs, were palpated, I sometimes felt pain, which was taken to mean difficulty in that organ. The same area when prodded according to acupressure techniques on the other side of my body did not reveal that pain. In other words, pain seemed not to have been produced by local pressure (as far as I could tell, the pressure put on both sides was equal), suggesting that indeed the palpated point was hooked up to, or reflective of, another organ which was the source of the painful sensation.

The advantages of diagnosis by way of acupressure are obvious, a probing finger on the outside of the body as compared, for example, to opening up the body to see what's wrong. One of the new alternative medical centers (Center for Integral Medicine, Putnam, Connecticut) reports considerable success in diagnosing otherwise inexplicable complaints with acupressure. My *shiatsu* masseuse, guided by her diagnostic probes, decided where to concentrate the acupressure of her fingers. I lay flat on the floor while she moved around me, pushing hands and fingers down on the selected areas. It was a lot less painful than Rolfing, somewhat less gentle than the Alexander technique. Afterward, I felt fine, though I could hardly say I felt any more fine than I would have after a Swedish or an Esalen massage.

Another diagnostic method involving energy is to take a picture of your energy, and ascertain from its color and shape your physical and emotional status. Yes, I did say *take a picture* of your energy. Kirlian, a Soviet electrician, invented the process bearing his name in which a high-frequency electrical current is passed through a subject and records on photographic film what are said to be energy field patterns. It is photography without a lens.

I have before me a Polaroid "photograph" of the pads of my four fingers, their black oval shapes surrounded by an approximately quarter-inch bluish green halo or aura. I had the opportunity of getting this "photograph" at one of the Silva Mind Control monthly meetings, a series in which diverse human potential and paranormal topics are presented. The speaker claimed to have taken Kirlian photographs showing the ethereal body apparently arising and leaving a corporeal body; he did not happen to have brought those pictures along. But there was no doubt of the remarkable pictures that he took of me and others there. What is doubtable is whether the flares are representations of energy and whether their characteristics are in fact specific to particular diseases. For example, is it true that the smaller the aura the more sick or more tired you are? Is it true that one can forecast disease by reading the auras of the etheric body? Does a blue-white aura mean that you are healthy, a purple one that you are intellectual, a gold one that you are pious and mystical? Are the flares stable, so that they are as identifiable of you as a fingerprint?

The Russians are said to have eleven institutes answering such questions. We have none officially sponsored by the government, just a few independent efforts such as those of Thelma Moss, at UCLA, and the Polyclinic Medical Center, in Harrisburg, Pennsylvania. With respect to the latter, *Brain-Mind Bulletin* reported that it was the only U.S. hospital where Kirlian photographs are routinely ordered for diagnosis. The hospital itself testily wrote me that Kirlian photographs are not routinely used for that purpose (". . . such statements come from news reporters born with overactive imaginations"). The hospital does agree that it has nonroutinely found correlations between finger-pad discharge coronas and a variety of physical disorders including cystic fibrosis and cancer. Some researchers say that these photographs are of minute variations in skin conductance and electrolyte balance which reflect metabolic or physiological changes associated with illness. That explanation, however, does not suffice for plants that have a part cut away yet the aura remains, the "phantom leaf." The counterculture clutches Kirlian photography to its heart as "proof" that we are energy fields, that our boundaries extend beyond our skin, that indeed we all are as one.

Actually, Kirlian machinery is necessary only for record keeping and research. Many human potential people, especially those of a psychic persuasion, claim that they can see auras with their unaided eyes, and in so doing can read the condition of a person's physical and emotional health. None of this need apply only to persons. Kirlian photographs show auras around plants and animals as well. Moral: all things are composed of energy.

In one study a psychic healer held water in a sealed flask, and when this water was poured on seeds, the plants significantly outgrew untreated seeds. If a depressed psychiatric patient held the flask of water, the growth of the seeds was retarded. Think of the implications: We may be sending and receiving healthy or noxious energy to one another all the time. There may be a concrete, physical basis for the common experience of feeling good in the presence of some people, bad in the presence of others. "You make me sick" and "I tingle at your approach" may be more than just figures of speech.

What would you say if I said that I had photographed energy with an ordinary camera on ordinary film? Well, hold your tongue for just a moment. I visited Uri Geller in his apartment-office in Manhattan along with author, artist, and photographer Peter Beard. Almost immediately upon our arrival, Geller enthusiastically began to do his psychic activities, attempting to bend keys and receive and send mental messages that would influence drawings. Wearying of these workaday phenomena, I set about taking photographs with a Rollei 35-mm. pocket camera. I took pictures of Geller doing his psychic work and shortly after, while he was posing at his desk. When my photo finisher brought out the developed prints, he asked what had happened; there were marks on the negative unlike any marks he had seen before. For once, I failed to lament imperfections in my pictures. The streaks on this 20-exposure roll occurred only on those pictures in which Geller was doing psychic work. The posed pictures were clear of them. Same camera, same roll of film, same photographer, approximately the same time. Geller said that imperfections and peculiarities have occurred in films of him before, but none that looked like the streaks that appeared on my pictures of him. Human potential people would not be as amazed as most of the rest of us. They believe that when someone sends you his energies, he might be doing just that.

On numerous stops during my odyssey, I have been taught to hold my hand several inches above someone else's body and feel the heat that is supposed to be a signal of the accumulation of psychic energy. Alternatively, the experience of heat could come from suggestion or the proximity of another's body. That it is actually psychic energy seems clear, however, to Harold Stone, the psychologist head of the Center for the Healing Arts, in Los Angeles, about whom we shall hear further in connection with alternative treatments of cancer (Part Five). He combines gestalt and some elements of transactional analysis and Jungian psychology with energy work in a process called "balancing the energy fields." I visited him in his office in Los Angeles with regard to his work with cancer. In the course of that discussion I learned about his energy-field work, and required no urging at all when he offered to show me firsthand what it was like to have one's energy fields balanced.

After putting a selection on his tape recorder (Ravel's "Pavane for a Dead Princess"), which he thought I would enjoy (he was right), he had me lie down on a waist-high table. Then he passed his hands over my body, satisfying himself that he was able to tell where I needed "work" or more energy. While he did this, we fell into some analytical exploration. His intention was, he said, to activate various archetypes through a dialogue between us, and between me and the various parts of myself. For example, he had me ask another part of me what was wrong with my life. "The other part" answered that I had left the body out of my life. After some intra-Stephen discussion, Stone talked to parts of me, and I answered as if I were solely that part. At one point he isolated out the figure of a stern, harsh taskmaster, and in the ensuing discussion I was portrayed as being in practically constant activity trying to escape from, or else follow, the dictates of this figure. It would have been pretty tragic except that this figure, or at least one of us in me, had a nice sense of humor, or so Stone said to one or another of us.

There is something funny about representing oneself as a collection of people within one's head talking to one another. Funny or not, something of the sort is at least implicit in most systems of psychology. In psychoanalysis the figures may be called "identities" or "internal objects" and abstracted as ego or superego. The figures seem accurately to represent factions in our personalities, speaking from disparate eras of our history, often at cross purposes with one another. In other words, we have various sides to ourselves. The dialogue method, such as that of Stone, makes these images helpfully concrete and dramatic. As to balancing the energy fields, the sample I had, made me feel no better and no worse, but it was clear that Stone thought he was moving a substance around.

As I listened and watched Stone balance the energy field of one of his patients, I made a number of inferences about the patient's personality and difficulties. I was troubled that these were not being dealt with, at least during this session. I imagined a day-long stream of patients getting their energies balanced while the crucial issues in their thoughts and feelings were left free to continue to harmfully influence their lives. What a gigantic self-delusion if there is no such thing as actual energy to be helpfully deployed! And what a great and overlooked opportunity in conventional treatment if there is!

Just as I was writing these pages on energy I received an announcement of a "new science," called "Integral Psychology," propounded by Robert Gerard, the psychosynthesist, my old UCLA classmate mentioned in chapter 1. "Human beings," Gerard writes, "are viewed as an energy system comprised of a series of interpenetrating energy fields of gradually higher frequency (physical, emotional, mental, intuitive, spiritual). Integral Psychology . . . has as its goal the formulation of the fundamental laws of psychological energies, their measurement (assessment and diagnosis) and transformation (psychospiritual growth and therapy) . . . our training will also focus on the discovery and practice of esoteric methods of energy transformation which have a direct impact on the psychological energy fields themselves, in order to improve the psychoenergetic structure and resultant functioning of the person in the world."

Indeed, among the alternative therapies there is no energy shortage.

7

The Twain Shall Meet

The Menninger Foundation is composed primarily of an East Campus, where most clinical activities take place, and a West Campus, where most educational and research activities take place. The distance between the two campuses is a couple of miles. They are very long miles. The two campuses serve as a microcosm of how two worlds can exist largely in ignorance of one another while harboring fantasies about each other's activities. Such fantasies frequently include an undercurrent of suspicion that the other is up to no good, and anyway is competing for scarce funds.

As a one-time superhawk citizen of the clinical East Campus, I ought to know. For over a decade Elmer and Alyce Green were doing their researches on biofeedback on the West Campus practically unknown to me and most of my colleagues. I had originally come to The Menninger Foundation to study with the pantheon of psychoanalytic ego psychologists whose works were famous in psychoanalytic circles and influenced much of the psychiatric work being done throughout the country. During visits to alternative-therapy centers, however, instead of being asked whether I knew Dr. So-and-So, the psychoanalyst or clinical psychologist, I was asked if I knew Elmer Green. And as I went through the human potential books on the new consciousness, biofeedback, and parapsychology, The Menninger Foundation was as fully represented as it had been in my old clinical texts, but in the persons of Elmer Green and his co-workers.

The word "biofeedback" provokes associations of modern technology, cybernetic loops, and futuristic dials and pointers. Albeit with a little help from its friendly Western electronic wizards, its essence is ancient Eastern yoga.

"The Greens" are Elmer Green, wife Alyce Green, children Judy Green, Pat Norris, and Doug Boyd. Though not a member of the family, Dale Walters is a long-time colleague. All are imbued with such usual human potential interests as yoga and parapsychology, and one interest that is less usual in the human potential movement, an affection for machinery.

Yoga, parapsychology, and machinery—the perfect background for biofeedback. It is a far better background than the colonial British in India had. They hardly knew what to make of the stories about the prodigious feats of the yogis which wafted up over the verandas and swirled around the teacups. Not that the colonial British were much different from any of the rest of us in Western society, where sleeping on a bed of nails and walking on hot coals were the province of cartoonists and Ripley's Believe It or Not department.

Instead of laughing, the Greens hooked up one of those Indians, Swami Rama, to a battery of electronic measures and had him do his things. I vaguely remember an announcement of this demonstration, but neither I nor most of my clinical colleagues attended. After all, whom had he ever analyzed? And he wore a sheet; it was all too fey.

Swami Rama went on to found the Himalayan Institute, which years later I attended hat in hand, seeking learning, as described in Part Four.

The Greens' machinery recorded that Swami Rama was able to change the temperature of two areas two inches apart on the palm of his right hand, making one cold and the other hot, then reversing the temperatures. But that was just a warmup (pun intended). On the next day the Swami did what he called "stopping" his heart. Actually, he sent it into "atrial flutter," a condition in which a section of the heart flutters at its maximum oscillatory rate without blood filling the chambers properly, the EKG signal going from seventy per minute to about three hundred per minute. In this condition the valves do not work properly, blood pressure drops, and there is no pulse. When a cardiologist examined the EKG record of this demonstration, he assumed that the subject had become unconscious. Instead, Swami Rama finished the demonstration and went on from there to give a lecture. On another occasion, he learned which feedback tones went with what state of his consciousness and could then produce beta and delta brain-wave patterns at will. Finally, he rotated through 10 degrees of arc an aluminum knitting needle mounted horizontally on a vertical shaft five feet away from him. He did this with a plastic mask over his nose and mouth, so that no one could claim that he had done it with air currents. Rather, he had done it, so far as anyone knows, as he claims: "by mind alone."

But you don't have to be an Indian and spend months in a cave or at the feet of a guru, though these seem to be helpful in developing such skills. Jack Schwarz, a Dutch mystic, seems to have honed his natural skills through self-study alone. Wired up in the Greens' laboratory, he pushed a five-inch sailmaker's needle through the biceps of his arm. He pulled it out after about thirty seconds of calm conversation, whereupon the wound bled slightly until he said, "Now it stops," and it did. He then repeated the demonstration without any bleeding at all. At no time did he seem to be in pain. The galvanic skin response indicator did not show any unusual stress when he was putting the needle through his arm; indeed, thermistors showed that his arms were warm, a sign of relaxation. As he inserted the needle, his occipital brain wave changed from beta to a combination of beta and alpha; it is in the alpha state that so many paranormal feats seem to be possible. For those who like audiovisual aids to learning, these feats by Swami Rama and Jack Schwarz, among others, can be seen in a Hartley Production movie made of the Greens' work at The Menninger Foundation and in India.

If we are not to consign these demonstrations to cartoons or seal them off in a portion of our minds, then we can hardly avoid the implications that a host of remarkable possibilities are there to be tapped, perhaps by anyone. Can these skills be learned without arduous training, transcendent consciousness, or remarkable, seemingly innate talents? Are there ways of making up for lack of such training and talent and nonetheless developing control over one's body to a degree previously never considered possible? Yes, say the Greens, and the way to do it is with biofeedback.

Here are why and how: Any task is learned with feedback. For example, one learns to steer a car by noticing that a turn to the right sends the car to the right. Perception of the onrushing curb is the feedback, the cue that teaches us. A succession of such cues teaches us to calculate how much to turn the wheel. Meanwhile we are very much aware of learning to drive the car, because in the process we use systems under our conscious control, the striate muscles. Other bodily systems, such as the digestive, circulatory, and endocrine systems, are ordinarily not under our conscious control. These systems go on silently, under ordinary circumstances out of our awareness, and obviously apart from our ability to do anything about them. Or so we thought. Not only do the yogis seem to be able to do a great deal about them, but in recent years academic psychologists have demonstrated, mostly with rats, that the so-called involuntary systems can be brought under control. Enter dials, meters, and beeps. Machines were pressed into feedback service, which gave cues from the body to the mind by which to learn how to master these erstwhile mysterious, automatic systems.

For several years the Greens have offered a two-day course in biofeedback at The Menninger Foundation during which one has the experience of being hooked up to biofeedback machines and learning to control oneself with their help. Participants come from around the country for a fee, while occasional "scholarships" are made available for Menninger Foundation staff members. In this generous and clever way a number of staff members have become exposed to biofeedback. The number, however, is not terribly large. I doubt whether the number would have included me had I not been embarked on this study. A prophet is rarely honored in his own country, and familiarity breeds contempt. Also, the logistics of taking days off from patients are difficult. One ought not overlook, also, prejudice against "those people on West Campus," meaning representatives of new therapies, a prejudice that expresses itself in ignoring them. Finally, the biofeedback message that one can have control of his body and health stirs up as much anxiety as hope. (More of that in Part Five.)

The course begins with meditation, which as we shall see

in Part Four need not be sectarian or encased in rituals, merely a way of slipping into an altered state of consciousness, presumably one in which one's brain waves change from beta to alpha and possibly theta. The Greens choose to begin meditation with autogenic training. Most of us were told at one time or another that the way to overcome insomnia was to go through the body willfully relaxing each section. That is autogenic training. It is the cornerstone of autogenic therapy, developed by Johannes Schultz and Wolfgang Luthe, popular in Europe, less so in the United States.

Participants in the biofeedback course followed these instructions: "Close your eyes. Place your hands in your lap with feet flat on the floor. Here are a series of phrases to aid your relaxation. After each phrase try to feel what that phrase suggests to you.

I feel quite quiet.
I'm beginning to feel quite relaxed.
My feet feel heavy and relaxed.
My ankles, my knees, and my hips feel heavy, relaxed, and comfortable.
My stomach, the whole central portion of my body, feels relaxed and quiet.
My hands, my arms, and my shoulders feel heavy, relaxed, and comfortable.
My neck, my jaws, and my forehead feel relaxed. They feel comfortable and smooth.
My whole body feels quiet, heavy, comfortable, and relaxed.
Continue relaxing on your own for a moment.
I am very relaxed.
My arms and hands are heavy and warm.
I feel very quiet.

My whole body is relaxed, and my hands are warm, relaxed and warm.

My hands are warm.

Warmth is flowing into my hands; they are warm, warm.

I can feel the warmth flowing down my arms into my hands.

My hands are warm, relaxed and warm.

Continue relaxing on your own for a moment.

My whole body feels quiet, comfortable, and relaxed.

My mind is quiet.

I withdraw my thoughts from the surroundings and I feel serene and still.

My thoughts are turned inward and I'm at ease.

Deep within my mind I can visualize and experience myself as relaxed, comfortable, and still.

I'm aware but in an easy, quiet, inward-turned way.

My mind is calm and quiet.

I feel an inward quietness.

Continue relaxing on your own for a moment.

The relaxation and reverie are now concluded and the whole body is reactivated gently with a deep breath and the following phrases: 'I feel new life and energy beginning to flow through my legs, hips, solar plexus, chest, arms and hands, neck and head . . . energy makes me feel light and alive.' Slowly reactivate yourself and open your eyes when you are ready."

Biofeedback has been called meditation with machines. Now that we were in the meditation, we turned to the machines. First, there was a thermistor, a device that measures temperature. Just as we did with the autogenic phrases, we told ourselves that our hands were getting warmer, we directed the flow of blood to our hands. Expectantly I watched the pointer, assuming that it would begin its triumphant course upward. Instead, it sank ignominiously down, indicating that my hands were getting colder! That is what I got for trying, trying in the Western, beta-wave, directed-attention, be-a-good-boy-and-you-will-be-rewarded kind of way. Instead, I was to take it easy, *let* the blood flow into my hands, get out of the way of it, observe it from a distance; there is nobody to please and nothing to do. Now, would you believe, the needle took off toward the heat end of the scale. I had learned to control the flow of blood, and also a new way of asserting control.

An electrode was placed on the frontalis muscle and I learned to relax that muscle. An electrode was placed on my head and I learned to change my brain waves, a reflection of changes in my consciousness. I did the same with my heart rate (EKG) and skin resistance (GSR). Whatever the bodily system and whatever the machine, control depended upon this new and peculiar set of doing by not doing, what the Greens and others call "passive volition." One way we used to know of passive volition was as reverse psychology: Tell a child what you don't want him to do, and he does it. Or portray something unpleasant as in short supply, and everyone wants it. That's how Tom Sawyer got his fence whitewashed. It all hinges on the yogic idea of detachment. You care while not caring, you participate while not participating. Jack Schwarz says that he puts the needle through his arm without feeling pain by detaching himself from the whole situation; it is not *his* arm, it is *an* arm. Some people conceptualize detachment as getting our usual consciousness out of the way and thus allowing the "unconscious" to take over. For example, people get over their fear of speaking extemporaneously, acting on the stage, or writing, by learning to trust their "unconscious," by just letting it come rather than laboriously designing and rehearsing each action. To the yogis it was mind over matter; mind can be taught to transcend body. We are no longer at the mercy of improper blood flow or pain, once we rise above these physiological manifestations and bring them under mental control.

All this can be made to sound rather mysterious. Recoil and disbelief are common reactions in our culture to assertions of mind power, for example that diseases can be overcome by meditation and visualization or by hypnosis. These phenomena are a lot less mysterious, and a lot less romantic, when one decides to go beyond one's culture shock and see the phenomena in physiological terms: A psychological stimulus sets off the limbic system, which in turn sets off the hypothalamus, producing hormonal changes via the pituitary and endocrine systems, and these bioelectrochemical phenomena result in tissue changes. The yogis talk of mind over matter, universal and transcendent energies, in part because they know little of matter. We of the West, who know of matter, minimize powers of mind, for we know too little of them. To each the other's expertise may seem mysterious, when in fact it could be all in the day's work of an ideally well-rounded scientist.

What can one do with the new kind of not-doing? The Greens regularly discover new practical consequences of biofeedback learning. You can now bring the following ailments to them for treatment/training: migraine and tension headaches, hypertension and cardiac dysfunction, Raynaud's disease, asthma, gastrointestinal and esophageal disorders, phobias, depression, inappropriate control of affectant actions, insomnia, spastic dysfunctions including torticollis, paralysis from strokes, accidents, or polio, intractable pain, hyperkinetic syndrome, and learning disabilities.

Here and there murmurs can be heard at The Menninger Foundation about a clinical facility being run by "non-clinicians" and without adequately established proof of effectiveness. The Greens are "non-clinicians" only if one defines clinician in certain formal ways. In practice they treat and apparently help people who bring difficulties to them, and in that sense of the term are indeed clinicians. It would be nice if they would run some precise studies of their effectiveness. Right now, they adduce mostly anecdotal evidence. A few studies have been done, and a few tentative numbers are available. For example, under the direction of Joseph Sargent, a Menninger Foundation internist, 80 per cent of migraine patients have improved with biofeedback, and this improvement has been maintained for five years.[1] As far as statistical outcome is concerned, the Greens are in about the same situation as is psychoanalysis. Both psychoanalysis and biofeedback are exploiting brilliant hypotheses, delineating the dimensions of their discoveries, and apparently helping a good many people along the way; both are learning by doing. Biofeedback, however, is in principle a much more easily researched method. We are justified in expecting from its practitioners solid statistical and experimental evidence of its effectiveness.

So much for the cure of diseases. As members of the human potential movement, biofeedback adherents are interested in self-improvement of all kinds, not just amelioration of disease. Such improvement may occur adventitiously in the course of curing diseases. For example, after traditional medications had failed to bring one patient's blood pressure down, he apparently brought it down himself with biofeedback, and he continues to maintain normal blood pressure without any medication. But he seems to have learned in addition that if he could be in control of his blood pressure he could be in control of the feelings and behaviors that led to the high blood pressure. He reported that in those situations in which he would have reacted with some variety of stress-producing anger he relaxed himself instead, a psychological analogue to his learned physiological relaxation.

Prisoners have been taught physiological self-control with biofeedback by, among others, Patricia Norris, one of Green's daughters, teacher of the training seminar and biofeedback clinician. Instead of disowning their feelings or acting upon them, prisoners learned that they could think of their feelings and maintain relaxation. Using this newfound capacity, they also learned that they could assert control over their coercive external world; they need not act in ways that inexorably draw the net tighter. The experience seemed not only to be generalizable but inspirational. Enthusiasts at their new skills, they eagerly took to visualization, guided imagery, and other psychological exercises. In the particular study reported by Norris,[2] prisoners who worked with her showed a recidivism rate of 13 per cent, as opposed to 33 per cent in Kansas and 70 per cent nationally for the same length of time, two years. Maybe they would have done as well just by having so much attention paid to them by the warm and gentle Patricia Norris. In rigorous research one would have to control for therapist qualities and special attention in general in order to isolate the value of the biofeedback training itself.

Children were trained in biofeedback in order to test the possibility that learned self-control could help prevent disease. If medication and visualization and a feeling of being in control can reduce tumors, as some clinicians claim, then how about all of these plus a tiny transducer inserted in an inoperable tumor which would give feedback cues and so further facilitate learning to regress the tumor? If theta waves are instrumental in both creativity and healing, then healing could be considered a kind of creativity and creativity might be learned just as healing is learned. If one can control one's body in the ways specified by biofeedback, what are the limits? Can one, for example, control the length of life itself? Perhaps the time of our death is determined less by the aging of our body than by our losing our will to live, a will that is founded on a sense of competence and control enhanceable by self-regulation skills. Fanciful, to be sure, but so are Swami Rama and Jack Schwarz.

Take a Western machine and cross it with Eastern capacities for self-control and there is no telling what will happen. As to the twain meeting, Kipling, you failed to reckon on the human potential movement.

8

And a Potential for Criticism

THE STORY CAN stand perhaps one more telling: Two men come to a wise man with conflicting points of view. The wise man, after hearing their positions, says to each of them, "You are right." His wife, having overheard, asks him how he could possibly have told each of them that he was right when they were diametrically opposed to one another. To which the wise man said, "You, too, my dear, are right." The wise man's attitude has a nice Zen feeling. More to the point, he was recognizing the "rightness" that can be found in any position. We only create problems for ourselves by casting arguments in extreme, conflicting terms. Rather, truth is much more likely to be found by way of perspective and synthesis between opposing points of view.

Stark dialectics tend to dominate thought, particularly upon the introduction of new ideas. Usually the new idea is expressed as a thesis, as an exaggerated assertion, often defining itself against what had been there before. This assertion stimulates a counterreaction, which is also usually exaggerated. If all goes well, this dynamic is followed by balance, synthesis, perspective, synergy. First black, then white, then gray.

The human potential movement was an antithesis to the previous several generations' Western society establishment. Now it has in turn become the center of a gathering antithetical storm. Representative examples are Edwin Schur's *The Awareness Trap*,[1] Peter Marin's "The New Narcissism,"[2] and R. D. Rosen's *Psychobabble*.[3] Among the litany of complaints offered against the human potential movement: A feckless prizing of feelings over the intellect, which substitutes mere indulgence of sensory experience for the hard work of conceptual thought. A de-emphasis of the past and future, which deprives the here-and-now of meaning, renders it superficial. A romantic deification of the animal, primitive, and child, as if a child could really lead us along the tortuous path laid out by the exigencies of the real world. The positing of a sublimely ineffable self that transcends mere social role, while in fact such a self is defined in part by social role and cannot exist independent of it. "Communicating" and "relating" become ends rather than means, as if the acts of "communicating" and "relating" are in themselves valuable regardless of what is communicated and why one is relating himself to someone or something. A language that gaily invites one to camaraderie while debasing the pursuit of meaning. The belief that the sky is the limit for a human's potential and achievable merely through the power of positive thinking, which turns attention away from practical, pragmatic means of bringing about change. The assertion that the way to change social ills is through changing individual consciousness rather than working directly on such social ills, which may also reflect an indifference to social problems.

Such an alleged indifference to social problems is a facet

of the most central criticism of human potential thinking, its alleged "narcissism," the tendency to deify the self, with consequent disregard of the needs and concerns of others. In the minds of some, the origin of this kind of narcissism also goes back to Eastern mysticism, among other religious disciplines. In *India: A Wounded Civilization*,[4] V. S. Naipaul calls Hinduism a "pernicious fantasy." He says that its romanticized personal detachment, its glorification of selflessness, is actually a selfish preoccupation that keeps the culture from examining and knowing itself. Self-centered escape is substituted for real history and real problems. Asceticism as a personal discipline, and to encourage better meditation, is allowed to proliferate into an indifference toward deprivation everywhere and in all forms.

Self-responsibility may be a powerful point of view both in individual change and in psychotherapy, there providing a needed corrective to morbid dependence and the blaming of circumstances for one's troubles. But self-responsibility, carried to its solipsistic extreme, results in a callous indifference to the fate of others, and paradoxically, through preoccupation with internal causes, it also leads to a minimizing of the self's capacity to solve external problems.

The controversy over "narcissism" in the human potential movement can be demonstrated in the varying understanding of Fritz Perls's Gestalt Prayer, postered lines that adorn many college and human potential meeting-place walls:

> I do my thing and you do your thing.
> I am not in this world to live up to your expectations,
> And you are not in this world to live up to mine.
> You are you and I am I;
> If by chance we find each other, it's beautiful.
> If not, it can't be helped.

These lines are presumably intended as a statement of yogic detachment. As such their message is a welcome corrective for those people who are tied to one another through guilt, who take on undue and unwarranted responsibility for others on the basis of neurotic fantasies rather than real need. The lines can also be taken as a teaching aid in overcoming the loss of self that many people suffer through designing their life according to the wishes of others, rather than hammering out their own philosophy and recognizing their own wishes. At a more primitive level, the message can be used as an aid to bringing about separation, a statement of the recognition that one need not be dependent on another for survival. The message can also be read as a declaration of solipsistic independence, the kind of self-preoccupation that results in heedlessness to the plight of others. Or, it could be read as a snarling declamation that the other person is not worthy of any more than a chance encounter. For example, here is a recently printed satirical version (1977).

THE GESTALT PRAYER

I do my laundry, and you do yours.
I am not in this world to listen to your ceaseless yammering,
And you are not in this world for any discernible reason at all.
You are you, and I am I, and I got the better deal.
And if by chance we find each other, it will be unspeakably tedious.
Fuck off.

No doubt the prayer is read and practiced in all of these ways. I think that it is most popularly and usefully understood as a corrective to those middle-class, especially intellectual, persons who are "well brought up," whose consciences burdensomely command that the needs and strictures of others should take precedence over their own.

Such consciences demand not so much that you be your brother's keeper, in the sense of taking care of him, but that you be his keeper in a shared prison. He is tied to you by gratitude as you are tied to him by a sense of guilty responsibility. A large measure of the popularity of the human potential movement lies in the proffering of freedom from such heavy responsibility, in the permission it gives to fulfill one's heretofore hemmed-in desires. To the extent that it provokes such an internal rearrangement, all other things being equal, it is likely to be helpful. To those people who excessively put their wishes first to begin with, it merely provides a rationalization.

To all of the accusations of the human potential movement there is one general answer: The criticisms are correct inasmuch as they indict an application of the human potential point of view to people or situations for whom it is inappropriate, and inasmuch as it is applied in an exaggerated, misguided fashion. No doubt the ideas are often abused; yet such "pilot error" should not, in and of itself, persuade us that planes cannot fly.

Both sides of the controversies are stopped short at the empirical issues: Is it or is it not possible, through human potential techniques and points of view, to solve some individual problems in living? Is it or is it not possible to change our society through changing consciousness of its individual citizens? Is it or is it not possible to begin, at least, with an upper-middle-class movement and encourage the spread of its ideas and values throughout other classes, ultimately to influence situations in order to solve social problems? Is it or is it not possible for each individual to strike a personally gratifying and socially useful balance between concern for self and concern for others? Is it or is it not better to continue personal and social struggles while maintaining traditional assumptions and consciousness. Or can only new assumptions and a new consciousness move us beyond our current dangerous mix of poverty, ignorance, destructive capacity, and all-around meanness to one another?

With respect to the human potential adherents' setting forth their thesis, and to their critics' setting forth the antithesis, I think they are both right. It remains for all of us to supplant being "right" with truth and usefulness.

As is summarized in the table of Contents, I have tried to organize the material I gathered into at least approximate categories. That is not the way it happened to me, however. I took whatever experience and information I could whenever and wherever I could. For example, during my week at Esalen to learn more about gestalt therapy and human potential life I was adventitiously introduced to Rolfing, the first of the body therapies I studied, and to massage. My attendance at *est*, in June 1974, only half-a-year into this work, contributed greatly to my immersion in the new world a-comin', though it is not taken up in this book until Part Three. If the organization of the book does offer a sense of coherence, it is one that I did not have at the time. I usually had, instead, a sense of chaos. When one of the human potential luminaries became apprised of my activities and the way I was pursuing them, she sympathetically warned me that I was doing it the hard way. "Opening up" myself to so many different activities and points of view in such an unsystematic way was bound to take a heavy toll of me personally, she thought, regardless of what effect it might have on my attempts to make orderly intellectual sense of my experience. I tried to tuck away the ominous aspect of her opinions in favor of trying to feel heroic. I really had no choice, anyway. I had to seize opportunities to experience and learn whenever possible, however much it may or may not have fit with "where I was" or "what space I was in" at any given time.

In this Part One survey of the new world of alternatives, I have tried to offer, along with the facts of its history, activities, and characteristics, a sense of it, a feel for it. But I doubt that anything I have written is as evocative of human potential experience and point of view as the following:

IF I HAD MY LIFE TO LIVE OVER

> I'd dare to make more mistakes next time. I'd relax. I would limber up. I would be sillier than I have been this trip. I would take fewer things seriously. I would take more chances. I would take more trips. I would climb more mountains and swim more rivers. I would eat more ice cream and less beans. I would perhaps have more actual troubles, but I'd have fewer imaginary ones.
>
> You see, I'm one of those people who live sensibly and sanely hour after hour, day after day. Oh, I've had my moments and if I had it to do over again, I'd have more of them. In fact, I'd try to have nothing else. Just moments, one after another, instead of living so many years ahead of each day. I've been one of those persons who never goes anywhere without a thermometer, a hot water bottle, a raincoat, and a parachute. If I had to do it again, I would travel lighter than I have.
>
> If I had my life to live over, I would start barefoot earlier in the spring and stay that way later in the fall. I would go to more dances. I would ride more merry-go-rounds. I would pick more daisies.
>
> By Nadine Stair, eighty-five years old
> Louisville, Kentucky[5]

PART TWO

What Is That Below Your Head?

PART TWO

What Is That Below Your Head?

9

Bodies Beautiful, and Healthy— Massage, Rolfing, Patterning

As far back as my earliest readings on the human potential movement, I was struck by its emphasis on breathing and the body in general. Though this emphasis was novel and mysterious to me, I paid only desultory attention to the subject for the first year of my study. Maybe it was because I was too busy with other aspects of the problem. Maybe it was because an opportunity failed to present itself. And maybe it was just because of the kind of person I am. To begin with, I am an ectomorph. In contrast to the rounded bodies of endomorphs and the muscular bodies of mesomorphs, I have 165 pounds stringily wrapped around my over six feet. According to the academic discipline whose members believe that personality characteristics are associated with each basic kind of body, ectomorphs like to keep their clothes on. While an obese endomorph might take his clothes off to relieve his perspiration and a mesomorph might wear a tank top to display his muscular arms and shoulders, an ectomorph shrouds himself in vestments. Understandably, with a body like that. I remember fondly the days before it was necessary to post a sign on a restaurant stating that a coat and tie are required, or, unbelievably, "shoes must be worn." These personal inclinations of mine are abetted by working in a community institution, and with a theory and technique that can justifiably be called conservative. So maybe it was not just happenstance that the need to study the body therapies crept up on me slowly. And it was no surprise that when Laura Perls began the gestalt session reported in Chapter 2 by calling attention to my bodily posture, she caught me unaware and nonplussed me.

Anyone who goes to the theater or movies knows, of course, that one can interpret thoughts and feelings from the way a person holds or uses his body. But I was unprepared to be asked by Laura Perls to look at my body and experience it. I dealt with my momentary consternation through trying to be witty and insightful, trying to feel secure again through the use of my mind. And that is the moral of the story.

In Western society we have become people of the mind, prizing intellect above all and ignoring the body except when it makes itself known through the promptings of instinct or disease, or when we select clothes for it. When we consider a person intelligent, we usually mean that his mind is intelligent, specifically that he is verbally intelligent. We usually ignore physical intelligence. Yet it is readily apparent when, for example, an intellectual is at the mercy of an automobile mechanic, that some people think very well with their hands, inarticulate though they may be.

One price we pay for this one-sided conception of self and others is to court diseases that might be prevented through greater awareness of the body's needs and by treating it better through exercise and diet. Another price we pay is to be "disembodied," to cut ourselves off from the wellsprings of feeling. The source of feelings is in the viscera, and the viscera are down there somewhere beneath the head. Perhaps this loss of the bodily aspect of the self lies behind the ennui, the lack of zest and enthusiasm, that brings some people to psychiatric treatment. And it may be one reason why we tend to feel better when we stimulate our bodies, as by taking a shower or a walk.

It was not always thus, as anyone who wanders through a museum will attest. In Greco-Roman times the body was idealized, immortalized in sculpture and painting, treated luxuriously in baths, celebrated in games. There was less conflict over the sexual and excretory uses of the body, less need therefore to put the body out of sight, to make believe it was not there. Hanns Sachs, an early colleague of Freud, suggested that the idealization of the body is in inverse relation to technological discovery. As long as the Romans idealized the body, he said, they could not allow its functions to be taken over by machines. Thus, even though they knew enough of mathematics and physics to have done otherwise, they restricted their inventions to those which could maximize the use of the body, rather than replace it. According to Sachs, the same thing happened when the classical love of the body, with relatively little internal conflict over it, was reinstated during the Renaissance in Italy. Although at that time Italy was economically superior to countries to the north of it, it was in those northern countries that the key inventions of firearms and the printing press were made. Coincidental with the demise of the body in Victorian times, the industrial revolution flourished. Free of the worship of the body and derogatory of its functions, members of modern industrial society have been free to worship automatized replicas of the body—robot substitutes for its frame and computer substitutes for its brain—while enshrouding the body in clothing and prohibitions.

"Splitting" is psychiatric jargon for when our minds separate people or things or ideas into all-good ones and all-bad ones. We are emerging from just such a culturally sanctioned intrapsychic exercise thrust upon us by René Descartes, a spokesman of the culture that gave rise to him. There was an all-bad, sinful body, a merely sexual, alimentary, and excretory machine; and an all-good soul, or mind. Such a sublime soul could not be considered a part or function of the body, so Descartes put it somewhere out in the atmosphere. How we must have wanted to believe in this split to have allowed it to influence us so long and so insidiously!

Even as we recognize the centrality of brain to mind, and learn increasingly of the connections between the brain and the rest of the body, we still struggle to keep body and mind separate. For example, we chronically pose the question, is a disease physical *or* mental? We often accept without cavil that a thought or feeling once put into words is solely mental. All this despite the fact that the mind is largely in the brain and the brain is in the body, and any time we think and feel, the body functions. All this despite our regularly noticing that when we feel embarrassed, our skin reddens, when our muscles are massaged, we feel relaxed, when we experience pain or terror, we perspire, turn cold, or our hair may whiten. Bodily ills can be given up under hypnosis, yogis walk on hot coals, ordinary citizens influence their metabolism, blood pressure, and temperature by meditation or with feedback cues from machines. Penfield stimulated an area of the brain and produced memories and emotion. "Rolfing," a method of manually rearranging the sheaths of the muscles, results at times in emotional discharge and the recovery of seemingly forgotten memories. And, increasingly, new disciplines are demonstrating that the mind can affect disease beneficially. Nonetheless, we have developed professions as an outgrowth of this split way of thinking: those which work solely with the mind and largely ignore the body, and those which work with the body and largely ignore the mind. I am not suggesting out of hand that in every instance this is not the best way of working, only that we have fallen into such professionalized activities *as if* body and mind were separate.

Sigmund Freud provides a case in point. He became professionally of age at a time when materialistic science had exhilaratingly moved from a theologically inspired understanding of human events of mind and body to exploring successfully and treating the material body in new ways. Rules of science were being rapidly codified, with the implication that sooner or later all human events would be understood according to the same scientific principles. Freud was trained as a laboratory scientist and became a practicing physician as a means to an end, in part simply to make a living. (He was in love and had the quaint notions of those days that one ought to be able to support a wife before one married her and that man and woman needed to marry to be together.) Out of patience with his four-year engagement, conducted to a large extent through letters, he somewhat reluctantly left the laboratory and went into the private practice of neurology.

Freud assumed he would go on diagnosing and treating bodies with his customary, recognized scientific methods. But, remarkably, patients came to him with physical complaints for which no bodily cause could be found. And when they unburdened themselves of feelings, thoughts, and memories concerning important events in their lives, *mirabile dictu,* their physical symptoms sometimes vanished. Freud was now at the heart of the matter. The connection between body and mind could no longer be ignored. True to his training, Freud first tried to cast his psychological discoveries in neurological terms. He called this the *Project for a Scientific Psychology*[1] (as if only when psychology is represented concretely in the body could it be "scientific"). Recently his model has begun to be confirmed through neurological explorations of the brain. At the time, however, his prescience was unsupported neurologically, and was all but lost to the world of ideas in the wake of his further dramatic and revolutionary psychological discoveries.

Declaring an armistice to the mind-body controversy, Freud decided to proceed in his investigation as a psychologist, collecting psychological data empirically and making sense of them inductively. But he would construe his observations according to such physical concepts as structure and energy, for such methods and concepts were consistent with his scientific conscience and training. He hoped that the physicochemical processes underlying psychological events would eventually be specifiable, but this was not to be his task. He had cast his lot with psychophysical parallelism, a solution that shelves the body-mind problem by dealing with each independently.

Abandoning his early experimentation with producing memories through putting his hands on the patient's forehead, he no longer touched his patients except to shake hands. The body remained very much an issue in his thinking: He recognized that the self is first experienced in bodily terms, which he called the body ego, and he understood the propensity of the body to express psychological events. But, as a child of his time, he collected and acted upon psychological data solely through psychological means, trying as hard as he could to remain with and exploit the forms of physical science. No wonder that I, as a child of *my* time, brought up in the training and atmosphere established by Freud, was taken aback when, first crack out of the box, Laura Perls called attention to my body.

In the past couple of decades, times have certainly changed with respect to the body. In a spasm of rebelliousness against Victorian prohibitions, we have disrobed, explored, and allegedly enjoyed the body zestfully if not flagrantly. And, sure enough, as our love affair with the body has begun, our love affair with the machine has begun to end. An article of faith in the human potential environment is a preference for the natural ways, to do without machines whenever possible and often to deride our technological achievements merely as the toys of our society.

The week after Laura Perls put a lens on my body myopia I had my first professional mixed-group unveiling. It, too, took place at Esalen, during the same week reported on in Part One.

Is there anybody here, the group leader asked on our first night, who has any reservations about bathing in the nude? Being usually the soul of honesty and always on the lookout for opportunities to provoke data, I responded in the affirmative. "What's the matter," she asked, "are you afraid your cock is too short?" To any statistically minded observer of the male human condition the question was a nonquestion. Practically every man seems to believe, however vaguely, that his penis is too short, just as every woman seems to believe, however vaguely, that she is overweight. After a few more opportunities to acclimate ourselves to what we all knew, indeed hoped, was coming, we trooped off to the famous springs of Esalen. Here, nestled on a cave in the cliffs facing the ocean, were spring-water tubs. Mercifully for many of us, it was night, and you could not see much of the virginal disrobees anyway, especially those cowardly ones who spent most of the time with only their heads above water. For most of us nudity comes easier in the heat of passion than on a chilly night under the light of the moon.

Later in the week the liberated ones participated in massage classes. Truth to tell, it seemed that the hesitancy about nudism was at least as much concern over saggy breasts, varicose veins, and protruding bellies as it was a fear of sexual display. And massage, once lifted out of the mental context of the massage parlor, is less sensual than sensuous. The oil-slippery hands performing one of the variations of massage, "the Esalen massage" in this instance, are soothing and stimulating. Their contact with usually ignored areas of the body reminds us of our physical totality, that this physical totality can be a source of pleasure, and that relaxed enjoyment of the body can come about not through cutting it off at the head but through being made gently and invigoratingly aware of it. Massage as an exploitation of the split-off, "sinful" body is represented in such institutions as "massage parlors," outright fronts for prostitution, or, as in Japan, storefront mixtures of sensuous pleasures, cleanliness, and optional sexuality. Massage as a sensuous bridge between sin and sublimeness is a means of nonverbal communication in a shared meditation state. In an altered state of consciousness the massage partners learn what could be available to their experience if they would allow and welcome it. As such, massage is another expression of the unity of body, thought, and feeling.

I suppose massage can be used all the way from temporary fun to a regular part of one's life, and mutual massage may contribute to a loving relationship as well as being a celebratory expression of it. Other ways of working with the body are grander in their aims. Their practitioners seek to overcome definitively some physical and psychological difficulties and to at least improve all of them. While massage is a sort of first aid to be repeated when necessary, Rolfing, the Alexander technique, and bioenergetics are designed to make fundamental changes in the body, and by implication these changes should last.

I first heard of Rolfing through reading a snide review of a book about it which left me feeling unclean. What is the world coming to, what is our society coming to, what is my cherished profession of psychological change coming to? What it seemed to be coming to was the, to me, bizarre belief that digging into people's bodies with one's hands would result in recovery of repressed memories, with consequent beneficial change in personality and in shape and tonus of the body. Fat chance, I thought, and proceeded to forget about it. But by the time I got to Esalen, with my policy of trying everything, keeping an open mind, and learning what I could, I knew I had to deal with Rolfing.

"Structural integration," which is the technical name for Rolfing, was, along with massage, an optional accessory to the basic week of Esalen activities. Assuming that the individual differences between Rolfers would be as great as those between psychotherapists, I set about learning who was best. Having ascertained that Beverly Silverman was the person to try to get, I signed up for her. There then ensued a dance, the like of which I was to participate in many times in making appointments for the new therapies. This minuet stems from the tension between two people having to be in the same place at the same time in order to accomplish a task and the reluctance on the part of the new therapists to submit to schedules. Add the mystical belief that people will come together if they are meant to come together, and you have a chaotic scheduling problem, which, however, usually does seem somehow to work out.

Beverly's schedule was filled, but by now wise to the

moves in these things, I approached her in the dining room and stated my case. I don't think she was much impressed by my quest for study and experience or the possible gain in making a convert in a prestigious institution. Rather, she looked at me from deep within her limpid eyes. She would see what she could do, would let me know, and then she drifted away into the Esalen / human potential abstractedness. I felt the inner person of me had been appraised. I approached her a few days later, and she said since I really wanted it. . . . She was, of course, late for our appointment. But, then, she did not have to be anywhere afterward either, so again it all worked out.

Upon instruction I stripped to my shorts and lay down upon a mat. In this first of the ten sessions comprised in the basic course of Rolfing, the areas concentrated upon are the throat and the chest. By "concentrated upon," I mean that Beverly pushed and probed my muscles, using her fingers, knuckles, occasionally her elbow, kneading my muscles according to the over-all plan of bringing my total musculature into alignment with gravity. Through stretching and loosening, the fascial envelope surrounding muscle fibers, bones, organs, tendons, and ligaments are repositioned for greater efficiency. Ideally, my "Rolfed body" should then be straight up and down, so that gravity would encounter the least possible obstruction in its relationship to me. By contrast, my un-Rolfed body had a variety of curves, bends, twists, and especially knots of tense muscles which fought with gravity, resulting in bodily and perhaps psychological strain. Theoretically, this conflict between body and surround should influence the way I held myself, and have consequences for my experience of self and the way I related myself to others. According to Rolfing theory, I could have gotten into conflicts with gravity as sequelae to real childhood injuries and from adopting positions in reaction to the threats and injuries I experienced from others in fact and fantasy.

The blood-red badges that adorned my body the next day were earned heroically: Rolfing hurt like hell. It was, however, a peculiar kind of pain. Beverly warned me about it, adding that all I had to do to stop the pain was to ask her to stop. I could, however, "go with" the pain, letting the pain be part of me rather than something I fought against, and learning to breathe in synchrony with it, "breathing through it."

These ways of dealing with pain make sense physiologically and psychologically. Much pain results from the tensing of muscles in response to an initial pain, making a bad situation worse. Pain is minimized by accepting rather than fighting it. We often tense ourselves in situations that we experience as evading our control. It would have been easy to feel myself a subject painfully manipulated by another person, but Beverly's offering of control and means of dealing with pain, along with the totally accepting atmosphere she created, offered me a sense of independence and autonomy. Paradoxically, the more I "went with" her point of view and procedures the more I felt in control. Here, in this homely example of the temporary management of pain, were the key human potential beliefs in the innate wisdom of the person and body, the need for the person to manage himself, and the belief that we minimize our capacities by yielding responsibility to others in assumed authority.

A variation of this issue, with important implications for the practice of psychotherapy, occurred later on in the session, when I found myself "chatting" following some intense psychological experiences brought about by the Rolfing and by some psychological interventions made by Beverly. I told her that I ought to stop the chatting, that I was intellectualizing, avoiding the opportunities for further work. Instead of appreciating my insightfulness and willingness to get back to work, Beverly said that it just seemed to be time for me to surface, that I would work when it was time again for that, that my body and mind knew when to do what.

Did she know better than I? My psychoanalytic self would deal with such turning from tasks by examining these as resistance, learning from them, ultimately giving them up and getting back to work. Was she simply playing into my resistances with her "democratic," *laissez-faire* attitude? At times, in other therapeutic experiences, I have pushed myself back to work, but with little success because it apparently was not the time to do so. In this instance I responded to Beverly's intervention by getting back to work successfully. She had, in fact, dealt with resistance, true to her principle of allowing me autonomy. Desirelessness turned out to be a powerful ally of desire. And if I could not have returned to psychological work successfully, what then? Perhaps I really was temporarily finished. I could have accepted Beverly's point of view without guiltily feeling myself a resistive failure. So long as I persisted in seeing my behavior as resistance, I would be adding self-reprimand to whatever else was ailing me.

In the course of having my chest worked on, I realized that my talk was in effect a free association and my associations were about my mother. Beverly, who is also a gestalt psychotherapist, invited me to let an image come to mind. The image was of iron bars. This could have been a reference to the iron-tense bars of muscle that Beverly was softening, or to issues of control in my relationship to my mother, or both. As Beverly worked on my body and encouraged me with occasional comments and suggestions,

Intro

Baby F

Roof, Alot, Bea,
Feld, Biop

Mend F
Gestanet, Presnd
E 55

Ilastic

Sp: Parflosgpn – Feltam
2-4, TM

bits of memories of the vicissitudes of my early life in relation to my mother emerged.

I greeted Beverly's telling me that we were finished both with relief that the pain was over and with sorrow that the experience was, too. According to Beverly, I now held my head, neck, and chest differently. That was difficult for me to corroborate, but beyond a doubt, when I began to speak, I realized that a remarkable change had occurred in my voice. Characteristically my voice is higher and more muffled than one would expect from a person over six feet tall. Now it was lower, louder, and more resonant. I was shocked at these new emanations from within me, and had to confront an aspect of what seemed a new person to be identified as myself. Shortly after, I called my wife on the telephone. She immediately said that my voice had changed. My acquaintances the rest of the day said the same. I was to have further opportunities to bring about this change, through the Alexander technique and several times through bioenergetics; in each instance the change was temporary. However, there is much more variability in my voice than there used to be, and I have learned a few techniques for dealing with the state of mind that brings about a choked, elevated voice as well as working directly on the physiological causes of this constriction. At the least, I can no longer simply assume that I was made with a bad voice. Rather, I know that it is something I make myself, and can do something about.

Arm in arm with Beverly on the way down from the high of my Rolfing experience and on to my next activity (dance therapy), Beverly told me of her husband and children and their life at Esalen. "I prefer," she said, "the craziness in here to the craziness outside." Simple sweet thunder.

Each of the basic ten Rolfing sessions is devoted primarily to one or another part of the body and done in preordained sequence. I was to have my third session, again with Beverly, in the course of a visit in Topeka. My other eight sessions (one of which included the interior of my nose and mouth—very uncomfortable) were with Tom Pathe, who set up shop in Lawrence, Kansas, every couple of months on a visit from the Rolfing headquarters in Boulder, Colorado. Tom is not a psychotherapist, and "material" such as emerged with Beverly in the first session did not emerge with him. Not only was Beverly a therapist, but I had been psychologically softened by the intense introspection generated by Esalen activities, being away from home, and in a culture different from my accustomed one, all of which may have played a part in the emergence of thoughts and feelings ordinarily held outside of awareness.

That psychological material should not have appeared in later sessions is in accordance with the original design of the procedure by Ida Rolf. Now in her eighties, she is an imposing, "Dutch aunt" sort of a person with a Ph.D. in biochemistry, an old shoe somehow caught in the midst of the sandaled set. She developed her method over half a century's study and experimentation, beginning with an attempt to discover how to help her sickly son, and her own spinal arthritis which threatened to confine her to a wheelchair. She and her son have long been free of their difficulties as the apparent result of "structural integration," her preferred name for the procedure. She seems tolerant, but just barely, of the psychotherapeutic uses to which Rolfing has been put. Her intention all along was to work solely on the body physically, to cure its deformities and illness, to produce straight bodies whose parts were in harmonious alignment with one another and with gravity. Naturally people would feel better generally, she thought, from such physical changes. In about a third of the cases, however, different areas of the body for different people resulted in intense outpourings of emotion, thought, and sometimes early memories. Such experiences give the impression that memories, with associated ideas and feelings, are "stored" in parts of the body apart from the brain. Since, for Ida Rolf, body and mind are one, intervening in either way ought to help the other.

I have heard many claims of cure of physical derangements through Rolfing. While many of these were only secondhand, such as increasing people's height, making a short leg longer, and many more, Beverly, among many other Rolfers, supports her alleged cures with before-and-after photographs. One of these cures was of a child, about to be put in a body brace for scoliosis, who apparently overcame her scoliosis through Beverly's Rolfing. As to the claims of straightening "normal" bodies of people through Rolfing, during the demonstration that Beverly gave, for which a Menninger staff member was the subject, she stopped after doing one half of his chest to let the audience observe the difference between the part she had worked on and the part as yet unworked on. The difference was unmistakable even to the untutored eye. One half of his chest was elongated and square, while the other was scrunched and rounded. We anxiously encouraged her to do the other half of him.

What of the durability of such changes? Some people need to take Rolfing sessions beyond the basic ten, notably practitioners of Rolfing themselves. Some critics from within the new therapies claim that the Rolfing implication of definitive treatment with only ten sessions borders on the unethical. Rather, continued extended work on the body is necessary, either through direct intervention or practice. Such continued practice is, informally, made available through an adjunct of Rolfing called "structural patterning," to be described shortly.

Valerie Hunt, head of the Movement Behavior Laboratory, at UCLA, studied the electrical activity of muscles before and after Rolfing. She found that after Rolfing one performs simple movements such as walking, lifting, sitting, and throwing with less neuromuscular static, less random tension, more-efficient patterns of energy use.[2] Julian Silverman, Beverly's husband and a research psychologist as well as human potential practitioner, measured brainwave patterns of Rolfed persons with the electroencephalograph and computer averaging. In twelve of his thirteen subjects the EEG average of evoked responses was significantly higher in amplitude and variability after Rolfing. He concludes that Rolfing creates a more spontaneous, open, rhythmic reaction to the external environment and to one's kinesthetic proprioceptive sensations.[3]

I have heard no reports of people's becoming psychotic as an apparent result of Rolfing, such as one hears about many other psychotherapeutic interventions. Temporary, mild disorientations following the sessions are not uncommon. I do know firsthand of a person who, in the midst of a series of Rolfings, for several weeks could not shake an attack of depressed feelings. Drawing on his previous psychoanalysis, he had tried to account for the depression with respect to events in his present life and his understanding of his vulnerabilities. But all his explanations were unconvincing; they could not be supported by dreams or associations in this self-analytic work. It was a great relief to him to find out from a Rolfer that such depressions may occur as a result of Rolfing, and that they clear up spontaneously, which in fact this one did.

What would it be like if someone in psychoanalysis were Rolfed and brought any newly released thoughts and feelings into the analysis? Could it be that Rolfing would speed up an analysis through removing blocks to warded-off thoughts and feelings? One of my patients provided a partial answer. Upon her return from her first Rolfing session (with a Rolfer who was uninterested in psychological phenomena) she expressed intense rage against me. She contrasted my sitting behind the couch out of sight with the direct, "human" intervention on the part of the Rolfer. She saw me as a person who persistently forbade her being spontaneous, taking initiative, who had in mind specific activities that I valued and which she was to follow. She had recently begun graduate professional studies and had inexplicably dropped them. Now, it turned out, she had dropped them as a rebellion against what she believed was my interest that she pursue them. While we had talked off and on for some time about her anger toward me, she was now caught up in these feelings and their associated meanings in a way that made them more alive, with an experiential importance that ordinarily lends itself to effective psychoanalytic work.

This experiment in nature was therefore encouraging. But, not too long afterward, this patient engaged in behaviors that threatened the course of the analysis, in part perhaps out of rebelliousness that was stimulated so quickly and intensely that it could not be integrated. Whatever the circumstances of this one case, it is plausible that "artificially" releasing thoughts and feelings, in advance of working with defenses against them and beyond the capacity of the ego to integrate them, would be a persistent danger in combining psychoanalytic work with Rolfing. One might still consider the possible helpful or harmful effects of recommending Rolfing as part of a regular adjunctive procedure, compared to its coming about inadvertently. The Rolfing itself could perhaps be changed, as by titration, in ways that best conform to a particular patient's needs in the context of a particular period of psychological work. The psychological work could perhaps be designed to maximize the benefits of the Rolfing while minimizing its dangers. These are some of the unexplored frontiers whose existence makes it impossible to declare out of hand that Rolfing has nothing to offer psychotherapy.

Another psychotherapy patient had as her chief psychopathological characteristic a masochistically weary acceptance of practically unremitting headaches. Still another one, with a severe and disabling psychosomatic symptom, had a subtle but deeply malevolent determination that nobody would succeed with him, that nobody cared enough and nobody was well enough equipped to make a difference in his life. Pleasure for him would be in demanding, on the one hand, and turning down, on the other. Both of these patients emerged from Rolfing with their characteristic attitudes and symptoms intact. The Rolfer, though untrained psychologically, was well aware of the psychological situation of these patients. He had learned through long experience that people benefit from Rolfing only to the extent that their personality allows them to benefit from anything. He thus shares with psychotherapists an implicit understanding of character, motivation, determinism. In Rolfing, as in psychotherapy, a diagnostic understanding of who is likely to benefit might save all concerned from needless expenditures or would help with the decision of who should have treatment procedures that are in short supply. While Rolfing may have beneficial effects on some aspects of personality, these effects are probably limited to reasonably well-integrated people and to superficial aspects. Tortuously complex and self-defeating characteristics, such as in the patients just mentioned, may fail to yield to the ministrations of

Rolfing, just as they ordinarily do to the ministrations of anything less than long-term, intensive psychotherapy, and even that is chancy.

Ex-dancer Heather Wing is a walking, standing, sitting, reaching, bending advertisement for "structural patterning," a discipline that teaches you how to use your body in everyday situations. Such situations may include activities that all of us do, as well as such specialized activities as serving in tennis, swinging a golf club, and holding one's body properly when playing the trumpet or guitar (according to my son, holding the body as prescribed by patterning improves one's playing of these instruments). I, on the other hand, was, in Heather's view, a barely walking advertisement for how not to use the body.

I got into this embarrassing situation because, like the mountain, it was there. Heather Wing came to the Topeka area every several months and gave hourly patterning sessions. I had heard about her through the local human potential grapevine and figured, what the hell she's here anyway. (Clearly, I have never gotten over my reluctance at dealing with the body.) Despite the unkind things Heather had to say about my body, we became friendly, and my whole family eventually joined me in becoming "patterned."

Heather's diagnostic acumen is eerie. As usual with the body therapies, she had me strip down to my underwear shorts so that she could make a visual diagnosis. Ostensibly she means, by visual diagnosis, spotting parts of the body that are held, in her view, incorrectly. However, in her slightly ethereal way, her remarks about the body begin to shade over into remarks about the personality. For her, body and mind indeed are one; without apparently thinking much about it, she diagnoses the whole person.

Heather takes Polaroid photographs before and after her

patterning instruction. Characteristically she claims to see a good deal of difference between one photograph and another. I must say that I could not quite join in her enthusiastic reporting of visual evidence of substantial changes. It seems to me that my facial expression determined a sense of change at least as much as any other change. (There I go again, relying on the head.)

Now, how was it possible that there was so much, to put it politely, questionable about my body *after* I had been Rolfed? Smiling through my disappointed tears, I asked Heather that. She said that as a result of Rolfing my body was basically okay; the problem was only that I did not know how to use my Rolfed body correctly. I tried to fight off the recognition that Heather is married to a Rolfer, lives where Rolfing has its center, Boulder, Colorado, and patterning is, after all, an adjunct to Rolfing. The problem may be less in the inadequacy of Rolfing than in what is claimed for it. Perhaps a more modest and accurate presentation of Rolfing would be that it is the first in a two-part series. A Rolfed body is a necessary, but in and of itself an insufficient, condition for achieving ideal bodily movements. For that one must submit a Rolfed body to the education of patterning.

My education was to consist of about a half dozen teaching sessions with Heather, separated by months between her visits, covering around a year and a half. Her method was to describe the exercise that she wanted me to practice and that was designed to bring about specific changes in my body. Perhaps I was a slow learner, but it always ended up that she had to implement her description and demonstration on my body with a demonstration of how she would perform the exercise. I had a terrible time remembering each of the minute movements that constitute a "pattern." It was a bit like playing golf; it seemed that each muscle had to be used in just the right way or the whole thing collapsed. According to human potential mores, it is gauche to take notes, and I tried to do without them. However, it finally became clear to me that my choice was to forget the patterns or to take notes. I took notes, which even now reside on my dressing table, sometimes to be helpfully used and sometimes to constitute a reproachful reminder that dust is being gathered.

Ideally, one should practice one's patterns for twenty to thirty minutes each day. They are supposed to be less a burden than an opportunity to enjoy one's body as one is training it to function well. That is the theory, and I daresay that for many human potential practitioners, and certainly for Heather, that is the way it is. For me, such daily exercises were daily chores. I felt virtuous when I did them, irresponsible when I did not. Instead of the meditative repose that one should be able to achieve in practicing one's patterns, I usually looked forward to their being over.

Here are some excerpts from instructions I was to follow daily.

1. *Settle down on a mat or foam rubber pad with a book or several magazines under your head, keep feet and knees parallel with legs drawn up so that knees are over the feet, and relax.* This is the basic starting position, which theoretically allows one to get ready to accept the invitation to enjoy and improve one's body.
2. *Breathe deeply, with the breath rolling back the head in a rocking motion. Be sure jaw is loose.* In this and other body therapies I have found a loosening of the jaw to be especially tranquilizing.
3. *Breathe into the right side of the back, the spine, the shoulder joint, then do the same on the left side, until you feel all of these areas opening.* Rolfers as well as patterners look you straight in the eye when they tell you to "breathe into" any area of the body by visualizing air going into that area, and that you can feel it going in and circulating.

Even if the area is your big toe. Strange as it may seem, by accepting their admonition and working a bit at it, I did have the distinct impression that air was entering and circulating in any area to which I directed it. I experienced such areas as opening, accepting air, becoming lighter and more relaxed.

4. *After circulating the air in each shoulder, pull the shoulder down ever so gently*. These are not calisthenics; one does not exercise muscles, one merely makes gentle, minuscule movements. Patterning is diametrically opposite from muscle building. Patterners want to lengthen and fine-tune muscles, while the visual definition of muscles comes about through brutish shortening of them. In Rolfing and patterning one is enjoined not to do activities that build muscles.
5. *The "pelvic rock" begins with breathing and consequent rocking back of the head, as in #2; then with the weight on the ball and heel of the foot you raise your waist, the hips rise and fall, without tightening of the buttocks and without sharp movements, just a slight rocking to and fro.* This exercise is designed to help you rotate your pelvis in such a way as to cradle your viscera, rather than allowing them to slip forward, thereby protruding the belly. Considering the ubiquity of potbellies, the pelvic rock should be a great hit.
6. *After the hint of a pelvis rock, let the legs collapse flat on the floor. Next, bring each arm up three or four times, as in levitation, then drop the arm by losing tension from the shoulders. Do these three or four times*. By now, if all has gone well, you should have a feeling akin to what it must be like to float on a cloud.
7. *Bring the knees up, the stomach relaxed, pull each knee alongside the ear, then with both knees alongside the ears, and fingers linked across the knees, breathe along the spine.* Second to potbellies, in numbers and in aggravation, is pain in the lower back. With this exercise, all the offending parts should be straightened, tension reduced, and low back pain an unpleasant memory.
8. *Roll over onto knees, with hands landing in front of jaws, toes under, then a) rock weight back onto feet, letting*

> *hands follow you, drop head, and your seat floats up; b) pelvis forward and knees straighten, balance on feet, not too far back on heels; then c) uncurl, let your chest up and "put your head on."* You have now correctly learned how to stand up from a lying position in a way that puts minimal strain on vulnerable muscles and organizes you for standing straight in a proper relationship to gravity. Indeed, having made it this far, and with the end in sight, I do feel taller than when I collapsed into the original, "resting" position.

The above is but a sample; there are many, similar exercises, each designed for any particular difficulties that a person may have. Whatever the exercises, they should be done as a treat, as a kindness to one's body and self, "time for yourself," rather than a duty, obligation, or chore in the service of frantic self-improvement. If I have repeated myself here, most of us require it. By contrast, human potential people, while not-doing, by being detached, almost accidentally, it seems, achieve their goal. It is a style that doesn't come easy in twentieth-century America. Most of us have to work at it (oops).

I did the exercises prescribed for me for several months, and in a minimal way enjoyed them. Whether as a result of the exercises or their serving as a daily reminder, I believe I walked, sat, reached, lay down, and got up more efficiently and gracefully than before. I learned that practically all chairs are designed to encourage incorrect sitting, usually because they tilt downward behind, where the tuberosities, or "sit bones," land. I replaced my desk chair with one that allowed me to position my weight on these tuberosities, with my feet flat on the floor, and I put cushions on the chair behind my analytic couch. I installed in my conscience the admonition to sit correctly and especially not to cross my legs while sitting. Did I follow through? Well, sometimes yes, sometimes no. So now I have to deal with new wrinkles in my conscience as well as twists in my body.

I do believe that with attention and practice we can learn to use our bodies better. It is also logical that in so doing we should lessen the danger of orthopedic injury. It could even be that we might feel better emotionally, too, and be helped in developing a straight-up-and-down, harmonious, efficient personality and way of relating ourselves to the environment. The problem is that those who are able to enter into, and maintain, these experiences and their applications may only be those who are already committed to the style of life that corresponds to it. Your typical Western pragmatist is more inclined to pump iron, and have some muscles to show for it, or to think he is too busy to have time for his body. The flesh may be weak, but the conservative spirit is strong.

10

Use What You Have, Correctly—the Alexander Technique

I MET ILANA RUBENFELD in Lincoln, Nebraska, in the spring of 1975; in Prairie View, Kansas, in the summer of 1975; in Dallas in the winter of 1976; in New York in the spring of 1976; and in San Francisco in the summer of 1976. Before, in between, and after, she could be found in other cities in the United States and throughout the world. That the Alexander technique is a fairly well-kept secret is hardly her fault. Nor is it the fault of Nikolas Tinbergen, who devoted his 1973 Nobel Prize lecture, in part, to the Alexander technique as an example of the usefulness of an ethological approach to medicine. Intrigued by what he called the "fantastic claims" made by Alexander and his followers, Tinbergen, his wife, and one of his daughters went to three different Alexander teachers to see for themselves. They noticed "very striking improvements in high blood pressure, breathing, depth of sleep, over-all cheerfulness and mental alertness, resilience against outside pressures, and also in such a refined skill as playing an instrument." Tinbergen concludes, "Although no one would claim that the Alexander treatment is a cure-all in every case, there can be no doubt that it often does have profound and beneficial effects . . . both in the mental and somatic sphere."[1]

In England in the 1930s, "going to Alexander" was fashionable. Among those who went, and declared the usefulness of the Alexander technique, were Aldous Huxley, Bernard Shaw, Sir Stafford Cripps, and John Dewey. Huxley's wife: "Alexander has certainly made a new and unrecognizable person of Aldous, not physically only, but mentally. . . ." Dewey: "[Alexander] gave people a positive standard of health and a means of attaining it."[2] I am inclined to think that Ilana's whirlwind teaching and publicizing campaign for the Alexander technique will succeed in making the technique popular once again.

I met Ilana in the course of one of her teaching demonstrations at the Nebraska meeting of 1975, and moments later was a demonstration subject myself on the wrong, or "misuse," way of getting in and out of a chair. It was a skill that I thought I had long since mastered. Not so, said Ilana, as she showed me how unevenly I distributed my weight, the unnecessary and stressful movements that I made in the course of what I used to think of as a simple act. My feelings became unruffled only when I learned that, according to Alexander standards, practically all of us misuse our bodies practically all of the time.

My first Alexander therapeutic session took place a year later. I arrived at Ilana's Greenwich Village, New York, studio and apartment perspiring and disheveled from a Kansan's difficulty finding his way around New York. By this time Ilana and I had met several times and had planned writing projects. So it was not remarkable that in the course of her showing me around her apartment she pridefully included in the tour one of her bathrooms. It was on a scale of Roman magnificence, with a huge open shower area designed for living as much as for cleaning. I was offered the use of this grand throwback to ancient times when the body was exalted, along with an exotic array of soaps and lotions. How perfect, I thought, that one who works with the body should have such reverential surroundings for its care.

Alexander work is done with the subject on a waist-high table. The Alexander practitioner selects what to work on and in what order, according to his visual diagnosis of the body. Instead of ten sessions, as prescribed by Rolfing and optionally followed by "patterning," a rule of thumb in the Alexander technique is that as many sessions are required as the number of years the subject has lived.

Alexander manipulations of the body, I was relieved to experience, produce hardly any pain. Indeed, the Alexander touch is usually so gentle that it seems nothing much is being done at all. And yet, demonstrably much is being done. For example, after Ilana had worked on one leg, she asked me to look down, and I saw that the one foot that had been worked on was pointed straight up in the air, while the other was lying at its usual, 45-degree angle. My voice was improved also, although not as dramatically as in the first Rolfing session; but, then, the area that produces the voice was not worked on as intensively either. (Some months later, Ilana was to show me that I could change my voice by biting on a piece of paper while jumping up and down on the balls of my feet. Impossible, you may think, if not bizarre. Of course. Except that it worked. At the same time, she showed me that with a bit of sugar or coffee on my tongue I no longer was able to prevent her pulling apart my thumb and index finger, which just previously she had been unable to separate. That is the way it goes on the human potential circuit.)

In the course of her work on my body, Ilana, as did Beverly, asked me to let an image come to mind. She picked one of my phrases, which touched on a *leitmotif* of my personality, and asked me to repeat it several times and sound as though I meant it. Following the manipulation and the associated therapeutic opportunities it provided, I was instructed in ways of walking and sitting, and in how to practice these. While Rolfing puts its emphasis on the physical rearrangement of the body, Alexander practitioners seem to emphasize equally the physical rearrangement and the learning and continued practice in correctly using the body—"use" rather than "misuse."

Ilana and I were an odd couple: she in Indian robes and I in a gray flannel suit; she constitutionally unable reliably to return phone calls and answer letters, I constitutionally unable not to do so; she able to enthrall an audience of hundreds but paralyzed at the prospect of attaching words to paper, while I in front of groups sometimes fight through waves of anxiety to find the words that troop tidily into place on paper; she with butterfly hands that do her thinking for her, while I laboriously direct ten thumbs with my mind. We each appreciated in the other what is missing in himself. As a gestalt therapist also, she fights the good fight to incorporate the words of psychotherapy into the body discipline of the Alexander technique. I consider the possibility of enriching psychotherapy with bodily interventions. Putting our ideas together, we came up with the following thoughts about a discussion of the relationship between the "Alexander technique and psychotherapy."

As with Ida Rolf, some Alexander practitioners assert that they are uninterested in the personality insofar as their work goes. They merely want people to prevent and overcome physical difficulties for aesthetic and health reasons. Others are interested in changing personality but believe that work with the body, in itself, will bring about desired changes in the way a person feels, thinks, and behaves. Some methods of work with the body facilitate work with the personality more than others do, whether the practitioner cares about that or not. The Alexander technique seems to be one of those that facilitate psychotherapy. F. M. Alexander, inventor of the Alexander technique, would probably not have liked that. He classified his work as belonging with those which adhere strictly to the use of the body.

There is every reason for Alexander to have seen his work as a subject-object modality, a mechanical procedure, in the mode, say, of a chiropractor. When he made his discoveries, in the nineteenth century, subject-object was a largely unquestioned interpersonal and professional mode of relating oneself to others. It was a culture in which children were caned and Cratchits cowered, when it was clear who was to give orders and who was to take them. Co-operation was only for those of equal rank; the rest were to be subservient.

Alexander made his discoveries intrapersonally, diagnosing and curing his loss of voice by himself. When the time came for him to apply his insights and techniques to other people, it would have been logical and expectable for him to go along with the duality of his time, accepting separateness—stratification—automatically, with its often concomitant experiences of emotional isolation. It would have been understandable had he used powerful directiveness, for he had the authority to do so by virtue of the student's* placing himself in Alexander's hands for the purpose of cure. Power could have taken the forms of cajoling, appealing to the student's conscious self-interest,

* People who come to an Alexander practitioner are called "students," not "patients," for reasons that seem more attempts not to infringe on medicine than substantive. Just as patients do students come with a complaint, expect to be cured, and pay a fee.

threatening, or pushing ahead heedless of the student's thoughts and feelings, as one would do in those surgeries in which the patient's attitudes toward his difficulties and himself are ignored. (Some people describe Alexander as the kind of person who would be likely to behave in these ways, that he was a child of his time and then some.)

But whatever kind of person he was, and however he conceptualized and described his work, when one looks at what he did and hypothesizes about his creative moments, one sees that he transcended his time. However unwittingly, he was a precursor of human potential, interpersonal, and dynamic psychology's beliefs and values.

Let us look closer at the process that occurs in the Alexander technique. The practitioner first observes a student's misuse of his body, then directs his own mind to the preferred relationship, creating in his own mind an image of how things should be for the student physically. He then puts that image into words, he tells the student that image. Then he manually adjusts and guides the student to redefine himself kinesthetically.

The basic model of theory and consequent technique in the Alexander approach could serve, in part, as a description of a psychotherapeutic approach as well. Alexander believed that in the natural course of events, which includes a certain amount of trauma, the person develops irrational ways of behaving.[3] Trauma may occur in the earliest years of life and set in motion life-long maladaptions.[4] Events become traumatic when driven by instincts that are inappropriate to an environment;[5] that is, an environment that is inimical to these instinctual expressions. Although the ways a person walks, sits, reaches may seem familiar and comfortable to him, they may nonetheless be examples of misuse in that they have harmful repercussions which may cover the whole range of bodily experiences and functionings. Equipped with the knowledge of his misuses, the student is in a position to inhibit what for him are natural, though inappropriate, tendencies, and to replace them with different, beneficial behavior.

A psychoanalytic psychotherapist might express these same ideas by calling attention to the ingredients of neurotic conflict: instincts versus the environment, the need to make conscious what has been unconscious, the recognition that when people become aware of the way they have been behaving and the consequences of this, they are then in a position to stop that behavior and find more advantageous ways of behaving. Also, Alexander recognized that in response to these "infantile" (his word) traumas, the person develops body blocks. These correspond analogously to mental blocks or other varieties of repression. In both systems these blocks are structures in a dynamic system, for the removal of them may lead to anxiety.

Alexander recognized that the teacher was intimately involved in many processes between himself and the student. He described a back-and-forth movement between observations of his own reactions, uses and misuses of his own body, and those of his students. These observations are analogous to the psychotherapist's awareness of his "countertransference" reactions and the use of them in order to understand better and deal with his patient.

A psychotherapeutic alliance is characterized by two persons working together on a common task. The same could be said for the Alexander process. Rather than the teacher's doing something to the student, the student works in his own way along with the teacher. Change is to be dependent upon his own efforts. And in between and after the treatment sessions themselves, the student is expected to practice, just as the psychotherapeutic patient is expected to engage in self-analysis. Both do so in order to keep available to awareness what has been learned, and to explore and exploit new knowledge in order to behave differently. The Alexander mode of "touching" provides a paradigm for the interpersonal mode of psychotherapy. Touch can be done harshly or gently, intrusively or cooperatively, take place in a context of surprise or of preparation. Alexander touching begins with a period of approach, a gentle "meeting of auras," which conveys that the tactile communication is to be one of respect and choice. The student has the opportunity to decide whether to move with the teacher or against him, to continue in what he has always done or to risk doing things differently. The teacher is neutral in the sense that he recognizes that people are as they are for their reasons, that they have to be ready to change, to have some sense of safety and security in the limbo between the giving up of old ways and the development of new ones. That is a good description of neutrality in the psychotherapeutic relationship as well. The psychotherapist knows that mental events have a variety of meanings and that these meanings perform interlocking functions. To change one is perhaps to change all. New solutions need to be available to supplant old ones, and the patient is the final arbiter of what, if anything, is to be changed.

Despite Alexander's discovery that habitual patterns laid down in the early years of life tend to continue, however inapplicable they may be to later life circumstances, Alexander devoted his life to finding ways of helping people change these patterns. In this he resembles Freud: They shared the therapeutic attitude that, however larded over with alleged pessimism and determinism, must at heart be hopeful.

So, despite his caustic attitude toward psychological thinking, Alexander seems to have intuited, in his physical therapy, the ingredients of a psychotherapy. Even more than does Rolfing, he raises the question of whether a combination of conventional psychotherapy and bodily therapy could be more effective, with some people at some times, than either one alone. It is a question raised still more pertinently by bioenergetics, as we shall now see.

11

One Part Interpretation, One Part Energy Release—Bioenergetics

By the time I had my first experience with bioenergetics I knew, from Rolfing and the Alexander technique, that the body was a kind of walking tape recorder. Stimulating parts of it in the course of trying to improve it physically could produce memories, thoughts, and feelings. Though improving the functioning and appearance of the body was important in its own right, as a psychotherapist I was even more interested in what psychological changes could be achieved by using bodily techniques to release thoughts and feelings designedly, rather than as a side effect. Most intriguing of all was the possibility of making substantial therapeutic headway by bringing the clinical theory of psychoanalysis to bear on thoughts and feelings seemingly released from the body. Would we not have, then, the best of both worlds—the world of the body *and* that of the mind? We might in this way deal with the objections to psychoanalytic thinking that too little emotion is brought into the process and too many memories remain buried for too long. We could in this way deal with the objection to body work that psychological material may be released but no one makes useful sense of it.

Bioenergetics seems the ideal therapy with which to test this line of reasoning. Its leaders include at least two psychoanalytically informed practitioners: Alexander Lowen and John Pierrakos; it was inspired by another psychoanalyst, Wilhelm Reich; and it comprises exercises specifically designed to release thoughts and feelings which then are to be interpreted psychologically.

I got my first chance to sample bioenergetics at the Lincoln, Nebraska, meeting of 1975. Eager not to miss out on this chance, I engaged the good offices of a convention official to make sure that I would find a place among the restricted number that John Pierrakos, M.D., was willing to have for his demonstration. Still eager, when he asked for a volunteer I thrust up my hand. I thought that he looked dubiously at me, as if wondering whether I knew what I was letting myself in for and he asked whether I minded taking off my clothes. Whether I minded or not, "yes" was the order of the day. He suggested that I might keep my shorts on, but then he rolled these up in a kind of bikini, the point being that he wanted for diagnostic purposes to see as much of my body as he could. He demonstrated his diagnostic procedure by holding a towel successively over my head, central, and lower parts, demonstrating to the audience the diagnostic differences. For example, he was immensely impressed with my head ("Look at that head!"). That I was inordinately pleased by this confirmed his inference that the head to me was all-important. He thought a good deal less of my chest and torso but had a few kind words to say about my legs, despite the shaky underpinning provided by my flat feet.

Pierrakos' diagnostic comments were cast in psychoanalytic terms, with particularly strong emphasis on the psychosexual stages of libido. For example, he said that I most likely suffered a trauma in the first days or weeks of life, resulting in an oral fixation. (In fact, I was untimely ripped from my mother's breast, because breast feeding was painful to her.)

Pierrakos tossed me a knotted-up towel, and we began a tug of war for it, while he encouraged me to become increasingly violent. I can attest (without impugning his head) that his middle—his chest and arms—are very strong indeed. At the same time, I found his strength reassuring and was increasingly able to deploy my own in our battle. I found it more difficult to do so when he had me repeat the tug of war with a woman he picked from the audience. To me it just did not seem right, which may be an expression of nineteenth-century manners, among other possibilities. Pierrakos was not saying, but that was only because this was a demonstration, rather than therapy. In therapy, he said, he would make interpretations on the basis of how I performed the exercises.

I was asked to make movements that correspond to the phrase "Get off my back," to say this verbally with facial grimaces and as much expression as I could muster. I was asked to fling my hands down at the floor violently as if in an attempt to pull down my shoulders, which Pierrakos thought were riding too high. He had me bend over backward, supported by a bed, and kick my feet.

Like primal therapists, bioenergeticists regard crying and screaming as highly effective ways of releasing blocked emotion and freeing respiration. Pierrakos had me scream as long and deeply as I could. As I was painfully to discover, later with Alexander Lowen, screaming and crying can also be brought about by the therapist's applying pressure at selected points. Pierrakos had me make a sound, and while doing this he palpated my chest, shoulders, and neck in order to loosen up my voice. He succeeded in lowering and opening my voice, though perhaps a shade less than occurred during the Rolfing experience. This, then, along with the Alexander technique was a third change in my voice, each brought about in a different way.

I was instructed to adopt the pose of an ape, to bare my teeth, and to come at him as if attacking. He had me swing a tennis racket over my head and down onto a bed repeatedly, encouraging me to use ever-increasing force and to shout. He told the audience that in therapy he would have had me do these aggressive actions with specific people in mind. (Actually, I did have some people in mind.) He chose to smile indulgently as, throughout all this, I did my usual bright repartee ploy. It wasn't easy, wearing only underwear shorts, though I suspect that made it seem especially necessary.

Following this workout, I felt both stimulated and relaxed. Bioenergeticists would claim that was because of the released energy. It could also have come about at least in part through having done something unaccustomed and surviving the experience. I have felt similarly relaxed after playing tennis. However, after tennis I was not busy thinking about myself. Although Pierrakos frequently reminded the audience that he was not "doing therapy" with me, that is not the same thing as saying that therapy was not being done. I was taking the experience seriously, set to allow the expression of feelings he was enabling me to bring to the fore, taking note of my reactions, and working at integrating all of this with my previous knowledge of myself. Any experience can be made into therapy if one intends it to be. Demonstration or no, I felt I had temporarily been "in therapy."

John Pierrakos and Alexander Lowen, both physicians, were long-time associates in bioenergetics. Now they have separated, and Pierrakos has developed in a direction called "the new age of man," which includes a psychic, mystical emphasis. I learned from Pierrakos' lectures at the Lincoln, Nebraska, meeting of 1975 and at the Association for Humanistic Psychology meeting in Estes Park, Colorado, that for him, too, energy is concrete: it can be measured and photographed. Like many psychically inclined people, Pierrakos claims to see auras, colored emanations from the body; but he says he sees actual figures in the auras as well. These figures and their activities give him diagnostic information. For example, he told of seeing in one aura a devil, and when Pierrakos asked the patient what was happening just then, the patient said that he had decided to deceive Pierrakos. These "visual" diagnoses are not, however, restricted to transient emotions and ideas; they afford Pierrakos information as to chronic physical and emotional conditions.

Pierrakos showed photographic slides that purported to show auras around flowers and people, and he conceptualized the body as a constant sender and receiver of energies. This energy is freely transmittable and results in excitement when there is free interchange, boredom when there is not. Energy is organized, as described in Eastern religions, in chakras, which according to Pierrakos are bell-shaped funnels about two to four inches in length. When a person is blocked, these chakras collapse and no longer serve as centers of centrifugal and centripetal energy. When blocks are dissolved, the energy is free to ascend the chain of chakras, providing liberated secular experiences, going on up to liberating mystical experiences and psychic capacities. Ideally, according to Pierrakos, these upper levels should be available to all of us as we free energy through bodily and psychological intervention.

My firsthand experience with bioenergetics and Pierrakos' comments inspired me to learn what I could of the genesis of bioenergetics. The search took me to my own library for a copy of *Character Analysis*, by Wilhelm Reich.[1] I have been assigned, and have assigned, that book a dozen or so times. Each time, the assignment included approximately the first half of the book's five hundred or so pages. Usually, some comment is made along the lines that if one should dip into the second half, he ought not be so put off by the insanity of it as to interfere with learning the assigned material. Reich was a physician and psychoanalyst who in the conventional view had much to offer to psychoanalysis, particularly to its techniques. But then he went crazy and left psychoanalysis to pursue his fancies. The conventional view is that everything he said outside the orthodox psychoanalytic tradition should be discounted. Yet, to many therapists outside the psychoanalytic tradition, Reich is a patron saint. His nonpsychoanalytic work has been fundamental to many of the new therapies. In particular Reich's stress on the linkage between body and mind, and on energy, are key contributions.

Reich's work might better be separated into three stages than only into psychoanalytic and nonpsychoanalytic ones. In the first of these stages, Reich described how people behave in characteristic ways designed to control anxiety and other unpleasant feelings stemming from unconscious conflicts. Such ways may include any expressive behavior, from key life decisions to the way one says, "Good morning." Reich was hardly novel in this point of view. Freud and Abraham had described typical kinds of character emanating from unconscious conflicts and libidinal fixations. But Reich was innovative in the emphasis he put on the use of the body as an expression of character, the way the body is groomed, the way it is held, the nonverbal communications it sends. Reich was innovative also in his forthright declaration that the pursuit of unconscious fantasies by way of dreams and free associations was fruitless unless one first dealt with defenses as these are embroidered into character. Moreover, he claimed that the analysis of character would, automatically, lead to the eruption of unconscious content, with consequent less need to analyze dreams and free associations.

Stage two, "vegetotherapy," stems from Reich's assertion that "character armor" (rigid behavior patterns) is paralleled by "muscular armor" (rigidification of the body). The inhibition of emotional and muscular responsiveness is maintained by an inhibition of respiration. As might be expected, then, resistance in the analytic process is keyed by an unconscious holding of the breath. In so doing the patient limits the amount of oxygen in the system, which in turn limits the metabolic and energic processes. And by the same token the natural motility of the body, inspiration and expiration, pulsation and counterpulsation, are restricted, with resultant chronic muscular tension. Particular areas of the body become tense in response to particular suppressions of emotion and are deformed in ways that are symbolic of thoughts and feelings.

According to Reich, if one worked manually with the body, one could break the character defenses and thereby speed and intensify the therapy. For Reich, psychoanalysis was no longer a verbal technique in which the analyst maintained a physical distance; it had become a truly psychosomatic enterprise. To his own satisfaction, at least, Reich had overcome the mind-body split.

While in the first two stages Reich deals with energy within the body, in the third stage he asserts that the universe, organic and inorganic, is composed of a basic energy, which he called "orgone." At this point, Reich is no longer a psychiatrist. His theories about this energy are couched in what I gather is pop biology and physics,[2] and he applied them to cancer and other physical illnesses, the creation of life, and the control of weather. Orgone energy is not a construct, as was Freud's libido, but tangible and "demonstrable visually, thermically, electroscopically and by means of Geiger-Müller counters."[3] Moreover, this energy could be stored in the notorious accumulators, called orgone boxes, the sale of which led to legal charges by the Food and Drug Administration and ultimately resulted in Reich's being put in prison, where he died of heart disease.

Before leaving Reich a word about sex is in order, since Reich's emphasis on orgastic discharge has been sometimes taken as a license, if not recommendation, for unrestrained sexual activity. Orgasm was, for Reich, the final common pathway of energy discharge. Chronic muscular tension prevented complete and therefore satisfying orgasm. However, the in some ways ascetic Reich did not recommend the practice of orgasm as a means of bringing about full discharge. Rather, such discharge was the consequence of loosening the emotional and muscular blocks. He did not recommend sexual activity as therapy any more than Freud did, though others have glossed over the distinction between sex as behavior and sex as therapy, between sexual activity as cause and as effect, and used Freud's and Reich's teachings as rationalizations for libertinism. On the other hand, when, as in bioenergetics, one participates with as little clothing as modesty permits, when exercises are designed to heighten sexual energies, when the atmosphere is conducive to overcoming inhibitions, it is not surprising that participants may feel disposed at least to check up on their potency.

Despite a recent chamber of commerce advertising campaign to the effect that Tulsa, Oklahoma, has everything, I was not fully prepared to learn that it is a regular stop on the bioenergetic circuit. The Tulsa Psychiatric Center serves as part of a loosely organized system of bioenergetics training centers, and from it radiates a good deal of local bioenergetics work. About six months after my experience with Pierrakos, I felt ready for more, so I was delighted to learn that Alexander Lowen was to conduct a day-long workshop at the Psychiatric Center. In his early seventies, Lowen looks and acts twenty years younger, a fine advertisement for bioenergetics. He is generally considered to be one of the leading and surely the most literarily productive of Reich's students.

Following a few warm-up exercises somewhat akin to calisthenics though with greater emphasis on stretching than endurance, Lowen spoke on the theory and practice of bioenergetics. Then everybody in this mixed group was asked to take off as much clothing as he or she was willing to. Lowen then led us through a series of exercises designed to loosen particular areas of the body held to correspond to particular psychological content and emotion. For example, inhibited impulses to cry, scream, and shout result in tension in the throat, chest, diaphragm, and abdomen. Inhibitions of reaching out for love, closeness, and help are associated with muscular spasticity in the shoulder girdle and thorax. Assuming excessive responsibility results in the shoulders being rigidly locked in an unnaturally high, stiff position.

Some of the exercises were strenuous, others were much like the stretching exercises of hatha-yoga, though in yoga one is cautioned not to strain oneself. In bioenergetics one does strain oneself, with the goal of feeling the flow of alleged released energy. Indeed, I was able to feel the desired trembling. However, I have no way of knowing whether such trembling is a manifestation of released energy or of fatigued muscles. (Since energy in Reich's formulation is real and measurable, it should be possible to determine mechanically and objectively whether energy has been released or not.)

While working on the thorax and arm regions, and simulating a reaching-for-help movement, we were asked if anybody required some individual help with the movement. Up, as usual, went my hand. Lowen came to where I was lying on the floor and pressed against my breast bone. I suffered immediate, excruciating pain, and burst into tears. These were not, however, tears of pain. For one thing, in response to physical pain I am more likely to curse than cry. For another, the tears continued long after the pain diminished. They came in convulsions and increased, if anything, as time went on, the episode lasting maybe ten minutes. I was not aware of any content to these tears, I did not think of anybody or any topic in particular, I did not feel sad except as much as anyone might feel sad simply through the act of crying. At the same time, I can warrant that those tears were heartfelt; they seemed to come from deep within me, as if expressing a pent-up sorrow. None of my patients, nor I during my own psychoanalytic hours, ever cried with the intensity, length, and feeling that I experienced as a result of this bioenergetic manipulation.

The pain I felt as a result of Lowen's pressing on my chest is not part of the planned procedure. In this instance it was iatrogenic: Lowen simply hit too hard on the wrong place and inflicted physical injury. It would make a better story to say that he had broken my rib, which I thought he had, considering the extent and type of pain I felt in subsequent weeks. However, upon X-ray examination, it turned out there was no break, just a severe strain. For what it is worth, some years previously, when I was hoisting myself into a boat, I "accidentally" injured the same spot, and I did it still another time in another way. It may be that both my unconscious and Lowen's clinical sagacity knew that I required emotional release from that area, and therefore saw that it was attacked. Most people go through bioenergetics therapy without suffering such bodily injury as I did. Perhaps strangely, I am without rancor about my experience. The physical sequelae were unfortunate, but I treasure the moments after the injury, the feeling of total emotional release, and I think back on it now and again with sobering recognition of the amount of sorrow that I, and others, can unwittingly carry. And I know now, for sure, that such feeling is approachable by way of the body.

The challenge to psychoanalytic therapy is clear. Either such manipulated outpourings of emotion are not integratable with an ongoing search for meaning, they are irrelevant to such a search, or they can deepen and hasten such a search.

There seemed no doubt in Lowen's mind that the exercises and manipulations offer material for interpretive comments, and that such interpretive comments are more effective than they would be if made in a traditional, exclusively verbal psychotherapy. Following the series of exercises, he worked interpretively with volunteers. After they made brief historical remarks and stated the difficulties on which they would like to work, he put them through selected bioenergetic exercises and manipulations and then offered fairly direct and deep psychoanalytic interpretations along with gestalt-therapy techniques. Whether through the aptness of his interpretive remarks, the bioenergetic exercises, or both, his demonstration patients seemed to me to be caught up in the procedure. One of them, for example, ended the sessions by falling into his arms. Whether they were caught up in the procedure to their therapeutic benefit is a question to which we shall shortly return.

While bioenergetics shares with primal therapy the importance of crying and screaming as ways of releasing blocked emotion and freeing respiration, their differences are more important than this similarity. Except for encouraging screaming and crying, Janov's approach is largely psychological, eschewing systematic work on the body. He commits what for bioenergeticists is the fatal error of going to fantasies while ignoring character as encapsulated in both psychological and muscular armor. To the bioenergeticist it is therefore understandable, and regrettable, that primal-therapy patients lose interest in sex. For their own patients they attempt to achieve the ultimate evidence of freed energy: complete orgastic discharge.

Bioenergetics therapy includes homework in the form of exercises. As an example, here are the exercises recommended to me to free my voice, as first aid before I give a lecture or to keep it permanently free to the extent that I do the exercises regularly:

> Bite down on a towel with back molars. Pull tongue forward while grasping it with a towel. Scream. Gag by putting fingers in one's mouth, or "dry heaving," vomit if possible. Grimace and growl. Shake head like a dog. Dig knuckles, horizontally, in muscles at the side of neck. Lying down on the floor, have someone "walk" across the upper back while exhaling, then breathe deeply on the release of air.

What kinds of changes result from approaching the mind by way of the body as in bioenergetics, and how durable are they? With respect to that issue bioenergetics is in no better a situation than are other alternative therapies. In watching the therapeutic sessions and talking informally with bioenergetics patients I often had the same dismaying feeling that I had toward participants in other new therapies. The patients seem long on having had experiences, even having learned something about themselves, but short, or indeterminate at least, in conveying an over-all sense of integration, purpose, effectiveness. I was especially dismayed when I learned from some of them that they had been relying on bioenergetics therapy for several years, having regular emotional experiences but with essentially the same life dissatisfactions. I am not saying, at this point, that no such comments could apply to psychoanalytic patients as well. A systematic discussion of that, and related issues as to results and desirability of therapies, is to be included at the end of this volume.

A major problem in evaluating bioenergetics, as with most of the new therapies, is the large number of uncontrolled variables. What we usually end up evaluating is only one person's way of working. The effectiveness of the approach may be limited by the selection and training of its practitioners, which, as with most of the new therapies, are less strict, less organized, and give less academic and practical training and supervision than is found in the psychoanalytic institutes. There is little selection of patients, so that the approach may be doing itself a disservice in attempting to apply what may be perfectly valid and efficient principles and techniques to populations of patients to whom they are unsuited. While some bioenergeticists and their patients work over a long period of time at frequent and regular intervals in individual sessions, much bioenergetic work is done in groups and whenever people have the opportunity to, or feel like, attending. Such scheduling may contribute to or detract from the effectiveness of the approach. The interpersonal relationship, with its possibilities for transference, is minimized, thus tending to deprive the process of a major means of achieving insight. Bioenergetics is also highly directive, thus increasing the danger that the fantasies dealt with may be more those of the therapist than of the patient.

Once again, I am bedeviled by the wish to know what effect bioenergetics work would have in the context of a systematic ongoing psychoanalytic treatment, whether done by another person or by the psychotherapist himself. Could such a treatment be speeded up or deepened? Could the emotional intensity of the bioenergetics event be channeled and integrated into the personality by way of continued disciplined psychological work, and would such work result in better and more durable change than the same psychological work done without intervention on the body? As far as I know, no one, literally no one, authoritatively knows the answers to these questions. Nonetheless, I left Tulsa and bioenergetics energetically alert to new possibilities and with a concrete reminder in my sore chest that a great deal lies below the head.

PART THREE

Fast Mood Chains

12

Latin for "It Is"—Est

UNDER THE GLASS that covers my desk, along with a stirring quotation from Edmund Burke and a beautiful drawing by my son, are the following two pieces:

LOVE		
Is giving someone the space		Here is where it is.
To be the way they are	and	Now is when it is.
And the way they are not.		You are what it is.
		Celebrate.

A lot more of such messages are available in *Up to Your Ass in Aphorisms,* a slender volume that Werner Erhard gives as a graduation present to each person who completes *est.*

The "love" message is on a red card that Erhard sent at Valentine's Day (signed "Love, Werner"). I clipped the "celebrate" message from a now-forgotten piece of literature from the *est* central office, one of what seems innumerable communications I have gotten since finishing the training. (That makes five years of a steady flow of information, reminders, and invitations.)

So what is that campy treacle doing on my desk? To

begin with, camp is another one of those sly ways that intellectuals have of smuggling a bit of primitiveness and romance into their sometimes arid lives, an oblique way of dirtying up their usually antiseptic field. So long as we make fun of it, call it names, we can allow ourselves a little sentimentality. I can laugh at the inanity of these adornments while rather enjoying and possibly benefiting from their messages. Most of the people I know would benefit from being able to celebrate the present instead of regretting the past and dreading the future. As to giving people the "space" to be the way they are and the way they are not, it may take a moment to follow the logic. But I do get immediately from these lines a nice feeling of tolerance and respect for people's struggles, and that seems a reasonable enough definition and expression of love. I have gotten worse valentines.

So that is the way it is with *est*, a campy theater of the sometimes absurd, but not without charm, and with important messages delivered by its somewhat jarring media.

Est (Erhard Seminar Training) was about three years old in 1974, when I first heard about it. Gardner Cowles, of *Look* magazine and the Minneapolis *Star-Tribune*, wrote to Roy Menninger, president of The Menninger Foundation, asking our opinion of *est*. The note of incredulity in Cowles's letter was one that I was to hear often from people upon first being apprised of *est*. Roy sent the letter on to me as "our man in the outer world," and we agreed that I would attend an *est* meeting in New York and report back. At that time the many magazine articles and books about *est* now available had not yet been published. I knew almost nothing about it. Because of other business, I left Topeka early for New York, and so I missed the letter informing me of how I should prepare myself. The preparations included taking care of bathroom and gustatory needs just before the meeting, as such needs could not be attended to at will during it. As luck would have it, I skipped breakfast the first morning of the meeting, an oversight to be regretted. But that is getting ahead of the story.

Customarily the story of *est* begins with its leader, Werner Erhard. *Est* minimizes most pomp and circumstance; it is democratic, espouses a no-nonsense approach to life. Nonetheless, there is a mystique about Werner Erhard that clearly identifies him as a leader. Indeed, one of the common criticisms of *est* is that it partakes of the Nazi approach to leadership. This association is, in part, probably stimulated by the now-famous story of how Jack Rosenberg, the son of a Philadelphia Main Line Protestant mother and a Jewish father, became named Werner Erhard. The story has a number of versions; the one offered here is the one that I heard Erhard himself relate. While he was on a plane that was taking him away from his old life with parents, wife, and children, he recognized that members of the life he was leaving might try to find him at a time when he did not feel like being found. Thus, a change of name was in order. In scanning a handy newspaper, he noticed the names of Wernher von Braun, the ex-Nazi rocket scientist, and Ludwig Erhard, the then leader of Germany, and appropriated their names. Some armchair psychologists have made much of this man with a Jewish name appropriating German ones and then establishing an organization in which he is the deified leader.

It is a little difficult to understand just how the leadership mystique has developed. At first, I felt it was because Erhard was much talked about but little seen. It turned out, however, that he is highly visible, as a participant on the lecture circuit, in humanistic meetings and conventions, and by way of detailing his activities in national media and in *The Graduate Review,* sent regularly to all graduates of *est* training, complete with pictures of himself. He is medium-tall, solidly built, probably in his late thirties. He is handsome in a Mediterranean way and dresses informally but impeccably. Maybe the mystique arises simply from the reverential remarks so often made about him by his co-workers. And, of course, there is always something of a mystique around practically instant success involving large numbers of people.

In some six years Werner Erhard parlayed an idea into one hundred thousand (geometrically growing) participants. Many of the graduates of *est* maintain their interest as a kind of extended family organization through reading the materials sent regularly to them from *est*'s central headquarters, in San Francisco, and from participating in one or another seminar designed especially for graduates. These seminars are organized around such topics as sex, money, communication, and are for special groups such as executives or psychotherapists. Graduates proselytize among their friends and participate in "Guest Seminars." The latter are free meetings for anyone who is interested, at which samples of *est* are given and greater or lesser pressure is exerted to sign up for the training. A casualty of inflation, the training fee has gone from two hundred fifty to three hundred dollars.

The basic training consists of some sixty hours, distributed between two consecutive weekends, beginning around eight-thirty in the morning and lasting until after midnight. In between the two weekends there is a meeting of several hours, which is recommended but not required.

Erhard is a former trainer of encyclopedia salesmen. Stewart Emery (who has left *est* to begin his own, similar self-improvement venture) was the leader of the training I attended. He used to be a fashion photographer and maker of television commercials. One of the chief executives of the organization is an ex-executive of The Coca-Cola Co. As might be expected from men with such backgrounds, *est* is highly organized, a slick operation. Almost everything it does organizationally can be viewed as simply good business practice. For example, the involvement it maintains with ex-graduates can be seen less as offering a continuing means of support, sense of community, and regular stimulation with ideas, than as a way of getting free salesmen to round up customers. Whatever the rank order of *est*'s motives, however, let us examine the product from the standpoint of its possible usefulness to participants.

To the extent that *est* leaders feel defensive, their defense is utter candor. Indeed, as part of the *est* philosophy, they assert that as successes in their previous fields, and having won that "game," they needed a new game to play, and that game is *est*. Conceiving of life as a game with numerous subgames is central to *est* philosophy. The *est* game is declared not to be therapy and not exactly education, either. Rather, it simply "is what it is" (another catch phrase of *est*). The experience is called simply a "training." Here is what my "training" was like.

Upon entering the *est* hotel headquarters, I was immediately struck by a rather harsh atmosphere. Each form had to be filled out fully and exactly. If one had imperfectly filled out his mailed-in application form, he found on his prepared name tag a little spot that could only be removed by filling out the form properly. (Even filling in "not applicable" in an empty space was necessary in order to get the spot removed.) There were two hundred and fifty trainees. An unstructured group of this size would be chaotic, and occasionally some events typical of unorganized group behavior did occur. But the meetings are highly structured, and errant group behavior was held to a minimum. Nonetheless, it turns out that even in a tightly organized meeting in a huge hotel ballroom, people can have intensely emotional private experiences.

Without any warning, we were informed that the doors would be guarded by the leader's assistants. We were told that they are perfectly nice people, but "they have ways" of enforcing the rules, and one rule is to not leave the room. This included not being allowed to go to the bathroom and not being allowed to eat or drink. Only water was provided. After perhaps four or five hours there was a perhaps twenty-minute break to use the bathroom, but not to eat. An hour-and-a-half eating opportunity was provided around nine in the evening. Keeping track of time was a problem, since we were not allowed to wear a watch during the meeting. Those who had not left their watches at home had to check them at the door. Thus, even on the breaks, one had to estimate the time to return, and there was an imperative in the atmosphere not to be late. No one was allowed entry without a badge. The whole atmosphere was rather Gestapo-like—hard-eyed assistants, rigidly enforced rules and boundaries, and little inclination for social chitchat.

The effect is somewhat disorienting. It is a bit like the primal-scream living conditions, also designed to aid one to put aside the usual ways of thinking and reacting in order to get the most out of a new experience. A moral to be drawn from the excreting-eating deprivation is that we give in to our bodies unnecessarily, that mind can overcome matter. We need not live as if we were just "tubes," taking in food and getting rid of it.

At first I resented the atmosphere and conditions. Then I began to appreciate them. I found it a challenge to adapt myself to these new circumstances, and especially to shift my position of receptiveness and expectation of getting my needs satisfied to one in which I could exercise capacities to get along without having to satisfy my usual "requirements." I appreciated the assertion of leadership as necessary to accomplish the task at hand, and recognized that establishing and maintaining boundaries, with concurrent centering on the main task, is a requisite for efficient group functioning. I had signed on voluntarily, after all, and until convinced otherwise had to assume that the structure was designed to advance the purpose of being there in the first place. Although there were moments when I would have preferred to be almost anywhere else, all things considered *est* was at least as easy to put up with as those plastic coffee-cup meetings in which "democracy" is maintained by way of hobbled leadership and the main achievement is the scheduling of another meeting.

Stewart, the trainer, turned out to be somewhat superhuman. For example, he talked without a microphone in this cavernous room for the marathon length of these meetings (members of the audience used microphones, and there were assistants rushing microphones to them as soon as they stood up and were recognized). He began by declaring that we were all "assholes" and "liars." He added that, by the time he finished, "fuck" will be as common a word to use as "spaghetti," and the only thing to figure out then is which one is better for us.

One can take the style of presentation and the content of what he presented as typical of what one could expect from all *est* leaders. They all somehow managed to look and sound like Werner. The training is organized in a notebook, which the leaders ostentatiously follow, so the training procedure is always the same.

While *est* people write a good deal about their work from the standpoint of its organization, they write practically nothing from the standpoint of science or related points of view. Indeed, there was in the air a contemptuousness toward science, writing, scholarship, as just so much "mind-fucking." One is forbidden to take notes during the meetings. While the trainer uses the blackboard to write down several concepts, he turns away any suggestions that these should be remembered as is. The learning is to come about through experience, awareness, and repetition. Principles, and often the experiences to which they apply, are learned through participating in exercises, what are called in *est* "processes."

The trainer used what one might call reinforcement by regularly thanking people for their participation, saying "I got it," "beautiful," "perfect," "thank you." And he suggested that when people offer their experiences the rest of the group should show its appreciation with applause. Curiously, I almost forgot that prearrangement, and felt as if I had said something "worthwhile" when it was greeted by hand clapping. However synthetically arranged, appreciating a fellow participant's contribution is consistent with *est*'s philosophy of nonjudgmental acceptance. But such unreserved acceptance is only for a person's genuine expression of his experience. Those comments which deny experience, such as intellectualized opinions, are emphatically not accepted. They are likely to be labeled, at the top of the trainer's voice, as "mind-fucking."

A central *est* concept is that we all live lies because we live according to belief systems that are unprovable. Those systems only appear to be provable, for the proof that is offered is simply another belief system. In other words there are no absolutes other than one's individual experience. The trainer gave an example of how Newtonian physics was supposed to be the truth, except that one time out of many thousands turned out to be an exception. This exception was explained away as an artifact until Einstein took it seriously and came up with the theory of relativity.

Est members are continually on the lookout for people's employing their system of beliefs, even their alleged *feelings,* as a means of avoiding experience.

"Experience" seems interchangeable with consciousness, and what *est* is after is being in touch with oneself, one's real consciousness, and the real consciousness of others. Consciousness can be raised or expanded through essentially meditative exercises. One consequence is to become more intuitive and understanding of others. Ideally we should communicate with others, rather than only apparently doing so while serving our own needs.

In fact, most of us most of the time are liars, avoiding consciousness in favor of illusions, delusions, false selves, and false values. The trainer continually pointed out the door or window to what he called the insane world, where so many proffered solutions to problems didn't work, though these solutions were usually pursued endlessly anyway, even after repeated failure. The same went for us "liars" and "maniacs" at the conference. Each of us tended to repeat the same old ineffective solutions to the same old problems, deluding ourselves, convincing ourselves that we were trying hard and were justified in our fruitless pursuits. Such behavior is, he declared, the definition of insanity. Instead of facing these truths about our bankruptcy we "yammer" and "run our tape recorders" (programmed minds). We "do our number," "practice our rackets" (neurotic patterns and character styles).

Stewart claimed never to have been in therapy himself or to have studied to become a therapist. Nevertheless, he demonstrated a remarkable clinical sensitivity. Members would tell of problems in their lives, and he would, in effect, work with these people therapeutically on the spot. Time and again in the course of these encounters, a person would go into his past and come up with an incident in which he had made assumptions about himself and others and adopted a defense mechanism or character pattern or style to deal with these assumptions. As this was brought to his attention he often enough resisted seeing what he was doing, which was highly instructive to the rest of the audience. Even after seeing what they were doing, people typically demonstrated how they recoil from the possibility of acting upon their new knowledge. Repeatedly, people pleaded to keep their customary beliefs and behaviors, though their lives, marked by these, were what they were complaining about to begin with.

In one exercise one seventh of the assemblage by turn stood up on a raised platform and faced the rest, after being instructed to remove coats and sweaters. We just stood there for a long period of time. This was to have everyone look at our bodies, and notice what, over this period of time, we did with our bodies—twitching, shaking, dropping one shoulder—with the trainer all the while pointing out what sorry messes we had made of our bodies through the years, what poor physical specimens we were. In the meantime we were practicing eye contact and looking directly at one or another person in the "audience." Some of the *est* assistants would come up and stand directly in front of us and make eye contact with us. This we were told was not staring but, rather, an attempt to see what it felt like actually to get into the consciousness of another and let another into the consciousness of oneself. One could learn to see and sense the difference between just staring, and insinuating oneself into another through looking "deeply" at him. It was possible to notice, even from a distance, how some people did one or another kind of looking, while others went back and forth between the two. I found it an eerily moving and somewhat sensual experience, as if I were indeed immersing myself in the person at whom I was gazing.

Various people in the group offered as their ways of dealing with their life problems the doing of good works in a social sense. The trainer pointed out how we devote much of our time and attention to solving such "distal" problems, none of which ever turn out to be solvable. For example, we try to solve wars in various ways, and yet there were three wars going at the very moment. Through the ages, all kinds of, in effect, external solutions have been tried and have failed, and yet the crazy world goes on trying and failing. By contrast, the proximal solution is consciousness. If one could be in touch with oneself and everybody else could be in touch with himself and each other, then the various issues that give rise to conflict would not exist.

The trainer asked us all to think of a period in our lives, or an event, that we would characterize as especially happy or pleasant. Then he said that he knew that this period or event followed directly after the solving of a problem. Indeed, it seemed that everyone in the audience agreed that this conformed to what he had thought about. In other words, here was a definition of happiness: the resolution or solution of a problem. In order to be happy one needs to have problems in order to solve them. The trainer vigorously contrasted this state of affairs with the ubiquitous fantasy that life should be without problems. Experiences are defined by polarities: there are no endings without beginnings, there can be no good without any bad, no up without a down, no happiness without pain.

The leader posited a universal need to solve problems. He gave a number of indications from industrial psychology of how we mistakenly give increasing rewards in the form of vacations and sick leave, which implies that staying off the job is much better than staying on it. By contrast, we ought to design jobs so that people can feel that they are solving problems, and then there would be a premium on staying with a job. Increased pay is simply a way of trying to make up for the fact that workers, for example on assembly lines, are not given sufficient opportunity to solve problems. He gave several homely demonstrations of how one could get much better service by presenting the other person with a problem, rather than making a demand or offering a solution that the other person only had to carry out.

One has to accept problems as part of oneself. Fighting against problems, for example pain, makes them worse. By making things separate we give them status, we create entities. As part of ourselves they become lost; they merge into our experience and are "handleable" that way. Thus, when a woman claimed that her husband was a drunkard, was ruining the family, and asked what she could do about him, she was told that she must accept the problem in herself, that she must find the solution in her consciousness, rather than putting it all on her husband and reacting to it as an external symptom. The same went for physical symptoms and manifestations of pain. We make things worse by taking distance from them, allowing them to hide behind medical names, by believing that they are diseases visited upon us from the outside. The trainer demonstrated with volunteers how to cure such symptoms as headaches and backaches. The main technique was to have the person invade the painful area with his consciousness. He was asked to define the symptom, give it a color, a size, a weight, an exact position in the body, to concentrate on it, even to exaggerate the pain. In both physical and psychological contexts cure begins with ceasing to locate cause outside oneself, in accepting our responsibility for cause and cure. For example, one is not *taught* things by traumatic incidents or difficult parents, one *learns* them by way of one's own, independent participation.

The leader gave instructions for setting one's inner alarm clock in order to get up at a certain time in the morning. As for insomnia, he suggested that people go through the parts of their body, beginning at the feet and on up to the head, "making a space" for themselves in each of the areas. ("Space" is an all-purpose term in *est* for feeling comfortably free in a sphere of operation.) A safe space is one in which one is free of criticism. A space can be enlarged to the degree that one can spread his sense of awareness wider, to include other people or become as wide as the whole planet. One has to learn what another's space is in order to understand him.

In one process for men only, each man in turn had to impersonate an eight-year-old girl. Finally there was only one participant left, a failure at the task. He rebelled, saying that he would not try it any more. He was challenged by the trainer with the threat that if he continued to refuse he would have to leave the training. He tried again, and the audience was asked to judge as to whether he had done well enough to be considered finished with the task. The audience seemed tempted to say that he was finished in order to get on with the exercises, to go to the bathroom, to get something to eat, or just to be "kind" to him. The trainer was furious with those of us who were willing to stop short of this last member's feeling that he had really participated to the best of his ability. The trainer would not give up on the man; he said that this man really wanted to get into the right space, he wanted to be able to do it, and being hard on him by forcing him to continue was the only way to be kind to him. The leader thought the rest of us were more interested in ourselves than in supporting our struggling colleague, and that was why "your fucking lives don't work." Sure enough, on the heels of this scene the man finally gave a creditable performance.

What we are used to calling reality is a construction of our mind. Nothing exists except as we think of it. Consensual validation of reality is simply an agreement based on our having similar receptors. For the most part, each person has his own reality. The problems of the world stem from the fact that we act as if everybody had the same reality, and we impose our reality on others. We should find out what the other person's reality is, see what is good in it for him, and then act creatively about any differences that might occur.

All activities are games. On the one hand, we must give it all we have, play the game up to the hilt, or it is no fun. The fun comes from solving problems. On the other hand, true power comes from really not caring whether we win or lose, from being able to give up the game at any point.

Another *est* catch phrase is "You get what you take, and you take what you get." This is a variation of desirelessness: you do your best but accept whatever comes. It matters, you see, but it does not really matter. Anyway, all you *can* take is what you get. The *est* implication is that this will turn out to be workable for you in the long run, because you can make any set of circumstances "work." Things are not "right" or "wrong," they just work or do not work.

One process involved imaginatively building a house, then an office in the house, then furnishing the office in any way one wished. This was to be one's physical "center," a concrete "space," one's ideal of a place in which to be. In this place one was to imagine helpers, guides, a man and a woman who would be available when needed to offer solutions to problems. Thus *est* picks up the tradition of many mystical movements and cultures, of having helping guides (often in the form of American Indians). These may be clearly imaginative or, as with some spiritualists, they may be reported as being "real."

About three quarters of the way through, we were told the climactic idea that man is only a machine, a continuous recording instrument. He is programmed by early events to experience later ones. He can do only what he does, and what he does is absolutely determined by past experiences.

Imagine the consternation. Here we had been told all along that the world is our oyster if we will only realize that and act accordingly. We were supposed to be the masters of our destiny, once we quit blaming others, and now we are told that we have no hope, no free will. We are just machines, without significance, consequence, or purpose other than to play out functions according to predetermined structures. We felt as if we had suddenly become the victims of a gigantic "sting."

At this point one of our members became openly psychotic. I previously had had a few informal contacts with him, and he seemed friendly, perhaps too friendly, but nothing more clinically noteworthy than that. Now he walked around the hall, calling out statements irrelevant to the topic of the moment, and then climbed up on the stage to join the trainer. All things considered, his wife, who happened to be sitting near me, did not seem unduly disturbed, from which I gathered that this was not the first time he had behaved in this way. The trainer, who had claimed not to have had any clinical experience, dealt with this man in a firm and reasonably effective way. He continually said that he recognized the space that the man was in, respected what he was feeling and doing, but right now what he had to do was to sit down and obey the rules like the others, which he sporadically did.

I believe that the man was, at least in part, responding to the prevalent horror in the room stemming from the portrayal of man as a machine. At bottom, this was a horror of death. The illusion of free will is one way we have of convincing ourselves that we might be immortal. Instead, we were told that there is nothing that we can do, about death or anything else, other than to play the tape until it runs out. On the heels of this portrayal of ourselves came the admonition to accept oneself as a machine, with no purpose, point, or goal. This, then, would make possible the second step, which was to choose among the many programs built in. We could "fine-tune" the machine as a product of the Mercedes-Benz factory, rather than a General Motors factory. We could choose the tape, and we could twiddle the dials to get the most out of it.

"Which do you choose," a volunteer was asked, "chocolate ice cream or vanilla ice cream?" After making his choice, he was asked why he made that choice. All the reasons he offered were judged as being wrong. He was then given the hint that his answer was not to advance a reason for his choice. Several of us (not including me) then got the answer, which was simply, "Because I chose chocolate [or vanilla]." In other words, we do what we do, and the reasons are irrelevant. They are outside of experiential space. The sound of one hand clapping *is* the sound of one hand clapping. If we get into all kinds of details about liking chocolate because of its being brown, being sweet, reminding us of other times in our lives, then we submit beliefs with which other people can disagree. Most arguments result from the clash of beliefs. The only unassailable position is that we chose vanilla because we chose vanilla. We do it because we do it.

As our meeting drew to a close, we seemed to be a bit rushed, the trainer saying that he was going to have to cover sex and children quickly. This seemed to be no problem for him. Human relationships, he said, go better when "screwing" is not involved. Screwing has practically nothing to do with love. You may enjoy eating a hamburger with someone you love, but you can also enjoy eating a hamburger by yourself or with someone you don't love. Sex can be reduced to, "When you're hot you're hot, and when you're not you're not." Very few people are able to have a good relationship in which screwing is an important factor. One should always ask himself whether he would have a particular relationship if screwing were not involved.

As to children, they are adults with small bodies. But, then, adults are children with large bodies. At the human potential meeting in Lincoln, Nebraska, elsewhere reported on in this book, Erhard declared that "children stink" and that adults who idolize children stink. According to him, children are manipulative and have zero sense of responsibility. Perhaps in an attempt to do something about this dreadful social blight, *est* holds a training for children from ages six to twelve, and one for teen-agers.

The problem with human relationships is that they require risk. They usually do not work, because people are unwilling to take these risks. People are further unwilling to respect the other person's space, to let him be as he is, rather than trying to pull him into one's own space.

Though I have tried to report the events of the four days factually and coherently, I have not offered much of a context in which to place the individual exercises and comments. Standing alone, they may seem at best truisms, at worst ridiculous. Embedded in the total context I found them less bumptious, less saucy, and more potentially useful than they may appear in print. More of that later.

The training can be classified into: 1) Information offered, lecture-style, from the trainer to the audience. 2) "Sharing," which consists of comments by individuals from the floor in the form of questions, reports on how the training is affecting them, or life stories. These offerings, particularly the last, often lead to "psychotherapy" on the spot. 3) "Processes" (guided imagery or meditative exercises).

I have just about exhausted the material from the report I wrote upon returning from my *est* experience. When I looked back at that report, I realized that I had forgotten much of the training. Evidently my memory suffers when my stomach is empty and my bladder is full. However, I had an opportunity to learn more of the theory of *est* from listening to Werner at a couple of subsequent human potential meetings. Fresh from having his back worked on with the Alexander technique, he offered a lecture-style presentation at the "Body, Mind, Spirit" human potential meeting of 1975 in Lincoln, Nebraska.

When I saw Erhard's name on the program, I wondered how he could keep from boring his audience in a straight lecture without the interspersed experiential work like that at the training, which in turn can at times be boring enough. *Est* has what might be called a clinical theory, couched in its own special language, which is interesting and easily applicable to ordinary activities. It also has what might be called a metapsychological theory, at times far removed from experience and applicability in behavior. That theory is dependent for understanding on a knowledge of physics as well as other esoteric ways of thinking. I should have known that being boring is not one of Werner's worries. He holds forth on abstract issues indefatigably during the training, either oblivious of or uncaring as to how much of the audience follows how much of what he is saying.

At this meeting Erhard was particularly concerned with the concept of "holding," by which he seemed to mean the forms in which information is held, independent of what the information may be. This would correspond in psychoanalysis to a structural, as against a content, point of view. We do not observe, Erhard said, we only see by way of our systems of belief, and these systems of belief are the way we gather and hold material. In the service of beliefs we use symbols. But while symbols are merely holders of reality, we tend to consider the symbols as being reality. The particular holder of information must be appropriate to the phenomena being held. Thus auras, the bodily emanations seen by psychics and photographed by the Kirlian method, are not appropriate to a means of holding called seeing, because you cannot see them. But that does not mean that they do not exist. We simply do not have a conceptual or operational holder for such information. Werner distinguishes "observing" from "perceiving." Observing, for him, is "being," experiencing, independent of systems of belief. Perception is how something is seen, as from a distance. For example, as a percept, Werner Erhard is a number of associations, responsibilities, characteristics. But Werner Erhard as a holder of "I," his experience, or the experience of him, is another kind of holder, and yields a different Werner Erhard. Our favorite holder for information is language. For all the advantages of language, it restricts us in that it is a different system from the experiential system, and it forces reality into available language models as much as it portrays reality. For example, if one holds one's hand up, this is "up" within the language system. Outside that system, it is either up or down, depending how high the observer is.

"Thinking" is better than believing in that it allows more latitude. For example, it makes possible the manipulation of symbols and the choosing between them. "Doing" is better than thinking or believing, for it is closer to experience and often develops proof that is founded in experience. Feeling can perhaps be illustrated by noting the difference between a great brain surgeon and an ordinary brain surgeon. The great brain surgeon has a "feel" for what he is doing; he holds his skill in his feeling, or feelings are the holders of his skill.

Metapsychologically speaking, however, feeling is not the end point either. There are 1) concepts, 2) feelings, 3) the system from which concepts and feelings come. Concepts and feelings influence one another as in a closed system; e.g., certain concepts give rise to feelings and certain feelings give rise to concepts. Only the system from which concepts and feelings come is totally free and uninfluenced. Werner calls this seminal system "abstraction" or "the generative principle." Paradoxically, if one explains what this principle is, that ruins it, because it then becomes a concept. Also, it cannot be directly experienced, it cannot be felt, it is just itself. This is the only truly spontaneous state of being human, not coming from outside the person but *sui generis*. It is created out of nothingness, by the person, from within. It is a self that is different from the selves that are products of other systems. If explainable at all, it is explainable by way of painting or poetry. What you feel or believe about, for example, the human potential movement is merely derivative. In Werner's scheme, therefore, it is no good. Goodness lies only in what is created from your generative principle, from your nothingness. To educate in any way other than allowing the person to generate, to create from nothingness, is to limit his capacities and to encourage a flawed result.

You cannot explain or educate. All you can do is give the person space to create his own beliefs, or whatever else he is creating. Prepackaged beliefs prevent experience. "Creating, being, experiencing" are identical; they all come from nothing. The belief in God, for example, needs to be given up because belief prevents the experience of God. One should systematically rid oneself of all beliefs generated by others, because they all stand in the way of one's developing one's own beliefs based on one's experience. Only in generating from one's personal void can one be free. In either a puckish or a brilliant application (I can't decide which) he suggests that "now" is not what is between the past and the future. If you look at it that way, then you are not responsible for it, for it is something given to you by our conventional system of beliefs about time. But if you generate "now" yourself, apart from such a system, then you are responsible for what you generate; now is up to you.

In order to illustrate the principle of abstraction, Werner drew a square that had a design within it. He pointed out that if an event occurs within that square, it changes the design. Rather than creating anew, it changes the old. He then drew an empty square. If something occurs in the empty square, it creates, there is nothing there to change. Nothing, therefore, is what everything comes from. By contrast, nothing as defined by something is no longer nothing, it is something. (Werner loves paradox.) The usual experience of love, for example, can come only from something, and if it comes from something, it is pretense. It is love that comes, for example, from need or obligation; it is derivative, a function of a belief system. A true experience of "love" can come only from nowhere.

Further gospel from Werner: If I know the truth I won't know it; if I don't know the truth, I will know it. In other words, if I know, it is according to some belief system; I will never know the truth, because I will be tied to the belief system. Truth can be discovered only out of nothingness, can only be created. The only true belief system is created by one's self from a void. By way of demonstration he asked the group "to experience," and the group naturally enough did nothing. He then asked the group not to experience, and people then did something, namely experienced; what else? The conclusion: Experience comes from nothingness.

I saw Werner again when he appeared on the program of the Association for Humanistic Psychology meeting at Estes Park, Colorado, a partial report of which has appeared earlier. "Neatly pressed" is the phrase for Werner, whether in reference to his clothing or his presentations, clean and sparkling, seeming brand-new, full of somewhat synthetic but relentless promise. It was summer, and his "bush" suit was at its fashionable height. The ideas were last year's models, but they rolled off with assembly-line newness. By now, you have read them here, if not elsewhere, before. But if you want the *est* experience you might just go ahead and read them again. They may be boring, or they may strike you, as they do many people, as infectious. You may also get some flavor of Werner's constantly new way of saying old things, or at least it seems like a new way. He was not a salesman for nothing.

Of course, he needs all the charisma he can muster. People are regularly offended by his abstractness, by his seeming iconoclasm, his regular put-downs of the beliefs cherished by members of the audience because they are beliefs rather than experience. At this meeting, where he was given a two-hour block of time, perhaps less than half of his original audience of a couple of hundred were there at the end. Since it was a free-spirited humanistic psychology group, several people interrupted the proceedings with parting shots. They especially seemed to resent Werner's failing to echo their enthusiasm for the ineffable beauty of feelings and the inspirational precepts of the human potential movement. They failed to "get clear" that Werner was not objecting to their or anybody else's ideas per se, only to the adoption of such ideas as somebody else's beliefs rather than the deriving of them by way of one's experiential self.

Here are some extracts from his talk.

"Now" is transcendent; it includes the past and the future. Experience transcends time.

If you believe in something, give it up. We are not interested in beliefs but in experience of the moment. Beliefs are delusions or illusions; we talk in facts.

Often we talk in facts as if facts were immutably real. Actually a fact is only an agreement. Words are not experiences, so they tend to be lies. Photographs or dossiers are not the person; the only thing that is the person *is* the person. Experience is not linear, positional, or in form—it is only what it is. We do not experience the present, only the record of it. By the time we can say or know what the experience of the present is, it has become a record.

Est's purpose is to show people how they are holding or organizing experience. *Est* has no content or position itself. The individual creates the world, or is created by the world, not according to any a priori position or belief. The person is the author of his own experience, and exploring that experience via explanation is a lie. Do not confuse explanations with experience.

Control comes about through creating conditions for

something to happen. If one needs force, then control has failed.

You do not see with your eyes, you just see. The eyes and cortex are ways of explaining the experience of seeing.

Since experience happens irrespective of time, place, or form, it is possible for any one individual to have the experience of being black, homosexual, or a city planner even though he has never been any of these.

In *est*, people see the roles that they play, founded upon beliefs, and they tend to give these up in favor of their experience. Werner demonstrated this point with an audience member who had survived a German concentration camp. Werner was, to some people, shockingly unsympathetic to this man's explanation of his present life as a function of his terrible experiences. According to Werner, only when he gave up this role, this explanation for his misfortunes, in favor of his present-day self and experience could he finally "leave" the concentration camp.

Experience transcends even the nervous system. How the nervous system functions is, after all, an explanation, something agreed upon by others. One's experience of self is subject to the nervous system so long as one believes that it comes from the nervous system. The only way experience can have complete freedom of creativity is to come from nothing else. Experience comes from the highest of all abstractions, nothingness. "The truth" is, paradoxically, a lie, because it is bound by forms, it is explanatory according to some system. Experience is without system. The purpose of *est* is to help you become aware of how you hold experience and information according to organized belief systems. Only when you understand that life is hopeless, cast in iron, that all things are determined, are you free to make changes.

Power in and of itself is neither corrupt nor good. The way we view power is corrupt, usually wanting it at the expense of others. Power is infinite, but people "in power" tend to be powerless. One can submit to power, one can struggle to overcome power, one can ignore power, and all these are useless. Instead, a person should give himself the space just to be, without roles, predetermined rules, or explanations. This is the only true and ultimate power.

So much for Werner himself, his ideas, and the training proper. Other *est* activities bring the graduates together in an extended family or fraternity that keeps the ideas alive and the organization growing. I have not attended any of the graduate seminars, such as in communication, self-expression, money, the body, sex. I have, however, attended a guest seminar, and an informal meeting of graduates to share experiences and, parenthetically, to encourage the bringing of prospective customers to the next guest seminar. Finally, I participated in graduation exercises of a training held in Leavenworth Federal Penitentiary, at Leavenworth, Kansas.

Each of these experiences began with a cheery phone call. I thought my wife's eyebrows lifted just a fraction as one of *est*'s honeyed, superfriendly voices asked for "Stephen." The relentless first-naming friendliness and slick organizational work that began with the phone call inviting me to attend a guest seminar and to bring interested parties, continued with the seminar itself. Synthetic and assembly-line though the friendliness was, it really isn't so bad when you consider the alternatives.

At the guest seminar two representatives of *est*'s central office took turns describing, and to some extent allowing us to experience, *est*. They started with the now-famous story about a rat in a maze trying to find a piece of cheese and after a while he learns not to go up the passageways that do not contain cheese. People, on the other hand, often spend their life repeatedly going up blind alleys, unrewarded, never seeming to learn that there might be another way. As alternatives some people seem to believe that going up more empty passageways might improve things, while other people just give it all up and drop out. The *est* way is to make the passageways work, to give up the beliefs that lead us into fruitless endeavor and to discover what we really need. We were told that 80 per cent of the training involves looking at the mind, noticing how we wear ourselves out listening to a voice in back of our heads instead of experiencing ourselves. We need to take a position, to decide. And "decide" has the same root as "homicide" and "suicide"—to murder the alternatives. Unwilling to do that, we remain undecided.

Interspersed with such lecture material were a couple of "processes." Two salesmen-lecturers were leading the discussion, and each *est* graduate who had brought along a non-graduate was also a kind of salesman. To make the sale easy, tables were placed at the side of the room and manned by people waiting to accept deposits. A nicely timed intermission before some promised further developments gave people the opportunity to sign up. A brochure with frequent questions and answers about *est*, along with information about the next and nearest training, accompanies home those who may still be unable to murder the alternatives. On the cover of the brochure is an example of Werner's psychoanalytic wisdom couched in his verbal sleight of hand: "Sometimes people get the notion that the purpose of *est* is to make you better. It is not. I happen to think that you are perfect exactly the way you are . . . the problem is that people get stuck acting the way they were, instead of being the way they are."

Est *Goes to Prison*

I had read in the *Graduate Review* some interesting reports of *est* training in prisons, so I was glad that the next of *est*'s inviting phone calls was to participate in a training graduation ceremony in the nearby Leavenworth Federal Penitentiary. Here is how that participation went.

A prison is in some ways the epitome of choicelessness. Everywhere bars, walls, guards that tell you where you can and cannot go; the daily schedule says what you can and cannot do. Yet *est* teaches that everyone is responsible for everything in his life, that he chooses his destiny. On the face of it, *est* training in prison might seem a nasty joke, an irony that has gotten out of hand. But that point of view would result only from a superficial reading of the *est* credo. Rather, *est* would have it that we are all prisoners, we all operate under constraints. Whether these constraints are external or internal, we have the opportunity to decide at each moment what is to be the quality of life. And indeed, from what one can gather from published reports and word of mouth, *est* has been successful in its prison "trainings." That, too, is plausible. For people whose choices are so limited by external circumstances, it is particularly important that they allow themselves internal choice, that whatever the circumstances, they realize they can decide on the nature of their experience.

Some fifty *est* graduates were needed to help graduate the more than one hundred prisoners of the Leavenworth Federal Penitentiary from the *est* training. In a remarkable testimonial to the enthusiasm of *est* graduates for their training, most of them had come over five hundred miles to help, primarily from Chicago and Denver. Most arrived just in time for the six o'clock start, recognizing that the training might continue until after midnight, and most of them were scheduled to return home at six in the morning. This selfless volunteer army is typical of *est*, which functions with a small staff abetted by hundreds of volunteers.

At our gathering point in a motel, we were told to divest ourselves of any valuables. We would be meeting with the prisoners after the graduation, and there was a small likelihood that our pockets might be picked. We were warned not to carry away any messages or do any favors.

The façade of the prison and its large rotunda reminded me of a cross between the nation's Capitol and a turn-of-the-century palace. To the side could be seen the high wall and control tower which revealed what it really was. From a control tower in the parking lot we were asked whether we had any assorted contraband such as guns, ammunitions, or drugs, and then were given entry instructions. As we waited to enter, the guard surveying the many of us gathered there said, "I don't know what the hell I would have done if they had any of that stuff on them."

Most of us could use whatever humor we could find. It was no joke to enter between sets of electronically operated barred doors in groups of fifteen. It was even less funny when we were told, once ensconced in the visitors' room, that the prison rule was that should someone be taken hostage, no deal would be made for his release.

Ed Forbes, who was responsible for our participation, had the typical presentation of self of *est* trainers: sharply pressed trousers, open-necked epauletted shirt, neat modish hair, and clean-shaven face. He, too, looked, talked, and acted like Werner. This was uncannily true of Ted Long, who was doing the training of the prisoners; he was practically a carbon copy of Werner's bodily movements, facial expressions, voice quality, and delivery.

Our job as assistants in graduating the prisoners was to

help each one to do a "personality assessment," which is a euphemism for a psychic exercise. This exercise has the implication of a final examination; upon its satisfactory completion, the *est* student raises his hand as a signal for the trainer to congratulate him and in so doing to graduate him. Our task was to fill out prepared cards with information identifying a person other than anybody present in the room. In addition to some physical characteristics of that person, we were to list things to which he might "react," adjectives that would describe his personality, and some of his interpersonal relationships. The *est* student was then to be told the name, age, sex, address, and body build of the person we had described on the card. The *est* student was to "get into his space, find his center," a quasi-meditative internal position learned during the sixty or so hours of the training. After the student signaled that he was in this presumably altered state of consciousness, he was to construct mentally, or sculpture on a platform imagined before his eyes, the person described on the card. He was then asked mentally to touch hands with this person, the better to bring himself into contact with the image of that person. Then he was given the personality characteristics written on the card and asked to choose between such opposites as whether the person is industrious or lazy, outgoing or bashful; to tell how that person would react to things, e.g. baseball, poetry, Italian food; and what quality of relationships he might have with friend, parent, child. These choices on the student's part were to be made on the basis of his experience of the imaginary person. He would allegedly be able psychically to duplicate in himself the experience that the imaged person would have.

Before administering this test to the prisoners, we underwent a period of training that included taking turns giving and taking the exercise with the person sitting next to us.

We further practiced "reinforcing," which is to follow *whatever* the student says with such remarks as, "I got it," "fantastic," "fine." Then we were asked to create with eyes closed the mental image of a blackboard, and to write on that blackboard, physically using our hands while we were imagining the writing. We were to "write" answers to such questions as what our judgments, opinions, ideas, criticism were, about giving and taking the personality assessment exercise. This central idea was worded and reworded in several different ways so that this mental writing took a very long time to do, and as with so much of *est*, it became boring. Nonetheless, it probably had a beneficial effect in helping people become aware of and perhaps work through their feelings about what they were to do, thereby allowing them to do it with greater satisfaction and efficiency.

Finally, after the completion of the 10 P.M. prisoner body count, our hands were stamped to identify us as being allowed to leave the prison, and we were led to the auditorium, where the training was to be held. This auditorium embodied society's ambivalence toward its prisoners, the conflict between prison as punishment and prison as rehabilitation. On the one hand, it provided the prisoners with the opportunity to see films, plays, and other entertainment, while on the other hand, the chairs were so uncomfortable as to make sitting through such entertainment a tribulation. As is the custom, the *est* students had not been told about our appearance, and they stared wonderingly as some fifty men and women nonprisoners suddenly appeared and sat down in a section behind them.

We listened to an hour or so of the final segment of the training. This consisted of a lecture on life being a cosmic game in which we were all, willy-nilly, participants. The only choice we had was to decide whether we were going to enjoy playing the game or to suffer playing the game, and that choice was made from moment to moment all through the game. After a few termination flourishes, including a stirring testimonial to Werner, who had, according to Ted Long, given him the "space" to make more of his life than he ever had done before, Ted's participation in the training was over. Now the prisoners were asked to line up at the sides of the auditorium while we took prearranged seats with empty chairs on each side of us to be filled by the people we would work with. (All this was interrupted by a body count, which showed somebody missing, and everyone had to return to his seat for another taking of the count.)

As we were a little short of help, I administered the ending process to four instead of two prisoners. At the end of the psychic exercise, they were asked, as per instructions, whether they were satisfied. For any occasional person who said that he was not satisfied with his performance we were prepared to offer the process again, with another imaginary person included on another card. Most trainees are, however, satisfied. By this time they want to graduate and be finished. It is one o'clock in the morning, they have worked for many hours, and they want to succeed, to believe that they have developed some psychic skills. They are given a good bit of help by the laws of chance, their suggestibility, and hints from the person administering the process. While we were not told to do so in so many words, the way we were trained to ask the questions allowed suggesting, chance, hints, and to conspire toward a subjectively successful performance. This is in contrast to the psychic exercises done at the end of Silva Mind Control, from which Werner presumably took this exercise (see next chapter). In Silva Mind Control, there is some but less opportunity for suggestions and hints. That exercise forced me to consider the possibility of the existence of psychic powers, while I had much more difficulty even considering that possibility during the *est* exercise. But, then, in Silva Mind Control psychic powers are much more central; in *est* they are a lagniappe.

As in most prison populations, the four prisoners with whom I worked ran the gamut from frighteningly cold and sullen characters who conformed to the stereotype of the hardened, slightly psychotic criminal, to a person about whom one could only wonder how he could have gotten himself into a maximum-security prison. The latter was a clean-shaven, blue-eyed young husband, innocent in appearance and style of interaction, who in the course of one process made a reference to Percy Bysshe Shelley. Through my judiciously emphasizing their correct responses, skipping over and minimizing or explaining away some of their misses, and passing over entirely the factor of chance, each of my prisoners was enthusiastic about his performance, and all graduated handily.

Prisoners and *est* staff and volunteer helpers mingled freely during the coffee-and-cake celebration following graduation. Reviews of the *est* training among the prisoners were mixed. They had the special *est* language down pretty well, and in the course of our conversations experimented freely with the ideas. Much like any group of recent *est* graduates, they were struggling to assimilate what they had learned, and groggy from the intense experience of it all. However, there seemed to me to be a subtle but important difference between these prison graduates and other graduates. Some of the prisoners seemed to find refuge in seeing *est* as merely one in a series of activities made available to them in prison. In the air was a paralysis of hope and trust, which diminished what otherwise might have been a greater expression of enthusiasm and hopefulness about their new experience. They had "seen it all before." One prisoner in his late twenties, handsome, ruggedly built, maybe six feet eight inches tall, did, however, rumble down from his height, "If only I had taken *est* ten years ago."

On the basis of informal questioning of thirty *est* graduates at least a year after their training, Marcia Seligson reported not finding anybody who had not found the training valuable. "About 85 per cent claim graphic, dramatic alterations in their existences." And she goes on to give several impressive examples.[1]

I had my experiences and opinions of *est* corroborated at, of all places, a convention of the American Psychoanalytic Association. For the past several years, at each of its semiannual meetings, discussions have been held on one or another of the new therapies. At the meeting featuring *est*, I offered some of the material presented here to some twenty-five psychoanalysts, most of whom knew of *est* only what they had read in the popular press or heard from one or two of their patients. One of these analysts, however, a writer and thinker of recognized high stature, had attended *est* with his wife as ordinary participants. This analyst's wife reported to the group that she had overcome a urinary-tract difficulty based on a narrowed urethra, which for years had required periodic opening. Moreover, she had developed an ability to win at tennis, for which she gave *est* credit. In her view, she had not really wanted to win before, because of her difficulties expressing aggression. Following *est* she beat her husband at tennis for the first time, and has continued her winning ways. Her insight in this regard was duplicated by a sixteen-year-old, reported on by her husband as having said at the beginning of the training that he was a poor pitcher, that he kept throwing balls instead of strikes. At the end of the training he got up and announced that he realized that his problem was not that he was a poor pitcher, it was just that he had not really wanted to pitch strikes. Another vignette, offered by this analyst, was that of a man confessing to the *est* meeting both his homosexuality and that he was going blind. At this point, members of the *est* group were in the palm of his hands, wanting to help him, to express sympathy, to do whatever they could, but the trainer would have none of that. He called the man's presentation a "number," that he was making a play for sympathy without exploiting his own capacities to the fullest. The same went for a woman grieving over the death of her husband, so busy grieving that she was overlooking her capacities to free herself of grief. My colleague psychoanalyst reported being greatly impressed by the lectures, particularly the discussion of free will versus determinism, in effect a mini course in philosophy and education. He reported he had gone, himself, only after years of urging from his children, and at first had adopted the position of the superior outsider. One thing that he had learned in the course of the training was that in respect to feelings and experiences he was no better than anybody else.

One or two other analysts suggested that *est* may bring about change the same way that any kind of brainwashing does. People give up their autonomy to an imperious leader, entering into a needful, supplicating relationship with such a leader and his ideas under the sway of the altered states of consciousness induced by some of the "processes." Being treated harshly and being deprived of amenities frighten the participants and lead them to an agreement with an apparently stronger group in order to make themselves feel safe. Further, while some people may be encouraged to muster their capacities when told that they are all right the way they are, and that they can solve problems if they but will, others may take this as a license to feel omnipotent.

I think these reasonings are sound, and probably do describe and explain the way some people react to the situation. However, as far as I could tell from observing myself and a number of others, the Gestapo atmosphere is clearly felt as make-believe after a while unless a participant needs, for reasons indigenous to his personality, to take it seriously. He simply takes it good-humoredly and concentrates on the use that can be made of the whole situation. If one therefore is relatively unthreatened, one has less need to think of oneself as omnipotent and less need to submit unreflectively. Others in this discussion group could see how, by focusing upon one's own responsibilities, *est* could help people take the crucial first step toward thinking psychologically. Members could see also that *est* would provide a way of thinking about oneself, a myth or version of life that would help to make order out of the common experience of chaos or fragmentation. Finally, the *est* attitude of detachment, as embodied for example in its assertion that life is only a game, interrupts morbidly intense self-preoccupation, affords a perspective that buffers unpleasant feelings, and minimizes the tendency some people have of making every untoward event into a life-deciding tragedy, rather than a transitory setback.

Werner "discovered" *est* by putting together what he had learned from the many self-help approaches in which he had participated. It shows. The training is a mélange of therapies and systems of thought. Gestalt therapy is represented through training in awareness of the present self, including experience of the body. Philosophy is represented by the solipsistic idea of creating one's own reality, with no absolute reality apart from this. Psychoanalysis is represented in *est*'s radical determinism, whereby people are alleged to have in their repertoire only those behaviors they have learned in the past; these behaviors often stem from traumatic events that generalize to later-life events. Game theory provides a context for seeing life as a series of decisions. Rational therapy is represented in the point of view that one decides how he will live, for example whether he will continue doing things in ways that resulted in failure or whether he will risk trying different ways. Zen Buddhism is included by way of some of the philosophical problems set for the members and in *est*'s detached perspective. Meditation is used to help put people in touch with their experience. Many of the processes involve guided imagery, as used in psychosynthesis. Mysticism is involved in the alleged capacity of people to expand their consciousness to the point that they can achieve communication that transcends the senses. Taoism, scientology, reincarnation, Dale Carnegie, the Bible, Ram Dass, Alan Watts, R. D. Laing, and others can all be found in the training. Werner's love of paradox is reminiscent of similar loves shown by Oscar Wilde, H. L. Mencken, George Bernard Shaw, and Voltaire.

Finally, there is a strong element of old-fashioned suggestion, such as at the beginning of the training, when one is told he will get more out of the training if he intends to get more out of the training, and less if he is there simply because he was sent by an institution or comes out of curiosity. For several hundred dollars and a lot of punishing hours one is inclined to intend that the investment be worthwhile, and to believe that it was. Finally there are the needs that pushed many people to sign up in the first place. These needs clamor for satisfaction, and fasten on to whatever help is putatively available.

Sometime after the training I remember clarifying through *est* strategies and points of view a decision about how to behave with regard to a problem in my life. I found myself thinking that I would act on this understanding if I could believe that the training was legitimate, if I could overlook the nonprofessional background of the trainer and the Gestapo, circus-of-the-absurd context. Now, get that. Here I had, in my opinion, an opportunity possibly to improve my life, and I was deciding whether or not to grasp it on the basis of whether I liked and trusted the context in which I had learned it. I would go up a blind alley looking for nonexistent cheese unless I could be persuaded to do otherwise! As if it were up to *est* to meet my standards of credibility more than up to me to use my wits and take my chances. I can hear it now, Stewart's ringing delivery: "You asshole, no wonder your fucking life doesn't work."

Of the hundred thousand people who have taken the training in the past half dozen years, most have taken it on the recommendation of friends. That the graduates recommend that others take the training, and donate their work to the organization in order that other people benefit as they claim to have done, seems to make a prima-facie case for some kind of effectiveness. During the training that I attended, one participant reported that, during the week between the first and second meetings, he had overcome his twenty-year fear of elevators. His was one of the more dramatic of several testimonials.

To its credit, *est* also asked officially and publicly the omnipresent question, "Does the training work?" It hired a research team, with the respected Robert Ornstein as principal investigator, to try to determine systematically the results of *est* training. The researchers, correctly and modestly, acknowledge that theirs was not, strictly speaking, a study of the outcome of *est*. It not only lacked matched control groups, but each subject could not serve as his own control, since he was not studied before and after the training. Rather, the researchers say that with their self-report questionnaire and telephone interviews, they merely set out to learn whether evidence gathered in this way would encourage further, more definitive studies. In other words, if people reported that *est* had made no significant change for the better in their lives, the matter could be laid to rest then and there. If they reported they had benefited, better means of testing the reality of that report would have to be found. One would, for example, want to study whether and how *est* itself brought about the putative changes rather than placebo, the passage of time, or other adventitious circumstances.

The report of the Ornstein study, *A Self-Report Survey: Preliminary Study of Participants in Erhard Seminar Training*,[2] was easily available from the Menninger professional library but marked "not for quotation or publication." Whatever that means. At any rate, an abstract of that study was mailed to *est* graduates, from which I do quote: "Respondents reported strong positive health and well-being changes since taking the *est* Standard Training, especially in the areas of psychological health and well-being and those illnesses with a large psychosomatic component. These are sufficiently strong to justify controlled follow-up studies of particular physical and psychological variables." The Ornstein group reminds us that the study does not demonstrate that people's health actually changes, but only that they say that it does. The researchers conclude, however, that "The reported changes are strongly positive and the findings are powerful enough to warrant further research in any of the areas noted as showing change for the better."

Among the positive changes most reported were general physical health; mental health; less use of drugs, alcohol, and coffee (but not tea); better relationships with significant others; fewer gastrointestinal problems, allergies, colds, sore throats, back, neck, and shoulder pain, and sexual difficulties; and less fear of doctors. Fewer than 7 per cent of the respondents to the questionnaire reported negative changes in physical or mental health. On the other hand, five people, only one of whom had a history of psychiatric disturbance, were reported in *The American Journal of Psychiatry*[3] as developing a variety of psychotic symptoms following their *est* experience. What may be implicated here is perhaps less the content of the training than the structure of it, the conditions of intense group participation. Sustained experiential studies in group process, such as those sponsored by National Training Laboratories (NTL) and the A. K. Rice Tavistock-Washington School of Psychiatry Group Relations Conferences, based on general systems theory, are well known to have their share of "casualties," two of which I observed myself. So, for that matter, do most medical procedures, including psychoanalysis and other expressive psychotherapies.

In another study, presented to the American Psychiatric Association in May 1976, Babbie and Stone report that more than half of 1187 *est* graduates assessed their training, on a scale of 1 to 7, as very favorable.[4] Following the training, improvements were claimed in work satisfaction, sexual satisfaction, emotional problems, relationships with significant others, among other dimensions of life. Possibly implying "suggestion" or determination for beneficial change, a high percentage of these people went to the training with high expectations for those areas of life that did change. Independent ratings were made by psychiatrists, psychoanalysts, clinical psychologists, social workers, and counselors of these same *est* graduates. They observed that 88 per cent of the participants had made changes for the better, on the same dimensions rated by the graduates. Finally, assessments of the training by *est* graduates made between nineteen and twenty-six months after the training were substantially higher than those made two to five months after the training. Of the many possible meanings of such a finding, it at least strongly suggests that positive evaluations of *est* are not due primarily to an immediate rosy glow such as is often observed following intense human potential experiences of other kinds.

I have met several people who told me of remarkable changes in their lives which they felt were due to *est*. Wanting more of such information, I was glad to be invited to attend a meeting of graduates in Kansas City, Missouri, organized (as usual by volunteers) to share experiences, get in touch with fellow graduates in the area, and co-ordinate efforts for the coming *est* seminar.

Around the circle of chairs we went: "I took the training eight months ago, it is still with me, a constant presence. So much was revealed to me. I no longer blame others, but take self-responsibility. Two years of psychotherapy, a psychiatric hospitalization, and TM failed to do as much for me as *est* did."

"I had taken scientology and done some primal scream, but I have the feeling that *est* is part of me, it is me."

"I'm intrigued by the idea of becoming, getting more out of myself, rather than competing with others."

"I went through life in a blur, but in the last two years, after *est*, I have been continuing to get its benefits. I am now clear and confident, I assume all will go well. I don't worry so much about the future, I am more easygoing. I can plan for the future but not be uptight about it."

"My experience is in the present. I can listen to others and not be so worried about what I am going to say next."

But one of the graduates reported how she had walked out of one of the graduate seminars, finding the "follow-the-leader mentality abhorrent." Someone else wondered how much we had been submitting here to group contagion, each person basking in the good feeling of warmth in this group and exaggerating how good his past experience had been. Were we in danger, someone wondered, of becoming *est* junkies?

Yet a mother and father reported that they had been trying for two years, with a wide variety of strategies (not including psychotherapy) to get their six-year-old to stop wetting the bed. Borrowing from their *est* training, they entered into an "agreement," an interpersonal contract in which the rules and regulations, the demands and opportunities for behavior, are set forth so that each person is clear about what he wishes to gain and what his responsibilities are. As an apparent result of this agreement, the child stopped wetting the bed. Shortly after, when the father appeared in a wet bathing suit, the little girl suggested that he go into his room, think over his responsibilities, and decide whether he wanted to continue that behavior. Here was, I thought, a beautiful example of how ordinary psychological principles are put into action through acceptance of the *est* philosophy and strategy of life. For two years the child had had things done *to* her, without taking her wishes into account. Insufficient opportunity had been provided for her to mobilize her conscious intentions and capacities. Since she was the one "doing" the symptom, she was the one to stop doing it if she so chose. The *est*-inspired agreement presumably gave her that choice.

One graduate reported that she had suffered for years with headaches, had been examined by a variety of neurologists, and had been told that nothing physically had been found wrong with her. She should just continue to use pain-killing medicines. During her *est* training she had volunteered for that portion of the training in which the trainer demonstrates to the group how one can overcome physical difficulties by getting into a quasi-meditative state and concentrating on the affected part, mentally seeing, feeling, touching, smelling it, and visualizing how one would like it to be. During the demonstration, she had overcome the headache and had used the recommended procedure to deal with subsequent attacks. Such headaches, however, became fewer, until now she says she hardly gets them at all.

A young mother reported that, when her husband was away on business, her daughter set up a great clamor for a cookie. The mother said to her that she knew that the cookie was not what the daughter wanted; what did she think she really wanted? The daughter replied, "I want my daddy," and that then was the end of the importuning for cookies. This seemed to me a nice bit of psychoanalytic work but was understood by the rest of the participants as another wondrous application of *est*. While no one made too clear a connection between the training and this mother's insight and strategy, I think it plausible to give *est* credit for having encouraged the mother to think psychologically about the situation. Not that *est* says to think psychologically in so many words, but the structure of the training and a good bit of its teaching encourage one to look inward. So it may well have been that *est* had created the conditions under which this mother could listen rather than act, and so recognize the covert meanings of her daughter's request.

As the meeting was breaking up, a young woman sought me out to tell me that with *est* she had overcome a fear of doctors, one of the major benefits reported in Ornstein's study. As a result of her having overcome this fear, she was able to get treatment for a physical symptom, which then cleared up. It was a nice story, but she seemed to have something else on her mind. She made some reference to my comments during the meeting, and she finally asked whether I thought psychiatry could have helped her with that problem and whether it was something she ought to consider. I pointed out to her that the symptom was presumably just that, a symptom. It was nice that she was able to overcome it, but now it was up to her as to whether she was interested in understanding the person who had the symptom. She seemed to get the message.

I hope so. The incident illustrates a danger of so many new-therapy interventions, that their very success may end a process of beneficial change far short of what it could be. I had tried to tell this group of graduates that *est* and psychiatry should not be in competition; in principle they are complementary. One can take *est* and get whatever benefits may accrue, may enrich the psychotherapy with material stirred up by *est*, may enrich *est* by applying to it some of the capacities developed by the psychotherapy. Forbidding *est* in the course of psychotherapy makes little more sense than forbidding reading, dancing lessons, eating health food, or going to college. Psychotherapy and other activities come into conflict only when the person or patient uses one activity in order to hamper the other. In psychotherapy, that can be dealt with, even turned to advantage, through analysis of the resistance.

I think I correctly understood the look in the young woman's eyes when she turned her attention from her symptom to herself. Almost palpable around us were the questions why she was unmarried, why she was fearful at work, what she felt when she awoke at three o'clock in the morning. *Est* was fine, but. . . .

13

From Laredo to the Planet with Betterment—Silva Mind Control

It was, as usual, a hot, windy desert weekend in Laredo, Texas, home of Silva Mind Control International. I had been invited by the founder and leader, José Silva, to address its yearly convention on the topic of how Silva Mind Control seemed to me as a psychologist and psychoanalyst. Eating under the stars, a few blocks down the street and across the border in Nuevo Laredo, Mexico, I had had the enjoyably disorienting experience of being in a foreign country. At the convention, also, I had my share of mastering a sense of being alien. After all, I had not been prepared for a wealthy businessman to tell me that some years previously he had barely been able to scrape up the fee for Silva Mind Control training, but by applying what he had learned from the training, he had transformed his life into a success. Nor was it my style to hobnob with people who, upon having a "negative" thought would counteract it by saying to themselves (or out loud), "Cancel, cancel." And it took a bit of doing to acclimate myself to having "How are you?" answered with a spritely "Better and better."

I was, however, more prepared than I would have been nine months earlier, before I had graduated from Silva

Mind Control training. Now the remaining sense of being alien and disoriented could be dealt with through concentration on the task at hand—namely, how to understand people's claims that they seemed in fact to be doing "better and better," and how to understand the new abilities that Silva Mind Control seemed to be calling forth from the devotees. I had accepted the invitation to attend and speak at the convention in part to pursue these new experiences and learning.

It had all begun when I finally took serious notice of the words "Silva Mind Control," which I had been hearing off and on for some time. A colleague of mine who had taken the training said something that I heard vaguely as having to do with diagnosing illnesses without seeing the patient. I knew that she had a penchant for trying out various offbeat activities, so I had more or less dismissed her comments. It was a good illustration of how information can be isolated through prejudice. Instrumental also in my initially ignoring her was the association that I and others have to the very words "mind control." To some they mean the control of the minds of others, as in brainwashing; to others they imply the need to control one's own mind, in the sense of keeping control, staying out of trouble, or exerting will power. As used in Silva Mind Control the term refers to the capacity to use one's mind in new and helpful ways, rather than merely to control it or anybody else's.

Silva Mind Control and *est* have a number of commonalities. Each has a central office that organizes and distributes the product, which is now sold in various cities throughout the United States and some other countries. Silva Mind Control is somewhat more of an out-and-out franchise, with its trainers, the people who lead the courses, having their own districts and keeping a percentage of the tuition, probably also a percentage of the profit from the books, tapes, and electronic devices they sell at the meetings. Both *est* and Mind Control run free introductory lectures and demonstrations to which graduates bring or send their families and friends in the hope that they will sign up for the course. Both meet on successive weekends, for long, intensive days and nights. Therefore, both require leaders of considerable endurance and loquacity. Each was founded and is led by one man.

José Silva, of Mind Control, a self-taught electronics engineer, formerly a television repairman without much formal education, observed that his children were not only answering his questions but seemed to know what his succeeding questions were to be. While many a parent has been bemused momentarily by similar experiences, he elaborated this observation into the Mind Control program, which includes apparently psychic phenomena as well as teaching other uses of the mind.

The structure of Mind Control meetings is similar to that of *est*, lectures interspersed by "processes"; and some of the lectures and processes are identical with those of *est*. In both, at various times during the meetings all but the most gullible or previously indoctrinated experience considerable skepticism at what is being propounded. Both call people who have finished the basic course work "graduates," and present them with diplomas in sometimes oddly moving ceremonies. The similarities are hardly coincidental. Werner Erhard is claimed by Mind Control people to be one of their graduates. Elsewhere, he is instead said to be a graduate of Mind Dynamics, an offshoot of Silva Mind Control.

The differences between *est* and Silva Mind Control are impressive also. Mind Control is intellectually homespun, offering a somewhat *Reader's Digest* level and quality of understanding people and society. *Est* is more psychologically oriented in a dynamic sense. Its use of one-to-one psychological analysis and its one-to-one psychological interactions employing concepts from psychoanalysis and gestalt psychotherapy, in particular, are not to be found in Mind Control. Mind Control meetings have fewer people, in small hotel meeting rooms, as compared to *est*'s two hundred or more people meeting in one huge hotel ballroom. The Mind Control fees are somewhat lower than those of *est*, its organization somewhat less slick. The radical chic that hovers around the edges of *est* is not to be found in Mind Control. The *est* clientele are perhaps on a somewhat higher socioeconomic and educational level. Mind Control people are less imbued with the atmosphere and mores of the human potential movement, the casual hippie clothes, "in" expressions, and foul language. The closest Mind Control comes to pornography, at least in the sessions I attended, were jokes about commodes—with a sly wink. In an informal conversation, my Mind Control trainer, Randy Youmans, clucked his disapproval of the goings on in *est*.

While *est* is free of religious values, as it tries to be of all values, Mind Control strides fearlessly into the land of values. Emblazoned in a prominent place in much Mind Control literature is the quotation: "To qualify as humans we must take part in humanitarian acts.—José Silva." Mind Control literature prominently displays "Dedicated to the betterment of humanity," and elsewhere many references are made to the goal of Mind Control as a movement "to make the planet a better world to live in." While Werner Erhard might subscribe to similar sentiments, central to his philosophy is the fundamentally amoral stance that all beliefs are arbitrary. He directs his attention to the well-being of the individual person more than to that of the planet. (Recently, however, he has initiated a campaign to solve the problem of world hunger, although still with an emphasis on individual consciousness as the means of bringing this about.) When José Silva writes, "What is wrong is when you are destructive, what is right is constructive and creative," he seems to have clearly in mind *what is* constructive, creative, or destructive, or at least it seems so from the atmosphere generated by his movement. By contrast with *est*'s sometimes academic lectures, Mind Control lectures sound sometimes like sermons. Randy Youmans lets his students know that he believes in God and at one time studied at a school held in a monastery, and he frequently quotes the Bible. I gathered that a good many of the participants were religious also, or at least were free in this atmosphere to sound religious, as they would less likely be in *est*.

What were four hundred thousand graduates of Silva Mind Control over the past ten years taught and encouraged to do in the course of their training? For one thing, old-fashioned positive thinking. Mind Control people are utterly unabashed at simply telling graduates to behave in uplifting ways. For example, "Take a kind interest in the cashier, salesclerk, gas station attendant, waitress, etc., and joke with them, look them in the eyes and smile." "Call another Mind Control graduate who was in your class and find out how he or she is doing. Help each other get better and better." "Mentally repeat beneficial phrases [learned during the training] while driving or riding, before sleep and upon awakening." "Listen to others and talk less, especially about the big 'I.' " "Guide conversations to areas of ideas, rather than people and things." "Give children a good positive label such as 'genius,' 'love,' 'sweetheart,' rather than 'brat,' 'dummy,' or 'stupid.' "[1] Simplistic as they are, such Mind Control devices, if practiced with even a small degree of tact, appropriateness, and sophistication undoubtedly oil the wheels of human interaction. Practically all of us have great areas of choice, many opportunities for self-help, which we overlook or put aside in favor of behaviors which, even on a moment's self-reflection or in the eyes of a casual bystander, could be expected to cause trouble. Mind Control serves the role of such a bystander. If one takes Mind Control seriously, he installs in himself a voice reminding him, "If you want your child to have a decent self-concept, then remember that people behave as they are treated. If you want decent service and pleasant surroundings, then look people in the eyes, smile, and joke instead of giving orders or ignoring them."

Among the less highfalutin ways of conceptualizing neurosis, there is the terse but wise "Neurotics are stupid."[2] Most of us know, intellectually, how to behave for pleasure and profit. We just act as if we did not know. We do so, of course, in large part for reasons outside of awareness, and moreover tend to defend ourselves in various ways from the facts and implications of situations. We wallow around in a morass of ancient, false assumptions and half-understood information, remaining oblivious to important other information. Yet, at times, with plenty of awareness of what we are doing and even why we do it, we still choose to step into mudholes. The positive-thinking part of Silva Mind Control simply reminds us with maxims and homely strategies to do good and be smart, and we'll feel better. More power, of positive thinking, to the people.

José Silva says, "Mind Control is a combination of several things. Yoga is its mother, and hypnosis its father. It is a child of both." He is referring to a central aspect of Mind Control, which is to "go to your level," the Mind Control phrase for getting into a quasi-hypnotic, meditative state. It is alleged that by following recommended induction procedures, one changes one's brain waves from the usual beta pattern, which facilitates focused attention, to the alpha state and sometimes the deeper states of delta and theta. Many of the exercises or processes are practice sessions in "going to level," often done with the aid of tape-recorded sounds as a backdrop to the trainer's hypnotic monologue. Tapes of these procedures are available for sale at the meetings and are recommended for regular relaxation. (One of the tapes is entitled, "Take an Alpha Break.") But the major purpose of going to level is to tap the powers alleged then to be available which are not available to our usual, waking consciousness. Most of the time, the training is spent in practicing going to level, there performing a motley array of tricks and self-help procedures. One is taught to put oneself to sleep, to waken oneself at a particular time, to learn how to remember dreams, to get rid of headaches, to lose weight, and to stop smoking. (With regard to the last, "Do it for your loved ones.") Further, one tries to learn to let one's hand rise "by itself," to rid an area of the body of the capacity for sensation in order to control pain and to prevent bleeding and hemorrhaging. One is taught William James's device for memory, associating numbers and words, a popular strategy used also in Dale Carnegie courses. (Yes, I attended one of those meetings too.)

With the so-called "three-to-one" method, one trains into himself the cue of bringing together the tips of the first three fingers of either hand, then counting from one to three, and in this way quickly and efficiently changing one's consciousness. In such consciousness one can develop a mental image of a mirror, the "mirror of the mind." On this mirror or screen one projects an image of a problem one wants solved, erases the problem image, changes the mirror's frame to white, and creates and projects an image of the solution to the problem. Whether my mind was too boggled at this invitation and method, or whether my problems are beyond solution, this proved for me to be a wholly inefficient way of solving problems. As a means of giving me a sense of my being in the wrong place at the wrong time it was surpassed only by the water-glass method of solving problems. In this exercise one is told to drink half a glass of water, then put the half-empty glass down and go to sleep. Upon awakening, one should finish drinking the water (by now tepid and dusty), and the solution to the problem would present itself to the conscious mind.

Another method of solving problems was, as in *est*, to mentally construct a laboratory and people it with "laboratory technicians," male and female counselors or guides who would provide solutions to problems.

I usually finish what I start, but at moments during the training I was tempted to drop out. However, I was encouraged to continue by the trainer's stories about the remarkable feats that were regularly accomplished by virtue of the power inherent in "at level" consciousness. The trainer's stories, moreover, were corroborated by various graduates I met informally. These people regularly claimed to demonstrate capacities ranging from finding a parking place and changing traffic lights at will to curing cancer. One woman maintained that she could diagnose the difficulties with her car by concentrating on it, in her presumed alpha state, although she knows little about the mechanics of automobiles. Her daughter, an ingenuous, refreshing fifteen-year-old, told me matter-of-factly that with Mind Control she had cured her scoliosis, improved her eyesight, and brought her school grades up, all through concentrating upon and visualizing what she wanted to achieve. Another girl, who had had a motorcycle accident only a week before, showed me her wounds, which were extensive but seemed almost healed.

The second weekend included exercises designed to help us experience ourselves as members of the mineral, plant, and animal kingdoms. In these exercises we were mentally to insinuate ourselves into these kingdoms, the better to observe them from the exterior and in particular their interiors. Doing this with animals was especially valuable as an aid toward getting us acquainted with what was to be the climax of the work, the capacity to immerse ourselves mentally in human bodies, there to diagnose and perhaps heal their pathology. Although for this purpose one need not know the physiology or construction of animal, mineral, plant, or person, we did get a quick course in gross anatomy. And we learned a few apparently universal symbols; e.g., seeing white powder signifies arthritis, seeing a black spot on the brain signifies hypoglycemia, and a healthy liver looks shiny.

I remember thinking, "They are really serious, they really expect that one can diagnose illnesses without actually examining the person!" Spooky. Finally, with some four hours to go in the scheduled course, the moment came. The group broke up into units of two in which, alternately, each member was to be the psychic, the one who was to work the case, and the other was to be the "orientologist," the one who was to help him get into his trance, encourage the process along, then finally disclose information about the patient. The orientologist could select a case of anyone he knew (excluding the people in attendance there and himself) or pick from a stack of cards that had been filled out during previous Mind Control trainings. These cards bore the name, address, sex, and age of the subject on one side, and the relevant medical facts on the other. The psychic was told only the name, address, sex, and age of the subject. My partner, a high school mathematics teacher and part-time minister, and I shared our anxieties with each other. We were sure that we would be failures, even though the trainer had assured everyone that students are 85 per cent accurate. We would be able to do it, he said, perhaps not in every detail or every time. But we would often enough clearly demonstrate that we had the capacity to make physical diagnoses simply by visualizing a person mentally.

I tried to take verbatim notes of these cases worked on when I was the orientologist, and I requested that the orientologist for my cases take down what I said verbatim. Here are five cases in which I was the psychic, done on that first night. In all case examples the only information I was given was the patient's name, age, sex, and address.

CASE 1:

Psychic: "Arms outstretched, she is black, I see a curved thing from the left hip to the right armpit, now the lower back, the left side, above the buttock, where the kidney is, tilted left higher than right at the hip, she's crippled, the idea of falling, the experience of falling. The arms have receded in my mind, the tilted pelvis and hip dominate the picture. I feel sorry for her. She is in severe distress, a cripple, muscles are affected. I can't see her head. I can't make much of her head, that seems not important."

Facts: This woman has multiple sclerosis. She is severely crippled, has been in a walker for some years, and her internal organs are severely affected. The orientologist's wife, a nurse, helps her with a catheter. The orientologist himself visits her in his capacity as part-time minister. He describes her as a person who refuses to give up, has been given a death sentence a number of times but persists in living, is convinced that she is going to be cured.

Comments: My references to her being crippled, falling, her muscles being affected, seem to fit with multiple sclerosis. The arms outstretched, then receding in importance, may be related to the falling image and the use of the walker. The emphasis I put on the tilted pelvis and hip area, beginning with the left kidney, may be a reference to the impairment of her internal organs. I had a pronounced feeling of dismay and sympathy as I was visualizing her. I was wrong saying that she was black. My partner said that he at first thought his subject, just preceding this one, was black also, though he did not say so at the time. Did he communicate this to me telepathically, was blackness in the atmosphere between us? Perhaps her good mental attitude was reflected in my calling attention to the head not being important in this work of locating pathology.

CASE 2:

Psychic: "I see her lying down on a hospital bed with her legs drawn up, some suggestion of straps that hold legs as in broken legs, and her head is turned to the left. Her hands are immobilized, she is sucking on a bent straw. Reminds me of paralysis; she may even have been in an iron lung. I see her in white. Sad parents are around the bed. (How did she contract what she has?) She was bitten by something or swallowed something." I was asked to put on the patient's head, as if it were a helmet, in order to experience myself as the patient. I had the distinct feeling of sitting in the chair in a way that felt precarious to me. I said, "I feel myself sitting in a chair like a paraplegic, a wheelchair. Her hands are curled into fists—'why is this happening to me?' Either it is paralysis, or she is numbing her hands trying to control her rage."

Facts: The girl has polio, and was operated on for it. (I do not know whether she was in the hospital at the time I "saw" her, or when the card was filled out, or before that.)

CASE 3:

Psychic: I first briefly thought of a brain, then scanned areas of the body up and down, then focused clearly on the pelvis/thigh area. "A very small person, sorrow, he has painfully severe trouble." I talked of half-moon shapes up and down his body, thought that the hip-pelvic area included enlarged hips, and enlarged testicles. The last reminded me of elephantiasis, his "plucky heart" was enlarged, and his eyes were large and round, his prostate gland was enlarged. "All of this enlargement doesn't fit, he has something that a child should not have. Emotionally he's a wreck." I put on his head, as in putting on a helmet. "I thought of the trachea area, it is Y-shaped, I have a feeling of fear, hands were lifeless, symbols of suicide, his legs roped together at the knee, from knee to foot, another Y shape. His problem affects his entire body, but the most serious area is the hip-pelvic area. There is a black spot on the top right of the brain." (Where do nerves from brain go?) "This nerve leads to the left side, the left hip." (Describe him.) "He has sandy hair, glasses, and brown eyes."

Facts: This child suffered a gunshot wound in the pelvic area which necessitated the amputation of his left leg. He has blue eyes.

Comments: He indeed has something wrong with him that a child should not have—a gunshot wound. The Y shape, with the legs locked together, suggested his body with one remaining leg. The fear I felt may have been the fear of the gunshot or what the boy is experiencing with regard to his amputation.

CASE 4:

Psychic: "Arms extended as in a crucifixion, dark cavernous eyes, head seen as a skull, he is blind to something. He has a muscular chest, hairy, but the left shoulder and chest are turning black, deteriorating, like gangrene, the shoulder is slipping down, the left hand is dangling, and now I see his toes, the bottom of his feet. He is on a bar like a gorilla on a trapeze. His chin is stuck out, a blue beard, once strong and handsome, but now has sexual problems, a feeling of weakness, feminine identification, all of which he covers up with a display of masculinity. Difficulty with his penis, gonorrhea, impotence. General problems with sexual life, something eating away at him, the lower half of his body. I see him afraid and suspicious, but determined to carry on, will not acknowledge his problems."

Facts: This man was in an accident and severely injured his left foot.

Comments: I had the injury on the left side, and implicated the feet, though I made early references to a dangling hand and slipping-down shoulder. The orientologist knew nothing of any specific sexual symptoms but said he has a general feeling of inadequacy, which he handles with a masculine sexual display. He is unable to get close to women, has been married two times unsuccessfully, and tries one woman after another.

CASE 5:

Psychic: I first saw his breasts enlarged and white, which made me think of what happens after treatment for cancer of the prostate with stilbestrol, arms outstretched, body whitish and flabby. This probable ratiocination of mine moved away in favor of a clear image of "the right side of the body dropping down at right angles to the shoulder, a clean drop between the neck and shoulder halfway up the neck. The whole right side of the body is squashed together. He seems fairly small, five foot six, flabby, dressed in dungarees or overalls. Face on the right side has an indentation as far as the nose. The head is half shot away, right side. Small area on left side between chin and nose. He is an absolute mess. I saw the upper left artery and a triangle below the eye. If it was brain damage, it was right-sided. (See any colors?) White, red, green bands around injury on the right side. More I think about this man the worse shape he's in on the right side. I see white work gloves, which would go with the dungarees."

Facts: This man suffered a heart attack which has left him a "vegetable."

Comments: If he is indeed a vegetable, then it is likely that his brain is severely involved, as I seem to be implying by seeing injuries to the head. The dropped-down, squashed-together chest is certainly suggestive of a heart attack, but I saw it on the right side. I kept incorrectly emphasizing the right side.

CASE 6:

Here is a case done by my partner as psychic of a person known to me. I acted as orientologist.

Psychic: "Bushy hair, not heavy, but a well-rounded body, breasts enlarged, one of them or both of them. No organ seems to stand out, but I am centered on the heart. Something about the joints, red streaks or bands on the joints. Head, nose—no, the problem is not in the head. The chest area, there is a brightness around the heart, things are flowing freely, as being washed. I'm trying to hold the heart in my hands. I feel a rapid pulsing in the heart when I'm holding it. The liver is shiny and so I assume it is normal, there is a spot somewhere below the stomach. (What stands out?) The strongest part is the joints, the cushions between the knee joints are dark, the right elbow, something rigid."

Facts: This person was suffering from high blood pressure at the time. Three days later her blood pressure was normal.

Comments: The initial remark about bushy hair seems significant in that the person had recently had her hair cut, an act which was of great psychological significance, and she complained that one part of her hair stuck up: "It is bushy." She does in fact have a well-rounded body with large breasts. The part-time-minister psychic said later that he had made his initial comment about her not being heavy because he was a bit embarrassed at the voluptuousness he "saw." Not seeing organs as standing out may have been a reference to not being able to see specific difficulties. Although he ended up by centering his greatest interest in the joints, his talk of red streaks, things flowing freely, rapid pulsing in the heart, and his centering on the heart are suggestive of high blood pressure.

CASE 7:

This case was done with the leader of the group as the psychic, while walking down the hall of the hotel, without his apparently even attempting to get into a trance. I was the orientologist.

Psychic: "Throbbing, pulsating chest mainly, like she is scared, a shimmering of blood vessels, hypertension. She's not like that type of person, a quiet type of person, I'm not attracted to organs, to the circulatory system. . . . With respect to her mind she is fairly bright but feels she could be a lot smarter, use more of what she has . . . tiredness. . . . A tremendous amount of symptoms, again a pounding in the chest . . . either irregular, erratic, or comes and goes. . . . The word 'milk.' . . . She's got a depressive syndrome, from her intelligence, a stickman type of image, like a spaghetti man, like a puppet, symbology. . . . She feels treated like a puppet . . . something in the chest. . . . I'm concerned mostly about blood, the way the heart is reacting, the blood is seen as watery or thin. . . . 'Milk' leads to eyeballs. . . . Depressions which come and go, they hit hard, they stay and let go. . . . Mainly it is blood and tiredness, anemia-like symptoms but not anemia. . . . Lack of protein."

Facts: This person had symptoms of anorexia nervosa.

Comments: At the time, this person consistently minimized her abilities, clearly felt she should be smarter. She had a variety of psychological and physical symptoms; one could say with only some exaggeration that she had "a tremendous amount of symptoms." She was subject to depression, which strikingly came and went. The stickman, puppet idea may have been a reference to her thinness from inadequate diet, or to the suggested experience of anorectic patients, that they are controlled by others. She did not have hypertension or circulatory difficulties. But she was tired, possibly in part from anemia. Certainly her diet was deficient in protein.

Consistent with a general principle of Mind Control—that one should never leave a situation in a "negative" condition—we were instructed to correct what we had discovered was wrong. We could imagine any cure that seemed appropriate; for example, blowing away the white powder that signified arthritis.

The Mind Control people are in utter earnest in expecting healing to take place. According to the leader, it ordinarily takes three days, and in one instance he planned repeated "treatments" every three days for a week.

We were told that psychic skill improves with practice. For example, José Silva writes that one should not participate as a psychic in research on the validity of Mind Control until he has done at least two hundred cases. The leader did a case with much less effort and greater precision than the students. Without practice the skill is said to atrophy. So these cases are presumably less accurate than subsequent ones would be.

Below are the instructions that we fledgling orientologists followed with our psychic partners.

1. a. Enter your basic level by the 3 to 1, 10 to 1 method. [Meaning count backward from 3 to 1 or 10 to 1, as you wish]
   b. If you have worked cases before, review a case that you were accurate on before working a new one.
   c. Let me know when you are ready. (When ready, continue.)
   d. I will now count from 10 to 1 to allow your mind to adjust to the specific level where you are going to be accurate and correct on the problem case that I am going to present to you. 10, 9, 8, 7, 6, 5, 4, 3, 2, 1. Your mind has now adjusted to the specific level where you are going to be accurate and correct on the case I am going to present to you.
2. a. At the count of 3, the image of the body of *name, age, address,* and *sex* will be on your screen.
   b. 1 - 2 - 3 (snap fingers). The image of the body of *name, age, address,* and *sex* is on your screen.
   c. Sense it, (Pause) feel it, (Pause) visualize it, (Pause) imagine it, (Pause) create it, (Pause) know it is there, (Pause) take it for granted it is there.
   d. Scan the body with your intelligence from where you know the head is to the feet, up and down, up and down, several times rapidly.

e. While scanning the image of the body in this manner, allow your intelligence indirectly to select three areas of greatest attraction (Pause).
f. Maintain the rate of scanning at one a second and mention to me the areas of attraction as they come to you.
g. This is a practice session; at this time let your experience come forth. Accuracy comes with practice.

As can be seen from these instructions, there is opportunity for the orientologist to reinforce diagnostic inferences that could have come about through chance and thus in effect to guide the psychic toward the correct information. Moreover, the instruction to say what comes to mind, to keep talking, increases the possibility of chance correctness to be reinforced and guided. At least one research supports that possibility.[3] Under the double-blind conditions of this research—that is, with the orientologist as well as the psychic unaware of the patient-subject's pathology—success in making diagnoses was no better than chance. When the orientologist knew the diagnosis, results were significantly positive. One could conclude from this study that success was due to cues that the orientologist gave, even without being aware he was doing so. Another possibility, of course, would be that the orientologist was giving the psychic information telepathically. This would be a somewhat different phenomenon from the one that Mind Control purports to demonstrate, though in itself a demonstration of psychic power.

The cases I have cited here could have been chosen from a far more numerous group of cases of obvious failure, thus creating the impression one could do as well as these cases any time. In fact I did choose those cases that encouraged me to believe that something was going on beyond chance. I was the psychic on eight or so the first night, and my partner approximately a half dozen. After our initial three or four cases, we were left on our own to do as many more as we wanted. I did not keep careful track of the totals, but I can report that, in my cases at least, the apparent successes far outnumbered the few clear failures. With regard to the trainer the case cited was one success out of one. But, whatever the statistics, when one considers the odds against being accurate (always keeping in mind the possibility of inadvertent guiding by the orientologist), then even a few cases of success at least stake a claim on our consideration of the possibility that information can be gotten psychically.

While doing the cases as a psychic, I often felt that I was forcing apparently random images. But then certain images, often areas of the person visualized, became sharply clear, like a suddenly lightening screen, and these seem to have been the most accurate. This experience suggests that random, chance guesses give way to real phenomena.

Throughout the Mind Control training, as we were going to level and performing various stunts, our brains were supposedly producing alpha waves. Mind Control offers several gadgets said to demonstrate this. With one of these, Mind Control Trainer I, one straps two fingers to the electrodes on a machine that emits rapid beeps, and one knows when he's gone to level when he slows the rate of beeping. Another machine, Trainer I PLUS, is hooked to a tape recorder you can "mentally" turn on by going to level, again by way of electrodes on your fingers. Presumably this altered state of consciousness allows you better to register and learn any material that the recorder plays. It is, indeed, a rather spooky experience merely through mental concentration to turn on a piece of machinery.

Whether or not alpha brain waves have anything to do with this remains unsubstantiated. Both these machines are based on the old standby in academic psychology laboratories, the galvanic skin response, or GSR. The electrodes react simply to changes in moisture on the skin. So going to level does demonstrate that one can change one's galvanic skin responsivity. No study was adduced by Mind Control that demonstrated a relationship between GSR and alpha brain waves.

In principle such a study ought not to be difficult to design. Mind Control has, on paper, a research wing. It cites in its literature a couple of studies offering some evidence that Mind Control induction methods do result in an increase of alpha. The hypotheses wait to be picked like little fruit hanging from overburdened trees, but as far as I can tell, little hard-headed research is produced. This may matter in the upper echelons of Mind Control, where academia and research are treated with reverence. To most of the Mind Control graduates I think it hardly matters at all. They either believe the pseudoscientific material offered in the lectures, or do not care one way or the other. "Science" makes no difference to those whom Mind Control has failed to help, while to those who have demonstrated hitherto unknown capacities in themselves to do things or to live better, it may matter even less.

Do psychotherapists practice a kind of Mind Control induction with their quiet voices and subdued offices? Do psychoanalysts increase this effect, perhaps greatly, by having their patients lie down on a couch, not even to be stimulated by a face-to-face view of the analyst? As a result of Mind Control, I was more sensitive than before to the state of consciousness of my patients as this varied with the kind of material they brought, the mood they were in, the events they were anticipating or reacting to. The genesis of psychoanalysis, after all, was hypnosis. After Freud gave up hypnosis for free association, he tried for a while to stimulate associations by placing his hands gently on the patient's forehead to promote relaxation. The characteristics of the psychoanalytic situation that encouraged an altered state of consciousness are legacies of this relaxing, hypnotic "going to level." The purpose of the psychoanalytic office conditions, which minimize distractions, is to enable the patient to relax his attentive hold on the external world, to promote the assertion of the inner world, to encourage thoughts and feelings ordinarily held in abeyance by directed attention and external distraction.

Every psychoanalytic patient, indeed every person, is somewhere on a continuum of consciousness, not just awake or asleep. In principle, when the patient is "deeper," "at level," or "in an altered state of consciousness," his thoughts ought to be more free and therefore more meaningful for the purposes of exploration and expressiveness. The analyst encourages this freedom at times simply by his silence, soft voice, or spare use of words. Yet at other times he may, for one or another purpose, raise his voice in volume and talk more. One of the main reasons for making this shift is to offer explanatory formulations, or interpretations. At these moments the patient no longer drifts in reverie the better to let ideas come to mind. He actively attempts to organize, integrate, synthesize, and learn new meaning and new perspectives. Perhaps such cognitions best take place when the person shifts his consciousness to ordinary, daily, problem-solving beta brain waves. Yet it may be that such learning takes place better in an altered state of consciousness in which thoughts and feelings are encouraged free production. Or maybe, for some kinds of interpretations, with some kinds of analysts and some kinds of patients, requirements are different for efficiency and durability of learning. In short, what state of consciousness best facilitates learning in psychoanalysis? It has not been an issue much dealt with in conventional psychoanalytic education and thinking. It may be irrelevant, or it may be an important uncontrolled variable. Whatever the answer to that may be, it is an example of how the experimentation in new therapies raises issues for conventional therapies.

I wondered, too, about the alleged effects of transmission of information apart from the five senses on the psychoanalytic treatment process and the psychological testing process. I was to wonder, off and on, many times afterward, to what extent, when asking for an association, I was at the same time inadvertently providing one. Sometimes, when asking for associations, I was unaware of having any in mind. But at other times I had one or more hypotheses as to what meaning a particular element in a dream or thought had to the patient. If my state of consciousness was in a "sending" condition, and the patient's was in a "receiving" condition, could I not transmit this information? As to my intuition, insightfulness, psychological-mindedness, perceptiveness, the ability to understand layered meanings of appearance, behavior, and thought in patients, that skill so often prized by psychotherapists and prized and feared by others—could that skill be thought of as stemming simply from a well-tuned receiver of "psychic" messages transmitted by the patient? This might help explain the experience of knowing without knowing how one knows, which occurs in doing psychotherapy (and elsewhere).

What part would such a process play in the administering and taking of psychological tests? I was reminded of the peculiar feeling I had often had in giving the Word Association Test, of somehow knowing what response the patient was going to make. Could I to any extent have transmitted those responses or was I picking them up in advance of the patient's enunciating them? When I administered the test in the course of my doctoral research, my career depended (or at least I anxiously thought it did) on patients giving responses that confirmed my hypothesis. Surely, here was a situation in which, if I could possibly influence responses, I was highly motivated to do so. I remember consciously hoping, one might say even mentally urging, patients to respond in desired ways. The test procedure I successfully used at that time has never been as effective for me since. That may be just because I have used it with different patient populations. But I never have quite been able to rid myself of the feeling that there was something in the situation of that research, charged with need, desire, and enthusiasm, that contributed to its results.

The Hunzas, of Kashmir, are often cited by nutritionists as evidence that proper diet will allow human beings to remain healthy and vigorous for well over one hundred years. The Mind Control trainer pointed out that, in addition to having a different diet from most other people, Hunzas meditate frequently during the day. So, if playing with psychic phenomena doesn't turn you on enough, how about living to the age of 125? Not only that, of course, but if you follow Mind Control principles, the long life you will then have will be healthy and enjoyable.

Apart from the guest seminars, which offer samples of Mind Control to encourage people to sign up for the course, every couple of months Mind Control offers meetings, usually free, to graduates. These may feature outside speakers or lectures by the trainer, along with some practice in "going to level." The topics range across human potential interests, especially those of a psychic sort. One of those I attended was a lecture and discussion of pyramidology. This discipline is based on the assertion that the form of the great pyramids of Egypt is a repository of occult powers. This was why their builders chose to use them for their mausoleums. One of the people I met at this meeting later showed me some vegetables that had been placed under a homemade paper pyramid; these vegetables were larger and healthier than comparable vegetables kept the same length of time without a pyramid over them.

In another graduate meeting I received my introduction to Kirlian photography, and have a color print of my fingers as a souvenir. The Kirlian procedure is painless and, with easily observed precautions, safe. There are variations in the apparatus. The one used to photograph me required total darkness and the putting of my hand on a copper plate. A few seconds of electricity, and a Polaroid print emerged of what I have no reason to doubt are my fingers, complete with aura radiating from them. Some human potential theorists cite the aura as evidence that we are not bounded by our skins, a view that fits with the ancient conception of the universe as being composed of patterns of cosmic energy, nothing separate, nothing hard, simply various swirling manifestations of the same fundamental "substance." Modern physics supports this model with its view of matter as subatomic particles in constant movement. This conception of the universe provides a context for better understanding unbounded movement of information as purportedly demonstrated by Silva Mind Control.

Mind Control people take seriously the power to heal at a distance. The trainer told me he had, on his own initiative, been at work trying to heal one of the cases I had tried to diagnose psychically. He had the whole group consolidate their healing energy and send it on a healing mission to a relative of one of the graduates. The motorcycle victim mentioned earlier said that her partner in the accident was scheduled to have his leg amputated. However, after she had organized a collective distance healing for him, much to the surgeon's surprise it was no longer necessary to amputate his leg.

While Mind Control does not offer the great array of graduate seminars *est* offers, it does occasionally offer extensions of the basic Mind Control training. One of these was led by José Silva in Kansas City, and while I was unable to attend the week-long course, I did manage to meet him there. He is a short, stocky man who looks to me to be in his early sixties. The first time I saw him, he was wearing a modish slack suit. Topping this off with an old-fashioned "butch" haircut seemed to capture perfectly the uneasy juxtaposition in Mind Control of the human potential futurisms and the old-fashioned "verities." Fundamentalist radicalism, if you can imagine such a thing. If Werner Erhard looks like the cat who swallowed the canary, José Silva looks like a rabbit enjoying himself. His generous jowls and dancing eyes seem to revel—in his discoveries? in his success? in his joy of parenthood? (He is the father of some ten children as well as hundreds of thousands of Mind Control graduates.) Shortly after our first meeting I received the invitation to address the annual International Convention in its administrative home in Laredo.

The atmosphere there was, indeed, that of one big happy family. I met the mother of my trainer, who herself was a Mind Control trainer and an all-purpose psychic. The program itself was at times one of numbing boredom.

The "rah-rah" was almost palpable. The fulsome and reverential introductions to one or another Mind Control functionary seemed to me far beyond the contributions offered. One encomium and hackneyed speech followed another, hour after hour for almost two days.

I suppose there were those who were bored by my talk, but not through any lack of trying on my part. I had a good many things I felt like saying and thought needed to be said. I expressed sincerely my gratitude to Mind Control for opening up for me the possibilities of psychic phenomena; I tried to put psychic phenomena in the context of human potential exploration, society's movement toward overcoming illusory limitations, people's attempts to explore and exploit capacities, however much these alleged capacities may fly in the face of conventional views about the nature of man and his abilities. I also appreciated being offered by Mind Control more examples of how the conscious mind can be exploited to help people live better. But, a little uneasily, I reminded the group of the unconscious mind, which in many of us has its way no matter what kinds of self-improvement we employ consciously. If we really believe in coming to terms with ourselves as whole persons, then both have to be taken into consideration. Competition founded on parochial professionalism is the enemy of us all. A scientific attitude followed up by a sober application in research could help us learn which people would benefit in which ways from what. I suggested that the scientific method might be a better way to advance man's betterment than separate groups behaving as if each had the final word.

It was not your standard patriotic Mind Control speech of the day. For some, I daresay, it lay there on the program like a dead fish. Others probably heard what they liked and didn't hear what they didn't like or want to deal with. And some people may have gotten the messages I intended to send and tried to make use of them. If the last is so, then Silva Mind Control and I have made a fair exchange.

PART FOUR

Go East, Young Robot

14

Climbing the Himalaya in Chicago—Yoga

BEFORE MY EXPLORATIONS began, yoga for me was something that women did in the evening in black leotards as part of their unending struggle to lose weight. Or it was Bernarr MacFadden standing on his head and holding out the promise that you, too, could live to be ninety, and perhaps become a wealthy owner of magazines, by standing on your head and eating only fruits, nuts, and vegetables. Or it had to do with people walking on burning coals or sleeping on a bed of nails, and Tyrone Power searching the Himalaya for Self, in 20th Century-Fox's production of Somerset Maugham's *The Razor's Edge.*

East is East and West is West is the way it used to be. Now East has invaded West; Eastern mystical traditions have provided inspiration, ideas, and practices to the human potential movement. Like Ram Dass, I could have made a pilgrimage to India to study the source. But, for my immediate purposes, that trip to the razor's edge was unnecessary. Ram Dass and others had paved the way for a procession of holy men and teachers from India to the United States. One of these was Shri Swami Rama, who founded the Himalayan Institute, in Glenville, Illinois, outside of Chicago. The aim of this institute, to quote from one of its brochures, "is to teach meditation techniques for the personal growth of modern people in their society, to make known the harmonious view of world religions and philosophies, and to undertake scientific research for the benefit of humanity." To implement these aims, the Institute offers therapy programs, biofeedback-meditation training, seminars, and workshops, and runs a graduate school that awards the M.A. and Ph.D. in yoga psychology and philosophy. Every three months, it holds a four-day training program for counselors and therapists. In this program the staff of physicians, psychologists, and counselors offer an understanding of the basics of Eastern and Western methods of treating mental and physical disturbances through lectures and through an experience of living and practicing yoga.

Each of my voyages to new-therapy centers required something of a wrench for me to free myself of my patients, schedule, and family, and to counteract those conservative instincts in me that railed against something new and disorienting. But the opportunity to study at the Himalayan Institute created additional resistances. I first had to get past my irrational and unfair prejudice against a drove of foreign holy men come to give the word. I tended to experience what may well be their tranquillity and composure as pompousness and arrogance, grandiosity posing as humility. Further, I do not like beards and men who wear dresses, even should the latter be called flowing robes. Topping it off was the news that in lieu of "regular dormitory space," I was requested to bring bedding, the better to sleep on the floor of the "Wisdom" room (women slept in "Peace," while we all studied in the main lecture room, "Bliss").

In the course of my many trips, I had become acclimated to motels. A Holiday Inn provides a passable welcome at the end of an airplane flight and a handy launching pad toward new adventures. But never before did a Holiday Inn seem so inviting as when I considered the prospect of dragging blankets through an air voyage, the better to curl up on the floor in communal sleeping. Muttering something about hardship pay, I borrowed my daughter's sleeping bag.*

The saving grace was that there was precious little time to squat, lounge, or otherwise try to be comfortable on the floor. The fourteen-hour day began at seven in the morning with instructions and practice of asanas, Sanskrit for "easy" or "comfortable." Asanas are hatha-yoga exercises designed to enable the student to assume an easy, comfortable position, the better to practice meditation free of distracting aches, pains, or cramps.

These exercises involve stretching parts of the body for as long as one can without strain—without excessive strain, maybe. It was clear from the instructions of the group leader that one should stretch to a point just short of discomfort, and hold it there. The exercises have such names as "cobra," in which, face down on the floor, you elevate your head and upper torso snake style, and "jackknife," in which you grasp your ankles with legs and elbows on the floor. Sarvangasana, meaning "all members' posture," is so named because it is supposed to benefit all parts of the body—arms, chest, shoulders, back, abdominal muscles—and to slim the legs and hips. It places gentle traction on the cervical vertibrae, keeping them flexible, and drains the veins of the legs, which is said to be especially good for varicose veins. It increases blood pressure and mechanical

* The Himalayan Institute has since moved its headquarters to Honesdale, Pennsylvania, where individual rooms are now provided to seminar participants.

pressure in the neck, which is supposed to improve the functioning of the thyroid and parathyroid glands, thus regulating body weight and metabolism. It also provides an opportunity to observe and learn diaphragmatic breathing. It is supposed to be a panacea for internal-organ ailments, especially those of old age, allegedly combating indigestion, constipation, degeneration of endocrine glands, a variety of problems of the liver, gall bladder, kidney, pancreas, spleen, and digestive system, as well as for healing acute and chronic throat ailments. No wonder that sarvangasana is called the "Queen of Asanas." This is how to do it.

1. Lie down on the back with arms at the sides, palms down and feet together.
2. Exhale, slowly raising both legs straight up until they are perpendicular to the floor. Lift the hips off the floor and bring the feet to the floor behind the head.
3. Place the palms as high up on the back as possible with fingers toward the center of the back, keeping the elbows in as close together as possible, not wider than the shoulders.
4. Exhaling, raise both legs straight up.
5. Keep the legs straight by tightening the back hamstrings of the legs and buttock muscles. Keep the stomach pulled in. The whole body should be straight and perpendicular to the floor.
6. Hold to your capacity. In order to gain the full benefits of the posture, hold one or two minutes at the beginning and work up to five.
7. Lower the arms to the floor, palms down. Slowly come down, one vertebra at a time, lowering the back to the floor.

8. Inhale and lower the legs to the floor.
9. Relax and breathe deeply, lying flat on the back.

These exercises were followed by instruction and practice in breathing. Pranayama, the science of breathing, implements the common observation that breathing often reflects emotions, as in the heavy breathing of passion, the breathlessness of excitement or suspense. Exercises in breathing are designed to rid the body of such emotional responses and thereby promote relaxation. Increasing the amount of oxygen and decreasing the amount of carbon dioxide is supposed also to be generally beneficial to health. (Breathing is also good for anxiety. Before stepping on the stage, asking the boss for a raise, or proposing marriage, take several deep breaths. It will work wonders.)

But breathing, in yoga, is not only an aid to relaxation for purposes of daily living. Rather, breathing is a stimulus for levels of consciousness, one means of achieving higher consciousness. How breathing is done helps determine how the person thinks, feels, lives; it is not just the inhalation and exhalation of air. Breath is energy (prana), and so breathing energizes the system. Prana underlies all activity, physical and mental. Like Freud's psychosexual stages of libido, prana is arranged roughly in ascending order of developmental sophistication. As a bridge between the mental and the physical, its source is physical but with development it moves toward the mental, ultimately achieving a balanced and harmonious distribution uniting body and mind. Exercises in breathing are designed to abet the flow of energy through the vertically ordered pathways.

Once its ultimate work is done and the person reaches the highest state of consciousness (samadhi), breathing can even stop. Yogis have demonstrated their ability to get along without breathing for periods of time that in a non-yogi would result in death.

Here are basic breathing exercises with which to prepare for meditation.

1. *The complete breath:* Exhale completely and slowly. Then inhale for a count of 16, or as close as you can come, then exhale again for the same count as your inhalation. Breathe through your nostrils, rather than your mouth, using your diaphragm and stomach muscles. Repeat three to seven times.
2. *Alternate-nostril breathing:* Place the index and middle fingers of your right hand between your two eyebrows. Rest your ring and little finger gently against your left nostril near the lower edge. Place your thumb on your right nostril near the lower edge. (Be careful! If you have the same difficulty following directions that I do, you may asphyxiate yourself. Press gently so that at least one nostril remains open.) Now block the right nostril with your thumb and exhale slowly from the open left nostril, counting to six as you exhale. Now inhale for another count of six. Exhale and inhale through the left nostril two more times. Now close the left nostril with your little and ring fingers and open the right nostril, exhaling for six seconds and then inhaling for the same amount of time. Repeat this two more times. When breath flows equally through both nostrils, you are promised calm and joy. For me, calm sort of; joy requires more than this.

It was now 8:00 A.M., and I was theoretically in condition for the meditation, which followed.

Meditation, in yoga, is not just another technique, although it is a technique. It is central to the practice and therefore to the quality of a yogi's life, the key to the consciousness toward which yogis strive.

For now, once over lightly with respect to meditation. We shall soon return to this important subject, to discuss meditation generally and other meditational practices as well as yoga.

Yoga meditation is a way of turning off the yammering of the senses, which prevent achieving unity with the "Cosmic Mind," the "inner light," our "true nature." Those who can achieve the highest states of meditation, who are able to follow the light to its source with undivided attention, are promised bliss and unbounded joy.

While we at the seminar had specifically prepared ourselves for meditation through the physical and breathing exercises, the context of our training during this weekend was, in part, a preparation and implementation of meditation. In keeping with the intent of turning off stimulation from the senses, we lived in an isolated community, without newspapers or television or trips away from the Institute. We lived an austere life, mainly work and study. We eschewed those foods yogis consider stimulating. This way of life was designed to enable us better to perform the central meditative technique of giving the mind one simple thought upon which it may be centered. The thought may be on sounds in the environment, or the spaces between sounds, as in Tibetan meditation; breathing and the movement of the diaphragm, as in Buddhist meditation, or upon a specific word or sound, as in yoga or transcendental meditation.

What does it mean that I now cannot remember what I concentrated upon during the meditations at the Institute? For one thing, it means that I have done too many meditations, of too many different varieties, to keep them all straight, which is exactly the kind of stimulus overload that meditation is designed to prevent. But in fact it hardly matters which I used. The purpose is only to develop "one-pointed" concentration on whatever the focus is.

That is easier said than done. Other thoughts intrude, so that it is difficult to maintain the focus. The meditation may turn into either a pleasant reverie or an attempt to solve problems presented by the errant thoughts. According to yoga teachings, such thoughts are spurred by unfulfilled wishes. Maintaining focus allows the mind to transcend such wishes and their interfering stimulation.

It is now 9:00 A.M. and those of us still hooked more on the body than the spirit are getting hungry. While yogis understand that meditation is liable to be interfered with if the meditator is starving to death, they seem more concerned at the possibility that meditation will be interfered with through overeating, as well as by eating the wrong foods. To insure against such eventualities, our diet was one meal, at midday, and two "teas," or light meals, one in the morning and one in the evening. I do not know whether it was according to a principle of austerity or not, but we were to serve ourselves and eat standing up or stretched out on the floor wherever in the compound we wished. The food itself was in keeping with yogic recommendations. Such allegedly stimulating foods as meat, spices, and eggs were not served. Also avoided were those foods that lead to lethargy through having their "life force" removed through spoilage or refinement, for example sugar and white flour, foods with preservatives, pickled foods, and leftovers. Instead, we subsisted on fruits, nuts, and seeds, raw and cooked vegetables, brown rice, and herb tea. Since, at the time, I was pursuing a macrobiotic diet (to be discussed), which conforms to all these principles, I had the rare opportunity of eating everything served. I was awarded a feeling of special nobility inadvertently by some of my colleagues, who, by the third night, had slipped out for a pizza.

After breakfast, and again after evening tea, there were lectures on yoga psychology. While the seminar was, as advertised, experiential in that we participated in a number of yoga practices and styles of life, it differed sharply from "experiential weekends" as practiced by human potential groups. In our midwestern Himalaya there was no hesitancy about immersion in textbook material. Also, no premium was put on self-disclosure or experiencing feelings. The only opportunity for the latter was in a couple of hours of "yoga encounter workshops." These workshops were designed along the lines of any human potential encounter meeting. People sat around on the floor, and the "leader" and "co-leader" opened the proceedings by offering the goal of learning to know oneself and relate oneself to others through free expression; when necessary they tried to nudge the process along. What this had to do with yoga was never made clear to me. I spent much of the time attempting to figure out where the leader and his coleader's ineptness began and where the possibly confusing mixture of yoga atmosphere and human potential techniques ended; which was more responsible for the fizzle? During this meeting, fresh from the lectures on the sublime, the new dimensions of human experience promised by yoga practices, I thought darkly that whatever you do you have to know what you're doing.

Another somewhat jarring expression of the mixture of the old and the new, the East and the West, came in the sessions on biofeedback. Hard on the halls of Peace, Wisdom, and Bliss, in this ancient, contemplative atmosphere, were machines with glowing dials, shiny knobs, nervous pointers, all encased in warm walnut, the sort of thing that draws crowds to stereo stores on Saturday afternoon.

I was told to lie down, present my head for electrodes to be attached to it, and through meditation enter an altered state of consciousness. In this state my brain presumably would be emitting alpha waves, as was alleged to occur during the meditations prescribed during Silva Mind Control as well. I then was to attempt, with my mind alone, to control the pointer on a dial. I was warned that the more I "tried," in the usual Western fashion, the less successful I would be. But should I simply allow myself to move the pointer, it would move, and indeed that is exactly what happened. I at first "tried" to move the pointer according to what I had learned, namely not to try. (The Western mind at work outsmarting the competition.) But trying not to try is the same as trying; just check with any electronic pointer. Only when I pretty much gave up on the task in frustration and figured I would just lie back and enjoy rolling with the alpha waves did the pointer take off in the desired direction. It is like the old description of psychotherapy: psychotherapy resembles feeding pigeons in the park; go toward them and they run away, stay still and they alight on your shoulder. It is like aikido, the Japanese martial art of self-defense in which one "defeats" one's opponent by moving in the same direction as he, rather than by opposing him. It is like a good salesman or diplomat, finding areas of agreement and side-stepping conflict. Through indirection, you let developments come about as you want them. Or, as the yogis would say, you are never more effective than when you are detached, the special yogic way of "not caring." None of this would be news to those who practice "reverse psychology"; e.g., a child threatens to run away, and the parent says to be sure to close the door on the way out.

Silence can be of many kinds. For example, the psychoanalytic patient who is silent may be angrily refusing to join in the agreed-upon task, may be enjoying a quiet time with his analyst, may be organizing and preparing his thoughts, or may simply be temporarily unhinged by some strong feeling and unable to find words. Yoga's attempt to encourage silence is another way of trying to achieve a meditative state of mind. If the pursuit of higher consciousness is hampered by incessant, often indiscriminate, stimuli, then turning off such stimuli, through living in a silent environment, enables one to listen better to one's own internal stimuli. So we observed silence daily from 5:30 to 7:30 P.M. and after 10:00 P.M. In addition we lived in silence from Saturday evening until Monday morning. (A pad and pencil were available for emergencies, and dispensation was made for asking questions in lectures and workshops.)

I did indeed find these periods of silence pleasant and tranquilizing. I tend, perhaps more than some other people, to find it easy and comfortable to go to a quiet, private place inside even when I am busily active. Silence may not be as pleasant for others. Periodically, I found silence to be stimulating as well as restful. In part that may be one reason why I broke silence to spend some of the quiet periods walking along with my pocket recorder, dictating thoughts as they freshly emerged. Personal style or a touch of misanthropy aside, silence is likely to provide a refuge from draining, low-level noise and the jabbing intrusions that divert attention outward and sometimes smother indwelling thoughts.

Those yogis who have not as yet achieved a state of consciousness high enough to control base feelings probably laugh in derision as they observe the "new" therapies. What's new, they might ask, in the human potential movement's assertions of wisdom and teaching practices long indigenous to yoga? What's new, of course, is the packaging, the distribution, and the amalgamation of millennia-old yoga ideas with the newly evolved human potential forms. Let us look at some of the ways yoga ideas are comparable to human potential ones.

The human potential downgrading of the objective, physical, and materialistic in favor of the subjective, mental, and sublime is basic to the yoga way of life.

Members of the human potential movement mend the Cartesian mind-body split by working with the body as well as the mind and by trying to relate themselves to people and experience them as whole. In Eastern thought, body is merely an expression of consciousness, a congealed field of energy, part of the person as a universal system.

As noted in Part One, the quasi-neurological wing of the human potential movement has asserted the "split-brain hypothesis": that the left and right sides of the brain are suited for different functions and that equal efficiency of both would result in a personality and style of thinking distinguished by harmony as well as effectiveness. In yoga much is made of the difference between characteristics of the left part of the body and those of the right part of the body. As we have seen, a basic breathing exercise is to block off one nostril at a time and breathe through the other one until the breath is flowing equally through both nostrils. When this is accomplished, ". . . you will find that you become calm and joyful."[1] If one is angry, one should breathe out the left nostril, for the right side is passive and peaceful. If one is depressed, one should breathe out the right nostril to activate one's active and aggressive side. The significance of left and right runs through the alternative therapies, as it does in the Jungian alternative to Freudian psychoanalysis.

The Eastern idea of struggling to *be*, as contrasted to

acting a role, surfaces in the new therapies' emphasis on finding oneself, eschewing the false selves we build up for purposes of defense. For example, in psychosynthesis there is alleged to be a "temple of self" which exists underneath and within the accumulated layers of social being.

Throughout the alternative therapies there is a shared understanding that we are more than our five senses, that our senses deliver to us only a portion of reality; or, as the yogis would say, our higher consciousness transcends sense data just as it transcends body, space, and time limitations.

The Gestalt Prayer epitomizes the belief that people do best when they maintain an optimal distance between themselves and other people and interests. The resulting steady, unruffled feeling is explicit in the yogic idea of detachment. When too closely attached, we are caught up in acquisition and maintenance, vulnerable to vicissitudes of gain and loss. Usually we are so engrossed in these pursuits that we lose sight of the values, purposes, and pleasures inherent in persons, objects, and situations in themselves. Both yogis and new therapists say that we do our thing and let the other do his thing, and work out a harmonious getting together if that is in the cards; and if not, that is the way of it.

Alternative therapists ordinarily do not strive to have their patients walk on coals, sleep on a bed of nails, or stop their heart from beating for extended periods, but they have been inspired by these feats to exploit "powers of the mind," powers that surface in altered states of consciousness. For example, the Simontons attempt to help patients reverse cancer growths by exploiting such powers (see Part Five). In human potential psychotherapy there is a strong emphasis on what can be accomplished if one simply sets one's mind to it.

Among these powers of the mind is expectation. We live

in a reality created by our minds, so if we expect something to occur it is more likely to occur than if it is not part of our reality and therefore not expected. One way to overcome cancer, according to the Simontons, is to expect to overcome it. One way to become the person you want to be is to believe that you have the capacity, that the ideal person lives within you, is part of your reality. This line of reasoning stems from the yogic belief that reality is a construction of the self. Our reality is shared by many, because they are subject to the same limitations of sensory input; we all agree that a tree is solid, because we are unable to observe, without an electron microscope, that it is composed of moving particles.

If we create our reality, then we are indeed responsible for everything. A highly evolved yogi would never be under a falling brick. That "accident" would never happen to him, because, responsible for his reality as he is, he would have anticipated its falling and moved elsewhere. As we have seen in so many different contexts, human potential thinking revolves around this central idea of self-responsibility; our problems are not from the instincts, not from our difficulties with our parents, not from early experiences, not in the stars, but in our conscious mind.

At the same time, we are not to be castigated for those behaviors often labeled as ill. Indeed, according to yoga philosophy, people are not ill at all, they merely have not yet learned to concentrate their minds so that they can benefit from yoga training and progress on the pathway toward higher consciousness. So, too, in the human potential movement the concept of illness is rejected. "Therapy" is offered to those who simply want to progress from the point where development is stalled. In gestalt therapy, they are merely "stuck." Or, as Werner Erhard says, people are perfectly all right as they are; it is just that they are living out some of their past, rather than realizing that they are all right and getting on with it.

Finally the easy tolerance, if not outright pursuit, of mysticism in the human potential movement is a legacy of its Eastern-mystical background. Such mysticism embraces not only the ideas of karma, reincarnation, and sublime superconsciousness but includes the state of mind and feeling that allows hope to soar, carries the expectation of help from above and beyond and the belief that anything may be true and possible.

I returned from my Chicago Himalayan expedition flushed with the excitement of a way of life and system of ideas theretofore new to me, my mind asizzle with the implications of it. One of these implications was the correspondence I saw between yoga ideas and psychoanalysis. Rather breathlessly, I suppose, I told one of my colleagues of this observation. He seemed to think that I was saying that Freud had stolen his ideas from yoga as he pointed out Freud's published records of the development of his thought across many decades of systematic work. He ended by suggesting, only half in jest, that I study yoga less and psychoanalysis more.

I was, of course, aware of the painstaking development of Freud's ideas across his lifetime, a precisely annotated adventure of the creative mind. It hardly detracts from this achievement to recognize that some of his ideas, such as the unconscious, were developed in gross forms by others before Freud. Rather than doing a disservice to psychoanalysis in noting how many of its ideas are to be found thousands of years earlier in yoga, such observations simply lend weight to these ideas. Their survival in one or another system of thought over such a long period of time suggests that indeed they told truths about human nature.

Be that as it may, for me it was inspiring and instructive

to find many psychoanalytic ideas in yoga. Here are some ideas held in common by yoga and psychoanalysis as noted in several texts by Himalayan staff members[2,3] and added to by myself.

Both yogic meditation and the method of psychoanalysis are designed to minimize external stimuli which might serve as distractions to the work of introspection. There seems a delicate balance between claims made on the mind by external stimuli and by internal promptings. When people are deprived of external stimuli, as in dim, quiet rooms, ideas tend to come to consciousness. Thus, psychoanalysis takes place with the patient lying down on a couch, which to an extent relaxes those bodily tightnesses that yoga exercises relax, minimizes bodily stimuli. The analyst is out of sight, so that his facial expressions do not intrude upon the patient. For long periods the analyst is silent. All these practices encourage the patient to drift inward toward his own thoughts, a practice central to yoga and psychoanalysis.

Both patient and analyst learn to practice detachment. The "free-floating awareness" of the analyst keeps him in contact with the patient's words, yet sufficiently removed from them so that inferences about what the patient says can be delivered to the analyst's consciousness unimpeded. He can remain relatively free of the kind of embroilment in the patient's ideas which would limit his capacity to hear and understand in dimensions not yet known to him or the patient. In yoga there is a similar process of observation, called "the witness," in which one forgoes judging or initiating action in favor simply of observing. As the patient, too, discovers the wider implications of his thoughts, perceptions, feelings, he learns to take some distance from them; they no longer make the same, often desperate, claims upon him. He recognizes ambiguities and possibilities, is less driven by needs and feelings to become positive and opinionated; in a word, he is more detached.

Both yoga and psychoanalysis recognize how not only fleeting situational stimuli can interrupt the goal of encouraging introspection but that the patient can get himself embroiled in activities outside the analytic hour which serve to drain his investment in the analytic process, so-called "acting out." In order to counteract this in both yoga and psychoanalysis, abstinence from such distractions is encouraged, as is asceticism in general. Both yoga practitioners and psychoanalysts accept a degree of suffering as unavoidable, and in fact as perhaps beneficial.

In both systems, meaning gained through introspection is more important than merely changing manifest behavior. Meanings are what is sought after in the meditative process and its associated "path," as they are in the analytic process. For the purposes of the analytic work, how one behaves is less important than why one behaves as one does and how one thinks.

Yoga works with the image of a toxic person who requires cleaning out, as can be seen, for example, in its various exercises to drain the nose and internal organs of mucus and wastes. This model is inherent in the yoga image of clearing the mind of base and interfering thoughts. Here, then, is the cathartic method of Freud's early days, which survives more subtly in the current psychoanalytic emphasis on bringing to mind, and thereby detoxifying, ideas and feelings hitherto warded off as noxious.

The psychoanalyst, like the guru, is enlisted for instruction and to help the patient through realms of experience that would be difficult and painful for him to master alone. Both relationships tend to be intense, with the guru or analyst endowed with fantasied attributes. The task of both guru and analyst is to point out and help the patient overcome these and other distortions. Throughout both processes, the patient is in control, however much he may try to give control to the analyst or guru. Unlike the typical doctor-patient relationship or as in hypnosis, in which the patient submits to the doctor's ministrations, the *sine qua non* for yoga and psychoanalysis is the patient's doing the introspective work, the main work of the treatment.

Karma means, among other things, that our present situation was brought about by past actions, thoughts, and desires, which constrain us to behave in certain ways. Such an idea could well be stated in a textbook of psychoanalysis under the heading of determinism. Moreover, though one's behavior is determined, one is at the same time capable of overcoming such impulsions through knowledge and consequent strengthening of will, in both yoga and psychoanalysis.

The psychoanalytic analogue of prana is libido, both being fundamental life energies that drive body and mind. In yoga as well as psychoanalysis, ideas are kept from awareness by the application of energy against them, as can be seen in the vigor and flowering of ideas, feelings, and behaviors when the binding energy is loosened and "repressions" are overcome.

The system of chakras, concentrations and distributions of energy, corresponds in important respects to the levels of psychosexual development specified by Freud. The stages or chakras are centered in areas or zones of the body, and are associated with characteristic behaviors and experiences. One can be fixated or stuck at any one of these, thereby depriving oneself of those experiences and behaviors available at the higher energy concentrations. To progress upward through the chakras, to "raise the Kundalini," is to release the energy for progressive flow. The first chakra is called anal, and is characterized by primitive experiences of fear, suspicion, danger—in short, the paranoid experiences relating to the anal stage in psychoanalysis and the paranoid position in Melanie Klein's version of psychoanalysis. The second, or genital, chakra is concerned with sexuality, procreation of the species, and has as its associated element water. In short, it corresponds to the phallic-urethral phase in psychoanalysis. The third chakra, centered in the solar plexus, with fire as its associated element, involves dominant, assertive, competitive behaviors—in short, those which psychoanalysis relates to the phallic-aggressive phase. The rest of the yoga stages do not have the same clear correspondence with psychoanalysis, though parts here and there do. The sixth chakra, which has to do with intuition, is called the "third eye." In psychoanalysis, when we are intuitive we are said to employ the "third ear." By way of the Kundalini energy system, yoga relates creativity to maternal nurturance, which is one psychoanalytic understanding of creativity also. Freud seemed to have something of this sort in mind in his remark, with reference to himself, that a boy who has had the unquestioned love of his mother is destined for greatness.

The central dynamic in yoga as well as in psychoanalysis is conflict: gross instincts press for satisfaction against prohibitions. In the course of expectable development, these instincts become harnessed, controlled, and refined by the psychoanalytic ego or yogic buddhi. The latter agency of the mind determines when, how, and under what circumstances the instinctual energy will be expressed; it is a center of choice, discrimination, and execution. Indeed, even Freud's imagery of the ego struggling to control the id like a rider struggling to control a horse is used in yoga to describe the same situation. The refinement of the instincts that results in behaviors of a higher kind, in yoga, corresponds nicely to sublimation. In addition to the formulations in yoga corresponding to id and ego, the psychoanalytic superego, with its parental ideas and conscience, corresponds roughly to buddhi. The yogi's description of the separation of functions in buddhi is similar to the psychoanalytic description of the superego as a split-off part of the ego.

Mind in yoga, as in psychoanalysis, is composed of layers. One layer is ordinary consciousness, material delivered through the five senses. Another level is material outside awareness that can easily be called into awareness, an exact definition of the Freudian preconscious. And there is the vast repository of material that is difficult to call into awareness, the unconscious. In both systems, material can get into the unconscious by way of being perceived outside the awareness of the perceiver, called "subliminal perception" in academic psychology, and as part of "secondary repression" in psychoanalysis.

In yoga, mental contents are stored in a memory bank, called *chitta,* a concept and image used identically by Freud in his discussions of how traces of past experiences are banked, so to speak, in the mind, there to be ready to exert continued influence.

One way neurosis can be conceptualized in psychoanalysis is as a narcissistic phenomenon, a preoccupation with the self which prevents satisfying connections with groups. So, too, in yoga; the path is toward loss of self-preoccupation in exchange for recognizing the identity of self with all others.

Practitioners of tantra yoga recommend that one improve oneself by indulging one's drives, though not for mere self-indulgence. Rather, internal pressures that make for attachment are diminished by being gratified, which allows for detachment. In early psychoanalysis Freud saw neurosis as a direct consequence of dammed-up, inhibited drives, with the implication that gratification would relieve the neurotic pressure. He is often misunderstood as having continued to recommend expressing drives directly as a cure-all and preventative, while in fact he opted for understanding, not simply action. Yet, still central to psychoanalysis is the recognition that a distinguishing characteristic of neurosis is inhibition of drive and that satisfaction of drive is an end and, in combination with understanding, a means of therapeutic movement.

Finally, in yoga as well as in psychoanalysis, the root of suffering is seen as ignorance, and the growth, or therapeutic, task is to surmount the false self, or defenses, in order to learn of the self they mask. In both systems, if one examines the contents of the unconscious mind, the resultant truth will set one free.

There are of course large differences between the two systems. Among these is yoga's insistence that its work is with ordinary people, not sick ones, for its system is one of continued and ultimately transcendental growth, for which all people should strive. Psychoanalysis, according to yoga, restricts itself to the lower chakras, is limited to empirical and verbally expressed events, and is heedless of the cosmic and transcendental.

But the similarities are to me more striking than the differences. That perceptive viewers of the human condition, though separated by their working in vastly different cultures and with thousands of years intervening, can have so much in common is an implicit validation of both viewpoints.

Not only psychoanalysis but modern physics can be found in Eastern mysticism. The Newtonian conceptions of matter, space, time, cause, and effect have all been revised in twentieth-century physics by way of the relativity and quantum theories in particular. Instead of matter being solid, objects are now understood as wavelike patterns of probabilities that can be understood only with respect to connections. No single part is fundamental, nor can any part be understood without reference to all other parts. According to the Eastern concepts of holism and changeability, all things are connected and fluid. Such a conception opposes the mechanistic belief in dead building blocks of nature, which led to the dualism of matter and non-matter, body and mind, as separate. As the mystics have said all along, in effect, mass is nothing but a form of energy; space and time are a unity; an object is an event, not a substance, and all of this is confirmed by modern physics. The hard-bitten Western mind might say that this confluence of a world view several thousands of years old and modern physics is coincidence. The committed Eastern mind might say that the yogis had achieved that ultimate consciousness which revealed the truth. Is wisdom to be found in Chicago or in the Himalaya? Let us press on.

15

The Electric Razor's Edge—Transcendental Meditation

TRANSCENDENTAL MEDITATION, OR "TM," is big business. Those who are put off by spiritual values being mixed with crass commercialism and those who dislike practical issues being enfolded in a haze of spiritualism are likely to be put off by TM. Many people do not fall into either of these categories, to judge from the popularity of TM now to be found even in hamlets throughout the country. About one million Americans have taken TM courses from ten thousand TM instructors. There is a Students International Meditation Society, an International Meditation Society, and Maharishi International University, which gives standard academic degrees and courses along with a heavy dose of the Science of Creative Intelligence, the theoretical framework of TM. The Science of Creative Intelligence is offered for credit at a number of colleges, including Yale and Stanford, and is part of the New York public school system. The Congressional Record includes testimony and testimonials by a TM teacher touting in particular its use as an alternative to alcohol and narcotics. I have before me a copy of a letter from Senator Adlai E. Stevenson III addressed to "Dear Meditator," promising to have an article by an official of the Maharishi International University summarizing the research on TM in rehabilitation programs introduced into the Congressional Record. Mr. Stevenson quotes from his already published Congressional Record statement to the effect that on the basis of scientific evidence TM should be continued or expanded in federal rehabilitation programs.

In addition to the Maharishi International University, in Iowa, The World Plan Executive Council, TM's parent organization, has extensive real estate holdings, including TV stations, and another research university in Switzerland, all bought with tax-exempt dollars. As befits such an enterprise, TM is a trademark. Honest.

While meditation in yoga is a means of enabling a person to learn about himself and pass to a higher consciousness, in the course of which he is likely to feel better, in TM the main purpose is to feel better, whether or not higher consciousness evolves. And benefits are expected after a week or so of minimal expenditure of time and effort. The other expenditure is $125. That includes the basic training, follow-up meetings, and the opportunity to attend low-cost further meetings and retreats.

Considering the alleged benefits, the cost is modest indeed. TM is supposed to make you sufficiently relaxed so that the day's stresses and strains fall away. You should sleep better and require less sleep. A wide variety of physical benefits may accrue, such as improving your eyesight, lessening the strain on your heart, reducing your blood pressure, improving physical co-ordination, and increasing resistance to psychosomatic disease. Students may expect to get better school grades. Narcotic and alcohol addicts can expect help in getting over their addictions. Prisoners can expect help with their efforts at rehabilitation.

Transcendental meditation was brought to the United

States, via Germany, by Maharishi Mahesh Yogi as part of his plan to enhance life throughout the world. In pursuit of this plan he has gone on tour with the Beach Boys and appeared on talk shows. I have seen him in the movies and in pictures, where he invariably shares the spotlight with flowers. Here is a sample of his prose: "The World Government for the Age of Enlightenment has been established with its sovereignty in the domain of consciousness. The philosophy that upholds the structure and activity of the World Government for the Age of Enlightenment and that underlies all its achievements is centered in the truth that consciousness is the prime mover of life and administrator of all action, and anyone who develops in himself the full potential of consciousness enjoys a natural authority over the whole field of actions and achievement." From the standpoint of English, logic, science, and art this sort of thing is clearly a disaster. But, once again, we must ask if there is something of value beneath the hoopla, beyond the commercialism, something that transcends questionable science and egregious style.

Several years previous to this study, I had attended a "Symposium on TM" given at the Topeka VA Hospital. The only flesh-and-blood TM person there was a director of the national organization. However, there was a movie of the Maharishi and closed-circuit television of a psychologist suggesting the use of TM in treating alcoholics, a psychiatrist conducting a study of the effectiveness of TM with psychiatric patients, and another psychologist summarizing scientific research on TM. Those were the days when my prejudices ruled. I had great difficulty getting past what I considered to be the flimsiness of the research findings so proudly presented. Further, when I asked what the diagnostic criteria were for determining what mantra should be selected for a given person, I was told that was a secret. Incredible! On the one hand the TM people were agog at the possibility of becoming accepted on the basis of scientific findings, and on the other they committed the scientifically unpardonable sin of keeping their thinking to themselves. More on mantras shortly. At any rate I let the whole thing lapse, just ignoring the newspaper advertisements featuring an attention-getting picture of the full-bearded Maharishi.

Once embarked on this study, I realized that TM was too big to be ignored. Further, I was encouraged by my yoga experience to consider still other means of exploiting powers of the mind. My introductory TM meeting was held in a bank, so far as I know not as yet owned by TM, which just rents a meeting room there after hours. My TM instructor seemed programmed; I later learned that he was. We were introduced to the basic plan—instruction in the technique, checkups to see how we were doing with our meditation, and further optional meetings. We learned how we could expect to benefit, and we were assured that we would be safe from any physical consequences. We would also be safe from sectarianism. No beliefs were required, despite the holy atmosphere generated by, among other things, Sanskrit prayers. For the beginning formal meeting, I was to report, free of drugs, with six to twelve fresh flowers, two to three pieces of fresh fruit, and a clean white handkerchief, as well as the fee. As I went cruising around town picking up these items, I thought that while TM might eventually relax me, right now it had my teeth on edge. Actually, I had been gritting my teeth off and on ever since I was subjected to the pop psychology, pop spirituality, and all-around banality of the teacher's lectures. Not that he was to be blamed, at least in the proximal sense. He had been taught what to say, apparently down to the periods and pauses. When asked a question to which he did not have an automatic answer, a question that might have required *thought*, he blanched.

This phenomenon was nowhere better illustrated than when the issue of the mantra came up again. The mantra is the word on which you concentrate, repeating it over and over again, at any speed you wish. It is your home base, where you go in turning away from interfering thoughts. The mantra is used in yoga and other practices optionally. But in transcendental meditation the mantra is a more or less separate technique; using a mantra is simply how it is done. In other meditation systems, no special to-do is made over what mantra is used. One or another collection of letters considered to be soothing and resonant, a common one being "om," is considered suitable. In TM, however, each person's mantra is especially selected for him, and he is enjoined to keep it a secret. Again I pushed for some understanding of how my mantra was selected for me. The smoothly programmed answer was that TM teachers learn how to judge each person with respect to mantras.

Some months later I attended a meeting of the American Psychoanalytic Association where I learned of research that demonstrated the beneficial effects of subliminally presenting the phrase "Mommie and I are one." This was held to be reassuring through its evoking the experience of the infant's symbiotic relationship with his or her mother. Not just any words carrying this idea would work. The "m" sound seemed necessary. As a side light, the experimenter Loyd Silverman, of New York University,[1] pointed out that in Herbert Benson's relaxation response[2]—meditation without the transcendental context—the mantra suggested by Benson is "one." According to Adam Smith's dialogue with Benson as reported in Smith's *Powers of Mind*,[3] Benson picked the word "one" more or less arbitrarily, assuming only that it would be meaningless and therefore not disturbing to meditation. Smith pointed out to Benson several mystical and religious associations to "one," which intelligence temporarily nonplussed Benson, though he ended by saying, ". . . 'One' is neutral to most people." If "one" unconsciously evokes symbiotic images as well, it is hardly neutral but may be soothingly healthful. Notice that the most commonly used mantra, "om," does have the "m" sound.

Now, here I was with a mantra that had a harsh-sounding, possibly disturbing "k," and the only slightly less harsh "g." Would it not be an improvement to my meditation to change my mantra to include an "m" sound?

When my instructor called to tell me about a meeting, I asked his opinion of my making this change. Speak of spitting in church! First of all he called it "gross" for me to say my mantra over the telephone, though presumably no one else was listening, and he and I both knew the secret. The next time we could talk without the profanity of a telephone, he explained to me that mantras were chosen on the basis of thousands of years of experience, and they work better than any makeshift mantra I could put together. As to the psychological and scientific reasoning for my alteration, back on his programmed track he did not want to deal with that.

When TM practitioners burble about how easy it is to learn to meditate, they are right. One simply sits comfortably, closes one's eyes, and mentally repeats one's mantra. As other thoughts come up in his mind, he turns away from them by concentrating his attention on the mantra.

The ability to concentrate on one thing only, called having a "one-pointed mind," is highly desirable. There is a Catch-22, however. One is supposed to meditate for twenty minutes. A cooking timer, a clock radio, an alarm clock, or some such device would seem ideal; just set it for twenty minutes and let it buzz when time is up. However, the instructor suggested that a jangling sound penetrating a meditative reverie would be bad for the system. He recommended a gradual, two-minute period of coming back to ordinary consciousness, and repeatedly warned against jolting oneself awake. An alternative would be to look at a clock, but to do that, the student would have to interrupt his one-pointedness and drift upward from the levels of meditation he had achieved. Instead, one just adjusts to the time automatically, or else makes the better of two bad choices.

At subsequent meetings I listened to more verbal Pablum and filled out several questionnaires about my experience meditating. At "checking sessions," the teacher and I meditated together. Invariably at the end of each session he would say, "It is easy, yes?" What could you answer without your contentiousness shattering the holy crystal, blaspheming the centuries of teaching from Guru Dev, Maharishi's teacher, on down? The checking sessions did serve, however, as encouragement to do the meditation: Each one began with my being asked when I last meditated.

My transcendental meditating career lasted just about as long as these checking sessions did. Part of the problem was that I have cassette tapes with suggested meditation procedures from the Simontons, the Center for the Healing Arts, Robert Monroe and "Astral sounds" (designed to help the student get "out of his body"), Silva Mind Control, and several others. On top of that, previous to all these I had learned a self-hypnosis technique for putting myself to sleep, which involved concentration on a point on the forehead. I have used it alone and in combination with other meditations as a handy device for changing consciousness. I suppose if I had what it took to meditate regularly, I would have decided to try one of these consistently. I think I was just glad to escape to the confusion of having too many, unable to choose one and stick to it. Of course, I tried once or twice to get away with the idea that I was too busy. My TM teacher said, "If you are too busy to meditate, you are too busy." About that, he was right. When I consider how I waste forty minutes in the course of the day, frequently because I suffer from the tiredness that meditation would probably help me overcome, my excuse seems hollow indeed. Nonetheless, I like to think that the early morning is when I do my best work, and I cannot afford twenty of those golden minutes. In the evening I can't relax until I read the mail and deal with the day's emergencies. In high dudgeon I am liable to say to myself, If I spent all that time meditating, how the hell would this book get written? The fact is that if I meditated regularly it might well have been written faster, easier, and better.

There are lots of reasons to believe that meditation is a great, relatively untapped source of various kinds of health. My own experience with cancer patients' doing the meditation-visualization procedure is suggestive of that (see Part Five). I have a friend who claims to have reduced his exophthalmos (abnormal protrusion of the eyeballs) through meditation. I have another friend who has found that meditation made it possible for him to give up smoking. (There is a good deal of research on its usefulness for addictions of various kinds.) Still another person claims that she finds it easier with meditation to go without her eyeglasses. It is not necessarily that her eyesight has improved, but she feels less needful of seeing things so clearly and more willing to assert her visual resources up to their unaided natural limits. Still another acquaintance, who has had limited but high-quality psychotherapy, claims that she and her husband have through meditation altered their lives beneficially in diverse ways, which did not occur during her psychotherapy. For example, she is less inclined to depression and insomnia. Her husband overcame chronic headaches.

TM workers are only too glad to let you know that scientific studies have demonstrated that changes are brought about by transcendental meditation: Skin resistance rises, lactic-acid levels markedly decrease, the need for oxygen is lowered, metabolism is lowered, alpha appears on the EEG, heart rate is slowed, and blood pressure goes down. These changes when one is doing transcendental meditation do not appear when one is sleeping or under hypnosis. Such findings on paper are impressive and probably did impress a good many of the million people who signed up for the course. Yet, as usual with research, there are problems. In addition to the common ones such as that other experimenters do not always get the same results, the original body of TM experiments, some done, others abstracted, by Robert Keith Wallace, did not use control groups.[4] Thus, the reported changes could have taken place in a matched group that merely twiddled their thumbs for twenty minutes twice a day. Bernard Glueck divided psychiatric patients into three groups, one group meditating, another group merely relaxing skeletal muscles, and a third practicing alpha-wave biofeedback.[5] The problem was that after a year the only group remaining was the group of meditators, the others having gotten bored with the procedures. This suggests that meditation was offering something that the other procedures did not, although one wonders whether the subjects knew of the experimenter's main interest and for a variety of reasons may have continued to do what he asked of them. Be that as it may, this study, too, ended without adequate control groups. It highlights another major problem in TM research: Those who practice TM twice a day over extended periods are, by definition, a special, highly motivated group, and it may be that the changes that occur are limited to such groups, as a result of placebo, suggestion, or determination.

However accurate the physiological measures may prove to be, TM puffs up its findings in a scientifically indefensible way.[6]

For example, TM claims through meditation an increase in skin resistance, indicating "deep relaxation, reduction of anxiety and emotional disturbances." An increase in skin resistance does not necessarily so indicate. And what "emotional disturbances" do they have in mind, anyway? A faster reaction time, due to meditation, does not necessarily, as claimed, "reduce dullness and improve efficiency in perception and performance." Perception of what, performance at what?

Fewer spontaneous galvanic responses hardly indicate, as claimed, such global bounties as "more resistance to environmental stress, psychosomatic disease and behavioral instability"—whatever behavioral instability is. This sort of thing reaches its nadir in the claim that meditators become more "self-actualized," as measured by two paper-and-pencil tests, from which the test taker can emerge being called "self-actualized." TM then goes on to list ten characteristics of self-actualized people as suggested by Maslow. These are all "good" things though rather unclear as to their empirical referents, for example "creativity," "increased integration and autonomy," and "increased ability to enjoy solitude." There is no indication that the paper-and-pencil tests are designed to measure these characteristics. Test scores may simply have been named as self-actualizations by the test makers on any number of bases, since self-actualization is one of those rubbery phrases that can bend at the whims and wishes of the user. Just listen to the TM conclusions to its scientific charts: "TM rejuvenates and normalizes the functioning of the nervous system, eliminates mental stress, promotes efficiency and effectiveness in life, harmonious and fulfilling interpersonal relationships, thus making every individual more useful to himself and others and bringing fulfillment to the purpose of society. . . . An over-all effect of fullness of life." In short practically everything is promised, in language that is diffuse and global but based on highly specific and narrow experimental findings, assuming these are valid to begin with.

But perhaps if there is essential value to TM it can be rescued from the fruit-and-flower set. So seemed to think Herbert Benson, a cardiologist at Harvard Medical School, who initially became interested in TM as a means of lowering metabolism and thereby treating hypertension. After lending his work and Harvard's name to TM, he retired to more accustomed surroundings and formulated what he called "the relaxation response." This response could be gotten in many ways in addition to transcendental meditation, and had for centuries been gotten through religious practices. The four common elements that produce this response and the associated changes are 1) a mental device, some constant stimulus such as a sound, word, or phrase, or simply gazing steadily at a point; 2) an attitude of passivity in which one is unconcerned about success or failure, just concerned with brushing away any interfering thoughts and continuing the concentration; 3) being comfortable, so that muscles can be relaxed; 4) being in a quiet environment as enhanced by shutting one's eyes. So it really does not matter which of my many cassette-taped meditations I choose to follow, just as long as each of them conforms to these requirements.

Any of the meditations would be cheaper than TM, and

on paper would work identically. However, a lot depends on the incipient meditator. Some people probably are attracted to TM's spiritual context, the feeling of continuity with the venerable past, the relationship with the instructor, and the feeling of being in a group with other meditators, part of the larger, worldwide meditation-movement group. Nothing is wrong with any of these, as they feed into or interact with suggestion. And the TM requirements of time and money are not unreasonable. The main thing is to do the meditation.

Just as the airlines are beginning to lower their fares, TM has come out with a series of four to eight one-week preparatory courses at a cost of $250 per week, and an advanced course at $375 per week to enable the student to levitate, fly, and dematerialize as well. It has been rumored that TM is beginning to wane in popularity, as measured by the number of people who take the basic course. One wonders whether this levitation product is a hype for a sagging gate. Already there are reports that levitation has been done, that it works! We wait for the glossy charts that offer scientific proof. But, inauspiciously, TM has refused a public demonstration unless no more than ten people watch and unless spectators donate at least one thousand dollars to the movement, or so said the Washington *Post*.[7]

I think it is a grave miscalculation on the part of TM to stir up a levitation hornets' nest unless it can deal with the swarm by way of public, convincing demonstrations. If some combination of commercialism and inbred delusion is responsible for these claims, the movement will not only have done itself a disservice but will have done a disservice to the possibilities for beneficial change through meditation. It would be too bad to have brought such benefits to so many people, only to destroy its credibility and abort its early success.

But whatever the ultimate fate of transcendental meditation, it has made us open to the possibilities inherent in meditation, or the general relaxation response, as a possible therapeutic tool and as another way of learning about the power of the mind. It took the advertising and distribution facilities of TM and the sanctifying work of the laboratory to do it, but now we in Western society increasingly recognize the value of what ancient cultures and religions the world over have long recognized and practiced.

The meditative process long ago was intuited as beneficial, and so found its way into ritual and doctrinal contexts. Sometimes the meditation has been acknowledged as a specific technique and other times it was implicitly built into ceremonial practices. Why do we feel good, for example, when we go to a house of worship? The reasons are probably many. Soothing our conscience is one. Becoming identified with a valued group is another. Having the feeling of pursuing the truth and of being aided by a force outside oneself are still more. It now seems that some of our feeling may be due also to meditation. Ritualized prayer, for example, shares attributes of meditation. The language of many prayers is sufficiently hollow and repetitious as to lull the mind, a process helped along by the reduction of other external stimuli. (But usually there is enough meaning in prayer to interrupt the somnolence.)

Why does meditation make us feel good? The physiologic explanation, backed by experimental findings, is that it shifts the person from the sympathetic to the parasympathetic nervous system. Much emotional and physical disease results from the unnecessary tenseness of the sympathetic system, which keeps the person ready to "fight" or "take flight," thereby providing the unremitting activation of a stress system designed to be used only in special circumstances. Western society can be crudely characterized as one of sympathetic activity, and Eastern mystical society as one of parasympathetic activity. Many of our problems are perhaps due to our hyperstimulation, and theirs to hypostimulation.

There are some hints, however, that encourage us to look at meditation from the psychological point of view also. One way to examine this possibility is to see for oneself. In a state of deep meditation, what kind of feelings arise, what are those feelings like, what kind of pleasure does one get, what kind of experience does the meditator have and benefit from? Some people report oceanic, merging experiences, which, according to psychoanalytic thinking, come from a primitive stage of development when mother and child are experienced by the child as being one in a sea of gentle, rhythmic security. All kinds of rest and relaxation probably partake of this experience, as does satisfactory eating. Periodically dropping out from the stress and strain of daily challenges may be likened to the baby's periodic nipping at the breast. Such experiences of fusion, yielding of oneself to a force, group, or idea, such as religion, and God in particular, have been described as an apparent consequence of altered consciousness such as can be achieved through meditation. This line of reasoning is further plausibly supported by the "m" sound as being prominent in mantras. "M" is the first letter of the word for "mother" in many languages, and "m" is a sound signifying the taking in of good nourishment, as in "mmmmmm." The very act of making an "m" puts together the sensuous lips in interstimulation. Such nurturing experiences are the major interactions in the fused, symbiotic mother-child unit.[8] They are recaptured in the identity of self with a higher Other as claimed through meditation.

If it is true, as seems likely, that many people who meditate feel better physiologically and psychologically, that they reduce stress, gain subtle gratifications, and return to daily challenges with greater energy, then why not prescribe meditation as one prescribes medication? One answer is that meditation is not in the U. S. Pharmacopoeia or the Physicians Desk Reference. A prescriber would have to familiarize himself with meditation on his own initiative. And he would have to have the courage to prescribe something outside the mainstream, in a gray area of professional sanction. His technical expertise would have to be accompanied by personal qualities of innovativeness and courage.

A more technical issue is whether feeling good is in the best interests of the ongoing psychotherapeutic process. Here we must distinguish between a situation in which a patient and a psychiatrist have feeling good as the major goal, rather than having internal change through psychological investigation as the goal. Some patients are not suited for the latter, either because they do not have what are usually considered the requisite psychological capacities and skills or simply because they lack the time, money, or access to regular meetings with a psychotherapist. In principle there seems no good reason why such people should not be offered whatever holds promise of helping them to feel better and be more efficient. Meditation looks to be one of those possibilities.

However, patients who are in a continued process of self-exploration are in much different circumstances. Without a sufficient amount of distress, many people find it difficult to do the necessary work. Some seek ways of feeling good in order to avoid painful self-reflection. Thus, temporarily feeling good used as a means of interfering with the arduous process of self-exploration can be inimical to the kind of beneficial change originally established as the goal. On the other hand distress beyond a certain level in itself interferes with psychotherapeutic work as it interferes with most tasks. Withholding opportunities to feel better in such instances is not only inhumane but in the larger sense poor psychotherapy. So, knowing whether to prescribe meditation involves knowing one's goals and diagnostically knowing one's patient well enough to be able to predict whether the meditation could be used to the benefit or detriment of the therapeutic process. Beyond these considerations there is nothing in meditation that is inherently contradictory to the conduct of a psychotherapeutic process. It offers, for example, no competing and possibly confusing ideologies.

Why should a psychiatric worker concern himself about an alien means of self-help, anyway? If he recommends meditation, then why not recommend diet, exercise, yoga postures and breathing, hobbies, marriage, divorce? Shouldn't he stick to his psychotherapeutic knitting and let the patient decide for himself what he needs, especially as the patient becomes increasingly aware of himself through the psychotherapy? We shall return to these issues in the final section. In the meantime it is nice to know that we carry within us by way of the relaxation response a means of finding sustaining, nurturing restfulness.

PART FIVE

Dusting off the New Medicine

16

Medicine Without Medicine—Alternative Medicine

I HAVE A complex and anomalous position with regard to medicine, quite apart from the fact that I am married to a physician. I am called Doctor, which is technically correct. What is incorrect is the implication, common in our culture, that "doctor" means "medical doctor." I spent most of my career in an institution that technically, legally, and socially is medical. Yet the work done in that institution—psychiatry, education, and research—has little to do with physical medicine. It employs more nonmedical professional people than medical ones, and much of the work performed there by nonmedical and medical people is identical, notably psychotherapy and psychoanalysis.

As a member of the American Psychoanalytic Association, I share membership and the common work of psychoanalysis with mostly medical people. Organized medicine in the United States has co-opted psychoanalysis as a specialty of psychiatry, which in turn is a specialty of medicine. I am one of a handful of nonmedical people who have received full psychoanalytic training under the auspices of the American Psychoanalytic Association by virtue of a loophole in its policy of restricting training and membership to those with an M.D. degree. This restriction was waived on the basis that I would use psychoanalytic training in my career as a psychologist, particularly for research purposes.

At the same time that I am a psychoanalyst, I remain a clinical psychologist, a member of a nonmedical discipline that has its own anomalies. Technically, the Ph.D. is an academic degree, having its roots in classical, nonclinical psychology. In the past thirty years, clinical psychology has become a specialty whose activities bring it closer to medicine, in many respects, than to its academic forebears.

Clinical psychology developed around psychological testing. The psychiatrists referred the patient for testing, and used the information gained thereby in the treatment. It became increasingly recognized, however, that adequate testing was dependent upon the testers' having training and experience doing psychotherapy. Furthermore, it was increasingly, though sometimes embarrassingly, recognized that in principle there was no reason to assume that psychiatrists were any more capable of doing psychotherapy than were psychologists. Little in conventional medical training was useful or relevant to psychotherapy, just as little in academic psychological training was. All of these paradoxes, peculiarities, and anomalies exist in the context of the general debate over the usefulness and accuracy of maintaining a body-mind split as concretized in medical and nonmedical professions, and whether medicine as organized and practiced in advanced Western countries is the most suitable way for dealing with psychological or physical unhappiness.

Knowing all this, and having participated in discussions, debates, and the politics of these issues, I nonetheless embarked on the study reported in this book mostly oblivious to the implications for medicine of alternative healing. I was unaware that anyone was taking seriously the paradoxes, peculiarities, and anomalies of how medicine is organized and practiced and the consequences of these and other factors, and doing something substantive and possibly definitive about the situation. My task, after all, was to study, evaluate, and compare with psychology and psychoanalysis alternative forms of psychotherapy, not medicine. My attitude was not idiosyncratic; it was a measure of the naïveté and insularity of many people who are imbued with the traditional practices of organized medical and psychological disciplines, whose professional affiliation keeps them behind conceptual bars.

It took the happenstance of my working in psychotherapy with a cancer patient to launch me decisively into the study of alternative medicine in addition to my study of the new psychotherapies. Once launched, I realized how vigorous and active a field alternative medicine is, remarkably so when one considers how young it is and how little of it is known to most conventional medical practitioners. Again, this is much less so if one lives in California. Even there, however, many physicians seal themselves off behind the walls of their traditional means of communication and education.

While the existence and extent of alternative medicine came as something of a surprise to me, upon reflection I wondered how I could have overlooked it. How could medicine not be subject to the same kind of searching questioning as so many other of our institutions in recent years: employer-employee relationships, sexual roles, industrial and environmental practices, consumer-products safety and advertising, and ordinary social regulations of dress, entertaining, marrying, and morals? Anything established has been fair game.

In some ways, traditional medicine easily and unfairly

incurs anti-establishment attack. When people feel the dependence aroused by illness, their needfulness is often reflected in demandingness. They place their putative healers on a pinnacle; how else to be sure that one is going to be healed? And the bigger they come, the harder they fall. The physician who fails to produce the wished-for cure becomes the target of the disappointment, disillusionment, and rage that children feel toward parents who disappoint them. To the extent that physicians accept being put on a pinnacle through acting the part, they encourage animosity. Also encouraging to eventual animosity is the implicit hope for miracles stimulated by the very successes of medicine. If there can be a wonder drug for tuberculosis, then why is there not one for diabetes? If you can transplant a heart, why can't you transplant a liver or a brain? Our instant communication outlets let everyone know about the gleaming new machinery with its implicit promise of escape from disease and death. So, if a physician fails to produce a cure for *your* disease, he becomes the target of disappointment, suspicion, and rage.

Even if one allows for the unfair emotions stirred by the need and anxiety engendered by sickness, there does seem much wrong with the American medical establishment. With the rise of specialization, the loss of the family doctor and his reassuring house calls, and the intervention of third-party payments, medicine has become experienced as impersonal, if not uncaring. Physicians themselves, who seem to work harder and harder and at greater cost to their own health, are often dissatisfied with the routineness of their specialization, much as assembly-line workers are dissatisfied with theirs.[1] Drugs increasingly, and sometimes irresponsibly, used not only quiet the patient and mask his symptoms without either party getting a chance to attend to the underlying disease but are often harmful in and of themselves. The eleventh-greatest cause of death in the United States is said to be the result of prescribed drugs, with estimates of hospital deaths due to drugs ranging up to 140,000 annually.[2] Out of every four patients who leave a hospital dead, one has been killed by drugs.[3] (That seems incredible to me, but that is the claim.) Several universities now include chairs of iatrogenic-illness medicine in recognition of the ills caused, with all good will, by physicians.

Medical-care costs have gone up 330 per cent in twenty years, while the price index has risen less than half that.[4] In 1975, 8.3 per cent of the gross national product, some $118 billion, was spent on health; a year later the amount had swelled to $140 billion. It is projected to be double that in five years.[5] While the physician still stands as the most trusted of all professionals, in the past ten years his prestige and authority have plummeted more percentage points than any other, according to Harris polls.[6]

In exchange for an enormous financial outlay, we not only have widespread dissatisfaction but disappointing results. Compared to other countries we are seventeenth in infant mortality and maternal deaths associated with childbirth, and nineteenth in male life expectancy.*[7a, b] Life expectancy for American adults has improved little since the 1920s; we are still hovering around the biblical three score and ten. It is true that many people live to old age as a result of medicine's successes with infectious diseases, some operations, and treatment of accidents. Yet at the same time, amid the splendor of exotic medical technology, a whole host of diseases are *increasing* all through the industrialized world, the so-called diseases of civilization: heart disease, cancer, stomach ulcers, high blood pressure, depression, anxiety, arthritis, and respiratory disorders. Ac-

* These figures may be misleading to some extent because of the differences between countries in record-keeping practices.

cording to adherents of the new medicine, more machinery, more specialization, more money spent will always be insufficient, since these measures fail to come to grips with the true nature of sickness and healing. The true nature of sickness and healing has less to do with circumscribed diseases than with whole persons. According to one study,[8] of every hundred persons who walk into a physician's office ten are helped, ten are harmed, and for eighty of them medical treatment makes no difference. Other physicians estimate between 60 and 80 per cent of people who come to their offices are not amenable to conventional treatment.[9] Conventional medicine fails because patients' malaise is more in their mind and its derivative effects on the body than it is measurable and treatable through physical means.

"Holism" is an old name and idea given fresh exposure and implementation in the new, alternative medicine. It is based on those same human-potential principles that underlie the new psychotherapies and the new, alternative ways of life. Holism usually refers to the taking into consideration of the whole person, not just his body or his mind. It also refers to consideration of the whole range of possible opportunities for amelioration of ills.

Let us compare and contrast conventional medicine with new, or holistic, medicine.

In conventional medicine the major responsibility is given to and accepted by the physician. The patient comes to him, symptoms in hand, and the physician assumes the task of diagnosing and treating those symptoms. The interpersonal mode is between subject and object, the physician *doing* something to or for the patient, who *takes* what is done to or for him. As an expression of the passive, subordinate, needful position of the patient, anger results when needs are not adequately and quickly enough met. According to Jerry Green, a humanistic lawyer from Mill Valley, California, most malpractice suits stem from this traditional relationship between doctor and patient. He suggests a new kind of contract between doctor and patient, according to which expectations are practical rather than idealized, with the patient assuming responsibility and thereby lowering his demands on the physician. Such a contract would not only diminish suits for malpractice but would enhance healing.

In conventional medicine the focus is on the body. Mind is split off into the specialty of psychiatry, if attended to at all. In the new medicine, body and mind are conceived of as one, with the choice for therapist and patient being which is the best way to approach the problem. Feelings, imagination, creativity, values, ethics, spirit are all implicated in any malaise. They help cause disease and the response to medicine, while imparting meaning to and thereby influencing the effectiveness of the treatment. Conventional medicine overlooks many of the ways that the mind can influence the body, such as through meditation, visualization, biofeedback, and plain positive thinking.

In conventional medicine reliance is placed on third parties or agencies, machines or drugs. In the new medicine reliance is placed more on the two parties to the contract, to the interpersonal participants; healing is brought about by the patient's body, which may sometimes use third agencies for this purpose.

In conventional medicine hope for the future lies in new inventions, new drugs, new surgical techniques. In the new medicine what's new is old. Dusting off the new medicine means to rediscover the past: herbs, homeopathy, naturopathy, and especially ancient oriental medicine. Ancient cultures produced portable cell batteries (they are in the National Museum of Baghdad), jet propulsion (in steam), descriptions of the coast of America fifteen hundred years before Columbus landed there, and the Parthenon, whose perspectives were based on a knowledge of mathematics and optics.[10] We can hardly assume that such sophisticated cultures were ignorant of medicine. Hippocrates, for example, preached the benefit of diet and mental attitude in the treatment of physical disease. Many ancient remedies are just now being established scientifically. Lithium, a newly discovered, now accepted, specific remedy for manic-depressive psychosis, was administered by the ancient Greeks to patients with disturbances of mood.[10]

While conventional medicine has always been largely empirical, it esteems experimental science and often realizes its objective of experimentally testing its practice. In the new medicine there is an even more frank use of empiricism, along with a relative lack of concern that what works be supported experimentally; it has an *ad hoc*, try-almost-anything attitude.

Conventional medicine is highly structured along organizationally professional lines. Its societies are exclusionary, and its policies maintain status and hierarchies both within the profession and between the profession and others. In part to maintain medical distinctiveness, it uses a special, technical language, which overawes more than communicates to laymen. In alternative medicine plain English is preferred, paraprofessionals are welcomed, organizations and status considerations are minimized.

Conventional medicine is stereotypically masculine in its assumption of responsibility, its intrusively doing something to someone else, its basis in such male-dominated fields as chemistry and physics, and its employment of machines. The new medicine is stereotypically feminine in its emphasis on caring, sharing, the natural rather than technological, humanistic rather than scientific values, nurturance rather than dominance.

In conventional medicine illness and cure are central. In the new medicine illness shares centrality with problems of living such as childbirth, aging, life crises of all kinds. Alongside cure is education in how to meet and master such challenges.

In traditional medicine diagnoses are most likely to be made by laboratory studies or exploratory operations. In the new medicine diagnosing by observation of the surface of the body is exploited. The eye, feet, palm, skin, tongue, ear are all held to provide information diagnostic of the condition of inner organs.

In conventional medicine symptoms are evidences of illness or the illness itself, and are to be gotten rid of. The patient who develops and uses his symptoms to avoid contending with those problems in living finds a ready partner in the conventional physician, who, for various reasons, may also avoid involvement with anything but the designated, traditionally categorized illness. In the new medicine symptoms are considered to be indications of underlying distress, and also as ways of the body's healing itself. To assume otherwise and automatically attempt to get rid of the symptoms is to interfere with the wisdom of the body, to undercut its own reparative efforts, as well as to conspire in the use of symptoms as a diversion from examining sources of distress.

In conventional medicine consciousness is in the body, a function of the brain; the body is solid, its boundaries physical and observable. In the new medicine the body is an expression of consciousness, is subordinate to it; the body may die but consciousness goes on. Instead of being solid, physical, and boundaried, the body is a congealing of energies that are in constant flux. For example, two and a half million blood cells die and are replaced every minute. Much relied on is Einstein's dictum that energy and matter are equivalent. As Kirlian photography purports to demonstrate, energy emanates beyond the skin. The assumed boundaries have really been determined by the mechanics of our apparatus of perception.

In conventional medicine the genesis of sickness is in bacteria, viruses, heredity. In the new medicine the genesis of sickness is in the way we live, think, feel. Germs, poisons, accidents are used, through unconscious design or as inadvertent by-products of our style of life, to bring about illness. What seems like genetic disposition may be karma. The way the pregnant mother lives and the way the baby is born predispose the baby toward illness, as do food, air, working conditions, stress in general.

Finally, practitioners of conventional medicine know and care little about health. The health-care system is really a disease-care system. If you try to get into the system without a disease, you are an unwelcome puzzle. The new medicine recognizes that there are many stages between health and disease, that, little by little, "dishealth" over a period of time leads to disease. Moreover, health is not to be defined merely by the absence of disease but as a positive state of well-being, vigor, enjoyment, which is at the same time a preventive against disease.

Thus far I have skirted the edges of the crucial question of what kinds of people are comprised in conventional and new medicine. Is it possible, first of all, to generalize about a profession? Although all generalizations are dangerous, and one can easily think of exceptions, there is reason to believe that generalizations about conventional medicine are plausible. This reason stems from the close control that conventional medicine maintains over the acceptance of students into its system, which results in homogeneity in important respects. Prospective medical students must begin early to lay the basis for their acceptance at medical school by concentrating their interests and studies in areas that are basic to conventional medicine. The desired areas are chemistry, physics, biology, and related disciplines. These usually difficult subjects require considerable intellectual capacities and specific turns of mind and personality. They put a premium on precision, efficiency, meticulousness, discipline, and they are impersonal.

It has long been argued that the population of adolescents who decide to become physicians and who are capable of and inclined to concentrate their interests in such sciences are a poor population from which to draw psychiatrists. While some psychiatrists are mainly interested in the physical aspects of their profession, usually drugs but occasionally surgery and diet, for the most part psychiatry is a humanistic and behavioral discipline. It puts supreme importance on language, subjectivity, and feelings. It is personal, warm, stereotypically feminine. Yet these qualities may be systematically excluded by virtue of admissions requirements and policies. In effect the deans of admission at medical schools select the people who are to become psychiatrists, and usually do so according to criteria that fit a substantially different calling. Moreover, since psychiatrists deal with life experiences, their work would be facilitated by many and varied experiences in their own lives. Yet the academic requirements of the calling release them to middle age with family life often postponed and a history composed largely of going to school. The new therapies, with their casual or nonexistent admission criteria, allow people naturally to select themselves for the work of psychotherapy, and at any age with any history. In so doing they have demonstrated the great amount of natural talent available among people with personalities and experiences much different from those who are accepted for medical training. (There is, of course, a price to be paid for this practice, namely that there are inadequate safeguards against people who select themselves incorrectly.)

The proponents of the new medicine now assert that the selective and restrictive practices of medical schools not only are inapplicable to psychiatry but in some respects to all of medicine. As we have seen, they claim that medicine in general is overmechanized, too impersonal, too narrow, precise, and limiting, too little interested in human values, motives, and the language in which these are communicated.

Such analyses and criticisms as these strike at the heart of conventional medicine—its raw material, its training, and its consequent practices. Such criticisms are to some extent a function of the M.D./non-M.D. squabble, which despite the merits involved is fueled by the same emotional wellsprings that underlie all struggles between "haves and have-nots," in this case the "haves" having degrees, social status, legal recognition, and often financial superiority (the typical physician in 1976 earned around fifty-six thousand dollars). Yet it is important to remember that the conventional versus alternative medicine debate transcends such parochialism, for the new medicine is in fact spearheaded by physicians. They have been stereotypically medical and scientific enough to have selected, been admitted to, and passed through the medical system, yet have emerged with a demonstrated strong devotion to humanistic, behavioral concerns, as exploited in innovative, unconventional careers. As renegades from an establishment, they are likely inclined to have revisionist, rebellious personalities.

Even within conventional medicine voices are being

raised along these same revisionist lines. George Engel writes, in the *Annals of Internal Medicine,*[11] that "physiochemical reductionism and the primacy of technology" have determined the narrowly defined preoccupation of medicine with illness, rather than with health and wholeness. He recommends that sciences basic to medicine should include social and psychological sciences.[12] A senior medical faculty member writing to the chairman of the department of medicine of a prominent medical school asserts (anonymously), "The ultimate products, i.e., the physicians we produce, are not related to the health-care needs of the people.[13] He goes on to detail his charge that the medical school trains students in esoteric diseases, employing the most sophisticated technology, which, by example if nothing else, underplays the basic skills relevant to the wide variety of illnesses they will be called upon to treat. Moreover, he raises the question whether the exotic and esoteric technology is, in fact, of greater benefit than less rarefied methods in many instances. For example, he cites a study "which seemed to show that a randomized study of individuals with acute myocardial infarction fared just as well at home as they did with the benefits of CCU (Coronary Care Unit) treatment." Malcolm Todd, president of the International College of Surgeons and former president of the American Medical Association, told a recent audience, "It is proper and timely that medicine should become informed and involved in some alternative programs of health care. If approached with caution, the concept of holistic medicine offers an exciting rejuvenation of our health system." He reminded his audience that Hippocrates said twenty-three hundred years ago that in order to properly diagnose and treat health-care problems the physician must consider the whole person. "We need to learn and evaluate skills derived from ancient cultural traditions, to integrate them with new technological discoveries."[13]

Informally, I have noticed in recent years that a small but growing number of recent medical school graduates who enter the Menninger School of Psychiatry are already imbued with the knowledge, values, and goals of the new medicine. There is a renaissance also of the family doctor, as the general practitioner "specialty" has begun a return to popularity among physicians. And some twelve medical schools have begun changing their criteria for selection in favor of students with a humanistic bent.[14]

To quote from its brochure: "The Center for Integral Medicine was organized in 1974 by a group of medical professionals who wished to help shift the perspective of health care from the diagnosis and treatment of illness to the development and maintenance of health and life. . . . The Center encourages a view of healing as a therapeutic partnership in which the health-care practitioner and patient share information, advice, and support. Professional and lay-educational programs support a whole-person attitude toward healing in which the mind, body, and spirit are treated as cooperative components of a single system that functions perfectly when proper research is paid to its intrinsic needs." The Center fosters research and professional and lay education, and is planning its own healing center.

The brochure statement should also have included a reference to alternative cures; both the maintenance of health and alternative cures were much in evidence at this organization's program exploring the interrelationships of mind, medicine, and health entitled "Mind as Healer—Mind as Slayer." This meeting took place at a hotel adjoining the Los Angeles Airport in February 1977. Among its distinguishing features was that it was in effect two meetings that shared the same faculty and presentations. One meeting was for physicians. The other was for everybody else. The content was much the same. I heard, informally, that the reason for two separate but equal meetings was that physicians would be more amenable to the ideas presented if they could listen to them with those of their own kind. However that may be, a crowd of two thousand overflowed both meetings. More than half of the thirty-seven-member faculty were physicians, with the rest including diverse representatives of the behavioral sciences. The content of the meeting can be classified according to the headings offered in a booklet distributed there of recommended readings: Acupuncture and Oriental Medicine, Nutrition and Health, Biofeedback, Meditation, Hypnosis and Self-Regulation, Environmental and Social Aspects of Health and Disease, Psychology, Parapsychology and Altered States of Consciousness, Preventive Medicine, and Pathways to Wellness from Birth to Aging.

Here are some of the participants, and briefly what they said.

Kenneth R. Pelletier, Ph.D., assistant clinical professor, Department of Psychiatry, University of California School of Medicine; director, Psychosomatic Medicine Center of Gladman Memorial Hospital: In the affluent nations the cost of medical care has increased; so have the technical aspects of medical services, which may justify the increased expense. But health has not increased: The incidence of cardiovascular and respiratory diseases, depression and anxiety, arthritis and cancer is on the upswing. "The facts are that medical care in the affluent countries has very little to do with health." Rather than further expanding the present system, we require a new conception of disease and health, the focus of which is the whole person—body, mind, spirit—rather than merely diagnosis and treatment of illness. Pelletier cited his research on "spontaneous remissions," in which he found that people who overcame illness, inexplicably by usual medical criteria, had in common having altered their diet, their relationships with others, their spiritual attitudes; and had worked long and hard at overcoming their illness. Since stress causes disease, whether internally or environmentally, it follows that changes should be made in ways of life that produce stress.

Robert Rodale, editor and publisher of *Prevention* and *Organic Gardening and Farming* magazines; author of books on organic gardening, diet, and health: Standard preventive medicine, such as inoculation and public sanitation, depends on technical expertise often not understood by recipients and not requiring participation from them. People-centered prevention depends on public and professional education, with shared responsibility, and is safer, more effective, and less costly. Along the way, Rodale mentioned examples of American dietary abuse such as that the need for salt is approximately five grams per day, while Americans average between twenty and thirty grams, one reason for their incidence of high blood pressure. The taste for salt, he alleges, will easily go away as salt intake is reduced.

Arthur Ulene, M.D., obstetrician and gynecologist, with a regular television program devoted to medical questions (Q: "Doctor Ulene, how do you get on television?" A: "You begin by becoming a doctor."). It is easy to see why Dr. Ulene is a television personality. In the course of sending his message he had the audience in stitches (no pun intended). He raised the question of who was the rightful owner of the body: Doctors act as if they owned it, they know more about it, they maintain control over it, one follows the doctor's "orders." The government acts as if it owns the body by making regulations about it without educating the public as to why. The drug companies own the body in that their enormous influence, by, among other things, subsidizing medical journals with their advertising, determines a good deal of what is done to the body. Since the 1930s, when Hans Selye demonstrated that disease is a consequence of stress, we have had the obvious option of minimizing stress in order to prevent and treat illness, for example by meditation. Physicians have ignored that knowledge and option in favor of "zapping with drugs." Yet 50 per cent of migraine headaches yield to biofeedback (meditation with machines), and 85 per cent of herniated lumbar disks are improvable with exercise and meditation. Drugs not only are often less effective with these and other ills but have deleterious side effects and are costly. Nonetheless, the American Medical Association opposes giving patients product-information circulars, including possible side effects, along with the drugs. In effect the AMA's position is that it is none of the patient's business. Yet physicians, delivered drug-information circulars by the hundreds, are in no position adequately to evaluate each and every drug. The drug companies often determine what drugs the patient will receive. But we are unfair, Ulene says, in criticizing the medical profession, as it is now constituted and organized, for failing to provide information and techniques relative to health, rather than only illness. As things now stand no one pays physicians for health, only for illness, and as a result they have had little training in the promotion of health. They labor under a conflict of interest; without illness they would have no livelihood.

James Fadiman, Ph.D., director, Institute of Noetic Sciences; lecturer, Stanford University; director of research, Institute for Executive Research; author and lecturer: Fadiman sketched out and contrasted the "mechanistic" and "vitalistic" traditions in medicine. In the mechanistic tradition both illness and cure are physical, therapy is specific to organs, patients have no responsibility, there is an unrealistic demand for swift cures, and low-quality medicine is offered at high cost. In the vitalist tradition there is no such thing as an isolated disease, only systemic ones. Symptoms are one of the body's ways of healing itself. The body is a mental phenomenon that has its inner wisdom; people make a decision to become or remain ill. The physician should become an educator and coach, enabling the patient more adequately to assume responsibility for his health and employ his own powers for cure. Illness is evidence of a failure in education. Fadiman cites the Flexner report, which restricted the number of physicians trained, as a milestone in the development of the exclusionary, guild mentality of traditional physicians, one result of which is our need in recent years to import foreign physicians.

Brugh Joy, M.D., formerly a practitioner of internal medicine and now a teacher of alternative diagnostic and therapeutic techniques at the Sky-Hi Ranch, in Southern California: I had met Dr. Joy through our participation in a discussion group at a Council Grove, Kansas, meeting. I first learned there, in a somewhat allusive way, that at Dr. Joy's ranch people are treated with a variety of unconventional, including spiritual, approaches. With impeccable educational credentials and a flourishing private practice, he nevertheless came to believe that he had discovered a greater medical wisdom than he had been taught and was practicing. This wisdom seemed in part to have stemmed from his own alleged psychic abilities. In his talk, "Exploring New Ways of Healing," Dr. Joy emphasized the healing powers available when one transcends ordinary consciousness. The body, after all, is "just a radiation field" which is a function of a person's consciousness. "Resolution of the death space" through a recognition of reincarnation, he said, is necessary in order to overcome the fear of moving into the new, healing range of consciousness.

Paul Brenner, M.D., chairman, Department of Obstetrics and Gynecology, Scripps Memorial Hospital, La Jolla, California; assistant clinical professor of obstetrics and gynecology, University of California, San Diego School of Medicine; coauthor of *Consumers Guide to Gynecology:* Disease and illness can be equated with Einstein's law of relativity, according to Brenner. Mass is no more than congealed energy. Thought is mass, it occupies space, so it can exert influence, he said. The positive emotion usually called love is an expression of an electromagnetic field. The interruption of the flow of this energy encourages disease. The refusal to accept and love oneself contributes to that syndrome. Brenner recommends that people not assume that family members, for example, know of your love, but, rather, one should demonstrate it in order to encourage the flow of health-giving energy.

Thelma Moss, Ph.D., assistant research psychologist, UCLA Neuropsychiatric Institute; author of *The Probability of the Impossible:* Illustrating her points with sound movies Dr. Moss delineated such types of healing as hypnosis, magnetic passes, the laying on of hands, and prayer and distant healing. Using Kirlian photographs, she showed that when part of a leaf was cut away visible energy nonetheless remained, which suggests that the "energy body" transcends the "physical body." We all send emanations of energy from our bodies, of various qualities as shown in their various colors. We may direct such energy through laying on of hands or directly from our minds.

David E. Bresler, Ph.D., director, UCLA Pain Control Unit; assistant adjunct professor, Department of Anesthesiology, Gnathology, and Psychology, UCLA Schools of Medicine and Dentistry and College of Letters and Sciences: In ancient Taoist medicine there are five levels of physicians; from lowest to highest they are the veterinarian, acupuncturist, surgeon, nutritionist, and finally the philosopher-sage, who effects cure by going to the cause of the problem, which is some form of inharmonious living with nature. The superior physician is one who cures before illness is manifest; the inferior physician can cure only the illness he fails to prevent. We become sick through such inherited predispositions as genetic factors and karmic factors; through early developmental programming such as from prenatal and birth experiences, childhood experiences including primal events and learning to be sick; through nutritional factors such as poor food and air, and inadequate electromagnetic, cosmic, and life energy. We can improve health by dealing with inherited limitations, reprogramming early experiences as with Rolfing and guided imagery; and achieving nutritional balance through changes in eating, attention to breathing and sensing, generating and attracting life energy. We need to raise our "serum fun levels," allow into life the joy that reduces stress and encourages life-preserving energy. People choose illness in an attempt to balance their lives, to achieve harmony. Part of education in health is to offer new and better ways of achieving that harmony.

These were the plenary speakers. In addition the conference included symposia and workshops on the following topics: metaphysical medicine, an exploration of psychic phenomena, energy fields and the work of Edgar Cayce, therapeutic touch, techniques to re-establish energetic balance in the muscles and organs, life-crisis instruction, ways in which seeming adversity can be transformed to growth-producing experiences, acupuncture and oriental medicine, instruction in the Bates method of exercising one's eyes to improve eyesight, nutrition, a discussion of medicine and politics, losing weight through the employment of consciousness, ways to promote healthy growth throughout all stages of life, the team approach with cancer patients, biofeedback and the relaxation response, methods of self-regulation of bodily processes, alternative therapies for hypertension, asthma, and chronic pain, and a ninety-day program for improving psychophysiological balance with resultant benefits of better health and longer life.

This was one of many such conferences held, usually in California, throughout the year. The Center for Integral Medicine is one of many organizations with the same philosophy, values, aims, and methods. My mailbox bears an almost daily reminder of such conferences and organizations. As I write this, a circular arrives advertising a conference in which the following workshops are scheduled to occur: Acupuncture, Massage, Biofeedback, Stress Management, Diet/Nutrition, Physical Education, Chiropractic, Birthing, Fasting, Mind as Healer, Autogenics, Rolfing, Patterning, Weight Control, Hypnosis, Pain Control, Dentistry, Sex and Health, Yoga, Food Safety, Naturopathy, Homeopathy, Cancer Therapy, Physiology of Exercise, and Relaxation. One can see from this list that some are illustrative of the catholic exploration and use of specific methods designed to alleviate illness. Others are designed to prevent illness and to increase health. These are the two main thrusts of the new medicine. The first can be combined with traditional medicine but can also be competitive with it. The second has no competition. In conventional medicine health has been synonymous with the absence of symptoms. In the new medicine, health is a condition that admits of many degrees, only the first of which is absence of symptoms.

For thousands of years, including their present Communist society, the Chinese have rewarded physicians for keeping patients well. Having to cure sickness is evidence of their failure at this primary task, and is less rewarded. New, experimental attempts are being made now in American alternative medicine to apply this ancient Asian practice. For example, there is the work of John Travis, M.D., and his Wellness Resource Center.† I have not gone through this program, probably unfortunately for my health and certainly unfortunately for this report, but George Leonard has. He details his experiences in the *New West* of May 10, 1976. I do have a bulky sheaf of information and forms that describe the program. To begin with, "well medicine" is not medicine at all, since no medicines are used. The term is used only to show that it is a type of medical practice. Though perhaps without obvious physical or flagrant psychological symptoms, many people are bored and depressed, tense, anxious, or generally unhappy with their lives, and these experiences in turn sooner or later tend to lead to physical disease through the lowering of bodily resistance; or they abuse their body through smoking, drinking, and overeating, which also lead to disease. Phase one of the Wellness Resource Center program is an evaluation of how you live and how you view life as these relate to your health. This evaluation includes a survey of your heredity, physical condition, physical history, smoking and drinking habits, personal care and home safety, sleep, nutritional and environmental awareness, physical and emotional activities, community involvement, creative self-expression, automobile safety, and behavior as a parent.

Phase two involves training in how to minimize stress, through biofeedback, massage and breathing, improving vision, and artistic efforts. (As to the last, Travis is interested

† 42 Miller Avenue, Mill Valley, Calif. 94941

in the hypothesis that much tension "is partially a result of inhibition of a person's creative energy, hence the emphasis on expressing creativity.") Travis also draws on his acquaintance with transactional analysis, gestalt therapy, and bioenergetics as bases for his offered group meetings. The wellness evaluation results, among other things, in a computer printout entitled Health Hazard Appraisal. With this appraisal one can compare one's actual age with one's appraisal age (the same risk of dying as a person of this age), the compliance age (the same risk of death as a person of this age if one makes all the recommended changes in one's life and behavior), and the risk of death compared with the average of one's age, race, and sex.

Another example of an innovative alternative medicine program, this one designed to cure illness, is provided by the Pain and Health Rehabilitation Center,‡ under the direction of C. Norman Shealy, author of *The Pain Game* and *90 Days to Self-Health.* Dr. Shealy was a neurosurgeon who at one time dealt with pain through cutting nerves. He now treats pain through "retraining the nervous system," with biofeedback, autogenic training, and other voluntary self-regulation techniques; transcutaneous electrical nerve stimulation; mechanical applications such as ice, massage, heat, and physical exercise; and counseling in order to achieve a life style that minimizes stress. He claims that 84 per cent of those who take and practice the program find relief from chronic pain. Dr. Shealy notes the interchangeability of pain and disease and other symptoms, the cure of one being replaced by another until the underlying feelings and attitudes that are bringing about these difficulties are adequately dealt with.

I have not been through Shealy's program, but I have met and discussed these issues with him. Our first meeting

‡ 615 South Tenth Street, LaCrosse, Wis. 54601

occurred during the Mind as Healer—Mind as Slayer Conference. I was in the midst of my macrobiotic diet and joking with the breakfast waitress about the relative amount of fat in margarine and butter (anything to break up the monotony of the dull breakfast required by the diet). A cheery voice to my left informed me that I ought to go ahead and have the butter, as it was better for me than margarine. I need not worry, he said, about fat and cholesterol. He knew of research that contradicted the link between cholesterol and cardiovascular disease, in fact demonstrated that high fat, especially butter, could reduce cholesterol and improve body metabolism in general. When Dr. Shealy said that he was from Wisconsin, he smiled thinly in recognition of what he knew must be going through my mind, that his encomium in favor of butter was influenced by where the research was done, namely at the University of Wisconsin, in the heart of butter country. I was to learn later of a supporting study done safely outside butter country, as reported in a later chapter. Through the course of several increasingly improving breakfasts, Shealy obliquely suggested that I get in touch with Dr. Hal Huggins, who he said has done some interesting research on the fat-cholesterol issue, among other things. This suggestion was propitious, as we shall see.

It is hard to quarrel with the new medicine assertions that the cost of conventional medicine has gotten out of hand and that the results of such expenditures have not kept pace with costs; surely there is no denying the increase in the "diseases of civilization." I am confident also that apparently physical ills are at least in part brought about and sustained for psychological reasons and that the mind, particularly in meditative states, can produce significant bodily changes. I think it likely that following a program of positive well-being and prevention will invigorate one's daily existence, probably prevent or minimize the development of disease, and maybe extend life as well.

I do think, however, that if these activities and benefits are to be made maximally useful, people in the new medicine need to be careful not to oversell themselves in the same fashion that conventional medicine has been oversold, with consequent anger and disillusionment. Unless lifelong training as a yogi has achieved its highest fruition for you, "anything is possible" is a promise of more than can be delivered. Yet, much more is possible than we ordinarily give ourselves credit for, and could be possible should we adequately educate ourselves and exploit our capacities. But, for most of us, "anything" is not possible. Such an idea, along with "mental health" and being a "perfect" parent, are fine goals to have and to work for, so long as no one really expects to achieve them. To the extent that the new medicine movement is fueled by unregenerate hope, it is in for a fall. This movement might well safeguard itself also against the inherent seductiveness of its values and promises. Such promises as love, caring, and blooming health can be so entrancing as to befog one's intellect; they may soften the hard resolve to think conceptually and to pursue the hard work of research.

Members of the new medicine movement would increase their persuasiveness if they kept relentlessly in mind that they are proceeding on the basis of assumptions about the nature of man and the universe that are not shared, understood, or often even heard of in conventional Western medicine and thought. To be effective proselytizers as well as contributors to new theory and practice, they need to be clear and logical and recognize degrees of confidence appropriate to their assertions. To allow sloganeering to replace discipline may be fun and bring the like-minded closer, but in the long run it will be destructive of the stated aims.

I am wary about the rebellious push behind the movement, as can be seen in some of the cheap-shot jokes about conventional medicine. Rebelliousness can be a helpful motive, but if too much reliance is placed upon it, then after victory not much is left for continued vigor. It is a good starter but a poor finisher, as witness other social and political movements which end simply by being new versions of their old antagonists.

What are the options for conventional medicine? It could experiment, formally and empirically, with these new medicine practices and think through concepts with the goal of integrating the conventional and the alternative. It could create a new specialty, particularly one that dealt with the prevention and improvement of health. Or it could relegate alternative medicine practices to the paramedical: administration, supervision, and support of these activities by people trained short of full medical training. It could incorporate the new techniques of healing—it already has somewhat gingerly done so with respect to acupuncture* and biofeedback—while leaving prevention of disease and improvement of health to others. These "others" would then have the responsibility of creating a new professional discipline, whether medical or paramedical.

Or it could ignore the whole thing. The latter, I believe, would ultimately be disastrous. The genie is out of the bottle. The imperfections of conventional medicine are too

* In many states [in the United States], physicians are forbidden to use acupuncture for anesthesia, despite such claims as, for example, that a patient whose prostate has been removed under acupuncture anesthesia can walk back to his room and eat lunch, in contrast to the protracted postoperative illness following conventional anesthesia. The outlawing of acupuncture in some states was brought about by organized efforts of anesthesiologists.

glaring, the dissatisfaction with it too rife, the alternatives to it too intriguing and possibly too effective for the movement to go away. The result of ignoring the whole thing would be a decrease in the support and prestige of conventional medicine and a missed opportunity to enhance conventional medicine's health and the health of the rest of us.

17

The Will to Have Cancer and What to Do About It

"When I got my cancer diagnosis, I decided not to take the medicine, just die," Mrs. S. said evenly, challengingly. She had already made two suicidal gestures. We were meeting in her hospital room, where she had come because of a dangerously elevated white blood cell count; she was staying there out of reluctance to resume her usual life. As we talked, I fought my dismay with an inner clenched-fist assertion: *You will not die.* As we discussed living and dying and the place of psychotherapy in this struggle, I felt it was as if God and the Devil were fighting within her over her soul. One by one, I dealt my therapeutic cards until there were none left, and then I made them up as I went along. The end of our meeting was signaled by her ringing for the nurse and saying, "I want to get the hell out of here."

One of my therapeutic cards was new. Until recently I would have seen her as a dreadfully unlucky person, the victim of cruel capricious fate, certainly not as having participated in getting her disease. I would have tried to help her understand the vicissitudes of her work of separation, been available as a supporting figure; in general I would have followed the teachings of Kübler-Ross[1] on how to help patients die gracefully. Now I was willing to extend to her the hope that she could get over her cancer by working with me according to the program pioneered by Carl and Stephanie Simonton: a meditation-visualization procedure to relieve stress, and psychological work from the point of view that cancer could be understood in the same terms that any symptom or behavior could.*[2]

At the time, I had more nerve than experience. Until a few months before, I had had no idea that cancer might be influenced by psychological means. In the course of a biofeedback workshop the leader parenthetically mentioned that the Simontons had been helping cancer patients by teaching them to control internal processes through meditation, a sort of biofeedback without machines. I tucked this information away for future reference.

When Mrs. S. was diagnosed, I checked further with the biofeedback leader. She reported that a local person had achieved considerable improvement with the Simonton approach, and here was the number to call. This was the beginning of a fascinating and helpful association with Carl and Stephanie Simonton. It was to include guidance for me in my initial work with cancer patients, attendance at one of the weekend workshops the Simontons have been giving around the country, listening to a presentation of their work at a Los Angeles convention on holistic medicine, contributing to two of their presentations, and spending a week at their Texas retreat with patients and with students learning how to conduct week-long trainings in self-help for cancer.

O. Carl Simonton is a radiation oncologist in his thirties whose life is illustrative of one way people can become cre-

* A portion of my studies of the Simontons' work was graciously supported by Dr. Dean Fritzler and his associates in western Kansas.

ative, productive, and innovative. While his mother was pregnant with him, Simonton's grandmother developed cancer. Perhaps in reaction to his mother's depression over her mother, he was a sickly infant. At age seventeen he developed a cancer on the skin, which was removed without sequelae. He grew up with the idea that he was to become a physician, and his ambition was to cure cancer. He further intended to be, in his words, "the world's best radiation specialist." When he realized that as a radiation specialist he was not going to cure cancer very often, he became depressed. He fought his way out of that depression in part by looking around for alternatives to radiation, surgery, and chemotherapy. He developed his approach by picking up ideas from various human potential therapies and beliefs and trying them out with his patients while continuing to give radiation therapy.

When I asked him what he would and would not like said about him, he said that he would like to be known as logical and hard-working, and he would not like to be known as charismatic. He is logical and hard-working. He is not flamboyantly charismatic. But as a man who has developed and is in charge of what many people assume is a lifesaving enterprise, and whose personality generates liking and respect, he is, I must report, charismatic also.

Stephanie Matthews Simonton is Carl's thirty-year-old wife and co-worker. She used to train business executives; now she counsels cancer patients. She is living testimony to the raw talent for doing psychotherapy available among people without the degrees that conventional psychotherapists tend to insist are necessary for the practice of psychotherapy. She is facile with words, gentle and evocative in style, clear-thinking, and dedicated.

During the past several years, the Simontons have spent a good portion of their time presenting their work at various human potential conventions and in their own workshops. When not doing that, they treated patients at their office facility in Fort Worth, Texas, to which cancer patients came from around the country for an intensive week of therapy. That week included instruction and practice in meditation and visualization, and group and individual sessions in which patient and spouse learned to think psychologically about themselves. At the end of the week a plan was formulated for continued treatment in the patient's home community or for follow-up visits to the Simontons. This way of working has been superseded by one in which patients and spouses live for a week with the Simontons and their staff in a forest retreat several miles outside Fort Worth. Much of the same work goes on there as went on at their offices but in the intimate and sustained conditions of a twenty-four-hour-a-day experience cut off from one's usual life and other distractions.

I spent a week at this retreat, learning their methods and living with the paraphernalia of cancer, the wigs and bald heads from chemotherapy, the replacement breasts, the scars, tears, and overpowering worry. I have also spent time in cancer wards, among the bulging eyes and emaciated bodies, heads bumpy with metastases, and the smell of death. I have consulted with people who have lost their limbs to cancer and whose cancerous lungs caused them to cough their way through the interview. All this for a person who gets queasy going to a hospital even to visit a friend.

When I first heard of the possibility of my working with cancer patients according to the Simonton procedure, I felt ridiculous. Not only was I abashed, but I felt something of *hubris* at my psychological knowledge being used to take on death itself, waging a campaign usually fought with gleaming instruments and daunting technology. Somehow death from cancer seemed more imposing than the psychiatric deaths with which I customarily deal. I remember being relieved learning that friends of Mrs. S. had already broken the ice by acquainting her somewhat with the Simonton approach. I continue to feel a bit defensive when describing this approach to some of my skeptical medical colleagues. In short, I have to struggle with the difficulty that so many of us have in overcoming the separation between mind and body, in recognizing that we are at one and the same time expressions of both, and in principle can be changed by work with one or the other.

I could help counter my queasiness by drawing on my psychoanalytic experiences and my studies of the new therapies. I had learned, for example, the effect on mind and emotion through manipulation of the body, as in Rolfing, the Alexander technique, and bioenergetics. I had made numerous observations, in my ordinary psychoanalytic practice, of thoughts and feelings being expressed in bodily symptoms that were given up when they were adequately understood and integrated. Both of my parents had died of cancer, and I knew firsthand the hopeless recognition that "nothing more could be done," an experience against which my being arose in defiance, with consequent openness to other possibilities. Finally, I knew that we were in the midst of an epidemic of cancer, an explosion of the disease in the past thirty years to the point that one in four people can expect to develop cancer, and at the current rate of increase, by the year 2000 one in two people can expect it. Clearly it was no time to stand on ceremony.

I also knew of a slender but persistent strand of research implicating a relationship between psychological factors and the development and course of cancer, beginning with Galen's ancient observation that melancholic women are most likely to develop cancer. It is a sign of our times and the way we think that conventional medicine mostly proceeds as if such psychological research did not exist or is only a curiosity. I had thought the same way, knowing of several of the studies years previously, having concluded, "There must be something there," and then having forgotten about it.

Here are some of the major investigations and key findings. A variety of stresses are alleged to precede, and presumably lead to, cancer in animals and people. Such stress in animals may be electroshock[3] or rough handling.[4] In people it may be a variety of changes, including those which on the surface might be considered happy changes. In one study, death of a spouse was the maximally stressful event, with minor violations of the law at the other end of the continuum, and marriage intermediate.[5] Either the human organism is conservative in that it finds any change stressful, or the change was experienced outside of awareness as stressful no matter how supposedly happy or advantageous it may have appeared on the surface.

In a retrospective study LeShan noted that cancer patients had difficult early relationships with their parents, a feeling of rejection and distance from them; in early adulthood they found important substitutes for the difficult early relationships, and when these were lost tended to develop cancer. He also found that cancer patients had a marked inability to express anger.[6] In a longitudinal study of hundreds of medical students Thomas and Duszynski were able to discriminate cancer patients from patients with four other diseases on the basis of the cancer patients' perceiving a lack of closeness in their early relationships with their parents.[7] In this first clear-cut longitudinal study of its kind Thomas was able to state predictively what LeShan and others said only retrospectively. Schmale and Iker were able to predict, before diagnostic biopsies, which patients had cervical cancer, on the basis of pronounced feelings of hopelessness elicited during interviews.[8] Cancer can, then, be seen as an equivalent to suicide, an action also taken under sway of feelings of helplessness and hopelessness. Both Blumberg[9] and Klopfer[10] were able to show an association between personality characteristics, as measured by psychological tests, and fast-growing rather than slow-growing tumors.

Particular personality characteristics have been related to particular kinds of cancer, just as has long been done with such more or less recognizedly psychosomatic diseases as heart ailments, ulcers, colitis, rheumatoid arthritis, and asthma. Bacon et al. noted an association between breast cancer patients and sex-role difficulty.[11] Kissen showed that lung cancer patients had poor outlets for emotional discharge.[12] Greene noted that leukemia and lymphoma developed in a context of emotional loss through death of a mother or mother figure.[13] Wheeler and Caldwell found cervical cancer to be associated with childhood deprivation to a greater extent than it was with breast cancer patients and people with no cancer.[14]

It seems plausible that amid the smoke generated by these and many other researches, there is the fire of feelings, beliefs, and attitudes playing a role in the development and/or course of cancer. And if that is true, then it may well be that a reversal of such feelings, beliefs, and attitudes plays a role in the overcoming of cancer. That possibility is central to the Simontons' theory: People are responsible for bringing about their cancer, and if they are capable of giving themselves cancer they are by the same token capable of getting rid of it.

The Simontons subscribe to the generally accepted "surveillance theory." Most of us have cancer cells in our bodies most of the time, but these do not proliferate and become seen clinically as "cancer" because the immune system keeps them under control. Where the Simontons depart from general medical understanding is in their belief that psychological stress leading to depression and despair can turn off the immune system. It does so by influencing the limbic system to influence the hypothalamus; that depresses the immune system while through the pituitary and endocrine systems it increases the number of abnormal cells. On the basis of tissue-culture studies, Hans Selye writes that "normal cells can pick out and destroy cancer cells. The cells that have this function are the very types that have been shown to be depleted during stress."[15] When a psychological intervention leading to hope replaces stress and despair, immune activity is increased, and abnormal cells decrease in number.

Conventional cancer therapy is directed toward eliminating abnormal cells by surgery, chemotherapy, or radiation. A start has been made toward stimulating the immune system with, for example, hormones, tubercle bacillus, and components of the patient's own blood. The Simontons also believe in aiding the body to deal with cancer cells through conventional means, and they recognize the adverse role played by food additives, smoking, and industrial poisons. Yet they believe that the major stimuli for the sequence of neurohormonal mechanisms that produce cancer are psychological.

The meditation-visualization instruction is available on a cassette tape as recorded by Carl Simonton. Three times a day the patient is to follow this induction procedure, which includes systematically relaxing each part of the body, one of many ways by which people can enter a meditative state. The yogis have for thousands of years demonstrated that in the state of consciousness loosely called "meditative" an adept can control bodily processes that appear uncontrollable in his ordinary consciousness. He can walk on hot coals and lie on a bed of nails without injury or pain. Moreover, he can control those silent, inner processes called (it turns out erroneously) "involuntary," such as metabolism, heart rate, and blood pressure. As with hypnosis, such a procedure should, in principle, put to rest the separation of mind and body through its demonstration that even a mild, quick alteration of the mind can drastically alter the way the body functions.

The Simontons exploit this "power of the mind" by asserting that one may influence a change in oneself through visualizing in the meditative state how one would like things to be. For patients with active cancer, the Simonton instructions are to visualize the cancer, preferably in symbolic terms, and to visualize the treatment that he or she is receiving for it, the white blood cells attacking and destroying the cancer cells, and the disposal of the cancer cells. He asserts, on the basis of cellular biology, that cancer cells, contrary to many people's fantasies about them, are weak and confused cells and should properly be visualized as something that can be destroyed. He suggests, for example, that one might visualize the cancer cells as hamburger, with the white blood cells as a lion gobbling up the cancer cells and expelling them as waste. The visualizing task may sound easy, but it is not. People with a flagging will to live characteristically visualize and symbolize the cancer cells as stronger than the treatment or the white blood cells, a poor prognostic sign. Others make a display of eradicating the cancer cells, but on close examination it turns out that they subtly have built into their visualization the seeds of their defeat. For example, one patient in the course of visualizing cancer as an agriculture product meant to say that insecticide was to be used against it, but in a slip of the tongue called the insecticide "fertilizer." The cancer cells may be envisioned as crabs or ants, which seem insignificant enough until one takes into consideration the hard shells of crabs and their capacity to hang on, and the difficulties, as for example at a picnic, of ridding one's blanket entirely of ants. The Simontons encourage patients to alter their visualizations in favor of the cancer's being effectively destroyed. To facilitate this, the patient is encouraged to draw his visualizations so that they can be examined in detail. This visualization technique can be applied to anything else one wants to change in one's body: the relief of pain, the overcoming of stiff joints, clearing of the skin. When the patient has been free of the symptoms of cancer for a year, he can visualize his body as being clear of cancer, kept so by various antiseptic and sanitary measures. Moreover, one can visualize nonbodily desires such as being on a longed-for voyage, maintaining one's composure instead of losing one's temper, having a different job.

Pictures, the proponents of visualization tell us, are indeed worth thousands of words. Visualizations stem from the primordial portions of the mind, are closer to experience than are the more verbal, calculating parts of our mind. They offer more faithful versions of what is really going on: feelings, attitudes, and intentions unobscured by defensive strategies and by the following of social and intellectual forms. So it is that a patient may claim his intention to overcome his cancer but give away his nihilism and despair in his visualized pictures. As the yogis have long said, reality is created in the mind; in order to bring anything about, one has to be able first to imagine it.

In assessing a patient, one takes into consideration whether he thinks or does not think psychologically, one characteristic of which is whether he is inclined to ascribe the cause to forces outside of himself or to take responsibility for it. These differences matter a good deal with respect to whether patients accept the recommendations for treatment, follow through on them, and benefit from them. Such differences exist even among a population of people who have identified themselves as having psychiatric difficulties by coming to see a psychiatric worker. Many more people have psychiatric disturbances but do not identify themselves in that way, often because they have little inclination to see their difficulties as internal and to think about themselves in psychological terms. If it is true that cancer patients have unconsciously chosen their bodies as vehicles of expression for their thoughts and feelings instead of choosing words or overt behaviors, then they would be expected to be highly resistant to seeing themselves as psychiatric patients. They would be reluctant to ascribe their difficulties to motives within themselves, rather than seeing them as something visited upon them from the outside, and resistant to thinking about themselves in terms of their emotions, feelings, and motives. The experience of the Simontons, myself, and others who have worked with cancer patients corroborates this. Even allowing for the cancer patients' physical difficulties and other situational stress due to having a life-threatening illness, they are often difficult to work with from a psychological point of view.

This difficulty is partially attenuated by the way the Simontons select their patients. In response to his phone call, the patient is sent written materials describing the Simonton approach, a copy of *The Will to Live,* by Arnold Hutschneker (detailing the point of view that people choose their illnesses and whether they are to live or to die),[16] and the taped meditation-visualization procedure. They are advised to work with the tape for two or three weeks and to learn from the way their bodies react whether this mode of treatment is appropriate for them. If they then wish, they may call again. A great many people are no longer heard from, whether because their trial at the meditation has not helped with their bodily feelings, they have been turned off by having a psychological point of view presented to them central to which is the idea that they are to assume responsibility for their disease, or, as has been reported to the Simontons, they have improved to the point of feeling that they do not require further work (such improvement could have come about partially or entirely from any medical treatment they were getting conjointly). So, by the time they have come to the Simontons, usually from long distances and at substantial though not unreasonable cost, they are highly selected and highly motivated. But only relatively. They are still cancer patients, often in pain and struggling with physical disability, and are the products of a socially accepted way of thinking that has taught them that they have "gotten" a disease through bad luck rather than any inclination on their part.

Living together twenty-four hours a day for a week in the Simonton retreat setting offers a new social system, a new reality, one in which everyone believes, or acts as if he believes, that people participate in getting their illnesses, whether these be accidents, the common cold, arthritis, or cancer. A patient can be by himself for purposes of introspection and, indeed, time is put aside for solitary thought, but for the most part he lives very much a part of this subculture, this therapeutic system. Surrounded by forests, without radios, television, or newspapers, patients eat, sleep, swim, play, and work with others devoted to the same task as themselves, which helps make their reorientation possible. A further aid in this task is the organization of the week, beginning with its title, "Cancer Self-Help Education." Seeing psychological treatment as education does no substantive violence to the procedure and makes it for some people much more palatable. Participants are given a workbook which gives instructions for exercises, provides work sheets, and offers the theory of self and treatment that lies behind the enterprise. The Simontons believe, in effect, in bibliotherapy, that selected reading can contribute usefully to psychological therapy.

While the Simonton cancer patients could be said to receive education under the guise of therapy, the students in the Simonton training sequence to some extent receive therapy in the guise of education. They come to the training week in Texas in order to learn the cancer education/treatment procedures, but the teaching method is to have them experience the training program as much as possible in the same way that the cancer patients do.

During the week I attended, there were some fourteen of us: an internist, a psychologist, ministers, teachers, and counselors, all called "therapists." The students, the Simonton staff, and patients swam, played Ping-pong, ate (and for all I know some may have slept) together. The staff took turns working with the cancer patients and with the education group, both groups going through many similar techniques, procedures, and exercises. Moreover, as it turned out, at least three of the students were themselves cancer patients as well as Simonton students and therapists. The Simontons recommend that the self-help course with patients be led by at least one person who has or has had cancer. During one exercise, Stephanie Matthews Simonton, who could probably make the phone book come dramatically alive, led us, following a meditation induction, to imagine ourselves as cancer patients who had just received the news of a recurrence. This exercise evocatively made explicit the time-to-time feelings of all of us that there was a wavering, and sometimes broken, line between ourselves and the cancer patients. At the same time, we were aware we were not cancer patients, and I, presumably among others, also experienced "survivor's guilt." The health and vibrancy that I felt in my body and my minimal anxiety about death as compared to that of the patients seemed grounds for self-reproach.

If you wish to experience yourself and your health in psychological terms, you may want to do the following exercises, which we students and cancer patients did. Think of a disease or injury you have had or have, then think back before that disease, six months or a year, and notice what marked changes there were in your life, particularly those changes experienced by you as a loss. Substantial research has shown that cancer tends to occur after major shifts and losses, and particularly after the death of a spouse or other loved one, and so perhaps do all diseases.

Now write down on a sheet of paper five ways in which you may have contributed to your illness. In what way, for example, did you do something that helped bring about the "accident"? Did you eat badly or sleep too little or go without your rubbers in the rain? What was your state of mind at the time and how do you now see that state of mind, and if there were problems then, how do you see that illness would in a way solve them?

Now write down those things that you may have gotten, or may be getting, out of your illness. Practically everybody will notice the so-called "secondary gains," the attention and concern of others for the poor, innocent victim. (One wonders why one has to be sick in our society to gain kindness and solicitousness.) But each person will, upon looking deeper, notice his own special "rewards" for being ill.

A fellow student maintained that she had never been ill, which was just as subject to psychological understanding as illness was. She thought that she had to be perfect, dominant, in control, with illness being just one evidence of weakness and submissiveness which she would not tolerate. When, in discussing these matters, someone used the word "tears," experienced by many people as an expression of weakness and passivity, she heard instead "rage," experienced by many people as active and assertive.

After my patient, Mrs. S., received a clean bill of health—no sign of Hodgkin's disease clinically or through laboratory study—it seemed awkward to continue the usual visualization of the struggle against cancer cells. "Have her set goals," Stephanie advised, three-month goals, six-month goals, and one-year goals. The setting of goals proved to be the catalyst one might expect; it got to the heart of those problems in living previously in danger of being solved irrevocably by cancer. When one sets goals, one comes to terms with one's wants, is confronted with choice, and summons or inhibits one's capacities to solve problems. One either takes action toward their solution or cannot avoid seeing how one contributes, through inactivity if nothing else, to their festering continuance. To a person with a life-threatening illness, the setting of goals also makes concrete the intention to live at least to the times stipulated for the achievement of these goals. Goals should be concrete and specific, they should be measurable so that one knows whether one is achieving them, they should be realistic, rather than setups for failure, and they should be balanced between work, play, family, and love.

If you are still inclined to learn experientially, you might get some Play-Doh, as we did during the training week. Pick a time before you were ten years old, and construct with the Play-Doh a family scene. Now identify the characters in the scene, describe the scene, tell what the people are thinking and feeling and how they are interacting. Now think of your present family and compare it with the one portrayed in the Play-Doh scene. How is it the same? How is it different?

I expect that some of you, by doing these exercises, have begun to discover aspects of your personality either new or recently overlooked in the hurly-burly of life. Such experiences are increased manifold when they are done, as we did them, in small subgroups, directed here and there with deft questions and comments by a staff person, with members presenting their experiences and observations to the group as a whole and listening to those of others. In other words, these exercises become part of and encourage the ongoing introspective process.

The Simontons require that spouses attend the meeting, out of the recognition that many problems in living that result in cancer involve other family members, chiefly the spouse. For the most part, spouses sit silently and observe the workshop and activities in which the patient participates. However, they also get the opportunity to learn about the roles people play in relation to one another, roles they can hardly avoid being sucked into by family-group forces in interaction with their own personality. An easy one for the spouse of a cancer patient to fall into is that of the "Rescuer," which often shades into being a martyr. If a cancer patient's spouse carries on well in the face of the strains and demands of the illness, he tends to be roundly complimented and so is encouraged to hide any signs of "weakness," e.g., ordinary human frustration and despair. He can then find himself in the role of the Victim, with the patient as erstwhile Victim, now the "Persecutor," the one responsible for the Rescuer's having to become the Victim. Some characteristics of "rescuing," rather than simply helping, are that the Rescuer often does things that he really does not want to do yet cannot acknowledge his disinclination; he agrees to get help with a task but then does more than half the work; he fails to ask for what he wants, so driven is he by the need to do for someone else. You might notice such roles in your next family interaction, how swiftly Victim can change to Persecutor to Rescuer, and around it goes. The only way out of this dizzying triangle is to be aware that one is in it: to recognize the forces that pull one into various roles, and the signs that one has fallen into them.

The week-long course has been collated into a workbook largely written by Jim Creighton, who, along with his wife, Maggie, were among the instructors. Again, here were psychologically sophisticated, sensitive people, yet with minimal formal training and degrees. A professional writer and organizational consultant, Jim participated with the Simontons in the writing of their book.[17]

Before leaving for the training week, I received, as did the patients, several psychological test forms to be filled out. In order to fill them out seriously, I had to get off my high horse. I had myself administered many batteries of individual tests, taught them, supervised those of others by the hundreds, and authored a book reporting the test results of a research in psychotherapy.[18] So I had some false and irrelevant pride to swallow as I filled out the forms.

Toward the end of the week with the Simontons, I stretched out in the sun at the pool and read the report of my tests. It by no means addressed itself to the deeper layers of the personality in the way individually administered projective tests do, but it did nicely delineate and illuminate important aspects of behavior, and to some extent the feelings that encouraged that behavior. As it happened, just the night previously at a group meeting, I had acted upon some of the more unlovely aspects of my personality, pointed out in the report, to which my colleagues had vigorously reacted. The combination of that memory and the test report encouraged in me a somewhat painful but usefully reflective turn of mind.

Feeling bruised, however, I did not look forward to Stephanie's offer to discuss my report with me, which one or another staff member does with patients and students routinely. And, anyway, what was there to discuss? I summoned up a few questions just so there would not be an awkward silence. I underestimated Stephanie. Although she did not fudge any facts, by the time she was finished I was feeling as if the report were a valentine. Instead of a documentary of accusations, the report became simply a recognition of the way things were, with implications for improvement. Along the way, she pointed out the characteristic test patterns of cancer patients who do well and those who do not do well. She ended by reassuring me, if that is the word, that according to my test results if I got cancer, I would probably overcome it.

The Simontons rely heavily on such tests, finding that they give an accurate picture even though it may contradict the patient's surface presentation of self. Moreover, the tests change in consonance with the patient's psychological changes, thus providing an objective, independent monitor.

With the development of their Self-Help Education program the Simontons now turn their weekend workshops around the country, which used simply to be presentations of their work, into mini versions of the training week in Texas. I attended a workshop prior to this change at Prairie View Hospital, in Newton, Kansas. This small, private Mennonite psychiatric hospital is an oasis of human potential ideas, geographically far from the major human potential centers but able to get major personalities and practitioners each year in a series of weekend workshops. Carl

Simonton began this one by asking of the sixty or so persons which ones had cancer. No one raised his hand. Simonton then said that he knew there were people there with cancer, and would they please let us know who they were. Seven people raised their hands, and after they met in private with Simonton they volunteered to serve as subjects for demonstrations. (One was a beautiful young woman, only recently diagnosed as having cancer, who popped up as my table-tennis partner more than a year later in Texas, she being there for a follow-up week of treatment.) Simonton moved right in with those patients, demonstrating his interviewing and counseling techniques while elucidating the principles by which we and they were to understand the role cancer played in their personalities. Selecting demonstration subjects and working with them publicly may seem to some professionals at best crass and at worst poor practice. I can only report that the atmosphere of caring and directness established by the Simontons facilitated the speed with which people were able to be candid with other participants and themselves and to focus on the learning task. It seems a matter of base line. When you tread delicately, one false step seems a disaster. When you stride purposefully, details do not matter so much. In a psychoanalytic session marked by relative silence, therapist anonymity, and a minimum of spontaneous action, the slightest departure seems momentous. In the free-wheeling atmosphere of human potential work one can kiss, hug, and dance, reveal confidences, eat and play together without momentous emotional consequences.

When, toward the end of the workshop, we got to the setting of goals, all the patients did so, except one, who precipitously left the workshop. In a note left behind she explained that she had no goals and could not face this exercise. Inadvertently she supplied the group with important educational information. According to Simonton, it is just the inability to view life with purpose and hope which offers cancer a medium in which to thrive. This person became my patient shortly after, so we had the opportunity to observe the vicissitudes of her flagging will to live, her experience of the pointlessness of existence, and her wish to use cancer to exacerbate and dramatize the deprivations in her life. Through our working on these things regularly over a long period of time, she (at least at this writing) has increased her will to live. It is likely that had she simply called the Simontons and received the usual trial packet of material, she would not have followed through. Perhaps sending out material is insufficiently inviting and encouraging for some people, who under other circumstances could be helped into treatment and benefit from it. Or it may be a highly useful screening device.

The Simontons report that more than three quarters of the people who inquire and are given information and tapes fail to follow through the next steps, and this has been my experience as well. On the face of it this "noncompliance" is remarkable. Here are people to whom conventional medicine has extended little hope for definitive cure, who submit to surgery, radiation, and chemotherapy, with their associated great expense and often dreadful side effects, and who pass up a relatively inexpensive and manifestly harmless opportunity to improve their lot. In "The Refusal to Take One's Medicine"[19] and with the Simontons at Research Hospital, in Kansas City, I offered some explanations for why people refuse to take the Simonton medicine.

The world of conventional cancer treatment comprises shining, impressive machinery—a technology that implicitly promises the best that Western science has to offer, the distillation of medical wisdom. To consider words, thoughts, and meditations as in any way more effective than conventional treatment may seem ridiculous. Moreover, the psychological meaning of doing something "unconventional" to many people smacks of rebellion and carries intimations of retaliation from authority. Sometimes such fears are real. There are physicians who forbid their patients to do anything apart from the physicians' expertise and control. More likely the patient is caught in a superstitious fantasy that if he offends the gods of medicine they will no longer treat him, or the medicine that they offer will no longer work. He may also fear that if he looks inward at himself, stirs up his sensed stressful thoughts and feelings, his disease may get worse.

If it is true that the cancer is a last-ditch, despairing effort to solve problems and therefore felt as needed by the patient, then he has to face the giving up of that solution through treatment. It is all very well to talk of developing solutions to life problems different from cancer, but the patient who has settled upon cancer is likely to be pessimistic that other alternatives are possible and reluctant to face again the gloomy alternatives that led him to settle on cancer. Moreover, he may be the kind of person who finds it difficult to accept the idea of self-responsibility, for his cancer or for any other eventualities in life, who imagines he can find comfort only in ascribing causes to others and the role of victim to himself. He may think he needs the cancer for the same reasons that people need many symptoms that inhibit their development: as punishment for fantasied misdeeds, as a way of preventing growth and success that are unconsciously equated with destruction, as perpetrating revenge on those who they feel have not met their needs, as the ultimate plea for succor, pity, attention, and concern experienced as having been withheld in the past and as otherwise unavailable in the future.

An example of the refusal to take the Simonton medicine was a man in his early thirties with extensive metastases, who was at the end of the months that had been allotted to him to live. An associate of his had heard of my work, called me, and then told the patient about me. A day passed with no phone call from the patient. I thought that this already was significant. One would assume that people in such dire circumstances, given a ray of hope, would immediately follow up on it. I checked with the original, referring person, who learned that the patient was in the midst of an attack of pain, unable to talk except to say that he had intended to call me and would do so.

Could this man have developed an attack of pain in order to avoid coming to grips with a possible opportunity to be helped? Such a possibility was affirmed during our first phone conversation. He called me the day after his attack of pain and told me that someone had already given him the Simonton tape meditation to try, as well as some articles detailing the Simonton point of view. However, he found that when he tried to do the meditation, his pain *increased.* As a diagnostic probe, I wondered aloud whether he had given some thought to the possibility that he was bringing the pain about, in the manner described in the articles. "Oh, you don't really believe that!" he said. Although he maintained that he wanted to meet with me, when I tried to settle on a time for an appointment, he brought up a number of reasons why he could not make the times offered. In the course of this he said he had no money. I asked about insurance, and it turned out that he had insurance that would cover most of the fee. He claimed, however, not to have thought about that. Finally, after several tries, we agreed upon an appointment for the next day, though his inclination was to wait several days. This casual attitude about time was all the more striking since he had just finished telling me of the metastatic ravages of his cancer and that his allotted time was up. He did not appear for the stipulated appointment but instead sent a message that he wished to reschedule it. When I called to do so, he again offered various reasons why he could not make any of the times that I offered. He behaved as if he were making an appointment for a tennis date. His wife seemed to conspire in the difficulty. I heard him ask her, "Honey, do you want to go to Topeka tomorrow?" and he reported that she said that she did not. Finally I said that I probably could find an agreeable time but I wondered in view of the many difficulties in getting together how serious he was about meeting at all. He remonstrated with me, again objecting to the implication that he was not 100 per cent devoted to getting help. Finally, he agreed to come, but he neither came nor called.

The Simontons have noticed that some patients, when they face the possibility that they are responsible for having caused their cancer, rather than fate having given them a way out, get precipitously worse and die more quickly than was anticipated. This has happened often enough for the Simontons to have given the phenomenon a name: "nose dive." One of my early experiences using the Simonton method may have been of this kind. When visiting a cancer ward, I was asked to see an emotionally upset cancer patient who was expected to live about another three weeks. I talked to her in the psychological terms just described and promised to have a Simonton taped guide of the meditation sent to her. During the interview, after an initial burst of anxiety her mood dramatically improved. Her mother sought me out elsewhere in the hospital to tell me how appreciative she and her daughter were of my ideas, how much more composed the daughter was, and she wanted to know where I could be reached in the future in order to continue the work with me. Two days later the patient was dead.

How effective is the Simonton approach? My several patients at this writing are doing well. Not enough time has passed to say definitively that they are "cured." They have received conventional treatment along with my work, and I have no way of knowing that their improved physical situation is not due entirely to conventional cancer therapy. I do know how much and in what ways their psychological state, plausibly relevant to cancer, has changed, but that may have nothing to do with their physical changes. Simonton describes himself as observing and learning and working with cancer patients with the hope that they will live longer, will live better no matter how long that may be, and if they must die of cancer will do so peacefully and without pain. He says he wishes not to be identified as a great healer who has produced a cure for cancer. Nonetheless, he offers the following not unimpressive statistics as of January 1, 1978: Of 139 patients (20 of the original sample of 159 were lost to follow-up evaluation), 55 per cent (76) died. Twenty-two per cent (14) of the living 63 show no evidence of disease, 19 per cent (12) show tumor regression, 27 per cent (17) have their disease stabilized, and 32 per cent (20) show new tumor growth. Fifty-one per cent (32) have resumed all their previous activities, 25 per cent (16) resumed three quarters, 9.5 per cent (6) resumed one half, 9.5 per cent (6) resumed one quarter, 1.5 per cent (1) resumed less than one quarter, and 3 per cent (2) are hospitalized. The living patients have exceeded two times the national average for living time after diagnosis. Even those who died lived one and one half times longer than the national average. The patients included in these statistics were all judged medically incurable before coming to the

Simontons, so changes for the better could not likely be ascribed to medical treatment.

These statistics have to be read in the light of some considerations. The Simontons' patients are probably not representative of cancer patients in general. Because they select themselves, after experimentation with the meditation-visualization procedure and exposure to the Simonton theoretical approach, they are by definition motivated to participate. In other words the Simontons work with patients who are self-selected as to taking initiative and who include a high proportion of "fighters." The patients who did best were distinguished by being cantankerous, generally aggressive, as compared to the compliant, "good" patients, who tended to succumb.[20] These findings systematize informal observation such as, for example, that of Loren Humphrey, professor of surgery at the University of Missouri at Kansas City Medical School. He notes that those cancer patients who do well are scrappy, conspicuously and often loudly determined to conquer their cancers. They "do not go gentle into that good night," as do his depressed patients.[21] Indeed, physicians have long observed that patients with any disease can be classified as fighters and as those who are inclined to give up, with the fighters ordinarily doing better. The Simontons' patients are also better educated and from a higher socioeconomic class than the general population. It is questionable whether these characteristics alone could account for the results, though such people may be better nourished and have gotten better medical care than the general population. But if with these advantages they are still judged as incurable, they may be even more ill in some ways than the general population. High educational and socioeconomic background probably are instrumental in helping to get the patients to take and work on the Simonton approach. At this writing, the Simontons are developing a control group for the possible effects of these factors.

We should also recognize that should an association between psychological factors and cancer be unquestionably demonstrated, there still remains the possibility that both are caused by a third factor.

What are some of the ways of understanding how the Simonton approach may work against cancer?

There is much in the Simonton approach that could be labeled "placebo" or "suggestion." Their patients are in a condition of heightened need, selected for openness to change, and have something in the way of self-esteem at stake in having chosen an unconventional treatment. They usually claim to have found more warmth and sustained attention from the Simontons and their staff than they have from their usual medical practitioners. They feel themselves, and are treated, more as people than as carriers of a disease, in an atmosphere of respect and hope. While taking responsibility for one's destiny can be unnerving, some people appreciate the feeling of being in control, and develop new hope coincident with the understanding that they have a say in the way their life and cancer go. Finally, the personalities of the Simontons, no matter how much they may modestly disavow it, can be considered therapeutic. They radiate concern and kindness, made all the more convincing by their down-to-earth realism. How much of their success is attributable solely to themselves as people? Homogeneous as they are in approach, each has better success with some kinds of cancer than the other does, suggesting that the personality of the therapist is a relevant, uncontrolled variable.

The Simontons' psychological work is in some respects much like preparation for, or early stages of, long-term, intensive psychotherapy. Their patients are taught to move the locus of responsibility from outside to inside, to look to themselves for the causes of life events. They are shown how the seemingly accidental, random, and disparate can be understood as a coherent pattern, one that in various forms the patient may impose repeatedly. They are engaged in a mutual task of self-exploration, otherwise called a "therapeutic alliance," and it is implied that these mutual efforts are likely to be successful, that there is in this adventure hope.

Perhaps what the Simontons do is sufficient in and of itself. Neither they nor their patients conceive of their work as merely preparatory for long-term treatment. Although the Simontons encourage their patients to continue the work in their own communities, they nonetheless offer the treatment and follow-up weeks with them as central and determining, indeed sufficient if the patient deems it so. The patients may benefit from the internal timetable that people impose on whatever time is available. They may gain a good deal more from the limited period of time than they would if that same period of time were a part of a long or indefinite course (an application of Parkinson's Law).[22]

The medium of a short period of therapy in and of itself conveys the central message, that people are self-responsible. Long-term treatment may, for some patients and some therapists, unwittingly convey or encourage the impression that, no matter how much self-responsibility is talked about, the therapist will do more than his share. He is, after all, in there for an indefinite period of time and the patient comes to him for an indefinite period of time, scarcely a mode to encourage full self-responsibility. Sometimes this factor may be too little emphasized and analyzed. At other times, such analysis may be impeded by the actuality of unlimited help, which, despite all interpretive efforts, may seduce the patient into unwarranted dependence.

The Simonton psychological approach borrows heavily from gestalt psychotherapy, transactional analysis, learning theory, and the application of conscious intention. It attends more to the surface than to the depths of personality. Their patients are not only asked to reflect but to do, to take roles different from their usual ones (for example to stop playing the role of the victim, and of the persecutor when their needs are not met), to express their wants more, to do the things in life they have wanted but prevented themselves from doing, for example finishing an aborted educational degree. It may be that under the time pressures created by the illness, with the kind of personalities that develop cancer, with the way patients are selected, the Simonton approach may be more effective than any other form of psychological approach to cancer.

Yet, one should consider the possibility that if some psychological thinking and work are good, more might be better. As I watched some of their patients being interviewed on videotape and went over the test materials and other forms filled out by these same patients, I could hardly avoid making my usual clinical inferences. These included inferences about diagnostic strategy occasionally different from, and certainly in addition to, those used by the Simontons. Sometimes I noticed that the Simontons dealt with the same issues I would but in different words and guided by a different theoretical background. But at other times I struggled with the feeling that they were missing the boat. Whether this is so, or whether they just got where they wanted to go in a different way from the one I would have chosen, neither of us knows. In my own, usually extended work with cancer patients, I have gone into the usual vicissitudes and complexities of unconscious processes as these are related to the cancer, and see no way to try to help patients work toward liberating themselves from the coils of such processes other than to work them through lengthily and at depth. To what extent such work is instrumental in influencing the cancer and to what extent psychological and physical headway could be made more quickly and with a different format, such as that of the Simontons, are questions that remain to be responsibly answered.

In doing so it is important to separate the derived understanding of the cause and maintenance of the cancer from the capacity to alter it beneficially. One should not be so taken with the fit and plausibility of psychological material as to let it lead automatically to the assumption that the unearthing of such material is an effective or best way of curing cancer. And one should not take the remission or cure of cancer as "proof" of all of the psychological influences. Understanding and cure should each be evaluated in its own right.

One first step in evaluating a variety of therapies is to see what they have in common. If several investigators independently develop confidence in a particular approach, then that approach is more promising than if only one person has found it useful.

At the National Federation of Spiritual Healers, in England, headed by a renowned spiritualist, Harry Edwards, cancer patients are treated in many ways similar to the Simontons', although with one important difference, as we shall see. I have so far been unable to observe their work firsthand, but I have learned about them through correspondence with Mr. Edwards and from his writings. Their theory of the development of cancer will by now sound familiar: In cancer patients the purpose of life is blocked, and the resulting frustration influences the cells to throw off pituitary discipline and "become demented, imbecilic," and to transmit this faulty "intelligence" to succeeding generations of mindlessly proliferating cells. The treatment includes a meditation-visualization procedure. For a half hour, once a day, the patient practices deep breathing, offers an informal prayer to God, then visualizes the dispersal of the cancer—"Yourself as you wish to be, free from disease and with a song in your heart." The patient may then go on, in this meditation, to thinking healing thoughts about others as well.

The second element in the therapy is not done by the patient at all. Rather, he is the object of "intercession" by a spiritual healer usually at a distance from the patient. The patient fills out a questionnaire acquainting the healer with him, and the healer concentrates on healing that patient. This is not faith healing, because the patient is not required to have faith; indeed, some patients are alleged to be cured even when the distant healing is done unbeknownst to them. Rather, the spiritual healer is the channel for healing done by the "spirit doctors," those who have "passed" yet retain the wish and power to heal. The spirit doctors are alleged to recognize that the cancer is the result of psychological stress, and through the healer they "soothe, calm, and remove the inner frustration."

Clearly, the spiritual element departs from the Simonton approach and in part contradicts the Simonton emphasis on self-responsibility. The patient does have the responsibility to meditate, to work toward developing calmness and a positive, fearless outlook toward cancer and toward his life, and by implication to try to solve life problems. But he is not worked with around those psychological issues which have allegedly led to the occurrence and maintenance of problems in living. The spiritual healers, like the Simontons, encourage patients to have conventional medical treatment as well. And as with the Simontons, a large number of people who inquire about the program fail to follow through after the initial inquiry.

After nine months of this treatment, eighteen of three hundred fifty patients had died; ten of the eighteen had either started the treatment a matter of days before their death or were being treated by the spiritual healer from a distance, sometimes even without knowing they had cancer or were being treated. Assuming that the diagnoses were correct and the data reliable—large assumptions, to be sure—these results are far better than would ordinarily be expected in a population of severely ill cancer patients treated only by conventional means. If we assume that patients are benefiting from this approach, then we have to credit singly or in combination meditation, spiritual and distant healing, or suggestion/placebo.

Simonton does not know of the work of George Francis Barth, of the Nova Yoga Center, in New York. Barth knows of Simonton, but his meditative work predated Simonton's by decades. Now in his early seventies, Barth began to develop his work at the age of eighteen, following a brief exposure to Émile Coué. Largely self-taught, Barth amalgamated his method from yoga, Pavlovian conditioning, and behavior therapy in general, positive thinking, and William James, and added a dash of psychoanalysis. His basic procedure is meditation, taught by way of instructions on tape cassettes. He acknowledges the comparability to his own of other meditative techniques, such as transcendental meditation and those induced by biofeedback; they all produce a change, he believes, from beta to alpha brain waves. However, he adds to the meditation imagery and visualization what he calls "the Yoga of the imagination." He suggests, in *Nova Yoga*,[23] that in the meditative state one can bring about changes in oneself by way of visualizing such changes and encouraging oneself to behave as one wants and by expecting that the visualized desired states of affairs will come about. One is further encouraged to back up this autosuggestion by behaving as one wishes, intending and expecting, doing things one has thought were beyond one's capabilities. Barth also recommends a series of hatha-yoga, or physical exercises, and yoga breathing exercises, along with a low-carbohydrate diet.

Although Barth reports useful introspections at some depth, he emphasizes consciousness and will power, as against underlying factors, to a greater extent even than do the Simontons. He offers his work as useful for general relaxation and in establishing an improved image of oneself; in these ways it is a means of overcoming difficulties in living. He provides tapes especially designed for hypertensives, heart patients, and insomniacs, as well as cancer patients. One may cynically assume that he offers his procedure to almost anybody in order to sell tapes and books, with cancer just being a convenient market. That may be true, but it need not be true. His theory of cancer and how his work contends with cancer is much like that of the Simontons, though they arrived at their ideas separately. In principle, if the theory is correct, it is difficult to see that it would not be applicable to a wide variety of physical and emotional disturbances.

Also, Barth sees cancer as developing from a failure of the immune system under prolonged stress, with stress being a function of emotional turmoil. Even when such stress does not result in cancer, it leads to the litany of psychological ills of modern man: compulsive eating and smoking, feelings of inferiority, sexual impotence and headaches, phobias, inhibitions, and underachieving. The Simontons, too, agree that the meditation-visualization procedures and their psychological approach should in principle be useful for a variety of physical and emotional disturbances. Barth offers only anecdotal evidence for the success of his approach. However, he shares enough thinking and practices with the Simontons for us to assume that, if the Simontons are successful, then it is likely that he is also, though not necessarily to the same extent. He may be more or less successful depending on the relative efficacy of what they do not have in common.

The cancer work at the Center for the Healing Arts† is directed by Harold Stone, Ph.D., who studied with the Simontons and is applying their clinical work in his own ways. He has organized a formal cancer-research program, which I learned about from *Brain-Mind Bulletin.* In philosophy the Center group agrees with Simonton about the individual's being responsible for his illness, that permanent healing can occur only through basic changes in patients' feelings, thoughts, and attitudes, and that the will to live is crucial. The Center people are explicit about the need for the healers and those to be healed to be part of a healing community. They are more explicit about group work than the Simontons, with group therapy, seminars, and workshops built into the treatment program. Their meditation-visualization approach is identical to that of the Simontons. They are somewhat more catholic in their activities, emphasizing body therapy such as Rolfing, diet, and the doing of writing and fine arts in general.

When I received the outline of the Center's cancer-research program I was elated. Here was an experimental design with which to study the effect on cancer of a Simonton-like approach, complete with control groups and objective measures to yield data that could be subjected to statistical treatment. Their experimental design called for

† 11081 Missouri Avenue, Los Angeles, Calif. 90025

questionnaires, psychological tests (including such individually administered tests as the Rorschach test), medical indices, reports on the current status of the cancer, the regular collection of patient dreams, and skin tests as a measure of immunological status. Their main comparison was designed to be between the patients in their program and patients who received conventional treatment only, matched for age, sex, nature of the cancer, and time of original diagnosis. And their patients were to be compared with national statistics for cancer patients. Correlations were to be done between the skin tests and other medical indices and current status of the cancer reports, and between the various reports and dream content. Other correlations were to be made between questionnaires and psychological tests and observations of the various therapists. In short, here seemed a group of workers who were to employ the conventional rule book of science systematically in order to determine the usefulness of a combined alternative-therapy approach to cancer. It is just the sort of thing that is so badly needed in the babble of conflicting and formally unsubstantiated claims.

But, nagging at my enthusiasm was the fear that the study, at least as described, would never be completed. In psychological research it is a rule of thumb, or ought to be, that every research project turns out to be more complex and difficult than it first appears, and this one appeared plenty complex and difficult to begin with. Moreover, one reason that such research is rarely done in the new therapies is the kind of people who characteristically work in that field. Such free spirits are, after all, ordinarily disinclined toward, if not contemptuous of, the rule book of science and all that it stands for with respect to Western establishment values and personality traits. Indeed, as we have noticed, the new approaches have developed in part in reaction to or rebellion against just such beliefs and ways of working.

I spent an interesting afternoon with Harold Stone at the Center, other aspects of which have been reported on in the section on energy. With respect to the cancer research program, I soon learned that my fears were justified. The experimental design had been given up. It just did not fit with the way people felt and worked in this, not unusual, subgroup of the new therapies. Indeed, Stone himself found objectionable even the organized training program of the Simontons, particularly the issuance of a certificate upon completing it and all that that stood for in his mind. Moreover, I learned from him of changes in his philosophy about cancer that had come about in the course of working with cancer patients in the ways described in the research. At the beginning the objective of his group was to "cure cancer," to prolong life. Members now believe that their mission is not necessarily to prolong life but to work with patients toward transforming whatever life the patient should decide to have, the quality regardless of the quantity. They now recognize the patient's choice to live *or* die. They can delineate with him the issues and possibilities, but the patient has the right to decide on the basis of the advantages and disadvantages of living or dying as he sees them; by having thought through his decision, however much time he chooses to try to have would be of better quality than it would have been otherwise. In a recent statement of his newly evolved position, entitled "From Cure To Transformation," Stone writes, "One does not seek to fulfill one's life as an insurance policy against future death. One moves toward actualization of the present so that the present may not be dead." He goes on to say that he hopes that the patient will transform himself "on this life plane; but, if there are too many barriers, internal or external, then death becomes not only a legitimate option, but a natural choice that is obeying the person's transformational design." The Simontons, too, try to recognize the time when, after all is said and done, the patient makes the decision to die. They then shift toward "death counseling" in order to enhance the quality of this aspect of life. The cynic might say that this is all a fancy excuse for failure. But, then, cynics don't create, they stay back from the awful cutting edge of experimentation. In order to gain an informal opinion as to the validity of these ideas one has to be there, in the cancer patient's experiential world and one's own experiential world as revealed in such moments of decision. In order to know formally and decisively, one has to take account, in some kind of experimental design, of what one has learned. And for the moment there we are.

I recently attended a meeting at which a prominent psychiatrist presented his experiences working with groups of cancer patients. This presentation seemed to me a quintessential example of the traditional thinking about cancer, with which we must come to terms if new methods are to be given a fair trial. The presenter's apparent goal in working with his patients was to ease their state of mind. This work stimulated philosophical reflections in him and his patients about how life changes when death is imminent, or at least when one has a life-threatening disease. When several members of the audience at this meeting raised questions about the possible curative effects of his work, we learned of one ex-patient, his co-worker, still living seven years after having had extensive metastases. The psychiatrist told us also that most of his patients had lived for a year, which was substantially beyond what was expected. Noting this, he told us, "I began to feel funny, as if I was omnipotent. But then a bunch of the patients died." It is all too plausible why a bunch of his patients died. He may have transmitted his "funny feeling" to them, that they were not *supposed* to live on. Thus deprived of hope and expectation of life, they obligingly confirmed conventional wisdom. He said of the Simonton approach that he had not studied it much, but he did know that Simonton had been unable to document his claimed success. In his next sentence he remarked that some of his patients believed that stress played a part in cancer and that they meditated in order to ease stress. "My patients pull me along in that regard," he said. Finally, in response to a fairly clear and direct confrontation from the audience about the patients' apparent will to live, he said that he always respected patients' "denial"; "I would never interfere with denial." In other words, for him the will to live in cancer patients was a denial.

Here was a somewhat celebrated authority, recipient of thousands of government grant dollars, functioning in one of the country's major medical centers, who apparently had failed adequately to study the field of psychological effects on cancer. He seemed content, if not complacent, at overlooking the possibilities for curing cancer, despite the evidence from his own patients who lived beyond expectation and on their own initiative were working toward self-cure. It was a grisly demonstration of the power of conformity, stultification, and nihilism. This psychiatrist, working in a helping context, seemed as hopeless for his patients as the stereotypical surgeon who dismisses the patient with, "You have six months to live; there is nothing more that I can do."

True enough, the data are not all in. It may be that such nihilism is justified. However, the options are few and clear. One can assume that one has a hopeless disease, that one's chances for survival are dictated irrevocably by the statistics attached to one's disease and its treatment. Or one can embrace the assumption that control can be asserted over the disease, that its development and maintenance can be understood according to psychological dimensions, and that if one works at it one may create a new set of statistics. It is a choice that the therapist, as well as the patient, has to make.

Postscript

Today, as I was editing these pages, I heard an announcement on the radio about a young woman who had died of cancer. I had seen her a few times through the years. Her father and I had played in the pit band for a stage show side by side in the saxophone section. On several occasions, most recently a month ago, mutual friends had asked whether I thought I could do anything for this young woman. Each time, I encouraged them to let her and her parents know that I would be glad to try. Each time, the report was that the family objected to any unconventional treatment.

If, by chance, we had again played saxophone side by side, I probably would have drawn the father out and perhaps might have been able to get him to have his daughter try the Simonton approach. Or maybe not. His reaction is familiar and understandable. He knew full well that there are many cancer quacks and charlatans. He may well have been afraid, realistically or not, of angering his daughter's physician, on whom he felt her life depended. He may have been tired from having tried many treatments already and daunted by additional expenditures of time, money, and work. My guess is, like so many people, he asked his physician, who discouraged him. While I might have drawn him out on a bandstand, I was reluctant to telephone him. I imagined how difficult it would be for me to answer some such question as, If I had something that might help in the treatment of cancer, why did not everybody have it and use it? Why did not her physician suggest it, or at least condone it? I also imagined being asked what business it was of mine. It would in fact have been none of my business; spontaneously telephoning people and offering services is poor professional behavior.

So the intermediaries went back and forth to no avail.

The statistical likelihood is that the young woman would have died anyway, but I would like to have at least tried to help her. An incident like this drives the point home. In a rational, humane health-care system there should be an openness toward, and eager support for, evaluating any method that meets even minimal standards of documented past experience and plausibility. Selecting treatment modalities should not be left up to harried families, and evaluating them should not be left solely to lone practitioners and investigators. The last place our record in the "war on cancer" allows us to stand is on ceremony.

18

Further Afield with Cancer— Diet and Other Alternatives

I GRADUALLY ACCLIMATED myself to my new and unexpected role of working with cancer patients. It wasn't hard to get used to, since I was mainly doing the same kind of work that I did with my usual patients. Apart from monitoring the meditation-visualization procedure, I worked with these patients in order that they might learn about and experience those intrapsychic factors that might be disposing them toward developing cancer. In principle these factors were no different from the ones that dispose other people toward depression or suicide. More unexpected developments were to occur, and in unexpected ways. These would take me even farther afield from my training and experience. I was to be involved, also, in another and personal way for which I was untrained and unprepared, although many of us think we are ready for such eventualities. The better to portray how life follows art, the march of gathering events, the rest of this chapter will be chronological.

Fall 1975: I accept an invitation to speak in April 1976 at an alumni reunion of the Boston University Clinical

Psychology Training Program, from which I had received my doctoral degree nineteen years before.

March 1976: Roy Menninger sent me a letter he received from Jean Kohler, music professor and pianist at Ball State University, Muncie, Indiana, who wrote that he had been cured of an inoperable, probably metastasizing carcinoma of the pancreas by following an oriental diet, part of the macrobiotic way of life. Since then, Mr. Kohler has been proselytizing. He wrote The Menninger Foundation on the supposition that it was a medical, rather than a psychiatric, hospital, suggesting that we try this diet at least with our terminal patients. Mr. Kohler sent along copies of his laboratory studies, his hospital discharge note, which indeed certified unequivocally his diagnosis of cancer, and a letter from his physician, from which I quote: "I've had the pleasure of treating and being associated with Professor Jean Kohler for several years. I originally saw him approximately 26 months ago at which time he was unfortunately found to have an inoperable carcinoma of the pancreas, and was treated with one five-day course of 5-FU. He refused further chemotherapy and, instead, has been religiously following a macrobiotic diet. Certainly somewhat surprisingly but happily, he has had incredible response and he remains essentially free of symptoms from his malignancy and already has had a very remarkable course with his disease. Certainly, this cannot in any way be ascribed to his single course of 5-FU."

Having answered the first question raised by critics of cancer treatments, namely whether the patient really had cancer to begin with, Mr. Kohler went on to deal with the second, whether in fact the cure was due to what he thought it was, in this instance the diet. Kohler offered evidence in the form of an elevated alkaline phosphatase reading, in the midst of his apparent recovery, which Michio

Kushi, the man who prescribed his macrobiotic diet, said must have come about through his eating prohibited spices. Having felt so well for some time, Mr. Kohler had in fact taken these liberties with his diet. When he reinstated his exact diet, his laboratory readings returned to normal. He also sent along stories and partial substantiations of other people's alleged cures from cancer, apparently through following the macrobiotic diet.

Mr. Kohler mentioned in passing that he had cast around among various alternative therapies to cancer, had read about Simonton's work, and had done some of the meditations. Furthermore, psychic studies had been a long-time hobby of his, an expression of his belief that many things are possible that seem impossible. Finally, he was the sort of person who would turn down chemotherapy in favor of his own devices. Thus, there is in his situation the uncontrolled variable of the determination to get well and his belief in the possibilities of doing so despite conventional medical opinion that it was impossible.

Nonetheless, spurred on by further correspondence and phone conversations with Mr. Kohler, I searched around and found that many investigators, even within conventional medicine, have recently specified and experimentally supported a link between diet and cancer. A report published in November 1975 in the journal *Cancer Research* pretty well sums up the diet-cancer relationship as developed by conventional medicine.[1] The evidence offered there suggests that a diet high in animal fat and alcohol, with deficiencies in vitamins A and C and containing certain food additives and natural as well as man-made contaminants of food is related to the development of cancer of the colon, esophagus, stomach, breast, liver, and uterus. Cancer of the colon occurs most often in people who excessively consume meat and animal fat while underconsuming fibrous foods. Seventh-day Adventists who have been strict vegetarians all their lives have two or three times less risk of developing colon cancer than those who at one time ate meat. Breast cancer was linked to a fatty diet in humans and animals. There is a fivefold to tenfold difference in the death rate from breast cancer between countries with low-fat diets and those with high-fat diets. Stomach cancer is linked to nitrates and other preservatives. Heavy consumption of alcohol is associated with a high risk of developing cancer of the esophagus. It is assumed that ingredients of the daily diet may be causing, directly or indirectly, half of all cancers among women and thirty per cent of those among men. Gio B. Gori, deputy director of the Division of Cancer Cause and Prevention of the National Cancer Institute asserted before the Senate Select Committee on Nutrition and Human Needs, "Today the accumulation of epidemiologic and laboratory evidence in man and animals makes this notion [dietary components lead to cancer and cardiovascular disease] not only possible but certain."[2] The National Cancer Institute is now spending around five million dollars to support studies investigating the links between diet and cancer. (While five million dollars may seem like a lot of money, fifty million dollars is spent annually to explore the links between viruses and cancer.)

Michio Kushi, Kohler's mentor, agrees with the conclusions about the link between diet and disease, though he reaches them in a far different way. Kushi is president of East-West Foundation,* a center for study, teaching, and research on macrobiotics. Trained as a lawyer in Japan, Mr. Kushi has spent the past twenty-odd years based in the United States while conducting seminars and lecturing throughout this country and much of the rest of the world. In addition he is president of Erewhon, a producer and dis-

* 359 Boylston Street, Boston, Mass. 02116

tributor of natural foods. According to him, cancer, along with the chronic degenerative diseases such as heart disease and arthritis, all stem from fundamental imbalances in the way we live, and "We must change our way of life from the very foundation—including our way of eating and our way of thinking." Coinciding with the epidemic spread of cancer in modern societies over the past fifty, especially the past thirty, years, our way of eating has become increasingly artificial and unnatural, he says. Through ingesting food additives, colorings, preservatives, and refined, chemicalized food, our bodies have suffered degenerative changes, the symptoms of which are the familiar diseases. According to Mr. Kushi, the food we eat and the way we think produce toxins in our body, of which diseases are merely symptoms, attempts of the body to eliminate such toxins. By treating the symptoms, as is done in conventional medicine, we interfere with these elimination outlets, which results in an accumulation and damming up of toxins. Examples are fatty-acid deposits and chronically troublesome mucus such as are found in vaginal discharge, ovarian cysts, and kidney stones. The greater the accumulation the more severe the symptom, with cancer only the last stage of a long process of bodily attempts to eliminate toxins ingested through years of eating the modern, unnatural diet. While cancer was largely unknown in the past, there were some scattered cases, and four thousand years ago in traditional Indian medicine a diet was prescribed with which to cure cancer. This diet proscribed dairy food and prescribed cooked whole grains and vegetables, recommendations that are central to the macrobiotic diet.

As a basic diet for all people, only slightly changed to deal with a particular illness, Kushi recommends that half of the diet should comprise cooked whole cereal grains, particularly brown rice. A meal should begin with a fermented-enzyme soup. One should eat mostly cooked, but sometimes raw, vegetables. For protein there are beans, particularly soybeans, and for minerals there is seaweed. Any foods with preservatives and chemicals, any artificially refined foods such as white sugar and white flour, are proscribed. Small amounts of fish or white meat or poultry are allowable if strongly desired, but never red meat. In general one should eat foods that are indigenous to one's geographical area. Thus, meat for an Eskimo is not harmful, while tropical fruits and juice in temperate climates, which include most of the United States, are harmful.

April 1976: I rather doubt that I would have pursued this lead provided by Mr. Kohler except for the happenstance that I was to be speaking in Boston that month anyway. So it was that I visited the East-West Foundation on that trip. Mr. Kushi was away at the time, but I met with others of his staff, including Sherman Goldman, editor of the *East-West Journal*,† a counterculture monthly centrally concerned with macrobiotics but covering a variety of alternative approaches to health and environment. I was, however, not to be denied my usual procedure of being the subject of my experiments. According to macrobiotic and other oriental traditions, one can diagnose internal difficulties through external manifestations such as the shape of the head and features, the condition of the eyes, lines on the palms of the hands, and by palpating spots on the body, which if painful implicate associated organs. Acupuncture and reflexology are applications of the same principle, that internal areas of the body are represented by points on the surface that may be at considerable distance from the organ or system in question. Edward Esko, executive secretary of the East-West Foundation, had been trained in this diagnostic art by Kushi and was willing to

† 233 Harvard Street, Brookline, Mass. 02146

apply his skills to me. I had always been in generally good health, and I fully expected that Mr. Esko would so certify me. Far from it. I had, according to him (corroborated and extended at a later date by Mr. Kushi), an irregularly beating heart, a tendency toward anemia, trouble in my lower intestines, fat deposits in particular in the left kidney, a poor gall bladder and liver, and poor sugar metabolism, and I needed more protein. All this merely from looking at me and prodding a few spots.

Somewhat shaken and suddenly not feeling too well, I was more than a little alert to the dietary recommendations alleged to cure my ills. My new-found mentors took me to my first macrobiotic meal, in a nearby restaurant. I was introduced to tofu, a soybean cake; miso, which is a soybean paste used as a base for soup; and a host of prohibitions: no coffee, no tea, except for cereal "coffee" and dandelion and a couple of oriental teas, preferably no liquor (though beer, sake, and scotch, were listed in order of increasing noxiousness), very little fruit juice and water especially during eating, no vinegar or mayonnaise, a minimum of fresh fruit and no bananas (since they are tropical), and no potatoes, tomatoes, eggplant, beets, sweet potatoes, asparagus, spinach, mushrooms, avocados, or citrus fruits. Recommended vegetables are carrot tops, diakon radish, azuki beans, turnips with their leaves, scallions, onions, watercress, radish, burdock and lotus roots, pumpkin, hard squash, broccoli, and cauliflower. I was given the book *Sugar Blues*, by William Dufty, the husband of Gloria Swanson, herself a long-time devotee and proselytizer for the macrobiotic way of life.[3] This book finished off most of the remaining foods, since it turns out that many of our foods are made with refined sugar. Indeed, if one goes through one's pantry, as my family did, with the intent to rid it of sugar, one will find at the end that the cupboard is mostly bare. Sugar is said to be addictive, creates hunger, and offers no food value of its own, just empty calories.

In *Sugar Blues,* Dufty details the history of sugar as well as its ubiquitousness. He reports, for example, how the infant Coca-Cola Company, then a struggling local concern in Georgia, was enjoined not to send its products across state lines, it having been legally judged by trial to be harmful to health. *Sugar Blues* is a well-documented, hard-hitting, and persuasive book. I recommend it but only at your peril. You will either decide to contribute to your health by ridding your diet of refined sugar, or else you will become less healthy through worry at not doing so.

But macrobiotics is not only diet. As I was to learn on this visit, and particularly through reading *The Teachings of Michio Kushi,*[4] diet is simply one manifestation and practice stemming from a philosophy of life and man. This was somewhat tartly pointed out to me in the course of discussing with the macrobiotic staff, at dinner, problems relating oneself to authority. I brought into the discussion the possible need to supplement the dietary approach with attention to those psychological issues which might underlie such problems. I was informed that the macrobiotic approach, "the right way of life," takes care of the mental as well as the physical. I spoke of unconscious forces against which diet and education and good intentions might well be helpful but insufficient. One of the group thought what I had said was interesting and bore further thought, while another rather loftily dismissed it, so convinced was he that macrobiotics was all that was necessary to solve any health problem. In such narrowness lies the strength of the new therapies, in that they commandeer all of the worker's energy and enthusiasm. It is at the same time a weakness if a particular approach has only a piece of the truth and its adherents are unable to continue to learn and expand. Furthermore, the hard work of research is made much harder if one is sublimely convinced of the conclusions anyway.

The ancient oriental teachings from which macrobiotics is developed permeate the human potential movement in general. For example, Kushi suggests that we have a limited concept of space and time, and that we fail to find transcendence because we base our beliefs solely on sense perceptions. But while the human potential people move in the direction of increasing freedom of behavior, the macrobiotic approach is a highly conservative one, its objective being to find, and live according to, natural order, including for example such recommendations as that one should honor one's parents, one should refrain from birth-control pills, and that men and women should have clearly defined, separate roles.

According to macrobiotics, all food is to be eaten slowly, each mouthful chewed fifty to one hundred times. This is said to aid digestion, and fits also with the reverent, contemplative serenity that devotees try to achieve. If all these strictures sound difficult in the reading, I assure you they are at least as difficult in the doing, and especially so when traveling. The next morning at breakfast in my hotel, I was ready to begin the new experiment, but the world around me was not. Consider: no breakfast meat, no eggs, no butter, no citrus juice, no commercial dry cereal, no sugar, and my hands flew up over the coffee cup just in time to stop the waiter's first, fatal splash. No tea or milk either. I finally settled on dry whole wheat toast and hot oatmeal with stewed prunes on top of it for a sweetener, very little water, and a small prayer that this breakfast would sustain me through my two-hour presentation at the alumni meeting.

For the next fourteen months every meal was to become

a contest of wits between me and the supermarket and restaurant pushers, and occasionally between me and myself (once in a while I succumbed to a Kentucky Fried Chicken fix). I was not nearly as strict as I could have been, but I did quite well, considering the difficulties. Ideally one should enter a macrobiotic communal-living arrangement for a while in order to learn the new way of life and especially how to make the oriental dishes with which to replace Western ones. Life took on a new dimension as I entered what for me had previously been a never-never land. I read a number of books on the subject, became a denizen of health-food stores, developed practically a photographic memory for ingredient labels and products, and took out my gustatory frustration by way of hauteur toward the misguided, junk-food life around me. But what may have looked at times like serenity was often tight-lipped resignation. To their everlasting credit, my children were also tight-lipped, quietly putting up with all this and taking their meals, whenever possible, elsewhere. My wife, venturesome, curious, and scientific, joined in, not only learning a new way of eating but a new way of shopping and cooking.

June 1976: A vacation apartment on the beach at Monterey, California. Outside, waves crashing; inside, dry gray stillness around the edges of which disbelief and panic fight for attention. Knowing of my studies, a very close friend called to say that she had discovered a lump in her breast that might be cancerous, and needed to know what to do. I had little time, and less inclination, to enjoy the irony of it all. When it comes right down to it, where do you turn, whom do you trust, what do you do?

On the assumption that it just might be a benign cyst, a chief of department at a medical school tried unsuccessfully to aspirate it. (We were told later by another cancer specialist that this is a dangerous procedure, which could spread cancer.) My friend had already begun the Simonton meditation. The Simontons were away, but the physician handling their phone calls advised me to have her accept the conventional procedure, probable mastectomy (removal of breast or breasts and sometimes surrounding tissue as well) if the lump is found to be malignant. This may make life more difficult in many respects, he said, but the crucial will to live need not be drastically affected and sometimes is intensified under these changed circumstances. Of course she should go ahead with the meditation-visualization procedure. Through my macrobiotic connections, I tracked down Mr. Kushi by phone. He wanted to see the patient and to prescribe a specific diet for her. When I raised the question of the biopsy, if not mastectomy, he urged that she not be operated upon. We should, he said, give the diet some three or four months, anyway. "Not to worry," he said. As luck, or irony, would have it, I was already in the midst of negotiations to meet with Rev. Rosalyn Bruyere, a psychic healer, as part of my studies. Her capacity to diagnose cancer is said to be more accurate than mammography, and she is alleged to have success in treating it as well. She was about to set off to see my friend when she was called away by an emergency in her family. Several phone calls to friends and specialists ensued, and final plans were made by friend and husband for the lump to be removed under general anesthesia. Frequently, if a biopsy reveals a malignant lump, a mastectomy is immediately performed, while the patient is already anesthetized. The classic scene is for the patient to awake from the anesthesia to learn whether she does or does not any longer have a breast, whether she is home free, having had a benign tumor removed, or has entered the twilight world of cancer patients. Little needs to be added to the imagination about the miserable consequences of having a breast removed. Moreover, some studies suggest that such extensive and irreparable procedures are no more effective than lumpectomy (removal of the lump only). Yet that is conventional medical practice. And conventionality, superstitious and irrational though it sometimes is, means a lot at a time of such emergency. If nothing else, it relieves one of the awesome responsibility of deciding on one's own, made even more difficult if the decision is counter to the recommendations of the certified agents of society. The jaws of guilt loom ahead, ready to snap should one make a false step. Yielding of responsibility becomes seductive.

Yet there are alternatives, some known already and some I have hints I will find upon further exploration. This is to be my immediate task. I go to work on this suddenly nightmarish vacation, while my friend enters the hospital with the following plan: A biopsy is to be done, but no further steps taken just then, no matter what the diagnosis.

Spread out before me, as I write this, are the notes I made during several days on the telephone. In spots the paper is crumpled, the way it gets after fluid dries, perhaps some perspiration, evaporation from a beer can, or something. "New York, Chicago, National Cancer Institute in Bethesda; Brookhaven, Long Island; San Jose, Newport Beach, San Diego"; surely out there somewhere is "the answer." Several of my leads came from John Steinbocher, executive director of the International Association of Cancer Victims and Friends.‡ This organization, along with the Cancer Control Society,* are the alternative therapies' counterparts of the American Cancer Society. They serve as educational clearing houses and general organizational centers for cancer information and recommendations, and

‡ 434 San Vicente Boulevard, Los Angeles, Calif. 90048
* 2043 North Berendo Street, Los Angeles, Calif. 90027

regularly publish magazines which they send to their members and sell in health-food stores.

Steinbocher was matter-of-fact; after all, such stories as mine were all in a day's work for him. He alerted me to alternatives to "cutting, burning, and poisoning" (surgery, radiation, and chemotherapy) both from within and without the conventional medical establishment.

Inside the establishment, though outside the mainstream of conventional treatment, is the work of Virginia Livingston and others,† of attempting to stimulate the immune response with enzymes such as BCG, a bacillus developed sixty years ago by Calmette and Guérin at the Pasteur Institute. Another and more experimental approach toward triggering the immune system is provided by Lawrence Burton. He creates a serum from the patient's blood, a concentrate of the person's own immune factors, and injects it back into the patient. Chemotherapy, I learned, could be available with less-harmful side effects and more efficiency at the Janker Clinic, in Bonn, Germany, where a variety of drugs in experimental combinations with other cancer treatments allegedly produce considerably better results than those available at even prestigious American cancer centers. I learned that if one knows the right people it is possible to get in the United States drugs considered in Europe to be highly effective against cancer but prohibited by the Food and Drug Administration.

I learned of psychic healers who have allegedly had considerable success with cancer.

I was put in touch by telephone with the wife and associate of William Donald Kelley, whose book *One Answer to Cancer* is subtitled *An Ecological Approach to the Successful Treatment of Malignancy.*[5] Kelley, an orthodontist

† Livingston Clinic, 3232 Duke Street, San Diego, Calif. 92110

now in the State of Washington,‡ claims to have cured himself of pancreatic cancer with purges, coffee enemas, enzymes, fasts, and diet. In his view cancer is the result of a pancreatic enzyme deficiency. Because of this deficiency, the body is unable adequately to metabolize protein. Cancer is alleged by Kelley to be present long before it is clinically manifest. This presence can be ascertained, he says, by the Kelley Index of Malignancy, a urine test. Treatment includes a variety of nutritional supplements; detoxification of the body through purging, fasting, and enemas and other cleansing measures; and following dietary rules. These include the eating of almonds, minimizing the work of the pancreas by drastically cutting down on milk, cheese, meat, and peanuts, and restricting animal protein consumption to before 1:00 P.M. (If the latter is done, according to Kelley, "83% of cancer in the United States could be eliminated.") Seeds and sprouts, fresh fruit and fruit juices, raw salads, beans, and eggs are desirable. All refined foods, particularly white flour and white sugar, are to be avoided, along with teas, coffee, soft drinks, vinegar, chocolate, tobacco, pork, and white rice. The nerve supply to the pancreas and liver should be stimulated through osteopathic or chiropractic interventions. Finally, the cancer patient is encouraged to have a spiritual attitude. Kelley mentions the importance of a "complete self-analysis to better understand your own emotions," but his emphasis is on positive thinking and faith in God. While one can journey to Winthrop, Washington, for an individually tailored nutritional program, such a program is available also through filling out a 935-item questionnaire, which is then run through a computer. However, your participation in this program must be initiated and monitored by your doc-

‡ The Kelley Foundation of Life, Castle Avenue, Winthrop, Wash. 98862

tor, who must swear that, among other things, he is not, in effect, a spy for any federal or state agency. In other words, as a dentist, Dr. Kelley must not and does not prescribe medical treatment; he merely provides a nutritional service to qualified medical personnel.

I posed, for Steinbocher, the classic question: What would you do if it were *your* friend or relative? I would, he said, do three things: get immunotherapy from Virginia Livingston, find a diet, find a psychological approach.

Phone rings dagger me; I rush to the receiver. If the voice in that receiver said yes it was malignant, then the first, crushing decision was here, how much of what if anything to remove surgically. Then more research, and further placing of bets. One may never be fully prepared, but I was ready. The answer was "no," no malignancy, a benign cyst, patient doing fine, wants to get out of bed and leave the hospital. Weeks later she and I agreed some good has got to come from this. I hope some of that good comes from this public recounting.

I have thus far only scratched the surface of the list of alternative approaches to cancer: educational organizations, books, and nontoxic methods. Among the latter are Gerson therapy, grape cure, Hoxsey treatment, the Koch treatment, psychotronics, and vitamin and mineral supplements. Given a lethal incurable disease and the desperation it engenders, one would expect a proliferation of quack cures, whether to make money or through misguided humanitarianism.

It seems reasonable that if someone really wanted to live he would not quietly accept the death sentence so often handed out by conventional medicine. But if he does not accept that sentence, he must set sail on uncharted seas and depend upon whoever has an opinion, informed or not, be swayed by one or another often irrelevant consideration, and sooner or later just take his chances. In any health-care system organized on rational, to say nothing of compassionate, grounds it should be possible to find out, definitively, what usefulness there might be in any of the approaches. That is not possible in the American health-care system. There is a class of researches of moderate respectability, notably on drugs. But the new therapies, even when propounded by physicians, lie mostly outside the pale. Nonetheless, one can get opinions about them from one's family doctor, through specialists and chiefs of service in prestigious medical schools, and from the American Cancer Society. But in the absence of experimentation and firsthand clinical experience these opinions have to be products more of prejudice than information. It is one thing to say that a particular approach is ineffective, after one has adequately experimented with it, and quite another to deliver an uninformed opinion backed up by authority and respect earned on the basis of other knowledge or in other fields.

Cancer treatment is a $20-billion-a-year industry. Nine hundred million dollars a year is now being poured into research by the National Cancer Institute, state and local governments, and such private institutions as the American Cancer Society, yet with little lifesaving gain. One might reasonably expect that in such a situation, with that kind of money available, there would be studies on any approach that showed promise. Or maybe just because there *is* so much money available, pressures to limit investigation in favor of one's own are intense. How *does* one explain such an irrational and ultimately cruel situation?

I called the American Cancer Society and inquired about the macrobiotic and William Kelley diets and the work of Simonton. My informant did not know what I was talking about until I pressed him, suggesting that surely he must have heard something of these approaches. "Oh," he said, "they must be in our 'unproven methods' files." Sure enough, there they were. I was then sent an article by the ACS on Kelley that begins, "After careful study of the literature and other information available to it, the American Cancer Society does not have evidence that treatment with the Kelley Ecology Therapy results in objective benefit in the treatment of cancer, or that the Kelley Malignancy Index is a proven method of diagnosing cancer in human beings." Fine, except that there was no list of references, no documentation of the "literature and other information available to it." Indeed, there was nothing in the article at all that would allow the reader to make an assessment of the American Cancer Society's assessment, not even to get any feel for what it is based on. The article sent to me on the macrobiotic diet begins, "Following a careful review of the literature and other data available, the American Cancer Society is of the opinion that the Zen Macrobiotic Diet poses a serious hazard to health and is not beneficial to the treatment of cancer." This article does include some references, but the articles are opinions, rather than experimental findings. One such listed opinion appeared in *McCall's* magazine, and was written by Frederick J. Stare, M.D. In 1960 Dr. Stare, then chairman of the Department of Nutrition at Harvard Medical School, spoke supportively of enriched white bread and food additives, opinions offered after Harvard received a gift of over $1 million from General Foods to expand the nutritional facilities in the School of Public Health.[6] This is the same Dr. Stare who has recently tried to blunt the growing criticism of junk foods[7] and who defends sugar and highly sugared prepared cereals. He is a paid "consultant" for the sugar and cereal industries. The ACS article reads as if macrobiotic diet #7, as propounded by the founder of the discipline, George Ohsawa, is what macrobiotic dieting is all about: "Today this is the most popular of the original ten diets." That is not so. Number 7 is the most severe of Ohsawa's diets, and one must work up to it, though most people stop short of it. More to the point, the writer of the article totally fails to take into consideration the work of Michio Kushi and others who apply the same general principles as Ohsawa but nowhere nearly as strictly as in Ohsawa's #7 diet. Indeed, as I know from firsthand teaching and observation, Kushi and his group encourage one to listen to the wisdom of the body, to avoid being rigid in the application of the diet, to apply its general principles slowly over a period of time according to how one feels.

With respect to the work of Simonton, the American Cancer Society merely sent a copy of one of his lectures. Some months later I again called the Society's main office in New York to inquire about Simonton and found out that the Society knew little or nothing about him. My ACS source, a physician, said that the Society had asked its Texas branch to investigate but that Simonton seemed a hard person to get to meet. He allegedly would make appointments and not show up, and my informant suggested that this seemed to be "the sign of a quack." As far as he knew, therefore, nothing had been learned firsthand about Simonton's work. I finally informed him about what I knew of the work. He asked if I would send him some of Simonton's materials. I suggested that it really was a simple matter to write or call Simonton and ask for the materials himself, as Simonton freely sends out materials about his work. Presumably he did not have the address and number, since he asked me for them. I further suggested that though Simonton and his wife are in almost constant motion between their every-three-week treatment retreats, and lecturing around the country, it is most likely that one can gain an appointment with them and that they would keep it. I mentioned in fact that they are eager for acceptance by establishment groups. Just that week, Stephanie Simonton had enthusiastically told me about being asked to participate in a program sponsored by the Los Angeles Medical Society.

In short the American Cancer Society was abysmally ignorant of the Simontons and their work, and was hardly making an effort to do anything about that ignorance. Nonetheless, I received a letter from the Kansas Division of the American Cancer Society, in response to my earlier phone call inquiring what they might know about Simonton. They acknowledged that they were "unable to locate any documented information" about him. However, "a discussion with the American Cancer Society office in Fort Worth revealed that that office 'did not know what his status is with the local medical society . . . but he is associated with the 'Freedom of Choice' movement. The American Cancer Society in Fort Worth does not consider his theories particularly reliable or reputable.' " Incredible! What does not knowing what his status is with the local medical society mean, other than as an innuendo that his status is questionable? Anyway, all they would have had to do to find out about his status would have been to call the medical society. Instead, they offer the "information" that he is associated with the Freedom of Choice movement, which is not only irrelevant to the possible usefulness of his approach to cancer but wrong. The Simontons are highly critical of that movement, unimpressed by the choices patients should be made free to have and critical of an approach that neglects the patient's self-responsibility in favor of a cure from outside. The Fort Worth office of the American Cancer Society commits character assassination in offering its uninformed, sniffing opinion of Simonton's work.

A confidant high up in the profession of cancer specialists, who for reasons soon to be obvious will be unnamed, characterizes the American Cancer Society as a bloated industry that uses the greatest proportion of every dollar it collects to maintain itself in not inconsiderable style. He points out that if cancer were cured the ACS would be out of business, a conflict of interest that could be insidious. The Food and Drug Administration, with whom he has regularly dealt, is in his view persuaded directly or indirectly by American drug manufacturers not to test and allow the importation of a variety of drugs used popularly, and with apparent success, in Europe.

The only possible defense, it seems to me, for not being informed and adequately testing an approach to the diagnosis or cure of cancer is that there is not even any face validity to the approach, although even this is a risky position to take. But many of the alternative approaches do have their adherents, their testimonials, and are often supported and practiced by some physicians. It seems that the medical establishment, including portions of the government and such putatively independent organizations as the American Cancer Society, have delimited the field of cancer treatment and research, which, no matter how ineffective, they stick to implacably. For them, apparently, there are no alternatives.

Whatever the effectiveness or lack thereof of macrobiotics in the treatment of cancer or in the promotion of health in general, I was able to gather some information suggesting that there may be a good deal to the methods of oriental diagnosis. I gathered these data in the course of a visit that Mr. Kushi paid to The Menninger Foundation. (He was a dinner guest in my home. Can you imagine fixing dinner for the nation's premier macrobiotic-diet exponent? The menu: miso soup, brown rice and shrimp, broccoli, sake and Japanese plum wine, and bancha tea.)

Mr. Kushi makes diagnoses with barely a look, even in social situations. We arranged, however, to accommodate twenty-six people who volunteered for diagnoses taking perhaps ten minutes each. I had each person fill out a questionnaire designed to ascertain what observations Mr. Kushi made of the person's physical and mental status, how accurate he was for each observation, and his prescriptions for the difficulties he diagnosed. He was diagnostically accurate in 42 per cent of the instances.* This was based on a total of 132 problems, with each person averaging approximately five and one third problems. So Mr. Kushi was apparently incorrect more than half the time. Some of the illnesses he diagnosed, however, might have been present but as yet unknown to the bearer.

More significant, perhaps, than the number of misses was the number of correct diagnoses. Those who have studied oriental medicine will hardly be surprised, as diagnosing from observation of the surface of the body is an accepted practice in this tradition. To the Western mind it seems like legerdemain. Western physicians do learn a good bit of information by visual inspection, and in certain instances can diagnose alcoholism or liver disease and other ills which are reflected on the surface. But, according to oriental physicians, a wide variety of diseases bear subtle indications on the surface, which require special training to observe, training unavailable in Western medicine.

If oriental medical people know that much which is unknown to us, it behooves us to consider the rest of what they have to say and recommend. Mr. Kushi also made inferences about the health and personality of the parents of

* Data were collated by Judith Koontz, M.D.

the people he saw, and of various behaviors of that person, remarking in one instance, for example, that the subject "had a tendency as a child to go away from the house [run away from home]." According to the respondents, he correctly spotted allergies, a heart murmur, a person with few medical troubles, atherosclerosis in the right anterior artery (it affected also the left one), mild depression and a memory that the person "would be better off to forget," sinus trouble, chronic bronchitis, breast cyst (though he missed that on another subject), and Hodgkin's disease. He correctly identified two cancers, and declared eleven other people to be cancerous or precancerous. I hope that he is not entirely accurate. He said that six to eight months previously I was on the way to developing a clinically manifest cancer, but that this no longer was a problem. As it happened, I had visited the East-West Foundation and begun my macrobiotic diet experiment eight months previously. He either made a public relations calculation, or was inaccurate, or possibly saved my life.

Four months later, Mr. Kushi gave me a jiffy diagnostic examination as we were standing around waiting for a meeting to begin. He pronounced me much better, but my eyes still showed traces of fat, and he said I must be using more than the recommended amount of oil in cooking. (True.)

Different backgrounds and professions, different objectives, different attitudes, and different parts of the world were brought together by the East-West Foundation in a conference entitled "A Nutritional Approach to Cancer," at Pine Manor College, in a suburb of Boston. One group of participants comprised cancer patients and macrobiotic leaders from various nations, and these participants for the most part offered testimonials as to how a macrobiotic diet had either cured cancer or dramatically relieved patients of pain even though they died. Jean Kohler was one of the participants. He is an articulate, energetic person whose story about the cure of his cancer is interesting and persuasive. However, as I have pointed out to the East-West people, his story and that of a dozen or so others is offered in a repeated series of publications from the East-West Foundation, which leaves the implication that this handful of testimonials is all that there is. If Kohler's kind of cure is really available to many people who have cancer, then surely there should be many others who can offer testimonials to a growing, rather than repeated, list circulated by the Foundation.

Another group comprised, largely, professionals who addressed themselves to the need to do research of a kind and quality adequate to convince the medical establishment that the macrobiotic diet belongs in the therapeutic armamentarium against cancer. Some of my prepared remarks were of this kind. I offered a plea to rise above chaos by observing the rule book of science, so that conclusions could be reached as to the effectiveness of which kind of diet for which kind of people having which disease and with which kind of goal under which environmental conditions. While observation and anecdote, each man his own experimenter, is an important early means of study, it was time to go beyond that.

Dr. Frank Speizer, of the Department of Medicine of Harvard Medical School, seconded my remarks, and added to them his own, more tartly and exhaustively put. He pointed out the, in effect, closed-mindedness of the macrobiotic people, which is just what they are accusing the medical profession of. He cited the macrobiotic disinclination to put much stock in the lung-cancer and smoking relationship. He questioned how serious the macrobiotic people were in wanting their ideas to be accepted if they demurred in supporting rigorous scientific investigations. In his view, only investigations of that kind stood a chance of influencing the medical profession or other scientific investigators.

The forthrightness of these remarks smoked out another segment of the group, probably resulting in the sort of overstatement the dynamics of groups tend to produce. Dr. Robert Mendelsohn, of the University of Chicago Medical School and chairman of the Illinois Medical Licensure Board, among other prestigious things, said, "I would like to dissociate myself from any attempt to set up medical scientists as gatekeepers to social or political action. I would also like to dissociate myself from any attempt to state that science as it exists today in medicine is any more valuable than anecdotal evidence. [Applause] I want to dissociate myself from any attempt to take a position that will ask for more funding for further medical or scientific research. I'm simply not interested in that. [Applause] . . . we are by no means convinced of the superiority of the medical or scientific approach." The stage was thus set for William Dufty (the author of *Sugar Blues* and husband of Gloria Swanson, you remember). He took an exceedingly dim view of the possibility of persuading anybody about macrobiotics or much of anything else: ". . . one is apt to be successful in changing people in inverse ratio to the amount of energy one devotes to it." With regard to the medical establishment, he said, "The hell with it, they are terminal. [Applause]" In his view, ". . . the best in Western science is slowly, tortuously arriving at the point where oriental wisdom begins, that the signs are all around us and we must celebrate the fact and that we are there with our arms open waiting for them and are not running to open arms waiting to be accepted by anybody else."

So what was going on here? The usual polarization, reducing complexity to simplicity, heat overtaking light. I had tried, in my prepared remarks, to address just this issue. I had sketched out the rationale for a psychological approach to cancer to range alongside the dietary approach. And I pointed out that even within the dietary approach there were contradictions; for example, Kushi forbids eggs for cancer patients, while Kelley recommends them. Thus, it was no time to be carried away in simplistic conviction that any approach, or any single theory, necessarily had the one and final answer. We should fight against the demands of each of our specialties that requires, or seems to require, a narrowing of attention, a fear of change, a dismay at dealing with the complexity of disciplines alien to our own. We have to recognize that each discipline tends to draw to it particular personality types, willing and able to pursue one line of investigation but ill at ease when confronted by another. We have to separate substance from ideas influenced by the politics of degrees, cultural expectations, organizations, and rewards. Instead of thinking in terms of single cause and single effect, we might better think in terms of what Freud called the complemental series, essentially a ratio: the more of one the less of the other. Thus, with a strong genetic disposition toward cancer, only a relatively small degree of psychological stress and exposure to cancer-producing environmental substance and only a moderately poor cancer-producing diet would be necessary to produce the cancer. With a small genetic inclination, little exposure to cancer-producing environmental substances, and a minimum of psychological stress, it would take a prolonged and highly cancer-producing diet to cause cancer. Treatment programs should be designed with recognition of the relative contributions from various causes.

In a postprandial discussion many of the participants

made the classic errors of bureaucratic planning for research. They papered over the fundamental philosophical differences as to the usefulness of research that had surfaced during the main meeting. Instead, they displaced internal difficulties onto the external world, occupying themselves with the alleged hostile lack of understanding in the medical and scientific communities. They concerned themselves with problems in getting research funds. They got into the minutiae of experimental designs. These flailings are expectable in early planning and shakedown experiences. However, I was all too familiarly reminded of many other initial stages of research thought that got nowhere beyond these blind alleys. I probably did nothing to add to my popularity by calling the group's attention to the dangers of expending its energies in these ways, energies that might better be spent on matters of greater substance. For example, how about clarification of philosophy and objectives: does the group really want to do research, or is this simply a grudging acquiescence to felt pressures? How about a list of specific questions that people are interested in and whose answers would be useful to the over-all objectives? Then it would be time to specify what activities would be necessary to answer those questions, in other words to design an experiment. Finally, one has to recognize that to be a good clinician or educator does not necessarily mean that one is a good researcher. The specialized skills of research planning and implementation require specialists; it is not an activity that usually goes well when done with a little time squeezed into a schedule of diverse activities. Are there the resources, human as well as financial, the talent, energy, and motivation necessary to conceive and carry through such a demanding task as formal research is? This meeting provided the podium for these thoughts, but they are just as applicable to any of the other alternative therapies. For that matter, they are often just as relevant and necessary with respect to conventional therapies.

I ended my macrobiotic diet experiment after fourteen months, under circumstances soon to be related. How to evaluate its effects? Some of my good feelings about my body and health could, I think, be traced to the effects of suggestion and to the gratifications of asceticism. At least three times a day I was involved in an orgy of self-deprivation, and for some people that is good for their souls; it absorbs guilt, it supplies the conditions under which other pleasures become acceptable, and it adds at times a nice touch of martyrish heroics. I enjoyed, also, thinking of my body as clear of those dreadful, toxic substances inflicted on us by evil industry, and I imagined myself free of cloying, demanding deposits of fat. I allowed to surface somewhat self-righteous feelings about not eating other living things (not much of them anyway, and fairly low down on the evolutionary scale, which seems to make a difference). I had little in the way of colds or sore throats, and no other illnesses, though that is not exceptional for me. My blood pressure and cholesterol readings were low, but they were low before the diet also. Whether due to the diet or not, a laboratory technician was amazed when she drew blood for a routine examination. Previously, she had had a good deal of difficulty finding my veins for an adequate insertion of the needle. Now she described my veins as "beautiful," for that purpose anyway. Unequivocal, however, was a weight loss of something over twenty pounds, maybe four or five of which I could have lost with profit. As a presumed consequence of this weight loss, I was physically weaker, and I think less energetic over all, requiring a good deal of sleep, and less able to produce my usual level of work in parts of the afternoon and evening. My digestive system improved in some ways and not in others. A slight pain, especially upon arising, in the bottom joint on the little finger of my right hand was unaffected by the diet. Presumably it was arthritic, though another oriental diagnostician said it was due to a vitamin deficiency. Of course the major benefit propounded by macrobiotic people is, if there are no diseases to cure, the prevention of degenerative diseases. I have no way of knowing, at this point, whether the fourteen months on the diet were useful in that regard.

Whatever its effects on my body, the happenstance of my being exposed to macrobiotics opened for me the whole question of the relationship between disease and nutrition, in turn an opening into the world of alternative medicine in general and oriental medicine in particular, as all these approaches were stimulated by the duress of my friend's cancer scare. Macrobiotics was the opening gun in a salvo of diets to which I was alerted, and some of its recommendations are most likely valid; at least they are shared by various other diets. I retain the prohibitions against refined sugar, refined white flour, nicotine, coffee, alcohol, and many dairy products. Due to macrobiotics I can never again be a typically gluttonous junk-food American, impervious to the likely importance of what he chooses to eat.

19

Are You Being Taken by What You Take In?

SUPPOSE, JUST SUPPOSE, that the standard American diet is injurious to physical and mental health. Then we would have the bizarre situation of people being given therapy in one part of a hospital while that therapy was being undone in another; e.g., tranquilizing the patient with medicine or interpretations while he is being stimulated by sugar and caffeine. Like pouring water into a bucket with a hole in it.

Many members of the counterculture, medical and psychological, believe that this Kafkaesque script is reality. Diet is another of the fronts on which they fight. While at the usual professional meetings restaurants are generally packed, at human potential group meetings restaurants may be strangely underpopulated. A not infrequent sight at human potential meetings is of brown bags of food pulled from knapsacks, the food eaten at any odd moment. According to the new nutritionists, bringing your own food is the only way to cross safely the gustatory mine fields of America.

It is understandable that the human potential counterculture should find its ideas compatible with those of the new nutritionists. Both groups show an affinity for the old-fashioned and basic; many of the alternative diet recommendations are taken from homeopathy. In the sociopsychological atmosphere of our times, the new nutritionists, too, experience themselves as wise underdogs amid overweening and destructive ignorance. Just as human potential people believe that our society pursues profit to the neglect of human values, the new nutritionists consider the huge modern food processing and distributing combines antithetical to human health: Under the lash of the need for profits food is "manufactured" for high markup and convenience: preservatives and other additives lower the cost of distribution, and dye makes food visually attractive, sometimes obscuring its defects and sometimes adding a harmful substance. Harmful or useless as they may be nutritionally, products that can be made popular, if not addictive, dominate the diet.

Ready for human potential parenting, diet is yet another area of ignorance and neglect left an orphan by conventional medicine. Nutrition is little taught in most medical schools, as part of a pattern of neglect of prevention of illness and of implementation of positive well-being. Instead, nutrition is consigned to nutritionists or dieticians, who may or may not know substantially more about the subject than physicians but are often handmaidens of the medical bureaucracy, faced either with going along or bucking the establishment.

Consistent with the human potential movement's proneness to hyperbole are the soaring benefits alleged possible from what alternative therapists and physicians believe is proper nutrition. According to these enthusiasts, almost any human ailment may yield to the right diet. As discussed in Chapter 17, diet has been put forth as a cure for cancer and also as playing a role in its development. Diet is also said to cure mental disorders and other illnesses. Good diet is said to lead not merely to the cure and prevention of disease but to the enhancement of vibrant good health and of such special capacities as insightfulness, empathy, even paranormal abilities. Psychic and meditative abilities, for example, are said to be improved by not eating meat.

The new nutrition is chaotic in ways similiar to the new therapies and medicine in general. It features a mixture of hypothesis, fancy, half facts, and beginning experimentation. It is a morass of largely separatist movements often in conflict with one another. As usual there are authorities but not always authority. Take, for example, the following article subheadline in *Better Nutrition,* a health-food-store giveaway: "Dr. Jean Mayer and Dr. Frederick Stare, both well known as newspaper columnists and nutrition consultants before government committees, take opposing views on sugar, as we have always known. But they are both off target in chastising the health-food movement for its nutritional contributions."

Even an occasional conventional physician or dentist will say that in the next five to ten years nutritional findings and practices may revolutionize prevention and treatment of any or all human physical and mental disorders. They may be taking their cue, in part, from Linus Pauling. Under the auspices of his institute in Menlo Park, California, cancer patients treated with high doses of ascorbate (vitamin C) are said to have lived over five times as long as matched control patients. Evidence is being gathered there that vitamin C is not only therapeutic but prophylactic in regard to cancer; further evidence is being adduced to show that it retards aging. Pauling's work is part of orthomolecular psychiatry, whose adherents believe that schizophrenia and other mental illnesses are best cured with nutrition, often with megavitamin doses. At the Pauling institute schizophrenic patients were shown to be abnormally low in ascorbic acid and some B-complex vitamins.[1] His institution workers are also trying to develop new methods of analyzing body fluids for early diagnosis and screening, which could lead to prevention of many diseases by way of nutrition.

My awareness of the discipline of nutrition began when my mother enrolled in a course in nutrition as part of the World War II home-front war effort. The family diet did not change much, but it was now backed up by "science." Like most other people, I was inculcated with the belief that the standard U.S. "good" diet was the path to good health. This diet was considered "balanced," in that it included something from the carbohydrates column, the proteins column, and the fats column. Up until World War II there was probably some truth to that approach. One could then easily purchase fresh, unprocessed, unchemicalized food. Practically the only way to do that now is to grow your own. In the past thirty years, as eating patterns have changed and food "manufacturing" has increased, so have the degenerative diseases: arthritis, cardiovascular disease, cancer. Correlation does not mean causation, but it does offer grounds for hypotheses.

As I began to study the alternative therapies and alternative-medicine cultures, I became exposed to the writings of Adelle Davis, and I subscribed to *Prevention* magazine. Enter the pill, pills of all shapes, sizes, and colors designed to "supplement" our nutritionally deficient food. This is the shotgun approach to nutrition: There are general rules about what "the body" needs, and no matter what body you have it is assumed that you will benefit from the standard doses of standard supplements. ("Standard" is used loosely, since various prescribers have various standards.) So, I took vitamins A, B, C, and D, dolomite, desiccated liver, folic acid, lecithin, kelp, and selenium. There may have been a few others from time to time; fashions change. Pantothenic acid was "in" for a while, now ginseng is hot. My macrobiotic phase put an end to the pills, or at least it was supposed to. I kept popping a few of my favorites, though according to macrobiotics a proper diet obviates the need for such packaged supplementation. *Sugar Blues* led to sugar mania. The white devil, sugar, was in the exasperatingly small print on practically every food-and-drink label consulted, and I learned to suspect that it could be found in every unlabeled substance as well. For example, I have before me letters from the Coors and Olympia beer companies. Upon reading in *Sugar Blues* that most beer includes sugar, I solicited these letters not only for scientific reasons. I hoped that I would be able to quaff an occasional beer without having to rationalize ingesting sugar as well as that other evil, alcohol. The Coors letter included unsolicited information, self-congratulatory you can be sure, as well as the following: "The only sugar in Coors beer is derived from barley malt. A small amount of sucrose appears in a lab check after cooking, but this is the first sugar to be consumed in the fermenting process." I delightedly showed this letter to Dr. Hal Huggins, of whom we shall shortly hear in detail. He called attention to the list of ingredients attached to the letter, which included "refined cornstarch," and said, "in other words, sugar." The ingredients of Olympia beer looked all right to me: barley malt, refined corn grits, rice, hops, and water, and so I now drink Olympia. I have not troubled myself to show the Olympia letter to Huggins, and every once in a while I wonder about those refined corn grits.

The moral of the story is that it is extremely difficult in this day and age in the United States to avoid imbibing refined sugar. If even a small percentage of William

Dufty's claims in *Sugar Blues* about the deleterious effects of sugar are true, then we are systematically making ourselves sick through what we eat and drink. Alongside the Rorschach test, according to Dufty, one would have to give glucose tolerance tests in order to rule out the possibility that mental illness was not a result of nutritional difficulties resulting from more sugar than the body can metabolize.

You may remember my previously mentioned chance breakfast meeting with Norman Shealy, and his throwaway line that I might be interested in some of the things that Hal Huggins was doing. I wrote to Huggins mostly out of dutiful completeness, and pretty much forgot about it. Months later, my next nutritional phase was ushered in by a phone call from Huggins, followed by some literature from him and reports of his research. He turns out to be a rather expansive and ebullient person whose enthusiasm and conviction could lead you to think that he either was going to relieve you of your valuables before the boat got to New Orleans or that he was offering brilliant iconoclastic contributions. Imbued with enthusiasm for his work, he seems to want everyone to be similarly imbued.

Early on in our initial phone conversation Huggins said that he was a dentist, the implication being that if I was one of those medical establishment types who wouldn't countenance what a dentist had to say we could stop right there. He wanted me also to realize that, as a dentist, he was not offering to cure or prevent "medical" illnesses. He had made some discoveries about how to treat dental problems nutritionally through treating the body as a system. If other symptoms or derangements should be prevented or cured in the course of his curing and preventing periodontal disease and caries, then that would be all to the good but accidental so far as his intention was concerned. He later informally told me anecdotes about nutritional cures of multiple sclerosis, cancer (especially Hodgkin's disease and leukemia), diabetes, paranoia, phobias, sleep disturbance, epilepsy, and of restoration of vision, all occurring under his nutritional regime for dental problems. His compound in Colorado Springs comprises a dental building, where he conducts a general dental practice, and an impressive laboratory building with, he told me, a quarter of a million dollars' worth of machinery for diagnostic testing of nutritional deficiencies. He spends about a third of the year giving workshops around the country in how to apply his nutritional approach, called "balancing body chemistries." These workshops take place mainly at dental schools or under other dental auspices and are largely unknown to physicians.

"Balancing body chemistries" is the umbrella term for bringing the body's vitamin, enzyme, and mineral readings into normal ranges, and some of them in proper ratio to one another. From a Huggins brochure: "There are systemic reasons behind why some people have degenerative disease and others have excellent health. These systemic reasons may be related to glandular malfunctions, improper metabolism of foods, or simply that a person is not eating what his body needs." All these sources of difficulty are dealt with through the Huggins program. His examination includes a blood-serum study of calcium, phosphorous, glucose, cholesterol, and triglycerides, basic to carbohydrate metabolism; and other studies basic to protein metabolism. He also analyzes those trace elements which frequently act as catalysts, or activators of chemical reactions, something like the ignition of an automobile. Trace-element assays could be made on tissues of the body, but it is much easier to do such assays by analyzing hair. A barber will cut a couple of tablespoons of it, close to the nape of the neck for greatest accuracy. No harm to your appearance, but you may have to contend with your barber's open or hidden concern for you.

Hair gives a reading of total-body trace-element metabolism in a similar fashion to the way the body values give a reading of metabolic activity. Hair analysis also tells the amount in the system of such injurious minerals as lead, cadmium, and mercury. All these data can be read so that one knows what is being helpfully used by the body, not simply what a person may be ingesting. For example, I was said to have a vitamin E deficiency even though taking 800 milligrams of vitamin E daily. Though I may not have been getting enough usable protein from my macrobiotic diet, it would not have substantially mattered had I been taking in more protein, for according to Huggins' tests I was insufficiently metabolizing it.

While Huggins could be considered as part of the new medicine, in that he questions fundamental assumptions and functions independently of the mainstream of dentistry and medicine, he does not share, indeed is more or less oblivious to, human potential philosophies and values. For example, he is traditionally experimental. Among his experimentally derived findings are the conclusions that bovine milk in the human diet inhibits the absorption of magnesium, which is "probably why Americans who drink a lot of milk also have numerous cavities." Another of his researches shows the possible role in the development of leukemia of mercury leached out of silver dental fillings.

High blood levels of cholesterol contribute to atherosclerosis and coronary artery disease, and cholesterol gets high through ingestion of saturated fats from eggs, butter, fatty meat, and a lot of calories, right? No; wrong, according to Huggins. He put a group of high-cholesterol people and another group, of low-cholesterol people, on identical diets of a minimum of two whole eggs and one quarter pound of butter daily (drastically limiting sugar) and found the following: People low in cholesterol showed higher cholesterol readings. People high in cholesterol showed lower cholesterol readings. Both readings stabilized at what he considers normal levels (about 220 milligrams per cent). Cholesterol is, after all, manufactured by the body; for example, it is important in the myelinization of the brain and in the manufacture of steroids. So one should not simply try to get rid of as much of it as possible. The usual studies of the cholesterol diet and cardiovascular disease relationship fail to control for sugar and other dietary considerations. The found relationships hold for the standard American diet, but according to Huggins do not hold for a diet that balances body chemistries.

Huggins' basic diet recommendations include a minimum of two eggs and a quarter pound of butter a day. They include also meat or fish every day, sometimes twice a day, with the addition of meat for breakfast. He reminds us that protein taken at breakfast is available for energy through the afternoon. Dairy products are pretty much proscribed, and carbohydrate intake is limited. White flour is prohibited, for it is not only low in nutriments but a drain on the system. No sugar, caffeine, nicotine, or alcohol (except a glass of European white wine with dinner, for digestive if not medicinal purposes). Then, on the basis of one's specific blood and hair readings a variety of supplements in the form of pills are prescribed.

In addition to the possibly therapeutic effects of following a fixed basic diet and supplementary vitamins and minerals, one also enters into a possibly therapeutic human relationship, at Dr. Huggins' clinic, which continues on. The laboratory results are first explained by a warm and friendly counselor who is later available by phone or letter and who monitors the patient's progress. Second blood readings are taken within the first week, hair and blood analyses are repeated four months later, then six months after that. These repeated studies give patient and counselor an opportunity to see whether they are headed in the right direction and to make commensurate changes. While the four-month and six-month studies can be done by mail, it is highly recommended that the introductory explanation and first implementation of the program be done at Huggins' laboratories* or those of others who balance body chemistries in the same way he does. There should be a good many such programs by now, since Huggins alone has given so many workshops and seminars throughout the country. Other dentists, chiropractors, and self-styled nutritionists teach and proselytize this work as well.

A psychotherapist friend of mine telephoned to say that a patient of hers insisted on nutritional counseling for her chronic, repeated depressions; could I recommend someone? No, I could not recommend anyone, but I could inform her about Huggins' work. The patient immediately went to him and started on the program of diet and supplements. Almost as immediately, she began to feel better. About four months later she came to tell me in detail of her experiences and to thank me for the "recommendation." She had had, in her words, a "cure which seemed like a miracle." This sixty-one-year-old woman had been hospitalized for suicidal depression at age forty-nine, and after hospital treatment received once-a-week psychotherapy for five years, a brief course of psychotherapy sometime after that, and for the last two years had had more intermittent psychotherapy. She had finally insisted on

* Analytic Laboratories, 100 East Cheyenne, Colorado Springs, Colo. 80906

nutritional counseling because she had a feeling that her disturbances, at least now, were not due to events in her life; she could not fit her disturbance into any of the patterns of thinking and behaviors she had learned about in her years of psychotherapy. They must be, she reasoned, something apart from or in addition to psychological causes. Until her recent reading about nutritional approaches, she had not paid any particular attention to nutrition. She spontaneously raised the question of the degree to which suggestion had played a part in her cure but noted that she had tried religion in addition to her years of psychotherapy and neither of these approaches produced cures by way of suggestion. Indeed, her low-key, no-nonsense attitude was reassuring on that score. Her husband volunteered, heartfully, that she was markedly changed; it was a great relief after all she and the family had been through for so many years. Not only did suicide seem the farthest thing from her mind, but for the first time in years she was awakening in the morning without a wracking headache. Previously, except for an occasional week, she would wake at five in the morning daily, head aching and with a feeling of not wanting to get out of bed. It may be of some significance in this case that Huggins frequently includes 300 milligrams of lithium daily among the prescribed supplements.

Several months later, a cancer was discovered in this patient's breast. Could it be that, deprived of one symptom, she developed another? Or perhaps the lifting of the depression allowed her to care for herself enough to discover the cancer and have it diagnosed. Any therapy may set a process of change in motion whose sometimes far-flung effects are difficult to predict.

Well, those are the reported facts and experiences about balancing body chemistries. What to make of them? Prejudice makes any positive conclusions of mine suspect. I find it reassuring to have numbers attached to statements, experiments to back up the meanings of these numbers, and to have repeated measurements that purport to show what is actually happening on the basis of which therapeutic measures are dictated. Possibly even more trenchant is the great change in my gustatory life, from the abstemious and demanding macrobiotic diet to the practically bacchanalian Huggins recommendations. I wanted badly to believe in the need for butter, eggs, and meat. All of a sudden my conscience had a new set of dietary rules; some of what previously was "good" was now "bad." When I did the "good" things, I felt better. Was this because of psychological change or the warm glow of inner approval? The breaking of a rule produced bad feelings, and perhaps an occasional physical symptom—consequences of diet or built-in punishment?

As we shall see in greater detail in Part Six, evaluation of the results of therapy is complex. To evaluate a diet that purports to prevent degenerative diseases and retard aging, one would have to wait until the end of life for assessment. To the extent that a diet offers cure of symptoms or diseases, one would have to be able to measure changes in these and to isolate the effects of other curative agents designedly or inadvertently playing a part. And one would have to conduct such studies with a sample of people large enough to cancel out any uncontrolled elements, as well as learning to what kinds of people the findings are generalizable. With respect to Huggins' blood and hair readings, one would have to know how much random fluctuation could be expected, whether meaning and degree of change varied according to the level one started from, and more. "Hey, didja get better?" just won't do.

If the standard American diet is injurious to physical

and mental health, the cost to us as individuals and as a society are incalculably high. Then, what of Hal Huggins and others like him? Either they have nothing to offer—neither impressive enough anecdotal information, experimental studies, nor logical and plausible theory and operations, and they deserve to be ignored by the mainstream of medicine—or what kind of society do we have, which fails to support, if not openly derides, such investigations as his? After all, there is always time enough, after responsible study, to turn down an approach. But there never is time to recapture time squandered in unnecessary misery, a casualty of our indifference or hostility to bold innovation and experimentation.

At least one source of indifference and hostility to nutritional change stems from the unconscious meanings of nurturance; for some people diet is one of the most inflammatory of subjects. Particularly resistant to diets are those soft, rounded, overweight people in whose personality passive, accepting trends are prominent, as countless watchers of weight have observed. I have learned that no matter how otherwise objective, sophisticated, well trained they may be, such people either bristle or quietly retreat into a desultory nod or change of subject when nutritional approaches to health are discussed.

The proselytizing situation is hardly improved by the conflicting claims even of the new nutritionists in alternative medicine. As a minimum try at improving oneself through nutrition, one might start with those recommendations which are pretty much agreed upon no matter how much disagreement there is in other respects. Agreed-upon recommendations include the proscription of sugar, processed/chemicalized food, caffeine, alcohol, smoking, and white flour. Medium agreement is achieved with respect to proscription of dairy products and carbohydrates.

The sharpest disagreements have to do with the usefulness or dangerousness of eggs, meat, fat, and oil. These last disagreements may be crucial. Mr. Kushi says that eggs, meat, and fat are productive of cancer as well as other diseases. Conventional nutritionists emphasize the relation of these to cardiovascular ailments and cancer. And here I am now taking in a dozen eggs a week, along with pounds of butter and meat. It all hinges on the assertion that with chemistries balanced, the sugar and other evils deleted, oriental and conventional wisdom no longer apply. At present no one can definitively say what to do; we have to take our chances. That is the present state of the nutritional therapeutic art, perhaps understandable for now. But are we doing all we can about it—or are we just resigned to being taken by what we take in?

In a sense, the foregoing chapters on alternative medicine, cancer, and diet have been a digression from my original aim of studying the new therapies, an inevitable digression given the new therapies' emphasis on the unity of body and mind. Now it is time to return to comparing, contrasting, and evaluating conventional and new therapies.

PART SIX

Passing Through Customs

20

What to Do? What to Do?—
Conclusions and Beginnings

In the course of my study I was frequently asked, in effect, "Are the new therapies any good?" The question is phrased in many ways, with many different undertones. I sometimes infer, from the careful, apologetic way that it is asked, that the questioner thinks I may have been doing something unethical or strange, that I have deserted my calling, am a turncoat. Some alternative therapists imply with their question the hope that I will portray them to academia and the clinical establishment in a way that will encourage acceptance of their methods. And sometimes, gratifyingly, the questioner has no ulterior motive, he just wants to know what conclusions I have come to and what use might be made of them.

Not being asked my conclusions tells something also. Some of my colleagues evidently would like to think that it is all beneath consideration, that the thunder from the Left will subside and go away. Some alternative therapists seem oblivious to conceptual comparing and contrasting; they do not question me for the same reason that they do not question themselves.

Just as both conventional and alternative therapists have

their doubts about my explorations, so, too, do I. Like most of the rest of us, I have difficulty remaining objective for purposes of evaluation. The image of the objective scientist remains an ideal, though it is mostly fiction. Scientists try to be objective, and one way to do that is to make themselves aware of influences that distort their view. But what is observed ends up a function of the observer. (Heisenberg said it elegantly on the way toward adding to the formulation of the new physics.)

Here are some of the influences I felt.

The sociopsychological field of our times is marked by an acrimonious polarization between those who are for the new therapies and those who are against them. It is only part fantasy for me to feel that should I espouse the new therapies and question and recommend changes in traditional work I will cut myself off from my colleagues. I would in that case lose the comfort of unquestioned membership in the group of my peers. And I would be in danger of losing credibility not only with respect to the topic of the new therapies but with respect to my other writings. Despite trying to be objective, a scientist's willingness to be persuaded by what a colleague says or writes is often determined by the reputation of that colleague, by what he has previously said. In effect much knowledge is determined by authority.

In addition to these pressures from the external world I must contend with my own conservatism, my fear of change and novelty, my inclinations to remain loyal to my psychoanalytic identity and to the medical ethos that has surrounded me, by not calling into question any of their commonly held beliefs and practices. Such loyalty could be at the cost of disloyalty to other scientific and ethical standards.

Most clinicians and scientists work away comfortably in

obscurity. Those relatively few who devote themselves to writing and lecturing are probably, to some extent, exhibitionistic, and thus subject to the temptations of show business. I sometimes feel a pressure to be provocative, to find or say something new, striking, attention-getting. If I said unequivocally that the new therapies were useless or harmful, or that they were valuable and helpful, I would be staking out a position that would be easily quotable, newsworthy, would clearly identify me. Good show business, bad science. Truth tends to be a mixture, a golden mean; it is found, or approximated, often after uneventful, painstaking, study rather than climactic breakthroughs.

At the same time that I would like to try to avoid overstatement just for news value, I feel the necessity to come to clear and decisive conclusions. I want to influence others in the directions that I think might be fruitful, and discourage others from those directions I think would be useless or harmful. As in doing psychoanalysis, the task is to remain both objective and subjective, or, rather, to be objective about objectivity and subjectivity.

In the face of felt pressure not to be taken in or deluded, I need to remain open, even temporarily gullible, so that any possibility can be entertained and perhaps learned from. At the same time, I need to be rigorous and critical. So, too, in psychoanalysis one "passively" accepts the patient's productions without question, without even too clearly attending to them, just letting them happen, the better not to miss any layers and nuances of the patient's experience and the meanings of these. Yet one also sifts among the impressions, organizes one's thoughts, and acts upon one's understanding judiciously.

In a maelstrom of blandishments threatening to tilt a balanced appraisal, the safest thing to do is to concentrate on following facts and inferences to their logical conclusions.

Suffering is everywhere. It comes from without, inflicted by others or by impersonal forces; or we make it ourselves, torturing ourselves with anachronisms. So, too, is joy everywhere. It, too, sometimes comes from without. At other times we find it in our own back yards, we are our own Holy Grail. Homeostasis is a nice idea of some utility, but it does not regularly win the day as a blueprint for life. Rather, we mostly want change: during suffering, time to get over suffering; during joyful times, to take risks or to get more. Those who claim to be satisfied are frequently in thrall to inhibitions of the wish to change and improve. Like patients who do not take their medicine, they find ways of remaining immobile and stagnant, acting out complacency, incapacity, lack of imagination. At bottom they are afraid to accept the impetus toward change and the fantasies connected with that impetus.

So we cast about.

The really great sufferers and the really infantile people wail for help. Their cries come from that time when night was changed by magic to day, when hunger was changed to satisfaction, when pain gave way to healing: Mother came when they cried.

Most of the rest of us sip from the same bowl. This bowl is the ultimate source of hope, and as long as we hope, we have the wherewithal to experiment, to try. Present reality, sober decision-making, willingness to work and to accept another's working with us implement hope. We have a finite number of years; it is plain logic that we should try to improve those years, and we have a notion that it might just be possible.

There is probably more suffering than joy. In the dark

night of the soul, as the insomniac F. Scott Fitzgerald told us, it is always three o'clock in the morning. We suffer a succession of losses, we live in the mortal shadow of losing everything. Religions try to provide a surcease from that suffering through the promise of solving earthly distress for us or else by extending to us an afterlife or reincarnation. Deep down, some people consider therapy a religion also, a way of life; and if one can change anything of existential dimensions, then perhaps one can change everything, including the finality of death.

So we turn to therapy. We once would have turned to medicine men, priests, to a neighbor over the back-yard fence, to our spouse or parent, or to the family doctor. But now we are too knowledgeable for magic, too sophisticated for religion, the neighbor over the back-yard fence has to get the kids to the orthodontist, the family is in disarray, and the family physician has yielded to specialists with whom one cannot get an appointment anyway. It is in just such times of dislocation that the therapist emerges. With external supports disintegrating, we are thrown on our own, and cry for help. According to Rollo May, when Greek civilization was in decline, around the first century B.C., philosophers became psychologists. They put aside issues of "being" and "truth" in favor of teaching how to develop security, and dealt with such symptoms as stage fright when playing the lyre. Technology masters the outer world in an attempt to still the tremors of the inner world, but to no avail. Instead we turn to technicians of the inner world, the therapists.

The evaluation problem begins with the word "therapy." It covers a lot of yellow-pages classifications: art therapists, educational therapists, physical therapists, poetry therapists, dance therapists; everybody, it seems, is some kind of therapist. We therefore are stuck in conceptual and practical mire. Where does therapy end, and anything that makes us feel better or teaches us anything begin?

It is heuristically handy and professionally useful to demarcate "psychotherapists" from all other kinds of therapists. But as we have seen throughout this book, that line is nowhere near as clear as institutionalized professions make it seem. Dance, poetry, music, and physical therapists may claim to affect the mind and emotions. If we turn to durability of change as a criterion, we learn that it is difficult to prove that the effects of one therapy are more durable than another. Treating symptoms, as compared to treating the whole person, is an unsatisfactory means of discrimination also. In clearing up a symptom, other and unintended changes may occur; in working to bring about change in personality as a whole, discrete behaviors and symptoms may be cured.

Practically all therapeutic, quasi-therapeutic, educational, and quasi-educational activities may include elements of learning, feeling better, and behaving differently, and hence may result in changes in thinking and in the experience of life. Much of what happens depends on the attitudes and capacities of the participants, sometimes irrespective of the goals and the techniques on which the work is based. An unmotivated or in some ways psychologically incapable person may render psychoanalysis merely a diversion, a superficial learning experience, or a vehicle for spending his parents' money. He may derive nothing that most of us would call therapeutic benefit (though achieving these other goals can, from the patient's point of view, be considered "therapeutic" in that they may help him to feel better, at least temporarily). Another person may take his participation in, let's say, a tennis match as an opportunity to confront himself with aspects of his personality: how he handles competitiveness, the wish to win versus the wish to lose, how he relates himself to partners and opponents and judges, how he deals with exhibiting himself, his self-control, his ethics. On the basis of such observations and increased self-knowledge, he may change himself.

Later in this chapter, I shall try to order "therapeutic" activities in a conceptual framework based on the substance of the activity, rather than on boundaries drawn for professional, legal, or linguistic reasons. But, for now, here we are in the yellow pages.

Whom to call? Where is help? Which is better? If only we could find an authority, consultant, counselor, a psychiatric wise man. At a minimum for that, one needs to find a person with firsthand experience with all of the therapies and with enough experience so that he can draw generalizations. He should have a solid foundation in at least one encompassing psychological system, extensive clinical experience, and a systematic, research turn of mind. It would be well also if he had at hand valid research findings based on technically impeccable investigations. In order to get all these qualifications he would have had to find the sustaining motivation to take risks, expend energy, and face again the insecurity and ambiguity expectable in the early stages of a career. He would have had to resist the blandishments of the marketplace, the success that could be his simply by practicing activities founded on supplying answers rather than asking questions.

These technical and personal constraints on finding an authority are compounded by the dynamics of groups. Among the most powerful and pervasive of these dynamics is the tendency of a group to consolidate itself against the world outside. In going from one therapy subculture to another, I had the surreal feeling of having just come from where I now was. In each subculture there were the same cast of characters, ideas, and emotions. Depending on which group they belonged to, people were either friends or enemies, ideas were either new or old, each therapy could do things better than other therapies could, each had a spate of studies or other evidence with which to "prove" its point of view, and each therapist had convictions, based on his own experience apart from any formal studies, as these seemed to him to be confirmed by colleagues and patients.

I had observed the same unfounded loyalties, the same mindless rejection of outsiders, in my work with therapeutic and educational groups regardless of who was in them or what their task might have been. I had the same experiences as I moved among, practiced, and participated in the subcultures of group psychotherapy as contrasted to individual psychotherapy, long-term psychotherapy versus brief psychotherapy, various theoretical persuasions and emphases within psychoanalysis such as the Sullivanian, Kleinian, Adlerian, Jungian, ego psychology, and id psychology. In the atmosphere of self-justification characteristic of such schisms, the objective struggle for truth often becomes a casualty.

As a consequence of all this, while there are a number of pretenders, the world of authorities on the choice of therapies has the population approximately of the moon. The choice for most people is to enter one of the self-contained worlds of solipsistic conviction and take their chances.

Luckily, whatever one chooses, one is likely to get better in some way, to some degree. People get better not only from the variety of psychotherapies and assorted other therapies but from the throwing of bones, the drinking of holy water, and the laying on of hands. With so many different modalities resulting in change, it seems likely that there are factors common to all of them, a multiplicity of silent influences that make it difficult to isolate the effects of a specific therapy. The most famous example is, when workers in a factory were subjected to various kinds of lighting in order to see which lighting increased productivity, productivity increased no matter what kind was used. Now at the center of the experimenter's attention, and presumably with the impression that management was looking out for their welfare, the workers responded by trying harder.

The existence of these "non-specific"[1] factors operating in any therapeutic field are fine for the patient, helping him benefit no matter what the putative therapy consists of. But it is not so fine for those interested in teasing out factors that bring about change, the better to improve therapies. We can at least be aware of these nonspecific factors, in order to try to ascertain their influence relative to a particular therapy.

One such influence is placebo. The sublime, however unsupported, confidence that some therapists have in the usefulness of their therapy can itself be therapeutic, which is one aspect of placebo, sometimes called suggestion. In some researches fledgling therapists have been shown to be more effective than experienced therapists, apparently because of their enthusiasm and optimism. This probably is the reason why new drugs, new psychological tests, new therapeutic techniques, and strategies of all kinds have their greatest success upon their introduction, when, especially on the part of their inventors, interest and hope are at their height.

A subject or patient can "administer" placebo to himself, whereupon it may go by the name of self-suggestion. Imagine the state of mind and feeling of a person winding around his neurotic circles, knowing he has nowhere to go except where he has unsuccessfully been before. Compare it with the state of mind and feeling of a person who has undertaken psychotherapy. The very act of getting into and remaining in therapy acts as a suggestion. The patient's attention has somewhere new to go, his energy has somewhere else to expend itself, and he has made a break with the past. In making the decision to enter psychotherapy he has acknowledged the wish to change, probably has made some headway toward recognizing what his dissatisfactions are, has summoned the resolve to make the initial telephone call, and now backs up his resolve with a commitment of time and money. He now seeks to break the repetitive patterns of his life, is no longer content with attempting the same old solutions to the same old problems, is by definition open to new possibilities. As in a self-fulfilling prophecy, he tends to get what he expects. All this can begin to take place before he has ever seen the therapist. Indeed, researchers have demonstrated that some people who call for psychotherapy and are put on waiting lists refuse the psychotherapy when it becomes available, because in the interim their symptoms have cleared up. The tooth stops aching by the time you get to the dentist.

Simple intention on the part of the patient sets the various therapeutic factors in motion. Intention is closely followed by attention as providing key therapeutic leverage. When one is doing a physical exercise or activity, for best results one attends to the area in question. In yoga-based visualizations, one attends to the state of affairs that one is trying to bring about. When therapy enters the life of a patient, he attends to the issues raised in that therapy. Some therapists, particularly alternative therapists, conceptualize this situation in terms of energy: The patient concentrates his energy in the direction pointed to by the therapy. The patient becomes imbued with this approach, and when he improves, even if by way of suggestion, he gives credit to the therapy, which has brought to his attention a way of dealing with his difficulties. He assumes a cause-and-effect relationship between his improvement and what the therapy purports to do, and is usually oblivious of what else has contributed to his change for the better.

Pretty near all therapists are decent, benevolent, and accepting; at least they are more that way than most patients imagine other people to be. While the patient may expect criticism, punishment, indulgence, or unwarranted control —any of a long list of expectations modeled on experiences in the past—he usually gets none of these from his therapist. He therefore learns that his expectations are false, he no longer forces others into an experiential world modeled on his past. In the language of learning theory, his characteristic responses have been extinguished. In psychotherapeutic language, he has had a "corrective emotional experience."

Psychological difficulties create aloneness, no matter how vigorously people may apparently relate themselves to other people and activities around them. Aloneness stems from the close ties between the person and figures from the past instead of the present. His interaction with this idiosyncratic population of internal images drains off the energy, attention, and meaning that would otherwise be invested in the present. Freud described a neurotic as someone who is unable to establish membership in a group; much of life's distress is due to this self-imposed loneliness. The mere existence of a therapy or therapist tends to interrupt the patient's festering apartness. He now has somebody on his side who seems devoted to loosening the ancient bonds and bringing the patient into more vivid appreciation of the new.

A therapist can help people put things in order and facilitate patients' feeling that their experience is understandable. Learning an organized story about oneself, a framework that encompasses what previously seemed to be disparate puzzling events, supplies confidence that one need no longer be taken by surprise, that there is a reasonable, logical context in which all eventualities can be placed. The patient is therefore no longer as subject to demoralization[2] as he once was. This surely occurs in those therapies which avowedly pursue understanding. But it probably plays a role even in those that do not. Even body therapies, for example, implicitly offer an understanding of distress by acting on their beliefs that this or that part of the body requires correction. The patient thinks that if his distress makes sense to the body therapist, then it must make sense. Many patients feel better just by getting a diagnosis, a name, which tacitly says that since there is a name for them they must be understandable. As can be seen from some altered states of consciousness and especially from dreams, the unconscious mind is chaotic. Many patients' conscious daily experiences, too, are often chaotic, marked by dismay, confusion, and loss of moorings. They benefit not only from internal order by way of understanding but often from external order. The very act of keeping scheduled appointments anchors life in a more orderly regime.

Need the life story that makes meaningful order of experience be true? Reconstructions of early life by way of psychoanalysis have sometimes been shown to be true through independent investigations; e.g., a parent will confirm an event from early life that was previously forgotten by the patient but revived during the analysis. Usually, however, the proof is in the form of logical connections, plausibility, "feel." It could be that any understanding that is persuasive to the patient is therapeutic. A true one would likely feel even more persuasive and be more therapeutic.

I have not exhausted the list of possible means by which most therapies seem to help their patients simply by being identified and experienced as therapies. But I do hope to have offered enough of such instances to help understand how it is that practically any therapeutic enterprise may seem to be helpful. So it is not surprising that I would go from therapy to therapy and meet with enthusiastic therapists, all claiming success though doing different things.

If the person looking through the yellow pages is now getting desperate, he had better get a grip on himself, for there is more bad news to come.

The person trying to become a patient has caused some of his difficulties just by the way he phrases his question: "Which therapy is better?" "Better" often implies an agreed-upon standard of health; one therapy helps patients approach that standard "better" than another does. This kind of thinking is another unfortunate consequence of casting therapy in medical terms, for in medicine the absence of observable and often measurable symptoms is a clear and useful standard leading to an empirical judgment of health (defined as the absence of disease). Not so with psychological difficulties. Whether someone is better or worse may vary according to who says so, the patient, the therapist, or society.[2] The patient may feel better, but so do people on drugs, winners of the Irish Sweepstakes, and patients who temporarily feel better in order to produce a reason for stopping further treatment. Much as my human potential friends will object to the idea as elitist, the therapist may know better. He may know that the improvement will be transitory, is irrelevant to underlying difficulties, and is enlisted for reasons outside of awareness. A patient who has been avoiding anxiety and depression by acting upon the environment through sexual promiscuity, the taking of drugs, or criminal activity may, after therapy, give up such attacks on the environment, and society will heave a sigh of satisfied relief, declaring him without question better. The patient, however, though spared the consequences of his difficulties with society, may now feel worse than ever, more anxious, more depressed, more in need of help.[3a,b]

The person searching the yellow pages may think correctly that since some of his tax dollars were spent on formal research, he has a right to information about what is good for what ails him. But he underestimates the difficulties in getting the answers by way of formal research. Research on whether traditional psychotherapy is effective or ineffective has, on the whole, been unconvincing. Studies can be cited to show that untreated patients do as well as treated ones, that patients change no matter what interventions they are subjected to, that the kind and extent of training of the therapist makes a great difference, and that they do not matter.

Such contradictory research findings are in some ways understandable. There is no such thing as *the* patient or *the* therapist. Patients vary greatly in ways that have a lot to do with the effects of one therapy or another. So, too, do therapists vary, also in ways that have a good deal to do with their effectiveness. The psychotherapeutic transaction is one of a kind, taking place in a particular way between a particular patient and a particular therapist, and it happens only once.

Another difficulty in comparing conventional and alternative therapies is the wide differences in the amount of training of their practitioners. Psychoanalysts, for example, usually have, in addition to undergraduate and medical-school years, three residency years and some seven to ten years of psychoanalytic training. Alternative therapists may have little basic education, and little training beyond their own experience as patients. Yet this wide disparity in training fails to tell the whole story. Extent and quality of training and effectiveness as a therapist are not in one-to-one correspondence. The great equalizer is talent. Therapist talent, much like musical talent, can simply override lack of years of training. Moreover, the likelihood of getting a good practitioner may vary with the kind of therapy. It may be more difficult to get a highly effective conventional therapist than it is to get a highly effective alternative therapist, not necessarily because of the individuals involved in the abstract but because the requirements of conventional therapy are such that fewer people, relatively, are effective at it. It may be that some of the new therapies can be relatively well done by a great number of people, even with comparatively little training. In other words one may aim higher with conventional therapy and run a greater risk of not achieving one's goals. Or one may settle for less with the new therapies, and be more likely to achieve it. But we will never know for sure without recognizing and controlling the issues of training and talent in any comparisons of therapies.

When do we decide that a patient is "better"? If psychotherapy were like other medicines, then "better" would be measured at the termination of the treatment. Yet the termination of psychotherapy is for most people a special and stressful time. At termination some patients tend to exaggerate benefits out of gratitude to the therapist or out of a need to justify their investment. Others are inclined to minimize their gains out of resentment at the ending of the treatment or because of their disappointment at not having realized their initial, fantasied hopes. When "better" is taken to refer to the nature of life, then treatment logically should be judged at the end of life, rather than at the end of treatment.

Most therapies, and all psychotherapies, are idiosyncratic enterprises, greatly influenced by the personality and skill of the therapist. Comparing conventional and new therapies usually involves not only a comparison of people with many years of professional training with people who may have little training beyond their own experience as patients, but people of differing personality types. The personality requirements for conventional and new therapies, and the styles of life that often go along with these respective practices, draw people from substantially different populations. It is likely that these personality differences are as much being compared as the differences in the so-called therapy itself.

Finally, different populations of patients gravitate to conventional and to the new therapies. Such differences may be economic, geographical, and social; they may involve such personality trends as rebelliousness toward conventionality, inclination toward ideas as compared to feeling, a task or work orientation as compared to a pleasure orientation, an inclination to persevere over long periods as against a preference for sporadic contacts. All these variables require control if there is to be definitive research on the relative effectiveness of therapies.

As should now be clear, it is too early to look in the yellow pages; rather, let us look to the drawing board. Here we may lay out some of the specific or generally recognized variables, the components, the characteristics of therapies. Let us subject them to that stage of research which follows the making of first-order observations, when one tries to organize impressions, compare and contrast with previously acquired information, and generate hypotheses.

A good many alternative therapists make much ado about the uselessness, even harmfulness, of insight. This position is usually code for criticism of psychoanalysis in particular, which is identified with the pursuit of insight. Yet many of the alternative therapies also deal in insight. Indeed, with some patients, there is no way to prevent insight. When the patient thinks psychologically, when he characteristically directs his attention toward meanings, he will make discoveries about himself willy-nilly. As we have noted previously, much of what gestalt therapists call awareness could just as well be called insight. Moreover, many of the interventions by alternative therapists are in effect interpretations, or at least part of the interpretive process. Much of the agitation against insight among the alternative therapists is politically inspired, something to rally around to build oneself up by putting down another. But there is substance in their position as well. Although they may clumsily frame their remarks as being against insight, what they really are against is intellectualization, using words and ideas to avoid experience. They are also against the image of an authoritarian therapist telling the patient meanings, sometimes experienced as telling the patient what is wrong with him. In these respects they are on solid ground. In principle, psychoanalytic therapists would agree with them. However, it is worth considering that a subtle intellectualization and authoritarianism does sometimes creep into some psychoanalytic thinking and practice. And for understandable reasons.

Psychoanalysis has an abstract, metapsychological theory in addition to the down-to-earth, empirical one that is directly derived from, and relevant to, work with patients. Sometimes the metapsychological theory infiltrates the clinical one, resulting in intellectualization, in moving from first-order experiences to verbal and conceptual abstractions. Again, we have to consider the kinds of personalities accepted for conventional psychotherapeutic training, namely people who have earned advanced academic degrees. Such people are, almost by definition, of high intellectual capacities, which often goes with using ideas to avoid experience.

The pursuit of insight runs other risks.[4] Some people can

take just so much self-awareness, at least under the conditions of some therapies with some therapists, without becoming suicidal or psychotic. Others simply do not have the wherewithal to improve their lives commensurately with increasing self-awareness, whether because of physical difficulty, age, or lack of intelligence or skills.

Some psychoanalytic thinkers believe, implicitly or explicitly, that overcoming repressions will do it all, that once self-knowledge is achieved, nothing else needs to be done. This is, I assume, the way that most of those few but notorious ten- to twenty-year analyses come about, analyst and patient hooked on discovery, on the assumption that enough discovery will result in change, that around some corner is the "crucial insight." Such long-run analyses may make for good Woody Allen jokes, but to me they are horror stories. Pursuing insight, making the unconscious conscious, bringing what is out of awareness into awareness, making overt what is covert is not an unalloyed good for everyone at all times. Whether for right or wrong reasons, the alternative therapist's criticism of insight can supply a powerful corrective to abuses of insight and so contribute to its effectiveness.

Closely connected to the claim that conventional therapists are concerned only with insight is the claim that conventional therapists are too little concerned with emotion. Psychoanalysts have long been aware of the dangers of those defenses which drain or suppress emotion. A major challenge in psychoanalytic technique is to infuse the process with feeling, with experience. I have previously written of the capacity to enliven ideas with experience as a special quality called evocativeness, as it appears in both therapist and patient.[5] I believe it is crucial to good therapeutic work, though rarely is it self-consciously taught and studied. But how much emotion is enough emotion? Those alternative therapists, such as Arthur Janov, who pursue emotion single-mindedly have demonstrated the explosive feelings that lie ready for expression. Their patients achieve an intensity of feeling that generally occurs only sporadically and briefly in conventional therapy.

Many patients caught up in the intensity of discovery and the often consequent fear of greater discovery tend to take actions that are designed to diminish anxiety and to subvert the process of discovery. Thus, in conventional therapy action is often thought about as something to be avoided. A more respectable context for action in conventional therapy is one in which it is explicitly set forth as an objective: The patient is supposed to learn to take actions that will be more beneficial than those he has taken, or has been afraid to take, in the past. He may do this on his own as his inhibitions are lessened. Or he may do it as the result of behavior therapy slipping in unnamed and unacknowledged. Since socially desirable actions may serve as confirmations of the effectiveness of the therapy, the therapist may be tempted to get the patient to take the desired action regardless of the degree of working out of internal difficulties. The patient may behave as he thinks he is supposed to behave either to please the therapist or to give himself the feeling of success, rather than as an organic outgrowth of choice based on knowledge and new, substantive effectiveness.

Action can also be a means of furthering the introspective, exploratory process. This opportunity comes about when inaction has been serving to ward off anxiety and associated thoughts and feelings. At those times the patient is sunk into a passive holding position, his thoughts and feelings constricted or seeking pathways apart from those conflicts he is contending with through inaction. These thoughts and feelings would be available for discussion if the actions were taken. An alternative therapist might deal with such a situation by directly getting the patient to perform the required behaviors; for example, by commanding him. The conventional therapist might take up the issue interpretively, showing the patient how he is behaving and trying to understand with him why he is behaving in this particular way at this particular time. Such interpretive work, if successful, would have the same consequence as a command: the patient would behave differently.

Action does not deserve the bad name that it has in some quarters. After all, sooner or later, if the therapy is effective, the patient is going to take actions, not for defensive purposes but because he is able to do what he wants to do. Much that is harmful about action can apply as well to inaction. It is the clinician's task to know when action or inaction is defense and when it is not.

The interpersonal relationship between patient and therapist can function as a potentially therapeutic experience in all therapies, even if unattended to. Both conventional and alternative therapists vary according to how much curative emphasis they accord the experience of the relationship itself, as against the opportunity the relationship affords for the development of insight and the summoning of emotions. Psychoanalytic therapists also emphasize the opportunities provided by the interpersonal relationship for modeling and ultimately identification, the patient taking into himself qualities of the therapist.

In many of the new therapies great value is connected to a particular kind of interpersonal relationship, one marked by "authenticity," meaning, as far as I can tell, genuineness, honesty, openness, warmth, and concern. These therapists offer the ideal of human relationships as a model, and correct the patient's expectations that people must be different from this ideal. In the service of this proffered relationship, alternative therapists may interact freely with their patients, may disclose much of their personal lives and psychological selves. Such behavior does indeed tend to make many people feel good, and is part of the glow that attends many human potential encounters. It is often held up as a beneficial alternative to the alleged cold, distant, impersonal conventional therapist, especially the psychoanalyst.

Once again, such criticism may be justified with respect to some therapists. The use of the couch, with the analyst out of sight, tends to encourage in some analysts an excess of emotional distance, as does high social, professional, and financial status. Many people with advanced educational degrees emphasize the mind over the heart, to the detriment of emotional connection with patients. The importance that the conventional therapist attaches to understanding, in the sense of decoding, interpreting, at times knowing more than the patient, may also dispose the therapist toward interpersonal distance.

On the other hand there are good, substantive reasons for maintaining some kinds of distance, reasons that have nothing to do with being emotionally cold or reclusive. The better the patient knows the therapist the less opportunity he has to become aware of his fantasies about the therapist and, consequently, about how such fantasies distort his view of others in his life as well. The more he interacts socially or occupationally in real life with the therapist the more hindered he is in maintaining the unique interpersonal stance that characterizes a psychotherapeutic relationship and from which it derives much therapeutic leverage.

The alternative therapist concerns himself with acting in a way that he wants his patients to imitate. This strategy has limitations. It overlooks the patient's unconscious creation of the therapist regardless of the therapist's behavior. Such creations have to be brought to awareness if they are not to be unfortunately repeated and reinforced.

What the best characteristics and conditions of the therapeutic situation are is a hoary subject of discussion in countless journals, from lecterns, and in clinic hallways. What are often overlooked in such discussions are the differing base lines, the vantage points from which the discussions issue. In psychoanalysis, with its carefully controlled and subdued conditions, designed to heighten the patient's awareness of his inner states, the tilt of the napkin on which the patient's head rests on the couch may provoke thoughts and outpourings of emotion that last for hours. ("You don't care enough about me even to put the napkin on straight.") To a psychoanalyst, who regularly observes the considerable psychological consequences of the smallest activity or deviation from the expectable, the rough-and-tumble interaction of alternative therapies seems like chaos. It is not surprising that he would be convinced that therapies full of personal, pointed, and gross interactions would be irretrievably burdened. By the same token, the alternative therapist can only be amazed and amused that so much could be made of so small a matter as the analyst's clearing his throat. What each of them overlooks is the patient's adaptation to one or another base line. The patient is probably not nearly as troubled or reactive to alternative therapists' behaviors as the psychoanalyst might think, since these behaviors are expected and normative. It simply takes behaviors of greater extremity to provoke the feelings and fantasies that a minuscule behavior might provoke when it occurs against the background of the psychoanalytic base line.

A final entry in this list of elements of psychotherapy is called "working through." In the new therapies there is a strong inclination to put discoveries about oneself into immediate practice. In psychoanalysis, discoveries are more likely to be put into the service of making more discoveries. Rather than being discrete findings, they are seen as connections and pointers to other aspects of the self, as additional elements to be integrated. Psychoanalysis is a discipline of patience, with respect for complexity, a kind of low-level skepticism about the truth of discoveries and a persistent questioning about the implications of discoveries. By contrast, the new therapies can be characterized as somewhat impulsive, simplistic, and ingenuous. Under some circumstances such characteristics can be economical and practical. And under some circumstances the psychoanalytic attitude can degenerate into indecision, intellectualization, and discouragement of constructive action. (If there is one maxim about clinical work that is most true, it is, "It depends on the circumstances.")

An example of differences with respect to "working through" and the use of transference: A person goes to a movie in which the theme of separation is prominent, and he gets an attack of anxiety. If that person is psychologically inclined in his thinking, he may first note the connection between the theme of separation and his anxiety. He may then proceed to find in his present life reasons why he should be reacting so strongly under the stimulus of the movie. Then he may look at other instances in his life when he has faced separation: leaving the family for school, school for work, changes in career, or his children leaving home. He may further find experiences of separation in his earliest years with his parents, separation from the breast as he may have reconstructed it from dreams, fantasies, symptoms; separations inherent in the developmental steps such as crawling to walking, independent control of bodily functions, steps away from home as implied in new interests, friends, activities, the separation from his being a person who gets love unsolicited to a person who gives love and competes for its return. The person in the theater realizes that anxiety and thoughts and feelings having to do with separation call for continued self-analytic work. He knows that his daily behaviors right now are likely to be influenced by thoughts and feelings having to do with separation and ought to be checked from that point of view before being acted upon. For example, if he is in therapy, he may develop the unsupported idea that his therapist is going to leave town, or perhaps feel the next interim between appointments as a painful separation. In other words he transfers onto his therapist his historical experiences of separation.

A person in one of the new therapies would have less training in noticing the connection between separation in the movie and his feelings of anxiety. He might "decide" not to have anxiety, at which he may or may not be successful. He may find like-minded people and attempt to lose his anxiety in the warmth of human encounter. He may indulge in a variety of activities he has found in the past have made him feel better—medication or massage, for example. He may meditate or try to find a philosophical state of mind that will enable him to overcome the anxiety. He may remember some remark or admonition of his therapist, but the therapist would likely be the actual person himself, a present-day ally more than a person remade by past images of others.

Thus far, in this somewhat airy and abstract discussion of comparisons between therapies, I have been blandly carrying on as if various conventional and new therapies *were* comparable. Although they are easily comparable in some respects, in other respects their differing characteristics make direct comparisons difficult.

Take, for example, where each stands with respect to happiness. Some conventional therapies function in a framework of abstinence and asceticism, with joy as something to be constantly striven for, expectable only when long-term, sufficient psychological work has been done. In such therapies even a small increase in the capacity for joy may be a criterion of beneficial change. Much more expectable is the puritanical resignation inherent in expending much time, money, and effort working toward far-reaching goals and indefinitely postponing pleasure until the soul is fully cleansed and the spirit is saved. By contrast, most alternative therapists set out to help patients discover joy almost immediately, and consider their work a failure should it not eventuate in a warm glow of hope, love, and happiness. Without joy the work is considered "heavy," an ambivalent term for unpleasant though possibly helpful experiences.

Esteeming goodness and joy as criteria for helpful change tends to limit the extensiveness of the new therapies' goals and consequently the scheduling and lengths of their meetings. The language of the new therapies sometimes sounds as if the goal is thoroughgoing personality change; for example, the patient may want to "get my head together," "change my life." Yet with "results" striven for so quickly and joy an end point, the inclination is to have brief and sporadic but joyful meetings. These *laissez-faire* meeting arrangements are media that send the message that no one is entirely serious about definitive personality change, though they may be deadly serious about change in some behaviors, overcoming particular distresses, and getting to feel good. Such goals encourage denial of evidence to the contrary while glorifying euphoria.

The slow struggle in conventional therapy in a context of deprivation and the avowed goal of thoroughgoing personality change may bring with it an unnecessary and burdensome fantasy of perfection. This fantasy may unduly lengthen the course of treatment, until fatigue or bankruptcy puts an end to it. It is as if the participants were unaware that even after analysis the unconscious continues to be alive and well, as can be seen in dreams which, though they may have changed somewhat over the course of the treatment, continue to be largely cast in the language of the unconscious. Conflicts are less resolved in an absolute sense than they are minimized and adapted to.[6]

Being temporarily joyful is no great trick. Drink, drugs, sex, and walking barefoot on the dew in the early morning work wonders for many people in that regard. The problem is that there is a morning after. But by that time the new-therapy meeting may be over. (As lacking in systematic follow-up as conventional therapy is, at least its regularity and length allow for continued observation of the vicissitudes of life and the meanings of these. The usually sporadic scheduling of the new therapies precludes such continued monitoring.)

Sometimes blithely ignored in evaluative comparisons of conventional and new therapies is the differing amounts of time and money invested in each of them. It is all very well for psychoanalysts to claim that their work produces fundamental, long-lasting beneficial change, while the new therapies produce merely a temporary "high"; but psychoanalysis may last five years and cost fifty thousand dollars, as compared to a comparative short time and handful of dollars invested in one of the new therapies. One would hope and expect that such greater costs would result in greater rewards. To expect results from conventional and new therapies that are equal in all respects is unfair. To promise them is even more unfair.

Finally, asking the question "Which therapy is better?" carries the implication that the patient has free choice to pick one or the other. In fact the choice for most people is limited. The requirements for psychoanalysis (for example, of time, money, and particular personality characteristics and capacities) make it feasible for only a minute portion of the population. Where someone lives, with consequent availability of a therapist, is in itself often a limiting and determining factor. For much of our population the choice is not so much between equally available therapies as it is between whatever therapy is available and nothing.

The question "Which therapy is better?" has its greatest usefulness as a point of scientific orientation and as an impetus to analyzing the components of therapies, attempting to assess each of these, the whole done in the realistic context of people's practical needs and resources. It is not a question of brand X versus brand Y. The yellow-pages approach to the problem comes about for want of anything better; it is a measure of the primitiveness of our present knowledge, our failure as yet to provide better ways of deciding how best to proceed toward self-improvement.

While not exactly providing a substitute for definitive knowledge, for rank ordering of therapies, and for specification of effectiveness of elements, there is at least one way of thinking about therapies that could be helpful in organizing our thinking about them. That way is to conceive of the range of therapies (indeed all activities that have a learning, potentially helpful aspect and whose goals are beneficial change) with respect to their relationships to consciousness and the unconscious.*

In those therapies in which the main focus is on consciousness, attention is less available for exploration of thoughts and feelings out of awareness. At the other ex-

* Conscious and unconscious is a rough dichotomy; in real life there is a range between these extremes, which may change from moment to moment. "The unconscious" often mistakenly carries the image of a discrete thing or place. The word is used here only as shorthand.

treme, where the emphasis is on the unconscious, little attention is paid to what is already in awareness.

This distinction is not necessarily based on what one does but how one does it. One can attend a boxing match introspectively and learn about aspects of the self ordinarily held out of awareness. And one can use words, write a poem even, more in the mode of action than in thought—some people talk and think, yet without being thoughtful; they are driven to master feelings and fantasies through action, rather than exploiting the potentiality for reflectiveness in speech and thought. But there are some activities, just as there are some therapies, that encourage one way of using the self as against the other. Team sports, for example, can easily be used to encourage interaction more than self-reflection. Those activities, such as behavior therapy, that emphasize living according to externally imposed rules render inner processes irrelevant; they discourage exploration of self. Those activities which depend for change solely on determination and resolve also minimize self-reflection. For example, Couéism, the power of positive thinking, and Dale Carnegie training adjure and teach that one can do better simply by deciding to do better and by following rules, ordained by others, that can be applied generally and mechanically. For them, introspection is therefore pointless. Therapies that require no active participation on the part of the patient, such as hypnosis and psychic healing, also minimize attention to internal processes and self-discovery.

At the other extreme is psychoanalysis. Stimuli external to and competing with the introspecting self are reduced by using a quiet room, by the analyst's quiet voice, and by his relative silence. The analyst encourages the patient to focus on underlying meanings, what may be implied rather than stated, covert rather than overt, impressions ordinarily outside of awareness that determine the meanings and experience in awareness. In short, psychoanalysis proceeds on the assumption that only through exploring what is unconscious can behavior be fully understood. Also unconscious are many of the ways that the person uses to maintain thoughts and feelings out of awareness. An examination of these devices, or defenses, results in their being relaxed, thereby allowing part of the unconscious to become conscious. Consequently the person knows more of himself, has more information with which to make choices, may be stronger since he uses less energy to keep material out of awareness. In a somewhat puckish but ultimately illuminating exercise, Lawrence Kubie[7] suggested that normality could be defined as complete awareness, the unconscious totally becoming conscious. Since the unconscious has the capacity to influence behavior unbeknownst to the behaver, if the behaver wanted full control of himself he would have to know fully all aspects of himself. Only then would he have all the information with which to choose how to behave, and only then would he be free of impulsions whose power is based on their being out of awareness.

"Examining, learning about, exploring the unconscious" may be useful jargon, but the verbs are crude metaphors for a subtle and beautiful process. "The unconscious" is not a thing that one can examine as through a microscope. Rather, it alludes to thoughts, impressions, fantasies, experiences, memories, and all with their associated feelings, that are outside of awareness but that in principle can be encouraged into awareness. Examining the unconscious is only a manner of speaking. Even in psychoanalysis one can work directly only with consciousness, can only infer what is unconscious. When, for example, a patient re-creates a dream, he does so with his conscious faculties. We never can know what exactly the dream was as delivered to the sleeping mind. We can only know what was reported by the awake mind. Indeed, if you ask a person to repeat a dream, you may get a dream that is different in some respects.

Awareness of previously unconscious material can come about through a variety of means: mind-expanding drugs, stimulus deprivation, fatigue, alcohol, sexual orgasm, humor. Some of these interventions are used intermittently in the new therapies; such transitory explosions of awareness usually have only transitory effects. By examining, learning about, exploring the unconscious, we refer to the usually slow, painstaking observation of material as it shows itself in symptoms and symptomatic behaviors, dreams, and fantasies, as these are delineated through collecting the patient's impressions and associations. In this systematic way, previously unconscious material is brought into relation with styles of life and behavior, the better to integrate conscious and unconscious, and presumably lead to durability of understanding and consequent change. This is the process that gave rise to psychoanalysis as a technique and therapy, and in so doing gave rise to the information about why humans think, live, and behave as they do on which psychoanalysis is based.

The discoveries made in this psychoanalytic way were earth-shaking. They are often said to rank with Copernicus' discovery that the earth revolves around the sun rather than the sun revolving around the earth, and Darwin's assertion of man's evolution from other forms of life. Freud, Copernicus, and Darwin struck blows against man's feelings of centrality and importance. People were no longer seen as the center of the universe or as a God-sent species, and instead of exercising free choice over their behavior they were seen as being driven by relentless forces unbeknownst to them.

An examination of those forces outside of awareness provided a view of people that was dramatically different from the ones they had been taught. Along with outrage came fascination. Ashamed and affronted as people were by the discovery of their unconscious life, they were nonetheless excited by it, and it became popular. Some people made of the discovery of the unconscious an excuse for continuing to perform unwanted behaviors or to avoid performing those they said they wanted; they claimed that their behavior was all the fault of unconscious machination. That attitude, too, contributed to the popularity of psychoanalysis.

Psychoanalysis' popularity, and notoriety, brought with it a downgrading of consciousness. Devotees of psychoanalysis looked down on doctors who told neurotic patients to take a vacation or gave them books to read. Patients, too, were sometimes disparaged for attempting to treat themselves by going to church, by exercising, dieting, or "taking the waters." These kinds of efforts were sometimes contemptuously dismissed as archaic on the supposition that help can come only through exploration of the unconscious.

But, then, there are those yogis demonstrating to a new audience in the West the power of consciousness, feats of body and mind possible only through highly developed consciousness, and without recourse to dynamic understanding of the unconscious. Their heirs are many among the alternative therapists, whether as exploiters of powers of the mind such as in biofeedback and meditation-visualization, or as an emphasis in all other new therapies.

Stimulated by such yogic points of view, I had wandered the Himalayan cold of Chicago and had dictated "Conscious Intention Revisited"[8] into my pocket recorder. This paper was an attempt to remind conventional therapists of the therapeutic possibilities of work with consciousness. As a paper written to make a point, to undo an automatic and unreflective emphasis on the unconscious, I think it was necessary. However, once balance has been achieved, it is crucial that it be maintained. To pin one's hopes exclusively on consciousness, at least for many people under many circumstances, could be disastrous. Again and again in my new-therapy travels I was struck by what I took to be the need for people to make fundamental changes in their personality if they were to approach salvation. True, in some ways they were benefiting and enjoying what they were doing, taken in small segments and episodes. But often this was taking place in the context of an over-all inhibiting, essentially self-defeating, existence. The way they behaved outside a particular therapeutic activity and the very stamp they brought to that activity were based upon a past outside their awareness, on inclinations over which they had inadequate control. Given less than half a chance, the unconscious will find a way to achieve its often self-defeating, painful ends, no matter how clever or devoted a person is consciously to self-improvement.

The most fundamental difficulty with many of the new therapies is their lack of respect for and understanding of the unconscious, especially its power. This may even be true of those who try to work with it, such as Janov; his appreciation of it, too, is limited. A good many people, including alternative therapists and some conventional therapists as well, who believe they know the power of the unconscious, in fact do not know what they do not know. One can learn a good deal about unconscious processes through reading, observing people closely, and practicing the new and conventional therapy. But one cannot know what he does not know until he has had a chance to experience as full a range and intensity of the phenomena of mind as possible. One such way of fully appreciating the power of the unconscious is to conduct a number of psychoanalyses, and so to participate for years in the vicissitudes of that power under conditions that maximize the observation and understanding of it. Another good, though not guaranteed, way is to be psychoanalyzed.

There is no way around it. People make what they will of any situation on the basis of their unconscious understandings, fantasies, and appreciation of it. The Rolfer may do a fine technical job of Rolfing in order to throw back the shoulders of a hunched-over person, and at the end of the ten sessions the Rolfer's efforts may be crowned with success. But six months later, when his patient's shoulders slip forward into their accustomed hunch, the Rolfer may be at a loss for an explanation, not realizing how this person needs to avoid direct confrontation, how unconsciously terrified he is of standing up to people, meeting situations head on, exposing his genitals which he experiences as vulnerable. By thus exposing him the Rolfer has adventitiously changed the patient's perception of himself and others, opening him to fantasied damage, and requiring from him a network of new psychological adjustments. Lacking the wherewithal to make these adjustments, the patient resumes his old, defensive stance.

Alternative therapists may assert freedom as a universal good, often helpfully counteracting the mindless morality and rigid values of society that are burdensomely built into so many of our personalities. But the encouragement to do what one wants to do, to set oneself free of the strictures of others, may lead seductively and thoughtlessly to the dropping of such "burdensome" commitments as getting an education, remaining married, working for a living. Some alternative therapists elide what lies between the recognition of a burden and the decision whether to take action to release that burden or to shoulder it voluntarily. They skip over the only real freedom that anyone can have, namely the freedom of choice. They tend to substitute obvious, concrete, and dramatic change as proof of liberation of the soul. Sometimes change is proof of liberation. But often one limited choice has simply been substituted for another. Those unconscious forces which made previous commitments onerous and burdensome are still there, to be expressed now in other ways. Old problems are exchanged for new ones or new versions of old ones. The divorced person contracts another unhappy marriage or is lonely in the midst of his busy new life. The youth released from a rigid educational assembly line finds a new persecutor by breaking the law, or after wasting ten years as a soldier of fortune decides, now with bridges burned, that he wants to "settle down," after all.

Again and again in my new-therapy experiences, I felt myself caught between the excitement and joy of experience itself and my recognition of the tenacious hold of unconsciously generated difficulties. I often felt by turn incredulous and sad as I observed what I believed to be self-defeating life patterns based upon unconscious conflicts being hyped with slogans, emotional turn-ons, the whole thing bathed in self-delusion. This possibility seems to me the most pernicious aspect of the new therapies. Their practitioners operate on the assumption, and implicitly propagandize to the effect, that what they offer is a definitive opportunity for life change. Instead, their participants may go to the grave heroically trying their best, believing that they are doing everything possible, but actually struggling with unconscious demons that they might have exorcised through psychoanalysis or other conventional therapies. Alternative therapists exploit the conscious aspects of the personality, and some make forays into the unconscious, but they never allow themselves the opportunity fully to come to grips with those forces which, like a magnet, suck into neurosis whatever one tries to do. I realize my prose has turned slightly purple on this point. The point deserves it; it denotes the biggest danger to the seeker of therapies.

It may be tempting simply to think of conventional therapies as having the goal of exploration of the unconscious, and the new therapies as having the goal of exploiting consciousness, but the situation is more complicated than that. Modern psychoanalysis includes an appreciation of thoughts and feelings outside of awareness (the id) and also a part of the personality that is in touch with consciousness as well as the unconscious (the ego and the superego). Psychoanalysts vary among themselves, between patients, and from time to time in the degree to which they may explore and exploit the conscious and the unconscious. The deep interpretations I frequently saw made by bioenergeticists and the assault on the unconscious past by primal therapists are probably the techniques most exclusively devoted to the unconscious. Examples of a predominant concern with consciousness are *est*, Silva Mind Control, working with the body without combining it with psychotherapy, yoga, and much of the philosophy underlying alternative medicine. Some alternative therapists seem to me to behave as if they were devoting themselves to consciousness, while in fact they are skillfully bringing to conscious awareness thoughts and feelings ordinarily out of awareness, heretofore unconscious. Their claim that they do not deal with the unconscious, though true in a sense, is largely naïve. Everyone who deals with people therapeutically and educationally deals with the unconscious.

The degree and manner in which the conscious and the unconscious are attended to can provide a dimension with which to measure all therapies, one with another, and with which to measure the vicissitudes of any one therapy. For therapists it is another means of organizing their thoughts about treatment, of providing themselves with guidance as to what to do in the course of the ever-changing circumstances of the patient's life and of the material he brings to therapy. It casts into relief the requirement that the therapist be ever appraising and self-conscious about selecting therapeutic activities. For the patient, such a dimension helps make clear the kind of decision he is making when selecting a therapy, the kind of stress he may be subjecting himself to, the feasibility of achieving his goals, and the manner of working toward those goals.

The use of such a dimension is part of a pattern of diagnostic thinking required to supplant the simplistic "Which is better?" It should be clear by now that such a simplistic question can result only in trumped-up, subjective, self-serving, and ultimately impertinent answers. André Gide is reputed to have said, "The answer is the disease of the question." In order to get more "healthy" answers about the usefulness of therapies, we need better questions. The proper scientific question and the question that ideally ought to be posed by the man looking through the yellow pages includes specification of a particular kind of patient, with particular goals and resources, in a particular social and cultural context, and with a particular therapist. Filling in each of these elements correctly would in principle eventuate in the selection of the most efficient therapy.

This set of specifications may seem wildly idealistic, practically implausible; and in many situations it is. To specify a particular kind of patient means to make a psychological diagnosis, to define and describe the person's strengths and limitations, the nature of his psychological difficulties, and the resources within his personality that may enable him to grow. This delicate task is often best done with the aid of psychological tests, but testers capable of using these instruments for such refined purposes are scarce. The misuse of tests by inadequate testers has contributed to a trend toward discarding the whole diagnostic enterprise as unnecessary and undesirable.

Even if many psychoanalysts and conventional psychotherapists content themselves with none or inferior formal diagnostic studies before embarking on treatment, they still make some attempt to define the problem they intend to treat, and assess the resources available for such treatment. By contrast, diagnosis hardly exists in any formal sense within the new therapies. Though there are exceptions, most alternative therapists accept for treatment anyone who applies. Therapists may, of course, exercise their talent, in or outside their awareness, to design and titrate their activities to fit what they think a person can absorb helpfully and safely. But this unsystematic skill is probably not as regularly effective for a wide variety of clinical exigencies as a systematic, comprehensive diagnostic appraisal would be.

The Menninger Foundation, among a very few institutions, provides a searching diagnostic examination, usually including an extensive battery of psychological tests, in order to provide a basis on which to decide what kind of treatment, if any, is advisable, with whom, under what circumstances, and how one might best proceed. In the course of such an examination, the patient has an opportunity to formulate his goals, to consider what changes he wants to make, under what circumstances, and to examine how determined he is to support such an enterprise. Whether it is to be done formally, with the systematic help of another, or done by his introspective self in conjunction with whatever he can learn or read informally, the person riffling through the yellow pages probably would be best served by stopping his moving finger at the entry "diagnosis."

Though some conventional therapists may be unaware of it, and more of them reluctant to acknowledge it, they, too, are in a search through the yellow pages. Every genuinely therapeutic conscience includes the wish to be as helpful as possible to patients, and most therapeutic identities include at least a quiet questioning voice: Am I doing as well as possible? Could the situation have been handled better? Is this patient getting the best help he can with his possibly one chance for decisive change in himself, his life, and the lives of those on whom his life impinges? What possibilities for bringing about desired change are there for my patients and therefore for me in the new therapies?

Why am I posing this question for a conventional therapist? Why is *he* to look to the new therapies, rather than alternative therapists looking to conventional therapy? The following discussion of options for therapists could just as well have been written from the point of view of an alternative therapist looking to improve his work. It is not, for several reasons. I have done my observations from the point of view of a conventional therapist, with an eye to how my work could be improved. Comparing, contrasting, and proving are valued in the conventional-therapy establishment much more than they are in the new therapies. Comparing and contrasting therapies requires wide and varied clinical experience and thorough knowledge of at least one encompassing system of psychology. That kind of experience and knowledge are in greater supply among conventional therapists than in the new therapies. All other things being equal, it would be easier for a conventional therapist to learn the new therapies than the other way around.

Parenthetically, I have no conviction as to whether there is more "first-rate intelligence" in the conventional or in the new therapies; but that might be good to know, for such intelligence is needed for comparing and contrasting. As F. Scott Fitzgerald put it, "The test of a first-rate intelligence is to hold two opposed ideas in your mind at the same time and still retain your capacity to function."[9]

Here are options for conventional therapists:

1. Conventional therapists can ignore the whole thing. If they do, however, they will become increasingly alone. Though the new therapies have their faddish aspects, in my opinion they are not all merely fads, they will not all go away. They are siphoning off patients who would otherwise be going to conventional therapists, they are beginning to make inroads into heretofore conventionally sacrosanct institutions, and they are setting up competing schools and degrees.

Moreover, for conventional therapists to ignore empirical phenomena such as are being provided by the new therapies is a dereliction of their duty as scientists, therapists, and citizens. Progress is dependent upon an openness and willingness to consider any reasonable possibility, and occasionally some unreasonable ones. Until we can say that we can be helpful to the greatest possible number and kind of people at the least expense of time and money and with the best possible results, the only responsible choice we have is fairly and objectively to consider all alternatives.

2. The conventional therapist can heed the siren song, respond to the intellectual and especially emotional appeals of the new therapies, drop out, and join the new movement. That scenario is often spun out in new-therapy publications and meetings: "I saw the error of my ways, my patients did not improve despite my earnest interpre-

tive efforts. They and I were both miserable living according to society's dictates. Now I have found joy. I gave up my wife and children, but in Eunice I have found a new love, a new life, and I radiate my joy to and with my patients." Maybe. But glow is no substitute for wisdom, and wisdom has more staying power. Let us be suspicious of extremes; 180-degree shifts turn us in opposite directions but on the same line. Those who drop out may have courage; they may have gotten clear about their own needs. But in the absence of substantiation I am as suspicious of them as I am of those who in this regard remain inert, complacent, and unquestioning.

3. Conventional therapists can refer patients to the new therapies, particularly when the patient cannot afford extended time or money, is unsuitable for conventional therapy, or seems highly suitable for one or another new therapy. Conventional therapists have in recent years widened the scope of those they feel can be helped by their work, and have made changes in their techniques commensurate with the requirements of this widened population. However, it may well be that the scope is still insufficiently wide; conventional therapies may still require that some patients who would be more effectively treated by other modalities be fit to a Procrustean bed.

But do conventional therapists have the right to recommend any of the varieties of new therapies? Do they know enough of the advantages, disadvantages, and risks? In principle they would not have the right until they had found out enough about the new therapies to be expert in their roles as consultants and referrers. In practice, any conventional therapist, just as any family doctor, is liable inadvertently to find himself inappropriately in a wise-man role, a person to whom a wide variety of troubles are brought, sometimes regardless of their fit with the consultant's knowledge and expertise. The therapist could refuse this role. But where would that leave the person asking for help? Who, then, would advise him? The putative patient might become the victim of advisers even less qualified than conventional therapists, or of self-serving advertising; or the patient might give up on the possibilities of change for himself. The harsh fact of the matter is that recommendations are often made by people in wise-man positions, notably physicians, beyond the recommenders' firsthand or sophisticated knowledge. For example, a physician may prescribe one of the dizzying array of drugs with which he cannot individually familiarize himself, on the basis of a detail man's pitch. As I have observed it, at least, conventional group therapy, family therapy, brief and long-term individual therapy, and psychoanalysis are also prescribed with varying degrees of knowledge and experience. So conventional therapists ought not automatically to shrink from the possibility of making referrals for a new therapy, though obviously they ought to learn all they can about how best to fit person and therapy.

Another referral possibility is with patients in the midst of a continuing therapeutic relationship to whom can be recommended one or another new therapy for a specific purpose. New thoughts and feelings generated from that new-therapy experience could then be used and integrated into the ongoing conventional psychotherapy (including what it means to the patient to have had his therapist make such a referral). Perhaps somatic symptoms, general health, or emotional disturbances could be improved by balancing the body chemistries, or by other dietary approaches. Perhaps the long, arduous time spent in analyzing defenses could be speeded up through such bodily interventions as Rolfing, the Alexander technique, or bioenergetics. Perhaps feelings trapped behind walls of prohibitions and social demands could be released and experienced through primal therapy, a stay at Esalen, or gestalt therapy. Perhaps a patient's emotional or physical distress could be eased by his learning and practicing yoga, especially meditation. Prescribing drugs as an adjunct to psychotherapy would be analogous to these prescriptions. True enough, with conventional therapy one might well work through the patient's difficulties without adjunctive measures, just as successful therapy can often be done without resorting to drugs. But perhaps the patient could be saved days or weeks of distress, and work through to understanding even more effectively than he could without such additional interventions. It is worth considering and studying. But one would have to evaluate carefully, as with the prescribing of drugs, whether one is considering such measures out of frustration, despair, or incompetence, and thus shortchanging one's patient, oneself, and one's method of treatment.

4. Conventional therapists can incorporate procedures from the new therapies into their own practice. While some of the new-therapy skills require a considerable investment of time, money, and ancillary study and specialized background, some do not. They are relatively simple to learn and to apply. This procedure would be like that of some general medical practitioners who, for example, use some chiropractic and osteopathy in their practice. Conventional therapists could, for example, teach meditation, breathing, and other loosening-up exercises. They could teach these as a general skill for their patients to use on their own. Or they could teach them and use them during conventional treatment sessions for specific purposes. I have, for example, used attention to breathing, and breathing exercises, to good effect with a number of patients, for specific reasons and at specific junctures.

These procedures have opposite effects with different people, suggesting that people use them for what they require at the time. Some patients have come into the therapy hours disturbed, confused, and anxious, and have responded a little, but not enough, to my usual interventions. With more of such interventions they likely would have worked through these spells as they had in the past. But they responded to breathing exercises quickly, and were able to reflect upon the causes of their disturbance sooner and with greater effect than I believe would have happened without such breathing exercises. Other patients have come to the therapeutic hour in a state of deadly, tight resistance, unproductive of thought and feeling. These people, too, in the course of our usual work over a period of time would likely have relaxed those defenses. However, as an apparent result of the breathing exercises, they allowed feelings and thoughts to emerge soon and effectively. The reactions of these patients could well have stemmed, at least in part, from my doing something unexpected and from their experiencing my behavior as, for example, caring or forceful. I encouraged discussion of such interventions so as to avoid any harmful influence on the over-all therapeutic context, and such discussions in themselves provided opportunities for new self-understanding. Patients' work with such breathing has also resulted in much information about specific difficulties, clearly demonstrable to both of us. For example, a patient with tendencies toward sexual frigidity noticed that she could allow the breath to seem to circulate in her body down to her pelvis, but there it stopped (or, as she came to realize, she stopped it there).

I have occasionally found modifications of gestalt-therapy techniques useful in otherwise conventional psychotherapy. The gestalt attitude of desirelessness toward resistances is not entirely foreign to the psychoanalytic attitude of desirelessness as related to neutrality. In both instances the therapist takes the position of serving as a guide, without predetermined goals for the patient; he is subject to the patient's going where he will and deciding as he does. Yet such over-all desirelessness and neutrality can, in conventional therapy, give way to the felt need of the therapist to follow technical rules to insure the process. Thus, when the patient is resisting, the therapist examines these resistances with the patient with the implicit expectation that they should be relaxed or given up. Gestalt therapists decry such an expectation, implicit or not. They take a radically neutral position, assuming that the patient has a greater wisdom than the therapist, and that the patient will give up the resistance only when he can make different use of the therapeutic process. The gestalt therapist may warm up the patient with breathing and physical exercises but usually lets the patient decide when and for how long he should "work." I think this gestalt attitude provides a reminder to conventional therapists of the importance of neutrality and patient self-determination, that unbeknownst to perhaps both the patient and the therapist there may be wisdom operating that is greater than that which is in the awareness of both of them. Nonetheless, I am sure there are many instances in which gestalt desirelessness plays into the patient's resistance, allowing him to avoid feelings and thoughts that might otherwise cause anxiety. Patient and therapist can then enter into collusion to leave certain areas of work alone, to attenuate or interrupt the organic growth of the therapeutic process. With such dangers and opportunities in mind, the therapist can be careful to become neither an incarnate conscience, mindlessly applying rules, nor a helpless observer of a process allowed to take its own, haphazard course.

Another technique that has proved useful to me is to

help the patient to exaggerate whatever feeling he is reporting, even an unpleasant one. Then I try to help him localize this feeling in his body. When he has a good hold on it and feels it intensely, I ask him for his associations, to tell me what comes to mind. I find associations offered under such circumstances to be especially revealing, and they tend to be experienced by the patient as emotionally real and important. Occasionally I have found it useful to have the patient imagine a person in his life sitting in the empty chair that faces him, and to talk to that image. This imaginary interaction tends to make the relationship between the patient and the fantasied figure on the chair emotionally vivid and revealing. Another gestalt technique worthy of experimentation is to experience oneself as an element in one's dream, and then tell how it feels to be that element, a special kind of free association.

There is, of course, no more magic in any of these devices than there is in any psychotherapeutic technique; sometimes they work and sometimes they do not. Effectiveness is likely to be related to particular patients, particular times used, and particular personalities of therapists. As a rule of thumb, these interventions pose less danger to the conventional therapy process the more that process departs from the ideal technique of psychoanalysis anyway. The psychoanalytic emphasis on a nondirective search, reliance on anonymity with respect to the use of the transference, and the working through of resistances would conflict with such new-therapy departures and require a good deal of interpretive work if traditional goals and means were to be continued.

5. Finally, there is much in the new therapies that conventional therapists can incorporate into their thinking without making gross and obvious changes. In so doing,

they can enrich their grasp of their own work and, likely, make themselves better conventional therapists.

Here are some examples. One aspect of meditation is already in psychoanalysis; the patient is lulled into altering his consciousness by lying down on the couch, by the quiet atmosphere, and by the contemplative task set before him. The therapist, enjoined by Freud to listen with a "free-floating awareness" or "evenly hovering attention," both attends and does not attend to what the patient says. He drifts with the material, thus allowing ideas to emerge of their own volition, so to speak, much like what occurs in somewhat similar frames of mind in meditation. Perhaps both patient and therapist enter the "alpha state" or "go to level," as the Silva Mind Control people would say. Perhaps learning occurs in that state more readily than in the state of alert intentionality. Since studying the new therapies, I have become more conscious of the meditative, altered-consciousness aspects of the process on the part of the patient and myself. I now sometimes designedly encourage that frame of mind in myself, particularly when I listen to dreams whose depth and consequent complexity tend to require a drift toward primary modes of thinking, as occurs in meditation. I use some of the techniques I learned from meditation and other methods of altering consciousness to move myself quickly toward "listening with the third ear."

Meditation is easily learned and for many patients is probably useful for its tranquilizing effect. Yet our cultural predilection for technology makes many of us feel queasy about teaching it. Although it has, if anything, only beneficial side effects, we might feel more comfortable prescribing a tranquilizing drug, often with possible injurious side effects.

Meditation as well as other measures can be seen in a

therapeutic context that is wider than their use as circumscribed tranquilizers for episodes of anxiety. This wider context has to do with the general problem of enabling people to feel better. Once past the fantasy that any kind of psychotherapy guarantees a life without internal conflicts and associated bad feelings, we have to face the issue of what to do with bad feelings when they occur. Conventional therapy is weak in this regard. It operates on the implicit assumption that if enough conflicts are worked through, with consequent insight, either the person will no longer suffer with symptoms and difficulties in living or he will "handle them better." Exactly how he will handle them better tends to be less explicit than it might be. In this sense the new-therapy critics are right when they indict conventional therapy as being overly concerned with pathology. Having grown up in the context of medicine, conventional therapy has unwittingly fallen into the traditional medical concern with what is wrong and how it can be cured, with comparatively little attention to a person's efforts to minimize "subclinical" distress and to prevent its eventuating in a call for the doctor.

Take, for example, a patient who has had, let us say, some five years of psychoanalysis. What does he do when he finds himself in psychological distress? He may think over what he has learned about himself that may be leading to the distress, notice its repetitive pattern, how environmental events have touched off reactions that stem from his early history and reverberate among his fantasies and the premises based on them. He may also think of what his ex-analyst might say or do. He may get freshly in touch with the feelings of competence, companionship, and concern that characterize his inner relationship with his ex-analyst.

As a result of these self-analytic efforts, he may feel a lot better, a little better, or no better at all. Even well-analyzed people have blue Mondays, red Saturdays, and may not feel too good or stay out of trouble throughout the week, either. All of this may take place at a higher level and in much improved circumstances than what might have been without analysis. Nonetheless, the problems in living are posed there to be solved or not solved.

Would it not perhaps be helpful if in addition to self-analysis the patient had a variety of other means of dealing with distress? We have already mentioned meditation as a substitute tranquilizer. The allied Eastern attitude of detachment can be another such handy aid. "Life is a waterfall . . . in a hundred years from now it will all be the same . . . we are merely grains of sand on the beach of time . . . this, too, shall pass . . . you win some and lose some, and some get rained out . . . who's to say that what seems like a miserable turn of events at the moment may not in the long run turn out for the better?" The words are less important than the feelings engendered by such aphorisms—feelings of tranquility, being safely in the observer's position even while being observed, confidence brought about by the recognition that all lies in the eyes of the beholder and one can be in charge of what he beholds. There are no wrong decisions, says Suzuki,[10] because all decisions are both right and wrong. Since there are no right ones either, one need not worry about meeting standards; meet them if you wish, but that is up to you. You choose chocolate ice cream because you choose chocolate ice cream, says Werner Erhard; no need to explain or justify your behavior. Honor your despair, says Ram Dass, so long as you use it as a stimulus to learn. Beyond that it is simply morbid, unnecessary, and you might as well give it up. Some of this Eastern wisdom finds its way into the Western "power of positive thinking": You have a choice between thinking positively and thinking negatively, so feel better by choosing to think positively. Aspects of this wisdom can also be realized through psychoanalysis, but not necessarily or always; psychoanalysis is inexplicit about such possibilities.

Breathing exercises are good for anxiety in general and are a specific antidote to stage fright.

You can also scream. I have had patients who said that they would like to scream but did not want to advertise their distress through the relatively thin walls of my office. Instead, they drove to a secluded spot, rolled up the windows of their car, and screamed, trying as much as possible to achieve a primal scream as described by Janov. They sometimes reported that such screaming helped them feel better.

As has been mentioned throughout this book, the new therapies' emphasis on self-responsibility can be a useful corrective to the passivity implicit in the language of the theory of psychoanalysis.[11,12] When the passive mode of the language infiltrates the therapy, it can result in an avoidance of assuming responsibility and taking commensurate actions, sometimes needlessly prolonging treatment and sometimes failing adequately to strengthen the patient's executive capacities. My studies of the new therapies have made me more aware of this danger, and of the opportunities an active stance provides. I now help the patient to notice in his language evidence of beliefs that forces are acting upon him out of his control, that symptoms happen to him, that feelings arise without participation of the executive self. I try to help him to see that he brings about all these events: he *does* symptoms, so to speak; he *causes* feelings. It is true that such feelings as guilt and embarrassment can be shown to have historical antecedents, and an examination of them can lead to early memories and consequent greater understanding of relationships with significant figures past and present. At the same time, such feelings, and even the psychoanalytic investigation of them can be used for defensive purposes. It is often of great benefit to question why the patient is producing guilt or embarrassment at a particular time and under particular circumstances, what he is attempting to achieve by reliving the past in these terms at this moment. A logical extrapolation of this point of view is to put proper emphasis on will and action as necessary adjuncts to insight in order for change to occur. Roles of will and action, eloquently enunciated a quarter of a century ago by Allen Wheelis, are less prominent in psychoanalytic thinking and teaching than they should be.[13,14] The new-therapy emphasis on self-responsibility rescues and dramatizes these roles. I now keep more careful watch on the patient's capacity for activity, initiative, effort. Without expecting more than he is capable of, I try to determine if he is selling himself short, unconsciously attempting to persuade me to do the same, to get me to do for him what he could do himself. Emphasizing the roles of will, action, and self-responsibility constitutes probably the single most important change in my conventional psychotherapeutic work, and has been similarly important in my teaching of young psychotherapists, and a good many not so young ones. This result of my study of new therapies suggests that conventional workers have been underestimating these factors. A new frontier is offered in conventional technique: how to emphasize and exploit the roles of will and action without falling into mindless behavior therapy or simplistic urging.

Emphasizing self-responsibility leads to a highlighting of the act of making choices and decisions. This act in turn highlights the frequent crossroads that patients and therapists face between "adjusting" to the demands of others and deciding one's destiny for oneself. At points in many conventional therapeutic relationships it is difficult truly to remain neutral.[15] A tone of voice, a flicker of expression, a choice of words, the choosing of one topic over another—especially in the context of heightened receptivity on the part of the patient to the therapist—can easily convince the patient that the therapist is in favor of one or another way of living. This is all the more true when the way of living fits with the surrounding culture and so can easily be considered an "adjustment."

Adjustment is sometimes taken as a code word for health. But adjustment may be at the cost of the patient's capacity to make independent decisions. As a result, decisions may not really be "his" and are therefore often difficult to implement in the long run. Taking the easy, thoughtless adjustment way also results in a lack of exercise of and confidence in the ability to blaze one's own path and accept the consequences, even should the path conflict with one or another aspect of society. Such conventionally valued achievements as marriage, children, completing school, and advancement in business are often set forth by conventional therapists as proof of the effectiveness of their work. That goals are cited in this way alerts us to the possibility that conventional achievements may have been consciously or unconsciously striven for by the therapist. However useful the attaining of these goals may be for the patient, subtle pressure toward them by the therapist can covertly undermine the patient's exercising choice, and diminish opportunities to understand the difficulties in making choices.

It is not uncommon in conventional therapy for a patient to assert the wish for certain things to come about, yet be unwilling to fantasy such occurrences. For example, one patient, plagued by a lifelong fear of warm and romantic relationships, which she said she wanted, nonetheless tried in various ways to avoid thinking about and discussing this very topic. In working with her I was reminded, and helped, by the yogi point of view that nothing exists except insofar as it is imagined by a person, that each person creates his own reality. My patient could produce only derivative and empty thoughts as long as she refused to admit to her mind the reality of what she wanted, the concretely realized hues, textures, dimensions, of specific people and relationships. The challenge to be specific, beginning with fantasy and progressing to words, helps overcome repression, avoids escape into vagueness, and focuses the therapy on clearly definable goals, thus counteracting obfuscation and drift.

Once having heard the primal scream—which is a way of saying having observed the extreme of the range of intense feelings available to people through a single-minded therapeutic pursuit of feelings—one can never again be sanguine about the amount of feeling that occurs in conventional therapeutic work. The hoary understanding in conventional therapy of the importance of feeling achieved, for me, a kind of supersonic dimension through my studies of the new therapies. I now work much harder, try to be much more ingenious in order to bring about the expression of the feelings that most accurately portray the layers, nuances, and intensity of a patient's experience.

21

A Station Stop Named Ending

So MUCH FOR conventional and alternative therapists, consumers of therapy, and science. Now, what of me? How has this study affected my personal life and behavior? I did, after all, participate in therapeutic activities as well as enlarge my knowledge of ways of promoting beneficial change.

Sedentary as I tend to be, I can never now, at least without added pangs of conscience, ignore or abuse my body. Sometimes I can enjoy the doing of exercises, Eastern and Western, and the tailoring of diets, and sometimes these become just another "should," something to have to do. As with psychotherapeutic progress in general, change often feels like a mixed blessing.

I have seen and experienced the release from undue and unnecessary self-restriction, a freedom that is so prized in human-potential thinking. As a consequence, I am more sensitive to life's pleasures often waiting just around the corner, and more aware of the self-oppression that sometimes prevents me from turning the corner. Such realizations are, on the one hand, comforting. On the other hand, they call for work, rather than resignation; courage and initiative, rather than cowed or resigned acceptance.

While I have not become a regular meditator, I now have available the capacity to alter consciousness for purposes of dealing with pain and sleeplessness, and to relax. As I write this, I have just returned from a New York City round of pressured meetings. On the way to one of these, fatigued from travel and general stress, I meditated in a taxi weaving its way through the noisy crush of five-o'clock midtown-Manhattan traffic, and emerged from the cab refreshed. Surely it was not I doing that? Oh yes it was.

I have devoted a good part of my life, energies, and attention to not making mistakes, to arranging my internal and external world in such a way as to be capable and blameless. I now at least intermittently am able to realize that what seems a mistake at the moment may turn out not to be one. Moreover, the mistake may be more in the self-laceration for being human than in falling short of a high-flown standard. And I am more accepting of the fallibility of others, in part as a reflection of greater self-acceptance.

The tranquillity that comes from tolerating apparent mistakes provides a comforting over-all blueprint for how to plan and decide the future. Such feelings and attitudes need not diminish ambition and drive. And they can be ignored at will; that, too, has its place, is not necessarily a "mistake."

I have become more at ease speaking in front of groups, and I write with greater facility. I am somewhat freer in my relationships. At the same time, I am more comfortable than before in pursuing lonely paths.

I am less troubled at the prospects of illness, in myself and others, than I was before; I now see illness more confidently as having large psychological components, and as a result feel better equipped to deal with it. As a result of my increased confidence in the psychological aspects of physical disease, I am devoting a portion of my career to research and treatment of cancer and other diseases through psychological means.

I have minimally changed my choice of language, clothes, and mores of interpersonal relationships and other customs. If anything, I enjoy Brooks Brothers clothing, the King's English, and the calling-card-on-a-silver-tray sort of thing even more than I did previously. I enjoy psychoanalytic thinking more also, and for the same reason: I have now more deeply examined these ways of thinking and living, compared and contrasted them with others, sampled others, and now feel more confirmed in my original choices, as well as seeing in them additional dimensions. I think I am also less needful of using my choice of behaviors and beliefs for acceptance and self-esteem, and am now more able to enjoy them for themselves. The fact is that I would rather live in traditional Western society, for all of its undoubted imperfections, than in Calcutta or Big Sur (except sometimes).

With study over and report written, do I resume business as usual? When I set off on this voyage, I assumed vaguely that I would. But you can't go home again, quite, or at least I can't. One reason I set off on the odyssey was to try to still the voice asking what, if anything, could be done better for patients. I responded to that voice with some new learning, attitudes, and techniques, and I think patients have benefited from these. But the voice has, if anything, only increased in volume. This study has allowed the development of more hypotheses than final conclusions, cleared away clouds only to expose horizons. I now find myself in a steady state of unsteadiness, a homeostatic alternation between seeking and finding.

You will notice in these remarks how often there are two sides to every question: advantages and disadvantages; each answer gives rise to a new question; each ending is a new beginning. This observation can be understood as an expression of my difficulty making up my mind, indecision, equivocation—character traits not unknown to me, indeed not uncommon to many personality types who get themselves professionally educated. And maybe that is all there is to it; but I do not think so. Rather, I believe that in nature there are no easy answers, that wisdom arises from conflicts, contradictions, paradoxes; one can never go wrong betting on complexity. I feel an affinity for yin-yang philosophy (for every front there is a back, for every up there is a down, for every right there is a wrong, for every step forward there is a step backward). I believe also in Western pragmatism and idealism. With all of the back and forth, with problems being created by solutions, with the scaling of mountains revealing new mountains, one nonetheless does move in one direction; that direction is forward.

Has my odyssey been a voyage ending with despair or hope, pessimism or optimism, as a discouragement or encouragement to the odysseys of others? In answer, here is the whole of the quotation from Scott Fitzgerald partially cited earlier:

> The test of a first-rate intelligence is to hold two opposed ideas in your mind at the same time and still retain your capacity to function. You should, for example, be able to see that things are hopeless and yet be determined to make them otherwise.[1]

If that seems enigmatic, ambiguous, vaguely unsatisfying, and slightly seductive, then it accurately conveys some of what psychotherapy is like: also difficult, frustrating, inspiring, an aesthetic delight, sometimes inexplicable, and a great opportunity.

Epilogue

I RECENTLY THUMBED through a book of my poetry written some five years ago. I found it difficult fully to believe that I had written it. I now creak toward experiences which, captured in the poems, I had fallen into. The poems were written at times when they were needed to absorb an overflow of thoughts and feelings. Now, in a more comfortable time, I find the poems faintly embarrassing. As I end this book I have begun to feel something similar about the explorations and experiences of my odyssey. I begin to notice feelings of irritation at the styles and excesses of the new therapies. I think I'll catch up on the psychoanalytic journals and take a few more patients with my newly freed time. I think of how well many of my patients have done with conventional treatment alone. Occasionally I wonder whether what happened to me did happen to me, whether the feelings I had were really mine. I have kept my mind open, suffered dizzying wrenches, and stumbled down halls of mirrors. Let me now escape to certainty, enjoy my prejudices, and lean on others and traditions for support, rather than having to think for myself.

I will have to work if I am not to succumb to these

blandishments. I will have to fight off the icy grips of disbelief and complacency. Those of my adventures and ideas and feelings that are to survive have to be consolidated, to become comfortably part of me. Those new ideas and experiences about which I feel more tentative have got to be allowed to continue to have their say and be evaluated. Those characteristics I no longer wish seriously to consider have to be laid aside, though with respect. All this has to be done not in cowardly retreat into orthodoxy but by way of coming to reasonable conclusions.

I have looked into myself and found there a microcosm of every person's struggle. However much psychotherapy may resemble and be sold as medicine, it is at bottom a new version of humankind's age-old quest to learn what life is about. Such odysseys as mine, at bottom a search for the ultimate, never end; they are just given up on. I expect many readers know what I have described: old world / new world, things as they have always been and things as they might be, the easy predetermined or the frightening leap into the unknown. Whether the context is psychotherapy or another path, we are always extended an invitation to an odyssey, and we are always tested in our resolve.

APPENDIX

A Psychoanalyst Looks at Gestalt Therapy

As a psychoanalyst writing about gestalt therapy, I am almost sure to write something that either a psychoanalyst or a gestalt therapist will disclaim as being not the way he does or understands his work. Individual practitioners behave and believe differently from one another although they nominally practice the same theory and technique. We shall have to allow as best we can for such individual differences, and make do with generalizations.

The sociopsychological nature of our times also contributes to the difficulty in providing a balanced discussion of psychoanalysis and gestalt therapy. The field of psychotherapy has recently become a highly competitive marketplace for men's minds and dollars. In such an atmosphere people tend to lose their identities and become fantasies in the eyes of others; ideas tend to be used as justifications or weapons rather than to be reflected upon. Psychoanalysis, because of its first and formidable claim to the field, its exclusive training practices, and its identification with the doctor-patient model, tends to be seen by gestaltists as the establishment authority against which other therapies must either rebel or measure themselves. The psychoanalysts' fantasy about gestalt therapists is that they are an errant younger brother scrambling for a place in the sun, reckless of the damage done to older institutions, and bolstering their shaky conviction with contempt for orthodoxy.

An added difficulty is that my gestalt experience consists only of the reading of some basic texts, discussions with gestalt therapists, and observation of and participation in a dozen or so gestalt therapy groups in Los Angeles, at Esalen and in Topeka. I have not practiced gestalt therapy except for an occasional use of some of its techniques and emphases within the context and structure of psychoanalytic therapy. I write of gestalt therapy, therefore, only as an informed amateur.

Interpretation

The delivery of insight by way of interpretation is probably the most crucial distinction between gestalt therapy and psychoanalysis. The extreme gestalt position would be that no interpretations are made in gestalt work; indeed, no active attempt is made to convey insight. The extreme psychoanalytic position might be that the major technique of analysis is to convey insight by way of properly timed and accurate interpretations. Both of these extreme positions collapse when one thinks of interpretation as a process of communication the goal of which is to enlarge awareness or consciousness. Such a process may include *an* interpretation; that is, an explicit statement of meaning. It also may include any behavior on the therapist's part which, because of its timing and the interpersonal and intellectual context in which it is inserted, can convey emotional and cognitive understanding. Silence, asking why a topic was or was not brought up, encouragement, tone of voice and rhythm of speech, all can be cues as to what meanings the patient might ascribe to his productions. On the basis of my experience, gestalt therapy will have to stand up and be counted as a highly effective purveyor of insight, however much gestaltists may dislike their method being characterized in this way. They cannot have it both ways: to encourage full awareness on the one hand and claim not to deal in insight on the other. It is true, however, that gestalt therapists minimize, and some no doubt abstain completely from, explicitly interpretive or "explaining" remarks. Thus, they try not to tell the patient about himself in so many words (although I *have* seen this done by some esteemed gestalt therapists along with hortatory, educative, inspirational, and summing-up comments). They do make highly educated guesses about what to emphasize, what roles should be played out in dialogue, what should be repeated louder, what elements in a dream should be attended to—all under a guiding clinical sophistication, reflecting *their* insight or awareness and encouraging the same in the patient.

I think a better distinction than insight and interpretation versus no insight and interpretation would be that gestalt therapists are hypersensitive to the invasion of the interpretive process by emotionally isolated cognition, and have designed their techniques accordingly.

Cause and Choice

Gestalt therapists regularly instruct their patients to substitute "I won't" for "I can't." This little but powerful device is an entry into what psychoanalysts would call character analysis. With it the gestalt therapist implies that he knows that the patient is inclined to minimize his ability and to see his difficulties as external and therefore apart from his control. Thus the gestalt therapist counters any of the patient's inclinations to be stubborn, petulant, or self-defeating. He implies that the patient has the capacity to solve problems, and that if he doesn't it may well be because he does not want to, all things considered. Such a point of view is in the tradition of psychoanalytic ego psychology, which posits a capacity for problem-solving that is partly independent of and partly an outgrowth of drives—a function of consciousness, will, judgment, decision-making, mastery, and self-determination. This view contrasts with the simplistic understanding of behavior as being solely determined by the id, instincts, or unconscious drives and wishes. The essence of psychoanalysis is internal conflict; the id is opposed by the ego, wishes contend with fears, and impulses compete among themselves. To argue against a conflictual view of human nature is to have misunderstood early psychoanalysis and to be oblivious of later psychoanalysis. Such an error is in a sense understandable, however; some psychoanalysts sound as if they, too, believe that drive, wish, and symbolism are all that is important in any given bit of behavior. Psychoanalysis has had difficulty moving from the discovery and drama of unconscious motives and symbolic meanings to the general psychology intended by Freud. It has remained for such innovators as Roy Schafer, Allen Wheelis, and others to make systematically explicit within psychoanalysis the place of action, reason, will, and the making of decisions as these take place with greater or lesser degrees of insight, awareness, and consciousness.

Determination in psychoanalysis is actually multidetermination. Saying that a behavior is unconsciously determined is not the same as saying that it is fully and inexorably determined that way. It merely asserts that unconscious motivation is an influence. In this sense, gestaltists, as they help people see and experience early relationships that are influential in the present, are no less deterministic than are psychoanalysts.* They are, however, more explicit, forceful, and perhaps more confident of people's conscious capacities to deal adequately with their troublesomely determined natures.

Memory and the Here-and-now

The gestalt therapists in their pursuit of the here-and-now of experience say such things as, "Talk to your long-dead relative now," "Say how you feel now," "Act it, be it, now," "Use the present tense." Their zeal for phenomenology is often accompanied by wild-swinging accusations that psychoanalytic work consists solely of the reconstruction of a figurative past on the assumption that reconstruction alone will bring about change, at best a half-truth. Psychoanalysts and gestaltists essentially agree that the most mutative experiences are those that involve the whole person, are most fully experienced, and take place in the present. The most powerful tool in psychoanalysis to achieve these experiences is the transference, which, by definition, is seen most clearly by the patient in the here-and-now of the psychoanalytic hour. Transference duplicates past relationships; indeed Freud described transference as a way of remembering. A past re-created in the transference may have a greater claim to being in the here-and-now than a past imaginarily re-created in gestalt role-playing and dialogues. Moreover, much of the here-and-

* People often sound as if they subscribe to single causes or determinants when they know better. Ambiguity, choice, weighting, and unsureness are all difficult to deal with, especially in the face of the anxiety generated by intensive work with patients. Sometimes one sounds as if one believed in unidetermination only because one has difficulty in thinking and speaking of more than one thing at a time.

now of group behavior and of the relationship with the therapist is ignored by gestaltists.

Gestalt therapists are far less innocent about the past and its uses than one might gather from some of their remarks. For example, a gestalt therapist might say to a patient, "Get into your time machine," as an invitation to remember the past. Their patients do, in fact, usually tell of past experiences that have seemingly played a major determining role in the difficulties they focus on in the gestalt sessions.

The Body

Psychoanalysts have always considered bodily symptoms, posture, gait, and inadvertent movements to be expressive of personality. Typically, however, these observations in the psychoanalytic situation are limited to the way the patient enters the office, his movements on the couch, and the way he leaves. Ever since the brief period when Freud attempted to stimulate reverie by putting his hands on the patient's forehead, direct use of the body has been eschewed in psychoanalysis, consistently with Freud's settling on psychophysical parallelism as his solution to the mind-body problem. By contrast, gestalt therapy emphasizes opportunities for observing the body, exaggerating its expressiveness, and for explicit manipulations of it. Observations are often abetted, especially in gestalt group sessions, by the opportunity people have for walking around and finding different positions on the floor. Assuming that the body is a carrier of memory and experience often outside of awareness, gestaltists attempt to release such experience through the direct interventions of urging the patient to concentrate on his body, to express himself with it, to change his breathing and body posture; and gestalt therapists often use bioenergetic exercises for these purposes as well.

Acceptance

Both psychoanalysts and gestalt therapists assert their nonjudgmental acceptance of the patient. Therefore, they both struggle with the paradox that even while claiming acceptance of the person as he is they are nonetheless engaged in a procedure designed to facilitate change. They usually say that they merely offer the conditions for change and it is up to the patient to decide what, when, and how changes should occur. This is a serviceable point of view for practical reasons, but it ought not to obscure the recognition that the therapist knows full well that when one goes to a therapist one wants to change something felt to be inimical to one's well-being. (If the patient were fully accepting of himself, there would hardly be any reason to come and to work; putative patients would just be dilettantes, "groupies," whom no therapy would benefit.) Gestalt therapists, despite the fact that they often claim the title "therapist," may assert that they are not interested in symptoms and cure, in any goals for the patient except that of increasing awareness, raising consciousness, encouraging a sense of whole from parts. In contrast, psychoanalysts expect patients to present specific symptoms or complaints. If the patient does not, most analysts consider it helpful to work toward the patient's recognition of what is alien and unwanted by himself. However, the psychoanalyst might similarly say he was interested only in making the unconscious conscious, in strengthening the ego, in the patient's integrating felt disparate parts of himself, and not in changing any aspect of the person held by the psychoanalyst as requiring change. One must distinguish an atmosphere of nonjudgmental acceptance of the patient and his productions within the context of treatment, from the over-all acceptance of something better coming of the work. The latter determines whether to embark on it and when to end it as a socioprofessional enterprise. Gestalt therapists seem unnecessarily exercised about acknowledging change as a goal, as though such acknowledgment leads necessarily to a lack of acceptance of the patient's production and where he "is" at any given moment during the treatment. Because of their medical training, and the medical role they assume politically, socially, and administratively, some psychoanalysts may have to struggle even more than gestalt therapists with maintaining the distinction between acceptance in the therapeutic hour and the unacceptability of symptoms and symptomatic behaviors.

Resistance

The issue of acceptance probably comes up most pointedly around the concept of resistance. Gestalt therapists at times seem to declare resistance out of court with their exquisite attention to, and premium placed upon, where the patient "is" at the moment. If that "is" does not include an openness to feelings and thoughts and a wish to exploit these, then the patient, at least in group situations, has the option of not "working." He stays off the "hot seat," and may or may not relate himself to others in the group. Instead, he may wander entirely out of the situation without his behavior being an object of particular therapeutic interest. Instead of analyzing resistance, gestalt therapists assert that the patient needs his resistances—but as a conscious option, rather than an unconscious compulsion. Nonetheless, gestalt therapists do work with the patient's struggle to be in touch with his thoughts and feelings. Often they use bodily tonus and stimulation to overcome what a psychoanalyst might call a condition of resistance. For example, they may have the patient attend to his body, breathe deeply, do exercises, get in touch with the lower levels of his mind by acting the parts of primitive people or animals. The gestalt therapist's seeming desirelessness about resistance makes for an effective way of dealing with resistances. For example, he may ask the patient to notice how he is resisting experience and to exaggerate such behavior until the patient feels tired, rueful, found out, or ridiculous at so defeating himself. If the patient expresses resistance by waking up before the dream is ended, the therapist may ask, "If you had not awakened, how would the dream have ended?" If the resistance is in the form of not remembering dreams, the therapist may ask, "If you had not forgotten it, what would the dream have been?"

"Going with" the resistance is a powerful technique. At one stroke the therapist may achieve all or some of the following: neutralize the patient's stubbornness and negativism by offering him the feeling of independence and control that oppositional people usually crave; recognize with the patient his need for resistances, thus underlining the therapist's human understanding and acceptance; stay out of the potential "countertransference bind" of wanting the patient to go at his own pace but also wanting to move the therapy along; stay out of the potential transference position of being seen as judging some behavior as having to be gotten rid of as if it were by nature bad; avoid acting in the paradigm of therapist activity, i.e., getting rid of the resistance, and in the paradigm of patient passivity, i.e., the patient's allowing the resistance to be taken away, which may be felt by him as a deprivation, attack, or loss.

I have been particularly impressed by the degree to which many patients take an analyst's interventions as prohibitions and criticisms, no matter how neutrally and non-judgmentally expressed and felt by the analyst. The analyst may know that his interventions are functional, rather than moral, but the distinction seems difficult for many patients to maintain, and it may not always be easy for the analyst, either. After all, he *does* value an intrapsychic situation that is relatively unimpeded by resistances, and he *is* inclined to describe a patient who can overcome his resistances as a "good" patient, and he *does* usually select for analysis only those patients who give evidence of capacities favorable to analytic success. The gestalt point of view and consequent feeling about resistances, even apart from the particular techniques used, helps minimize any such tendencies toward being judgmental.

Dreams

In psychoanalysis the dream is the guardian of sleep in that it allows partial expression of impulses by symbolically fulfilling the wishes that are psychological expressions of such dammed-up impulses. In gestalt therapy a dream is described as an existential message from one part of the self to another part of the self. On the surface, these viewpoints might seem quite different, but the differences are more apparent than real. Even as stated, there is nothing necessarily contradictory about these formulations. After all, unfulfilled wishes and their consequences are most of what existence is about. And there is at least a bit of psychoanalytic lore to the effect that if one traced all the possible associations to any one dream, the whole personality would be revealed.

Any seeming differences are even less apparent when one moves from metapsychology to the way psychoanalysts use dreams in practice. The dream is not always taken as an actual event of the night but, rather, a communication from the patient to the analyst in the here-and-now of the psychoanalytic hour. Thus patient and analyst may learn from when the dream was mentioned, how it was told, and what the patient does with it once it is told. The analyst may understand the introduction or report of a dream at a particular moment as an avoidance of the here-and-now; he may call attention to that or simply ignore the dream. Or he may react to it *as* an existential message that the patient, for defensive reasons or through lack of conscious awareness, is unable to express in less coded ways. Rather than offering an explanation (which many gestalt therapists seem to think he would invariably do), the psychoanalyst would likely encourage the patient not only to associate to elements in the dream but to come up with his own understanding. Just as a gestalt therapist might do, the psychoanalyst might remind his patient that the dream was a creation of the dreamer's mind, rather than a representation of people or events apart from himself.

While both kinds of therapists are likely to collect associations to dream elements, gestalt therapists do employ a special technique of having the patient *be* a person or element in the dream, and say, in effect, what comes to mind as this person or element. Proceeding on the belief that everything in the dream reflects aspects of the person, gestaltists assume that a spoon, window, or coffin can represent the self just as can such more obvious self-representations as people or animals.

In recent years, the importance of the dream in psychoanalytic technique has diminished to the point that some analysts claim to ignore dreams entirely. It may be that these analysts have learned that at least their way of using dreams has led to dreams being used more as resistance than as a useful point of entry into the inner life. It seems to me worth the while of psychoanalysts to explore the gestalt techniques of role-playing with elements in the dream, as a possible aid, and in some instances as a rejuvenation of the recognition of the therapeutic usefulness of dreams.

Object Relations via Dialogue

Constructing a monologue or dialogue based on dream parts is only a variation of the major gestalt therapy technique of having the patient "play the parts" of himself and people significant in his life. This technique, too, is foreign to psychoanalysis, and might well be investigated for its possible effectiveness. Such a procedure, among other things, dramatizes what the psychoanalyst informed by object-relations theory might label as the "inner world of objects." It provides dramatic illustrations of the relationships between self and others as these are carried out within the mind of the patient. It demonstrates the interchangeability and empathy that one can have with the people who constitute oneself. Improved self-awareness, and by implication greater tranquillity and effectiveness, come about by owning up to, rather than disowning, these "introjects," as one forgives, adjusts to, or otherwise integrates them into a workable, less conflict-laden whole.

Free Association and "Working"

Initially I was surprised at how articulate gestalt-therapy patients were in talking about their personal problems and difficulties in front of a group. I wondered whether I would be able to "work" adequately on the hot seat at all. Such fears were unfounded. In a short time I was able to shift gears into a state of consciousness not unlike what one experiences on the psychoanalytic couch, which facilitates free association, openness to experience, and reverie. Maybe the inhibiting effect of a face-to-face confrontation is diminished by there being many faces; maybe the atmosphere of acceptance so prevalent in gestalt work helps one overcome inhibitions; maybe observing others doing the same thing allows for a sense of community that helps allay fear and embarrassment; maybe impeding the development of intense feelings between patient and therapist is helpful in this regard.

Articulateness and verbal productivity in a gestalt session seem to stem in large measure from the free-associative process. Some gestalt therapists may be surprised at my applying such a term to the flow of ideas when a patient is "working," but I think that might be due to a common misunderstanding of the term and phenomena of free association. "Free association" is a misnomer. Associations, by definition, follow rules. Psychoanalysis posits that associations are determined by motives or impulses and are therefore meaningful. What is "free" about the phenomenon is a state of mind that allows thoughts to come, unhampered by judgments as to whether they are moral, intelligent, or important. Freed of such strictures, the patient is helped to allow the rules of determination to operate "freely." Psychoanalysts make these conditions formal with the basic rule: tell whatever comes to mind. The atmosphere provided by analysis is enough to encourage the association process without the rule, just as seems to occur in gestalt-therapy sessions. However, the explicitness of the task denoted by the basic rule is a powerful adjunct to the basic free-association process, making for wider-ranging associations and for the emergence of resistances whose analysis becomes central to the understanding of the personality. By contrast, "working" gestalt patients go quickly and emotionally to more restricted topics. Essentially, however, "working" comes about by letting one thought lead to another; i.e., free association.

Pyschosexual Stages

Frequently during gestalt work I found myself translating back and forth between the language of the gestalt session and the language of psychoanalysis. An example occurred when Laura Perls discussed the issue of intimacy. The problem of intimacy, she said, was to find a comfortable and effective point between a clinging need for others (which might be labeled grossly, in psychoanalytic terms, orality) and excessive distance, a hyperdiscrimination between self and others with rigidly prescribed means of interpersonal contact (which might be labeled grossly, in psychoanalytic terms, anality). The comfortable and effective midpoint between these extremes allows an integration of both of them, in the service of discharging effectively the task of intimacy, getting the most from and giving the most to relationships (which might be labeled in psychoanalytic terms phallic-genital).

The Fritz Perls model of taking in through the mouth what is compatible and spitting out what is not seems identical with the oral-dependent/oral-aggressive paradigm in psychoanalysis.

Encouraging Change

Gestalt therapists often use what could be labeled "corrective emotional experience." They encourage their patients to try out thoughts, expressions, and behaviors to see what feels right for them. They depend on the nonoccurrence of the unconsciously expected bad consequences as being reassuring to the patient, thereby encouraging him to use these new behaviors and be emboldened to try out still more new ones. This idea seems to underlie "risk-taking": "Sure you feel anxious," the gestalt therapist says, "but don't let that hold you back; try it out, go ahead and see what happens." Gestaltists do this to increase awareness, rather than simply to encourage mindless new behavior, as some therapists do out of a belief that behaving differently in and of itself is beneficial. The traditional though not exclusive psychoanalytic approach would be to try to help the patient understand what is making him anxious. With the consequent diminution of anxiety, the patient can proceed with the behavior that had been inhibited by fear. Some psychoanalysts probably are convinced that in all instances insight precedes change, and consider encouraging the taking of action and the assertion of will by the patient as outside the range of psychoanalytic work. In my opinion the roles of will, action, the making of decisions, and an openness to the possibility that changed behavior can precede and bring about insight are inherent in psychoanalytic thinking, though perhaps they are only recently becoming fully recognized. The use of understanding, insight, or the psychoanalysis itself as a possible defense against the anxiety of changing one's behavior is, or should be, well recognized; as Freud said, sooner or later a phobic patient must face, rather than merely talk about, his phobias. Some psychoanalysts may encourage understanding beyond a point where taking on extra-analytic challenges should be encouraged (such encouragement can be done analytically, through interpretation, as well as through exhortation). Gestalt therapists probably avoid this kind of error with their de-emphasis on insight as an explicit goal and their emphasis upon the immediate taking of risks, if only in speech during the gestalt sessions. The danger is that they merely inspire the patient to behave differently, based essentially on suggestion and borrowing the strength of the therapist. Away from the therapeutic influence the changed behavior might well collapse, or the patient may be unable to deal with the consequences of the new behavior.

Time

The gestalt-therapy attitude toward time is flexible, soft, and maternal: There need never be endings; gestalt patients may continue attending group or individual sessions indefinitely, and the sessions themselves may go until their idiosyncratic conclusion. How one feels at the particular moment is all-important, with the understanding that this feeling may change in an instant. The demands of continuity, predictability, beginnings, middles, and ends, which some identify with the masculine elements in personality, are relatively unattended to. Some patients may experience such a point of view as reassuring; it lightens the burden of commitments; it relieves the need for promising and being responsible in the future. Yet the relatively brief time usually allotted to the therapy puts a premium on solving problems quickly.

By contrast, psychoanalysts are rigid about time boundaries of each session, often make gross predictions of the length of treatment, and are attuned to the psychologies of beginnings, middles, and ends. This scrupulousness about time lies in uneasy apposition with the implicit timelessness within the time period—what is not dealt with today can be dealt with tomorrow, the wheel comes around again, themes will recur, four or five years of four-or-five-times-a-week treatment is unremarkable. For some patients the stipulation of a period of time of treatment may imply that they cannot change their behavior until the treatment has been concluded or has taken effect. The analyst has to alert himself and the patient to the immanence of now, the capacities for self-help that can in principle operate at any given moment. He and the patient must overcome the passivity implicit in waiting, and must come to terms with the illusion that a period of time and treatment, even when it is a long period of time, can in and of itself result in an improved life ever after.

Closure

Both gestalt therapists and psychoanalysts sound at times as if they have closure as a realizable goal. In gestalt therapy lack of closure is "unfinished business," an unexpressed and unintegrated tangle of thoughts and feelings relative to a person or situation which by implication at least can be untangled and thus "finished." Psychoanalysts set forth goals such as the resolution of the transference, resolution of conflicts, and a full and complete psychoanalysis. Yet, at the same time, both gestaltists and psychoanalysts also hold as a goal the patient's developing tools with which he can help himself in the future through self-analysis or through the capacity to make himself increasingly aware. This suggests that neither field considers that its formal treatment efforts provide an absolute solution to the patient's problems. In one systematic research of psychoanalytically oriented psychotherapy and psychoanalysis, little conflict resolution was found to have occurred, at least as judged from psychological tests. Other changes in conflicts, such as awareness of them in consciousness, occurred more frequently. Reanalysis or further brief analytic work is not uncommon (although Freud's dictum that every person should have further analytic work every five years is honored more in the breach than in the observance). Gestalt patients often attend continued workshops, where they are reminded that what is true for one moment need not be true for the next moment and that determination or ambition for too much change over too long a period of time is inimical to awareness ("trying is lying").

"Closure," or "resolution," is most clearly applicable to those moments during the therapeutic work when something is integrated, usually signaled by a feeling of liberation and relief, and the patient is released toward new challenges. It is paradoxical to apply the language of closure—termination, ending, and completion—to the treatment as a whole, while at the same time believing that the patient should deal with continuing conflicts in new, perhaps ever-changing ways. This is a particular issue for psychoanalysts, who posit comprehensiveness, if not completion, as a purpose and justification for the considerable time and expense of analysis. Such an implication is made concrete by the work's having a fixed ending and being offered in the social context of the health-sickness model (inapplicable as that model is to psychoanalysis). In that model, with a prescribed treatment, one hopes to cure a sickness.

Gestalt therapists are more easygoing in this respect. They are satisfied with fragmentary interventions with respect to the personality and to the structure of the treatment. While some gestaltists may use a regular schedule of appointments with a fixed ending, others give patients the option of coming or not coming and, when there, of working or not working. This may open the way for patients' resistances. They may either keep attending gestalt workshops, and in that way appear to be trying to improve themselves even though not achieving greater awareness; or in response to the anxiety of emerging, unintegrated awareness, they may simply stop attending.

All those who work toward human change might benefit from asking themselves whether "closure," "resolution," "completion" are satisfactory words and concepts at all, whether the human condition permits or admits of them. Rather than achieving enduring solutions or lasting joy, the patient, like everybody else, has to learn to live with the quest for awareness itself, with recognition of the mystery, profundity, and ambiguity of human life and its ultimately unsatisfactory, and in many ways incomplete, ending.

Relationship with the Therapist/Analyst

The following personal experience is consonant with the gestalt therapist's indifference to a differentiated interpersonal relationship between patient and therapist: I had to be late to a gestalt workshop, and therefore missed the new therapist's self-introduction and preliminary work. Feeling the need to "work," however, I took the hot seat as soon as I could, and achieved intensely experienced new insights. I left the workshop not yet knowing the name of the therapist who asked me the right questions, told me the right things to associate to in dreams, interrupted a defensive tangent, made an aspect of my inner world live, and found ways to encourage its intense emotional expression.

Insofar as the temporary gestalt experience may be concerned, the lack of a differentiated sense of the therapist could be helpful. In the example just cited, I was absorbed with an internal puzzle, and in a low-key, unself-conscious way was sufficiently satisfied with what I had seen of the therapist's working with others to be content with knowing what was expected of me and what was to be forthcoming from him. Transference characteristics of the therapist, even a "real" relationship with him, could conceivably at that moment have been an impediment. If, however, having an extended individual relationship with a benevolent other is in and of itself important to enduring change, then its absence from gestalt therapy may be an important loss for some patients. Some psychoanalysts—such as those of the so-called interpersonal school of Sullivan, Will, and Fromm-Reichmann—are much more convinced and explicit about the curative effects of such relationships than are other psychoanalysts. Whatever the curative effects of the relationship, psychoanalysts focus upon the relationship between patient and analyst not for purposes of practicing interpersonal relationships or to provide a corrective emotional experience but as a powerful aid to learning about internal relationships. If a transference relationship is the best way of learning about oneself, then this is an opportunity lost to gestalt patients.

Self-selection of Gestaltists and Psychoanalysts

There seems no reason to exempt the choice of gestalt therapy or psychoanalysis, by practitioners or patients, from the participation of unconscious motives. The life styles typically practiced by the two groups suggest fundamental differences in their personalities. Gestalt therapists are more informal than psychoanalysts, less inner- and goal-directed, more direct in their interpersonal relationships, more responsive to the primitive and romantic in man, more optimistic, hedonistic, and socialistic. Aggression seems less central in their personalities and in the group atmosphere. The defensive purposes served by the contrasting life styles of psychoanalysts and gestaltists probably interfere with their attempts to appreciate the intrinsic worth of one another's theories and practices. Instead, both groups tend to see in each other caricatures of the warded-off parts of themselves: the uptight, rigid, button-downed, hyperintellectual, unfeeling, materialistic, hidebound psychoanalyst; the sloppy, child-like, fuzzy-faced, fuzzy-minded gestalt therapist. It is a sad commentary on people who espouse wholeness to split off and project aspects of themselves—sad, but all too understandably human. In principle at least, an integrated psychotherapist could adopt insights, techniques, emphases, and values from wherever they might arise toward increasing his effectiveness. He could do the same with himself as a person.

Corrections for Psychoanalysts and Others Whom It May Concern

The gestalt emphasis upon the immediacy of experience, self-responsibility, and mind-body holism could provide a correction for possible errors in psychoanalytic technique. The danger of such technical errors is part of the cost that psychoanalysis pays for its elaborate theory, whose avowed purpose is to understand all human behavior, motives, adaptations, morals, art, and social groupings. It is a price, too, that psychoanalysis pays for comprising several theories (metapsychological, clinical, and experiential), which were set forth over a period of three quarters of a century, each generation of analysts learning somewhat different versions. That is a lot of theory to keep in mind, sort out, and pick from when working with patients. Gestalt practitioners have no such ambitious goals as formulating a science, and their theory is by comparison compact and homogeneous.

Gestalt techniques were in part designed to counter alleged errors in psychoanalytic technique and theory. Gestalt criticisms can join with such revisionist trends within psychoanalysis as dropping the structural and economic points of view and emphasizing phenomenology, process, and experience—all of which have implications for change in technique. The gestalt challenge may serve as a helpful stimulus in reraising, in novel ways, issues of flexibility, empathy, concreteness, present-past emphasis, and the capacity and autonomy of the patient.

Corrections for Gestaltists and Others Whom It May Concern

One way psychoanalysts can contribute to gestalt therapy is to assert the need for an encompassing, differentiated theory of personality on which clinical sophistication and flexibility for differing clinical emergencies can be based. While for the most part I found gestalt therapists remarkably sensitive, selecting patient material and techniques that to my mind were responsive to the patients' needs, I have seen instances in which I thought a better over-all clinical understanding of patients, based in theory, would have increased the gestalt therapist's helpfulness to them.

In one such instance, a patient seemed to be smugly complacent about a way of life and kind of self that made others responsible for him and in which aggression was masochistically bound rather than constructively available. In my opinion the therapeutic task and ethical responsibility were to test the limits of his apparent contentment. If he really was without workable or usable conflict, then the therapist should not interfere with his chosen way of life, and in fact could not make headway with it anyway. Yet patients presenting themselves as satisfied frequently respond to probing diagnostic interventions by becoming anxious, and become aware that they wish they could feel and live differently. In this instance one such intervention could have been to confront the patient as to why he was participating in the gestalt-therapy workshop. But such an intervention could not be made when a perfectly acceptable reason for being there was simply to "enlarge awareness" or to "raise consciousness." As with any jargon, such phrases can obscure motives and deflect potentially unsettling intrusions. Moreover, as I ruefully found out, such confrontations were alien to the spirit of the therapy group and fell on unreceptive ears. This patient may go from one gestalt-therapy group to another, increasing his awareness and raising his consciousness, without ever coming to terms with the conflicts that, I suspect, are depriving him of choice as to his way of life.

In another example a woman portrayed herself as not being able to find a man who could provide her with as much joy as did her lover in the occasional moment when he had time for her. The therapist seemed to accept at face value that no other man in the world could satisfy her, ignoring the information that when she was not available, her lover's interest in her increased. In my opinion her need for such a sadomasochistic relationship is preventing her from finding other kinds of gratification. To suggest, as was done, that her task was simply to decide whether the joy she was able to get from this relationship was sufficient or not, and to proceed accordingly, could help spell the end to her stated hopes for marriage and motherhood.

I am concerned also about the casual attitude on the part of some gestalt workers toward shaky ego functioning —an attitude with the potentiality for injuring the patient through encouraging more psychological work than he can master. Their attitude may stem from an inability to assess such dangers, often a difficult task for anyone, no matter how well trained, which sometimes requires hours of psychological testing. Gestalt workers claim that the patient should be given credit for the ability to maintain himself. I think it is likely that there is a range of instances in which psychoanalytic clinicians might step in with support too soon, minimizing the patient's capacity to help himself. I think it is just as likely that there is a range of instances in which the patients cannot sufficiently help themselves, and if unsupported, needlessly develop symptoms, act on the environment in harmful ways, commit suicide, or become psychotic. I saw no such instances myself; indeed, I saw a gestalt therapist deal effectively with such a danger by unwinding the patient from an emotional pitch that threatened to get out of hand primarily through helping the patient to anchor himself in his bodily experiences. I do think, however, that some patients, if subjected to gestalt work without interpersonal or environmental supportive measures being available, would risk being harmed. Deciding if, when, and how such measures should be used seems to me to require a comprehensively trained clinician with a wide range of interpersonal or environmental options available.

Such clinical mistakes as I have suggested occurred should hardly be surprising. Gestalt therapists say, on paper, that they are in favor of systematic training of practitioners, and compared to some schools of psychotherapy they do have extensive training and high standards. However, compared to that of psychoanalysts, the training of gestalt therapists is limited, being shorter, less systematic, and providing less wide-ranging clinical experience. The surprising thing to me is not that there were occasional errors (or at least times when I felt at odds with the strategy and conclusions) but that I saw so few. Without adequate comparative studies, we are left with the questions about the usefulness, for the treatment of patients, of the therapist's knowing developmental theory, general psychology, the differing psychologies of men and women, psychopathology, and other aspects of psychoanalytic training. But the training issue cannot be solved without at the same time resolving questions of differing goals of the treater, and with respect to different capacities and wishes of the patient. Training has to be commensurate with task, although to ascertain what a particular therapeutic task should be ordinarily in itself requires considerable expertise.

A View from Above

We may ask ourselves in what way the over-all system, the culture, our world, is being served by the emergence of gestalt therapy and the many other therapies that have developed in recent years. We are encouraged to take this perspective by the fact that these therapies seem part of a cultural revolution; they are not just technical or scientific emendations and discoveries. One not only practices gestalt therapy instead of psychoanalysis, but often does it without shoes, using first names, with psychedelically inspired pillows, while being casual toward time boundaries, nourished by organic food, hostile toward material possessions and Western culture, and admiring abstemiousness and Eastern philosophy. In short, gestalt therapy is cresting a wave of frustration and revolt, of regret for the past, distrust of the present, and pessimism about the future, while at the same time formulating an optimistic response with ancient antecedents. The present generation of world citizens is the first to have been born into a world in which death to the whole community, from nuclear destruction, is always a hairbreadth away. Rather than being unduly fanciful, it seems parsimonious and hardheaded to me to understand current resentment of how we got here, and determination that the future will be different, with reference to this atmosphere of imminent extinction.

Psychoanalysis began as an intellectual rebellion, as a decisive new chapter in Western man's thoughts about his nature and the world in which he lives. But through its association with science and materialism and emphasis upon reason, psychoanalysis is seen as a social and administrative arm of the Western establishment; it is legally and socially sanctioned by it. As such, many people feel it is something to be rebelled against. In principle this should not matter. The substance of psychoanalysis still remains a powerful means of systematically understanding all of human nature. Psychoanalysis still offers the ultimate freedom that lies in being able to think all of one's thoughts and liberate all of one's behavior from constraints unknown to the person. Psychoanalysis is itself always in rebellion against much of what is wrong in our culture. Unfortunately, many workers in the human potential movement have only a smattering of knowledge about psychoanalysis, and they conflate its social and legal position with its substance. In large part, psychoanalysis has only itself to blame for this. Its exclusive training practices have made it impossible for many people interested in and capable of working psychologically with the human condition to learn psychoanalysis. That such people should find a new path, perhaps in part founded upon resentment at being excluded, is hardly surprising.

From a general systems point of view gestalt and the other new therapies have been used by the over-all system to bring about corrections, additions, and emphases beneficial to the whole of the science of human improvement and change. The human mind, scientific or otherwise, works in dialectical ways, polarizing, going from one extreme to the other. In sharp contrast to the "activity" of a traditional medical practitioner at the turn of the century, Freud discovered that "passivity" encouraged the emergence of information about the mind. Psychoanalysis is now identified with being passive, and may in some ways indeed be too much so. Also perhaps overestimated are such psychoanalytic discoveries as the importance of unconscious motivation and the influence of the past on the present. Within psychoanalysis the dialectical pendulum has been making its way back toward a more balanced view as analysts become more active, as they take multidetermination more seriously, and as they increase their recognition of the implications of autonomous ego functions, neutralized drives, manifest dream content, and the power of consciousness. Further rethinking and corrections are implicitly being offered by gestalt therapy, among others, as part of the over-all scientific system.

If any of us are to benefit from the ideas and experiences of others, then the whole has to be defined not as psychoanalysis alone, nor as gestalt therapy alone, but as knowledge. Only knowledge can unite disparate schools, techniques, and views of man and change. Only knowledge is boundaryless and infinite.

References

Part One

Chapter 1

1. Arthur Janov, *The Primal Scream* (New York: Dell, 1970).
2. Richard Corriere and Joseph Hart, *The Dream Makers: Discovering Your Breakthrough Dream* (New York: Funk & Wagnalls, 1977).

Chapter 2

1. Ram Dass, *The Only Dance There Is* (New York: Jason Aronson, 1976).

Chapter 3

1. Karl Menninger, "Hope," *American Journal of Psychiatry*, 116, 481–91, 1959.

Chapter 4

1. Ram Dass, *The Only Dance There Is* (New York: Jason Aronson, 1976).
2. Artie Shaw, *The Trouble with Cinderella* (New York: Collier Books, 1963).

Chapter 5

1. George Leonard, *The Transformation* (New York: Dell, 1972).
2. George Leonard, *The Ultimate Athlete* (New York: Viking Press, 1975).

3. Will Schutz, *Here Comes Everybody* (New York: Harper & Row, 1971).
4. Will Schutz, *Joy* (New York: Grove Press, 1967).
5. Wilhelm Reich, *The Sexual Revolution* (New York: Noonday Press, 1962).

Chapter 7

1. Joseph Sargent, "A Followup Evaluation of the Menninger Pilot Migraine Study Using Thermal Training," *Headache*, 17(5):198–202, 1977.
2. Patricia Norris, "Working with Prisoners, or There's Nobody Else Here," unpublished dissertation, 1976.

Chapter 8

1. Edwin Schur, *The Awareness Trap* (New York: Quadrangle, 1976).
2. Peter Marin, "The New Narcissism," *Harper's Magazine*, October 1975, pp. 45–56.
3. R. D. Rosen, *Psychobabble* (New York: Atheneum, 1977).
4. V. S. Naipaul, *India: A Wounded Civilization* (New York: Knopf, 1977).
5. Nadine Stair, "If I Had My Life to Live Over," *Association for Humanistic Psychology Newsletter*, July 1975, p. 2.

Part Two

Chapter 9

1. Sigmund Freud, "Project for a Scientific Psychology" [1895]. *Standard Edition*, 1 (London: Hogarth Press, 1966), 282–397.
2. Valerie Hunt, "A Study of Structural Integration from Neuromuscular Energy-Field and Emotional Approaches," unpublished manuscript, 1977.
3. Julian Silverman, *Confinia Psychiatrica*, 16:201–19, 1973.

Chapter 10

1. Nikolas Tinbergen, "Ethology and stress diseases," *Science*, 185:20–27, 1974.
2. Franklin Pierce Jones, *Audio-Awareness in Action: A Study of the Alexander Technique* (New York: Schocken Books, 1976).

3. W. H. M. Carrington, "The F. M. Mathias Alexander Technique," *Systematics*, 1(3):233–47, 1963.
4. A. Frank, "A Study in Infant Development," *Child Development*, 9(1):9–26, 1938.
5. Peter MacDonald, "Instinct and Functioning in Health and Disease," *The Alexander Journal*, 4:2–11, 1965.

Chapter 11

1. Wilhelm Reich, *Character Analysis* (New York: Farrar, Strauss & Cudahy, 1961).
2. Charles Rycroft, *Wilhelm Reich* (New York: Viking Press, 1969).
3. Wilhelm Reich, *Selected Writings* (New York: Farrar, Strauss & Cudahy, 1960).

Part Three

Chapter 12

1. Martha Seligson, *New Times*, Oct. 18, 1974.
2. Robert E. Ornstein, A *Self-Report Survey: Preliminary Study of Participants in Erhard Seminar Training* (San Francisco: *Est* Foundation, 1975).
3. Leonard L. Glass, Michael A. Kirsch, and Frederick N. Parris, "Psychiatric Disturbance Associated with Erhard Seminar Training: I. A Report of Cases," *American Journal of Psychiatry*, 134(3):245–47, 1977.
4. Earl Babbie and Donald Stone, "What Have You Gotten After You 'Get It'? An Evaluation of Awareness Training Participants," presented to the American Psychiatric Association, May 1976, Miami Beach.

Chapter 13

1. Newsletter, *Mind Control*, 5:5, 1974.
2. John Dollard and Neal Miller, *Personality and Psychotherapy: An Analysis in Terms of Learning, Thinking, and Culture* (New York: McGraw-Hill, 1950).
3. Bob Brier, Gertrude R. Schneidler, and Barry Sevits, "Three Experiments in Clairvoyant Diagnosis with Silva Mind Control Graduates," *Journal of the American Society for Psychical Research*, 69:263–71, 1975.

Part Four

Chapter 14

1. Swami Ajaya, *Yoga Psychology* (Chicago: Himalayan International Institute of Yoga Science and Philosophy of U.S.A., 1976).
2. Swami Ajaya (ed.), *Psychology: East and West* (Chicago: Himalayan International Institute of Yoga Science and Philosophy of U.S.A., 1976).
3. Swami Rama, *Yoga and Psychotherapy* (Chicago: Himalayan International Institute of Yoga Science and Philosophy of U.S.A., 1976).

Chapter 15

1. Loyd Silverman, "Unconscious symbiotic fantasy: a ubiquitous therapeutic agent," *International Journal of Psychoanalytic Psychotherapy*, 7, 1978 (in press).
2. Herbert Benson, *The Relaxation Response* (New York: William Morrow, 1975).
3. Adam Smith, *Powers of Mind* (New York: Random House, 1975).
4. Robert Keith Wallace (ed.), *Scientific Research on Transcendental Meditation* (Los Angeles: MIU Press, 1972).
5. Bernard Glueck, "Biofeedback and Meditation in the Treatment of Psychiatric Illnesses," *Comprehensive Psychiatry*, 16(4):303–21, 1975.
6. Robert Keith Wallace (ed.), *Scientific Research on Transcendental Meditation* (Los Angeles: MIU Press, 1972).
7. Cited in *Clinical Psychiatry News*, September 1977.
8. Ralph Greenson, "About the Sound 'Mm . . . ,'" *The Psychoanalytic Quarterly*, 23:234–39, 1954.

Part Five

Chapter 16

1. Stuart Miller, "A New Humanism in Medicine," *Synthesis*, Spring 1974.
2. George Leonard, "The Holistic Health Revolution," *New West*, May 10, 1976.
3. Irving Oyle, "Interview," by Alan Vaughan, *Psychic*, November/December 1976.

4. George Leonard, "The Holistic Health Revolution," *New West*, May 10, 1976.
5. George Leonard, "Beyond Getting Better," *The Graduate Review*, March 1977.
6. Stuart Miller, "A New Humanism in Medicine," *Synthesis*, Spring 1974.
7. a) *Pediatrics*, 60:304, 1977; b) *Demographic Yearbook*, 153–57, 1976.
8. As quoted by Shealy.
9. Irving Oyle, "Interview," by Alan Vaughan, *Psychic*, November/December 1976.
10. Donald Law, A *Guide to Alternative Medicine* (Garden City, N.Y.: Doubleday, 1976).
11. George L. Engel, "Enduring Attributes of Medicine Relevant for the Education of the Physician," *Annals of Internal Medicine*, 78:587–93, 1973.
12. Anonymous, "Directions in Medical Education," *The Esalen Catalogue*, October/December 1977.
13. Malcolm Todd, as reported in *Brain-Mind Bulletin*, 2:17, July 1977.
14. James Fadiman, Mind as Healer–Mind as Slayer Conference, Center for Integral Medicine, Pacific Palisades, Calif., 1977.
15. C. Norman Shealy, *Pain Game* (Millbrae, Calif.: Celestial Arts, 1976).
16. C. Norman Shealy, 90 *Days to Self-Health* (New York: Dial Press, 1977).

Chapter 17

1. Elisabeth Kübler-Ross, *Death and Dying* (New York: Macmillan, 1969).
2. Carl Simonton, Stephanie Matthews Simonton, and James Creighton, *Getting Well Again* (Los Angeles: Tarcher, 1978).
3. R. C. LaBarba, "Experiential Factors in Cancer: a Review of Research with Animals," *Psychosomatic Medicine*, 32:259–75, 1970.
4. V. Riley, "Mouse Mammary Tumors: Alterations of Incidence as Apparent Function of Stress," *Science*, 189:465–67, August 1975.
5. T. H. Holmes and M. Masuda, "Life Change and Illness Susceptibility." In *Separation and Depression, Clinical and Re-*

search Aspects. American Association for the Advancement of Science (Washington, D.C., 1973), 161–68.

6. Lawrence LeShan, "An Emotional Life-History Pattern Associated with Neoplastic Disease," *Annals of the New York Academy of Sciences*, 125:780–93, 1966.
7. C. B. Thomas and D. R. Duszynski, "Closeness to Parents and the Family Constellation in a Prospective Study of Five Disease States: Suicide, Mental Illness, Malignant Tumor, Hypertension, and Coronary Heart Disease," *The Johns Hopkins Medical Journal*, 134:251–70, 1974.
8. A. H. Schmale and H. Iker, "Hopelessness as a Predictor of Cervical Cancer," *Social Science and Medicine*, 5:95–100, 1971.
9. E. M. Blumberg, "Results of Psychological Testing of Cancer Patients." In J. A. Gengerelli and F. J. Kirkner (eds.), *Psychological Variables in Human Cancer* (Berkeley and Los Angeles: University of California Press, 1954), 30–61.
10. B. Klopfer, "Psychological Variables in Human Cancer," *Journal of Projective Technique*, *21*(4):331–40, 1957.
11. C. L. Bacon, R. Renneker, and M. Cutler, "Psychosomatic Survey of Cancer of the Breast," *Psychosomatic Medicine*, 6:453–60, 1952.
12. D. M. Kissen, "Lung Cancer, Inhalation and Personality." In D. M. Kissen and L. LeShan (eds.), *Psychosomatic Aspects of Neoplastic Disease* (Philadelphia: J. B. Lippincott, 1963), 3–11.
13. W. A. Greene, Jr., "The Psychosocial Setting of the Development of Leukemia and Lymphoma," *Annals of the New York Academy of Sciences*, 125:794–801, 1966.
14. J. I. Wheeler and B. M. Caldwell, "Psychological Evaluation of Women with Cancer of the Breast and of the Cervix," *Psychosomatic Medicine*, 17(4):256–68, 1955.
15. Hans Selye, *The Stress of Life* (New York: McGraw-Hill, 1956).
16. Arnold Hutschneker, *The Will to Live* (New York: Cornerstone Library, 1975).
17. Carl Simonton, Stephanie Matthews Simonton, and James Creighton, *Getting Well Again* (Los Angeles: Tarcher, 1978).

18. Stephen A. Appelbaum, *The Anatomy of Change* (New York: Plenum, 1977).
19. Stephen A. Appelbaum, "The Refusal to Take One's Medicine," *Bulletin of the Menninger Clinic*, 41:511–21, 1977.
20. Jeanne Achterberg, Stephanie Matthews Simonton, and O. Carl Simonton, "Psychology of the exceptional cancer patient: a description of patients who outlived predicted life expectancies," *Psychotherapy: Theory, Practice and Research*, 14, 416–22, 1977.
21. Personal communication.
22. Stephen A. Appelbaum, "Parkinson's Law in Psychotherapy," *International Journal of Psychoanalytic Psychotherapy*, 4:426–36, 1975.
23. George Barth, *Nova Yoga* (New York: New American Library, 1974).

Chapter 18

1. Gio B. Gori, "The Diet, Nutritions, and Cancer Program of the NCI National Cancer Program," *Cancer Research*, 35(11): 3445–47, November 1975.
2. Gio B. Gori, "Dietary Goals of the United States," Staff Publication of the Select Committee on Nutrition and Human Needs, U. S. Senate (Washington, D.C.: U. S. Government Printing Office, February 1977).
3. William Dufty, *Sugar Blues* (New York: Warner Books, 1975).
4. Michio Kushi, *The Teachings of Michio Kushi* (Boston: The East-West Foundation, 1972).
5. William Kelley, *One Answer to Cancer* (Beverly Hills, Calif.: Int'l Assoc. of Cancer Victims and Friends, Inc., 1974).
6. Peter Barry Chowka, "Money Talks," *East-West Journal*, 7(3): 30–31, March 1977.
7. "Stare vs. Mayer on Sugar and Health Food 'Faddists,'" *Better Nutrition*, 37, #10, 1977, 30–48.

Chapter 19

1. Linus Pauling and Ewan Cameron, *Proceedings of the National Academy of Sciences*, 37, #10, 3685–89, October 1976.

Part Six

Chapter 20

1. Jerome Frank, *Persuasion and Healing* (Baltimore: Johns Hopkins Press, 1961).
2. H. H. Strupp and S. W. Hadley, "A tripartite model of mental health and therapeutic outcome: with special reference to negative effects in psychotherapy," *American Psychologist*, 32:187–96, 1977.
3. a) Stephen A. Appelbaum, "The Dangerous Edge of Insight," *Psychotherapy: Theory, Research, and Practice*, 13:202–6, 1976.
   b) Stephen A. Appelbaum, *The Anatomy of Change* (New York: Plenum, 1977).
4. Stephen A. Appelbaum, "The Idealization of Insight," *International Journal of Psychoanalytic Psychotherapy*, 4:272–302, 1975.
5. Stephen A. Appelbaum, "Speaking with the Second Voice: Evocativeness," *Journal of the American Psychoanalytic Association*, 14:462–77, 1966.
6. Stephen A. Appelbaum, *The Anatomy of Change* (New York: Plenum, 1977).
7. Lawrence Kubie, *Neurotic Distortions of the Creative Process* (Lawrence, Kan.: University of Kansas Press, 1958).
8. Stephen A. Appelbaum, "Conscious Intention Revisited," *Psychotherapy: Theory, Practice and Research.* In press.
9. F. Scott Fitzgerald, *The Crack-Up* (New York: New Directions, 1956).
10. Shunryu Suzuki, *Zen Mind, Beginner's Mind* (Rutland, Vt.: John Weatherhill, 1970).
11. Roy Schafer, *New Language for Psychoanalysis* (New Haven, Conn.: Yale University Press, 1976).
12. Roy Schafer, *Language and Insight; the Sigmund Freud Memorial Lectures* (New Haven, Conn.: Yale University Press, 1978).
13. Allen Wheelis, "Will and Psychoanalysis," *Journal of the American Psychoanalytic Association*, 4:285–303, 1956.
14. Allen Wheelis, "The Place of Action in Personality Change," *Psychiatry*, 13:135–48, 1950.
15. Stephen A. Appelbaum, "A Therapist's Garden of Paradoxes."

In Sydney Smith (ed.), *The Human Mind Revisited; Essays in Honor of Karl A. Menninger* (New York: International Universities Press, 1978).

Chapter 21

1. F. Scott Fitzgerald, *The Crack-Up* (New York: New Directions, 1956).

Index

"Abnormality" ("normality"), 47–48, 61
Abraham, Karl, 183
Abreaction, 21, 23, 24. *See also* Catharsis
"Abstraction" ("generative principle"), *est* and, 214–15, 218
Acceptance of the patient, gestaltists and, 481–82
Action, role of, 435–36, 466–68, 478, 489
Acupressure, 117–18
Acupuncture, xvi, 41–42, 89, 116–18, 326, 332, 378
Addictions, 290, 296. *See also* specific kinds, therapies
"Adjusting," 72, 467–68
Adlerian psychology, 424
Aggression (aggressiveness), xxi, 31, 181, 227, 358, 496
Aging, 39, 86; diet and, 260, 403, 412
A. K. Rice Tavistock-Washington School of Psychiatry Group Relations Conferences, 233
Alcoholism (drinking), 446; behavior modification and, 32; and disease, 328, 375, 376, 400, 405, 409, 413
Alexander, F. M. (Alexander technique), xvi, 79, 90–92, 99, 118, 153, 157, 169–77, 457; evaluation of, 173–77; theory and technique of, 169–77
Allport, Gordon, 45
Aloneness. *See* Loneliness
Alpert, Richard, 55. *See also* Ram Dass
Alpha brain wave. *See under* Brainwave patterns
Altered states of consciousness (expanded consciousness), 97–98, 152, 428, 462, 470, 497 (*see also* Awareness; Consciousness); drugs and, 59, 62, 72; *est* and, 223; Mind Control training and, 243 ff.; Ram Dass and, 59–74; TM and, 290; yoga and, 271–72, 273, 277, 279, 288
Alternative vs. conventional therapies, 48–51 (*see also* specific aspects, concepts, kinds, problems, therapies); comparison and evaluation of, 417–68, 470–71, 475–501; gestalt therapy and psychotherapy compared, 433, 475–501; and medicine, 307–33, 334–72, 373–400, 401–14
Altruism, 27, 28, 82
American Cancer Society, 384, 388–92
American Center for the Alexander Technique, 79
American Indians, xii, 209

American Journal of Psychiatry, 233
American Medical Association, 323
American Psychoanalytic Association, 227, 233, 293, 307–8
Analytic Laboratories, 410 n
Anger, cancer and inability to express, 339
Antabuse, 32
Anxiety (fear), 30–31, 69, 72, 93, 311, 321, 328, 429–30, 435, 439–40, 463, 465, 489 (*see also* Phobias; Stress); behavior modification and, 30–31, 33–34; breathing exercises and, 271; TM and, 290, 299, 302, 303
Arthritis, 221, 311, 340, 377, 400, 404. *See also* Rheumatoid arthritis
Asanas, 269
Assertion training, behavior modification and, 30–31
Association for Humanistic Psychology (AHP), 103–9
Asthma, 340
"Astral sounds," 295
Astrology, 47, 51
Attachment. *See* Detachment
Auras, 118–21, 176, 182, 213, 261
Aurobindo Ashram, x
Autistic children, ix
Autogenic training, xvi, 129, 130
Automatisms, 33
Awareness (self-awareness), 11 ff., 80 ff. (*see also* Altered states of consciousness; Consciousness; Introspection; Mind; specific aspects, kinds, problems, therapies); bodily, 49, 50, 78, 87–90, 99, 145 ff.; descriptive, 82; *est* and, 202, 203–8, 214, 223; evaluation of new therapies and, 433–34, 438–39, 443 ff., 478 ff., 486, 491–93, 497 (*see also* specific problems, therapies); feeling therapy and, 23–24; gestalt therapy and, 11–16, 41, 42–43, 433–34, 438–39, 443 ff.; human potential movement and, 80–82 ff. (*see also* specific kinds); Ram Dass and expansion of, 56–74; Silva Mind Control and, 243 ff.; yoga and, 282–83, 286
Awareness Trap, The (Schur), 173

Babbie, Carl, 233–34, 504
Bacon, C. L., et al., 340, 507
Balancing the body chemistries, 407 ff., 457
Barron, Frank, xiii
Barth, George Francis, 364–66
Bates method, improving eyesight and, 327
BCG, 385
Beard, Peter, 120
Beer, use of, 405
Behavior, 4, 11, 19, 29–35, 71, 110–23 (*see also* Action; specific aspects, concepts, developments, kinds, problems, therapies); Alexander technique and, 174–75; choice and, 83 ff. (*see also* Choice); determinism and (*see* Determinism); *est* and, 203 ff., 230; evaluation of new therapies and changes in, 422 ff., 435 ff., 475–501 *passim* (*see also* Change; specific kinds, therapies); feeling therapy and, 23–24, 25; group (*see* Groups); modification therapy, 29–35; motivation and (*see* Motives); neurotic (*see* Neurosis); psychotic (*see* Psychosis); psychosynthesis and, 26–27; self-responsibility and (*see* Self-responsibility); Silva Mind Control and, 243 ff.; yoga and, 280–81, 283–88
Beliefs (belief systems), 465–66; *est* and, 202–3, 204, 210, 213–15, 216, 217, 218, 220, 240–41
Benson, Herbert, 293–94, 299
Bertalanffy, Ludwig von, 4
Better Nutrition, 403
Bible, the, 230, 242
Bibliotherapy, 346
Bioenergetics, xvi, 62, 70, 153, 157, 178–91, 451, 457, 481; evaluation of, 190–91; technique and theory of, 178–91

Biofeedback, xvi, 124–35, 148, 275; new therapies and, 313, 323, 327, 328, 332, 335 (*see also* Brain-wave patterns; specific aspects, problems, therapies)
Birth trauma, primal therapy and, 19, 21–22
Blame (blaming), 83–84, 138 (*see also* Self-responsibility); *est* and, 209
Blocks, body, Alexander technique and, 175–76
Blood pressure (high, hypertension), 19, 148, 169, 311, 322, 365; biofeedback and, 132, 133–34; TM and, 290, 297, 299; yoga and, 269–70
Blumberg, E. M., 340, 507
Bodily symptoms, human potential therapies and, 11, 18, 19–21, 24, 34, 49, 51, 70, 84–85, 91–92, 101, 145–68, 169–77, 297 (*see also* specific aspects, kinds, problems, therapies); alternative medicine and, 315 ff., 377 ff. (*see also* specific kinds, therapies); biofeedback and, 124–35, 148; choice and, 84–85; evaluation of new therapies and, 428, 451, 458–59 (*see also* specific problems, therapies)
Body (*see also* specific aspects, problems): bodily awareness, 49, 50, 78, 87–90, 99, 145 ff.; and bodily symptoms (*see* Bodily symptoms); and control (*see* Control); and exercise (*see* Exercise); and health (*see* Health); importance in human potential theory of, 49, 50; and mind dualism (*see* Body-mind split)
"Body, Mind, Spirit: Self-Unity" workshop (Lincoln, Nebr.), 95, 98–100, 212–13
"Body-Mind-Spirit" workshop (Dallas, Tex.), 77–94, 95
Body-mind split (body-mind unity), 110–23, 124–25, 146–51; alternative therapies and, 313, 316, 338, 495 (*see also* specific therapies); Cartesian dualism, 148, 278, 288; holism and (*see* Holism); Reich and, 183–84
Boston University Clinical Psychology Training Program, 373–74
Boyd, Doug, 125
Brain, the, 90, 97–98 (*see also* Brain-wave patterns; Consciousness; Mind); and body-mind dualism (*see* Body-mind split); split-brain hypothesis, 111–13, 278
Brain-Mind Bulletin, 111, 119, 366
Brain-wave patterns, 97; alpha, 243–44, 245, 256–57, 276, 297; beta, 243–44, 258–59; biofeedback and, 126–27, 129, 131–35, 297; Rolfing and, 160; TM and, 297
Breast cancer, 340, 375, 376, 382–87, 411
Breathing (breathing exercises), 11, 12, 70, 98, 145, 155, 165–66, 169, 184, 459, 460, 465; and altered consciousness, 98; emphasis of human potential movement on, 145, 155, 165–66; for meditation, 272; yoga and, 270, 271–72, 278
Brenner, Paul, 325
Bresler, David E., 325–26
Breuer, Josef, 18, 21
Brown rice, macrobiotic diet and, 377, 393
Bruyere, Rev. Rosalyn, 115, 383
Buddha, the, 62, 102
Buddhi, yogic, 285, 286
Burton, Lawrence, 385
Butter, use of, 330, 381, 408–9, 412, 414

Caffeine use. *See* Coffee
Caldwell, B. M., 340, 507
California State University, 29
Cancer, alternative medicine and therapies and, 24, 93–94, 121, 134, 245, 309, 311, 337–42, 373–400 (*see also* specific kinds); American Cancer Society and, 384, 388–92; diet (nutrition) and, 341, 374–400, 402, 403, 404, 407, 414; evaluation of, 357–72, 387–

400; immune system and, 341, 385, 387; meditation-visualization therapy and, 279, 280, 296, 335–38, 340–62, 363–64, 365–66, 368, 369, 370, 371, 373, 383, 388, 390–92; personality (psychological) factors and, 337–42; Reich and, 184; self-responsibility and, 340 ff., 354, 360, 363, 366, 391; will to have, 334–72 *passim*
Cancer Research, 375
Cardiovascular disease, 330, 376, 404, 409, 414. *See also* Heart disease
Carnegie, Dale, 230, 244, 444
Cartesian dualism. *See under* Body-mind split
Catharsis (*see also* Abreaction): primal therapy and, 18, 21
Cayce, Edgar, 326
Center for Feeling Therapy, 10, 11
Center for the Healing Arts (Los Angeles, Calif.), 121, 366–71
Center for Integral Medicine (Putnam, Conn.), 117–18, 320–27
Cervical cancer, 340
Chakras, 61–62, 182, 284–85, 287; yoga stages of, 284–85, 287
Change (changed behavior), human potential movement and, 46–48 ff., 56–75, 77 ff., 80 ff., 93 ff., 137, 339 (*see also* specific aspects, kinds, problems, therapies); behavior modification and, 29–35; body therapies and, 153 ff., 159 ff., 172 ff.; *est* and, 227–37; evaluation of new therapies and, 420 ff., 469–72, 475–501 *passim* (*see also* specific kinds, therapies); gestalt therapy and, 38–43, 488–90; nutrition and (*see* Nutrition); primal therapy and, 22; psychosynthesis and, 26; Ram Dass and, 64–75; TM and, 296–97, 304
Character Analysis (Reich), 183
Chemotherapy, 337, 341, 374, 385
Children: *est* and, 211; psychosynthesis and rearing of, 26; Silva Mind Control and, 243
Chitta, 286
Choice, freedom of (free will), human potential movement and new therapies and, 28, 83–87, 95, 391, 424 ff., 446, 449–50, 464 ff., 477 ff., 494–95; and determinism (*see* Determinism); *est* and, 209–10, 218, 221, 224–25, 228, 235; role of, 466–68; and self-responsibility (*see* Self-responsibility); Silva Mind Control and, 243
Cholesterol, 84, 330, 399, 407, 408–9
Chung-Liang Huang, Al, 80
Civil rights movement, xii–xiii, 45–46
Clairvoyance, 62
Clinical psychology. *See under* Psychology
Closure, therapy and, 491–93
Cobbs, Price, xiii
Coffee (caffeine), use of, 379, 386, 400, 401, 409, 413
Cognition, feeling and, 69–70. *See also* Intellectualization, therapy and
Colon cancer, 375–76
Communication. *See* Language (communication)
Communitas, xxi
Concentration, "one-pointed." *See* "One-pointed" concentration
Conditioning, behavior modification and, 30 ff.
Conflict: neurotic (*see* Neurosis); yoga and psychoanalysis and, 285–87
"Conscious Intention Revisited" (paper), 447–48
Consciousness, human potential movement and therapies and, xv, 12, 26, 46–47, 51–52, 56 ff., 80 ff. (*see also* Awareness; Mind; Unconscious, the; specific aspects, concepts, developments, problems, therapies); altered states of (*see* Altered states of consciousness); and alternative medicine, 315–16, 324–25, 327, 331, 338 ff.; "at

level," Silva Mind Control and, 245, 254 ff., 462; brain and (*see* Brain; Brain-wave patterns); criticism and evaluation of therapies and, 136–41, 428 ff., 443 ff., 478–501 *passim; est* and, 203–8, 214, 223, 230; higher (*see* Higher consciousness); meditation and (*see* Meditation); and unity of body and mind (*see* Body-mind split)
Control (self-control), 128–35, 284 (*see also* Choice; Power; Self-responsibility); biofeedback and, 128–35 (*see also* Biofeedback); *est* and, 217–18; Silva Mind Control and, 238–64
Conventional vs. alternative therapies. *See* Alternative vs. conventional therapies
Corriere, Richard, 23–24
Coué, Émile (Couéism), 364, 444
Counterculture, 8, 44–47, 49, 401 ff. *See also* Human potential movement; specific aspects, developments, individuals, movements
Cowles, Gardner, 196
Creativity, 134–35; *est* and, 218; healing and, 313, 329; Rollo May on, 96
Creighton, Jim, 350
Creighton, Maggie, 350
Criminal behavior, 86
Cripps, Sir Stafford, 170
Crying (tears), 180–81, 187, 189; gestaltism and, 13–14, 15, 16; primal therapy and, 18, 20
Cues, behavior modification and learning of, 32, 33, 34
Cures. *See* Healing; specific aspects, kinds, problems, therapies

Dairy products, use of, 413–14. *See also* specific kinds
Dallas, Tex., "Body-Mind-Spirit" workshop in, 77–94, 95
Dance (dance therapy), 11, 41, 47, 157
Darwin, Charles, 446
Davis, Adelle, 404
Death: cancer and will to have, 334, 337 ff., 347, 368–69, 387–88; choice and, 86; and "death counseling," 369; new therapies and, 210, 329, 421; and nuclear threat, 499–500; and reincarnation (*see* Reincarnation)
Decision making, problem solving and self-responsibility and. *See* Problem solving; Self-responsibility
Dental problems, diet and, 406–7, 408
Depression, 72, 132, 160, 311, 321, 328 (*see also* Anxiety; Despair); cancer and, 338–39, 341, 358, 373; diet and, 410–11; lithium and, 314; new therapies and, 429–30; TM and, 297; yoga and, 278
Deprivation, sensory-stimuli. *See* Stimulus-deprivation experiences
Descartes, René, and dualisms, 148, 278
Desensitization, behavior modification and, 30
Desirelessness, gestalt attitude of, 459–60. *See also* Detachment
Despair, 464 (*see also* Anxiety; Depression; Hope); and cancer, 341, 354; and growth, 72
Detachment (attachment), 62–64, 65, 97, 139, 464 (*see also* Desirelessness); *est* and, 208, 229; yoga and, 276–77, 279, 282–83, 286
Determinism, 60, 71, 478–79 (*see also* Choice); conditioning and, 30 ff.; *est* and, 209, 218, 221, 228, 229–30; karma and, 284
Dewey, John, 170
Diagnostic thinking, 452–54
Dickens, Charles, 73–74
Diet. *See* Nutrition
Disease (illness, sickness), 307 ff. (*see also* Health; specific aspects, conditions, kinds, problems, therapies); alternative vs. conventional medicine and therapies and, 307–33, 334–72, 373–400, 401–14, 470–71, 475–501; biofeedback and, 132–35 (*see also* Biofeed-

back); body awareness and, 146, 148–49; cancer and (*see* Cancer); choice and self-responsibility and, 84–86, 89–90, 91–92, 93–94, 95, 97, 340 ff.; energy fields and, 115–23; *est* and, 206–7, 232–33, 235–36; evaluation of new therapies and, 417–68 (*see also* specific aspects, problems, therapies); mind and, 148–49 (*see also* Mind; specific problems); nutrition and (*see* Nutrition); TM and, 290, 296
Distant healing, 325
Dollard, John, 504
Dreams (dreaming), 19, 25, 60–61, 113, 183–84, 428, 442, 461, 484–86; gestalt therapy and, 42–43; psychotherapy and gestaltism and, 484–86; symbols and (*see* Symbols)
Drinking. *See* Alcoholism
Drugs (drug use), 62, 72; and altered states of consciousness, 59, 62, 72; new therapies and, 310–11, 317, 323, 388, 446, 457, 458, 462
Dualisms (duality), 50–51, 111–13, 146–51. *See also* Splitting; specific kinds
Dufty, William, 379–80, 396, 405–6
Duszynski, D. R., 339, 507
Dynamic psychotherapy, 48

Eastern philosophy, religions, and traditions, x–xi, 48, 49, 62, 68, 73, 80, 115, 125, 138, 267–88, 464–65, 499. *See also* Oriental medicine; Yoga; specific concepts, developments, therapies
East-West Foundation, 376, 378, 394–99
East-West Journal, 378
Ecology therapy. *See* Kelley, William Donald
Edwards, Harry, 362–63
Eggs, use of, 381, 386, 397, 408–9, 412, 414
Ego, the, 285–86, 424, 451, 478, 497
Ego functioning, 497
Ego psychology, 424, 478, 497
Einstein, Albert, 316, 325
Emery, Stewart, 198–99, 201, 203–4, 231
Emotion. *See* Feelings; specific kinds, problems, therapies
Encounter groups (encounter experiences and therapy), xiv, xv, 10, 20, 78–79, 80 (*see also* specific groups, kinds, problems, therapies); *est* and, 203 ff., 233, 235; group dynamics and (*see* Groups); primal therapy and, 20
Energeticists, 114–23. *See also* Energy; specific therapies
Energy (energy fields), xvi, 88–89, 100, 114 ff.; and auras (*see* Auras); balancing, 121–22; bioenergetics and (*see* Bioenergetics); body as a congealing of, 315–16; body-mind unity and, 110–23; chakras (centers), 61–62; and healing, 115–23, 324–25, 326; new medicine and therapies and, 324–25, 326, 426; yoga and, 271, 278, 284–88
Engel, George L., 319, 506
Erhard, Werner, 195, 197–98, 201, 211, 212–19, 220, 222, 225, 229, 240, 241–42, 262, 280, 464. *See also Est*
Esalen Institute, x, xiii–xv, xviii, xxi, 11, 36, 40 ff., 73, 77, 94, 99, 141, 151 ff., 476
Esko, Edward, 378–79
Esophagus cancer, 375, 376
Essence, choice and reincarnation and, 86
Est (Erhard Seminar Training), xvii, 141, 195–237, 451; basic training, 198 ff.; concepts, 202–3 ff.; evaluation of, 227–37; *Graduate Review*, 198, 220, 221; graduate seminars, 118, 219; leadership mystique and, 197–98, 201, 216, 228, 235, 240; "processes" (exercises) in, 202–11, 212, 220, 223–27; psychic exercises, 223–27; Silva Mind Control compared to, 239–41; and training in prisons, 221–27

Evocativeness, therapy and, 434–35
Exercise (exercise therapy), 41, 51, 146, 458–59, 460, 465, 481; bioenergetics and, 186–88, 189; breathing (*see* Breathing); structural patterning, 164–68; yoga, 269 ff., 365
Existential psychoanalysis, 96
Expectation (*see also* Hope): reality and, 279–80
Experience (experiencing), xxi, 87, 97 (*see also* specific aspects, kinds, problems, therapies); emotional, gestaltists and, 488–90, 495; *est* and, 202, 203, 206, 213–16, 217–18, 220, 226, 229; evaluating new therapies and, 427 ff., 488–90; feeling therapy and, 24, 87; gestalt therapy and, 82–83; group (*see* Encounter groups); here-and-now (*see* Here-and-now, the); past (*see* Past, the)
Eyesight, Bates method to improve, 327

Fadiman, James, 323–24
Faith healing, 363. *See also* Psychic healing
Farson, Richard, 100
Fasting, 89–90, 98
Fat, dietary (fatty-acid deposits), 330, 375, 376, 377, 394, 399, 408–9, 414
Fear. *See* Anxiety
Feedback. *See* Biofeedback
Feelings (emotion), human potential movement and therapies and, 48–49, 51, 59–75, 83, 86 ff. (*see also* specific aspects, kinds, problems, therapies); behavior modification and, 30–35; bioenergetics and, 180–81, 184, 187, 189; body awareness and, 146–47, 148, 159, 161; breathing exercises and, 271; and cancer, 338 ff.; *est* and, 203, 214, 217; evaluation of new therapies and, 434 ff., 457 ff., 461, 464, 465–66, 468, 482–83, 488–90 (*see also* specific kinds, therapies); feeling therapy and, 22–25; gestalt therapy and, 41–43, 488–90; and healing, 313, 317; meditation and, 302; primal therapy and, 11, 16–22; psychosynthesis and, 26–28; Ram Dass and, 59, 69–75
Feldenkrais (Moshe) exercises, 80, 90, 99
Fifth Annual Southern California Conference on Behavior Modification, 29
Fisher, David, 32
Fitzgerald, F. Scott, 421, 455, 472, 510
Flexner report, 324
Flour, refined, white, 378, 386, 389, 400, 409, 413
Food (*see also* Nutrition): additives and preservatives, 341, 375, 377, 378, 402, 413
Food and Drug Administration, 392
Fool, the (foolishness), 78, 97
Forbes, Ed, 222
"Forces of Life" workshop (Lincoln, Nebr.), 95, 98–100
Free association, and "working" in gestalt therapy, 42–43, 486–88
Freedom (free will). *See* Choice
Freedom of Choice movement, 391
Freud, Sigmund, xxii, 18, 22, 23, 48, 60, 61, 67, 79, 110–11, 112, 114, 115, 147, 148–50, 176, 183, 185, 258, 397, 427, 446, 462, 478, 479, 480, 489, 491, 501 (*see also* Freudians); and mind-body controversy, 148–50; yoga and, 281, 284, 285, 286–87
Freudians, xvi, xvii, 23, 30, 110–11, 278. *See also* Freud, Sigmund
Friedman, Maurice, xiii
Fritzler, Dean, 335 n
Fromm-Reichmann, Frieda, 494
Fuller, Betty, 79, 89
Future, the. *See* Goals; Here-and-now, the; Expectation; Hope

Galen, 338

Games (game theory), *est* and, 199, 208, 224–25, 230
Geller, Uri, 120–21
Gerard, Robert, 26–27, 28, 123
Gerson therapy, 387
Gestalt Prayer, 138–40, 279
Gestalt therapy and therapists, xvi, xxi, 29, 35, 36–43, 63–64, 69, 70, 80, 138–40, 279, 280, 458, 459–61, 475–501; choice of therapists and, 424 ff., 494–95; and insights and interpretation, 433, 476–77, 489, 493; and psychotherapy evaluated and compared, 433, 475–501
Glueck, Bernard C., 297, 505
Goals (goal setting), 64, 69, 467–68 (*see also* Hope; Values); cancer and, 348, 352–53; new therapies and, 441–42, 491–93 (*see also* specific therapies)
God, 87, 215, 242, 302, 363, 386
Goldman, Sherman, 378
Goldstein, Kurt, 45
Goldwater, Barry, xii
Goodman, Jerry. *See* Smith, Adam
Goodman, Paul, 37
Gori, Gio B., 376, 508
Graphology, 47
Green, Alyce, 124, 125–35
Green, Elmer, 124–35
Green, Jerry, 313
Green, Judy, 125
Greene, W. A., Jr., 340, 507
Grof, Stanley, 98, 105
Groups (group dynamics and processes), 107–9, 396, 423–24, 480; encounter (*see* Encounter groups); *est* and, 233, 235; gestaltists and, 12–16, 41, 480
Guided imagery, 27, 134, 212, 230. *See also* Imagining; Visualization
Guilt feelings, psychosynthesis and, 26. *See also* Blame; Shame, feelings of
Gulliver's Travels, 55
Gurus, 283–84
Gustaitis, Rasa, xvii–xviii

Halifax-Grof, Joan, 97
Hampden-Turner, Charles, 104, 106
Happiness, 58, 69, 441 (*see also* Joy); *est* and, 205
Hart, Joseph, 23–24
Harvard University, ix, 299; Medical School, 395
Hatha-yoga exercises, 269–71, 365
Hayakawa, S. I., xiii
Headaches, 235–36, 297; biofeedback and, 132, 133, 323; migraine, 132, 133, 323
Healing, 308 ff. (*see also* Disease; Health; specific aspects, kinds, problems); alternative vs. conventional medicine and (*see* Alternative vs. conventional therapies); biofeedback and, 132–35; distant, 325; faith, 363; psychic, energy fields and, 115–23, 324–25, 326; Silva Mind Control and, 245, 246–56, 261–62
Health, 49, 50, 51, 85–86 (*see also* Disease; Healing; specific aspects, concepts, kinds, problems, therapies); Alexander technique and, 169–77; alternative vs. conventional medicine and, 307–33, 334–72, 373–400, 401–14, 470–71, 475–501; energies and, 115–23; evaluation of new therapies, 417–68 (*see also* specific problems, therapies); nutrition and, 373–400, 401–14; Rolfing and, 154–59; Silva Mind Control and, 245, 246–56, 260, 261–62; TM and, 290, 296–97, 299; yoga and, 269–70
Heart disease, 84, 85, 311, 319, 340, 368, 377. *See also* Cardiovascular disease
Hepatitis, 85
Herbs (herbal medicine), 313
Here-and-now, the, human potential movement and, 48, 82–83, 102, 137 (*see also* Past, the; Present, the); memory and, 479–80
Here Comes Everybody (Schutz), 79, 503

High blood pressure. *See* Blood pressure
Higher consciousness (*see also* Altered states of consciousness): TM and, 290; yoga and, 271–72, 273, 277, 279
Higher self, the, psychosynthesis and, 26, 28
Himalayan Institute (Glenville, Ill.), 267–68 ff.
Hinduism, 138
Hippocrates, 314, 319
Hodgkin's disease, 85, 407
"Holding" concept, *est* and, 213
Holism (holistic therapy), xxi, 312, 319, 321, 335
Homeopathy, 313, 402
Honesty. *See* Truth
Hope (hopelessness), human potential movement and therapies and, 51–53, 101, 420, 472 (*see also* Expectation); and cancer and immune activity, 340, 341, 353, 354, 355, 359; goals and (*see* Goals); yoga and, 281
"Hot seat," gestalt therapy and, 13–16, 42, 482–83, 486, 493
Howard, Jane, xvii–xviii
Hoxsey cancer treatment, 387
Huang, Al Chung-Liang, 80
Huggins, Hal, 330, 406–14
Humanism (humanistic psychology and values), 44–47, 64, 69, 70, 75, 77, 103–9; new therapies and, 313, 315, 317, 318 ff.; success and, 69, 70, 75
"Human Potentialities" (Huxley lecture series, 1961), x
Human potential movement, ix–xxii, 9 ff., 44–54, 55–74, 75 ff. (*see also* specific aspects, concepts, developments, individuals, movements, problems, therapies); conventional therapies vs., 48–53 (*see also* Alternative vs. conventional therapies); counterculture and, 44–47 (*see also* Counterculture); criticism and evaluation of, 136–41, 417–68, 475–501 (*see also* specific aspects, concepts, individuals, problems, therapies); emphasis on body-mind unity in, 110 ff.; gestaltism as central to, 36; gestaltism and psychotherapy compared, 475–501; oriental influence on, 381; use of term, 47; and workshops and meetings, 76–109; yoga compared to, 277 ff.
Humphrey, Loren, 358
Hunt, Valerie, 160
Hunzas, the, 260
Hutschneker, Arnold, 344, 507
Huxley, Aldous, x, 4, 45, 170
Hyperactivity, altered consciousness and, 98
Hypertension. *See* Blood pressure
Hypnosis (self-hypnosis), 59, 97, 116–17, 243–44, 258, 295, 325, 342. *See also* Suggestion

Iatrogenic-illness medicine, 311
Id (id psychology), 26, 285–86, 424, 451, 478
Iker, H., 339–40, 507
Illness. *See* Disease; Health; specific aspects, kinds, problems, therapies
Imagining (imagination), 92–93, 156–57, 171–72, 182, 313, 420, 468 (*see also* Visualization); guided, 27, 134, 212, 230
Immune system, and cancer, 341, 385, 387
India: A Wounded Civilization (Naipaul), 138
Indians. *See* American Indians
Insights (and interpretation), new therapies and, 432–34 ff.; gestalt therapy and psychoanalysis compared, 433, 476–77, 489–90
Insomnia (sleeplessness), 365, 407, 470; Alexander technique and, 169; *est* and, 207; TM and, 297
Instinct(s), 114, 175, 285–86, 478
Integral Psychology, 28, 122–23
Intellectualization, therapy and, 439. *See also* Cognition, feeling and
International Association of Cancer Victims and Friends, 384–85

International Meditation Society, 289
Introspection (self-analysis, self-discovery, self-reflection), 87, 282, 283, 303–4, 345, 349, 354, 365, 435–36, 439–40, 463–64. *See also* Awareness; Insights; Self-responsibility

James, William, 244, 364, 465
Janet, Pierre, 18
Janker Clinic (Bonn, Germany), 385
Janov, Arthur, 10, 11, 16–17, 20, 21, 22, 23, 189, 435, 465. *See also* Primal therapy
Jesus Christ, ideals of, 103
Johnson, Lyndon B., xii
Joy, Brugh, 324–25
Joy (enjoyment), xxi, 53, 58, 278, 326, 420–21, 442, 450, 456, 497. *See also* Happiness
Joy (Schutz), 79, 503
"Joy Is the Prize" (Litwak), xiv
Jungian psychology, 278, 424

Karma, 281, 284, 316, 326
Keen, Sam, 96–97, 100
Kelley, William Donald, and cancer and ecology therapy, 385–86, 388–89, 397; and Foundation of Life, 386 n; and Index of Malignancy, 386
Kennedy, John F., xii; Museum (Dallas, Tex.), 77–78
King, Martin Luther, Jr., xii, 45, 46
Kirlian photography, 115, 118–21, 213, 261, 316, 325
Kissen, D. M., 340, 507
Klein, Melanie, 285, 424
Klopfer, B., 340, 507
Koch cancer treatment, 387
Koestler, Arthur, 45
Koffka, Kurt, 38
Kohler, Jean, 374–76, 378, 395
Köhler, Wolfgang, 38
Koontz, Judith, 393 n
Krippner, Stanley, 105
Kubie, Lawrence, 61, 445
Kübler-Ross, Elisabeth, 335, 506
Kundalini energy system, 284–85
Kushi, Michio, 374–75, 376–79, 382, 390, 392–94, 397, 414; *Teachings of*, 380–81

Laing, R. D., 230
Language (communication), 72–73, 137; conventional medicine and, 314, 317; new therapies and, 441, 465
Laredo, Tex., Silva Mind Control International in, 238–64
Laying on of hands, healing and, 325
Learning, 78 (*see also* specific aspects, concepts, developments, kinds, problems, therapies); altered states of consciousness and, 258–59; behavior modification and, 29–35; biofeedback and, 127–35; *est* and, 207, 214–15, 219–20
Leavenworth Federal Penitentiary, *est* training in, xvii, 221–27
Leonard, George, ix–xxii, 57, 78, 95, 100, 102, 104, 105–6, 502, 506
Lerner, Max, xx
LeShan, Lawrence, 339, 507
Leukemia, 85, 340, 407, 408
Levitation, TM and, 300
Libido, 114, 115, 179–80, 185, 284–85
Lies (lying), *est* on, 202, 203, 217. *See also* Truth
Lilly, John, ix, 98
Lincoln, Nebr.: "Body, Mind, Spirit: Self-Unity" workshop in, 95–98; "Forces of Life" workshop in, 95, 98–100
"Listening with the third ear," 285, 462
Lithium, use of, 314, 411
Litwak, Leo, xiv
Livingston, Virginia, 385, 387
Loneliness (aloneness), 100, 427
Long, Ted, 222, 225
Look magazine, x, xiv, xvi, 78, 196
Love, 73, 97, 100, 104, 152, 331; altruistic, 28; *est* and, 195–96, 215; psychosynthesis and, 28

Lowen, Alexander, 179, 181–82, 186, 187, 188
LSD, use of, 62, 98
Lung cancer, 340, 395
Luthe, Wolfgang, 129
Lymphoma, 340

MacFadden, Bernarr, 267
Machines, people viewed as, *est* on, 209, 210
Macrobiotics, 374–82, 388, 389–90, 392–400 *passim*, 405, 412
Maharishi International University, 289, 290
Maharishi Mahesh Yogi, 291, 295
Mantras, xvii, 291–94; TM and, 291–94
Marijuana. *See* Pot smoking
Marin, Peter, 137
Martin, Bob, 13, 15
Maslow, Abraham, 45, 298
Massage, 41, 51, 117, 118, 141, 152 ff.; Rolfing and, 152 ff.; *Shiatsu*, 117, 118
Maugham, Somerset, xi, 267
May, Rollo, xiii, 45, 96, 100, 103, 104–5, 421
Mayer, Jean, 403
Mayman, Martin, v
Mead, Margaret, 4
Meat eating, vegetarianism and, 376 ff.
Medical schools and students, new therapies and, 316–18, 319–20
Medicine. *See* Alternative vs. conventional therapies; Disease; Health; specific aspects, concepts, problems, therapies
Meditation, 47, 51, 128–31, 132, 148, 203, 212, 236, 260, 323, 330, 458, 462–63, 464, 470; breathing exercises and, 272; and cancer therapy, 335, 337, 341 ff., 363, 364–65, 370, 373; mantras and, 291–94; relaxation and, 290, 292, 293–304; Silva Mind Control and, 243–44; TM and, 289–304 (*see also* Transcendental Meditation); yoga and, 268, 269, 272 ff., 282, 283
"Melodrama," Ram Dass on, 62–63
Memory (memories), 178, 244 (*see also* Past, the); body therapies and, 159, 161 (*see also* specific therapies); and the here-and-now, 479–80
Mencken, H. L., 230
Mendelsohn, Robert, 396
Menninger, Charles Frederick, 4
Menninger, Karl, v–vi, 4, 52
Menninger, Roy, vi, xix, 4–5, 196, 374
Menninger, Will, 4
Menninger Foundation, The, v–vi, xix, 3, 4–6, 10, 196, 374, 392, 453; East Campus, 124; School of Psychiatry, 5, 6, 320; Topeka Institute for Psychoanalysis, 5, 6; West Campus, 124 ff.
Menninger (C. F.) Memorial Hospital, 6
Mental health (mental disorders). *See* Mind; Neurosis; Psychosis; specific aspects, concepts, kinds, problems, therapies
Meridians, energy, 116
Migraine headaches, biofeedback and, 132, 133, 323
Miller, Neal, 504
Mind (*see also* Awareness; Brain; Consciousness; Unconscious, the; specific aspects, concepts, therapies): alternative medicine and therapies and, 315–16, 324–25, 327, 331, 338 ff.; and body dualism (*see* Body-mind split); Silva Mind Control and, 238–64; in TM, 294 ff.; in yoga and psychoanalysis, 286
"Mind as Healer–Mind as Slayer" conference, 320–29, 330
Mind Control. *See* Silva Mind Control
Mind Dynamics, 240
Minerals. *See* Vitamins and minerals
Monroe, Robert, 295
Mores (morals), 44, 45

Moss, Thelma, 119, 325
Motives (motivations), 69, 71 (*see also* Behavior; Change; specific aspects, kinds, problems); and cancer therapy, 358; and determinism (*see* Determinism); new therapies and, 422 (*see also* specific therapies); unconscious (*see* Unconscious, the)
Murphy, Gardner, xiii
Murphy, Michael, x–xi, xiii, xx–xxi
Muscles, body therapies and, 154 ff. *See also* Exercise; Relaxation; specific problems, therapies
Mysticism (the occult), 47, 67, 80, 138, 230, 281 (*see also* Psychic phenomena; specific aspects, concepts, individuals, kinds, movements); physics and, 287–88; pyramidology and, 261

Naipaul, V. S., 138
Narcissism, 63, 81–82, 137, 138–39
National Cancer Institute, 376, 388
National Federation of Spiritual Healers, 362
National Training Laboratories (NTL), 233
Nature (natural environment and resources), xxi, 45, 51
Naturopathy, 313
Neurosis (neurotic conflicts, neurotic patterns), 17, 20–22, 38–39, 41, 115, 139, 175, 203, 243, 285–87 (*see also* specific aspects, concepts, individuals, kinds, problems, therapies); acupuncture and, 41; evaluation of new and conventional therapies and, 417–68 *passim*, 475–501; gestaltism and psychiatry compared and evaluated, 475–501; nutrition and (*see* Nutrition)
"New age of man, the," 181–82
"New Narcissism, The" (Marin), 137
"Non-specific" factors, new therapies and, 425 ff.
"Normality" ("abnormality"), 47–48, 61
Norris, Patricia, 125, 134
Nova Yoga Center, 364–66
Nude bathing, 41, 151–52
Nutrition (diet, eating, food), human potential movement and new therapies and, 47, 51, 89–90, 101, 146, 260, 314, 317, 322, 326, 327, 330, 374–400, 401–14 (*see also* Overeating); and aging, 260, 403, 412; and cancer, 341, 374–400, 402, 403, 404, 407, 414; macrobiotics and, 374–82; orthomolecular psychiatry and, 403–4; yoga and, 273, 274–75
"Nutritional Approach to Cancer" conference, 394–99

Occult, the. *See* Mysticism
Ohsawa, George, 390
Onassis, Jacqueline, vi
One Answer to Cancer (Kelley), 385
"One-pointed" concentration: TM and, 294–95; yoga and, 274
Only Dance There Is, The (Ram Dass), 38, 53–54, 56–75 *passim*
Orgasm, 59; bioenergetics and, 185, 189; Reich and, 185
Orgone energy, Reich and, 184–85
Oriental medicine, 313–14, 326, 328, 374 ff., 392–400, 414 (*see also* Eastern philosophy, religions, and traditions; specific kinds, problems, therapies); Chinese, 328; and diagnosis, 393–94
Ornstein, Robert E., and *A Self-Report Survey: Preliminary Study of Participants in Erhard Seminar Training*, 231–33, 236
Orthomolecular psychiatry, 403–4
Overdetermination, 71
Overeating (obesity), 413; behavior modification and, 31, 32
Oyle, Irving, 116

Pain (misery, suffering), human potential movement and new therapies and, 18, 206, 287, 329, 420 ff., 470 (*see also* Anxiety; Stress; Traumas; specific aspects,

concepts, conditions, diseases, kinds, problems, therapies); bioenergetics and, 187–88; detachment and, 65; memory and (*see* Memory; Past, the); primal therapy and, 17–22; Rolfing and control of, 155–57
Pain and Health Rehabilitation Center, 329–30
Pancreatic cancer, 386
Paradox(es), 62, 72, 103; *est* and, 214, 215, 218, 230; Ram Dass and, 62, 72
Parapsychology, 125. *See also* Psychic phenomena; specific kinds
Parks, Mrs. Rosa, 46
Passive volition, biofeedback and, 131
Passivity, psychoanalysis and, 501
Past, the (past experiences), 196, 281, 284, 427–28 (*see also* Memory); detachment from, 65; feeling therapy and, 23–24; here-and-now and, 479–80 (*see also* Here-and-now, the); human potential movement and, 48, 56, 69, 137; primal therapy and, 17–22
Pasteur, Louis, 84
Pasteur Institute, 385
"Patients" ("patient" role), 47, 48
Pauling, Linus (Pauling Institute), 403–4
Pelletier, Kenneth R., 321–22
Penfield, Wilder, 148
Perception, 58, 60, 213
Perls, Fritz, xiii, 36–37, 38, 82, 488; and Gestalt Prayer, 138–40
Perls, Laura, 37–40, 146, 151, 488
Personality (personality factors): and cancer, 340, 349–52, 373, 397; new therapies and changes in, 427 ff., 441 ff. (*see also* Behavior; Change; specific aspects, kinds, problems, therapies); and therapist-patient relationship, 431–32
Personal relationships. *See* Relationships, interpersonal
Phobias (*see also* Anxiety; Neurosis; Psychosis): behavior modification and, 31
Photographs (photography): bioenergetics and, 182; Kirlian (*see* Kirlian photography); Rolfing and, 159, 163–64
Physicians, alternative vs. conventional medicine and therapies and, 307, 311, 312–14 ff.
Physics: Eastern mysticism and, 287–88; new, 418
Pierrakos, John, 179–82, 186
Pike, Bishop James A., xiii
Placebo influence, 425–26
Pleasantness (unpleasantness), conditioned behavior and, 30
Please Touch (Howard), xvii–xviii
Poetry (poetic feelings), 70, 73
Polyclinic Medical Center (Harrisburg, Pa.), 119
Positive thinking: cancer and, 386, 444, 464–65; Dale Carnegie and, 230, 244, 444; Silva Mind Control and, 242 ff.
Pot smoking, 103, 104
Power (potentiality), human potential movement and, 52–53, 61, 100–1, 102, 105–6 (*see also* Energy; Will [will power]; specific aspects, concepts, kinds, therapies); cancer and, 342 (*see also* specific therapies); *est* and, 219; of mind (the unconscious), 447, 448 ff. (*see also* Unconscious, the)
Powers of Mind (Smith), xvii–xix, 293–94
Prairie View Hospital (Newton, Kans.), 351–52
Prana (energy), 271, 284
Pranayama (science of breathing), 271–72
Prayer(s), 325, 363; meditation and, 301
Present, the, 56, 65, 68 ff., 102, 137 (*see also* Here-and-now, the; Memory; Past, the); *est* and, 196, 215, 217
Prestera, Hector, 41–42
Prevention magazine, 322, 404

Pribram, Karl, 4, 79
Primal scream, 17, 20–21, 70, 180–81, 189, 465, 468
Primal Scream, The (Janov), 11
Primal therapy, 10–11, 16–22, 23, 24, 25, 29, 70, 188–89, 451, 458
Primary-process thinking, 60
Problem solving, 140, 354, 478, 490 (*see also* specific aspects, concepts, therapies); behavior modification and, 32–33; *est* and, 205–8, 230–31; self-responsibility and (*see* Self-responsibility); Silva Mind Control and, 241–42, 244–45 ff.
Project for a Scientific Psychology (Freud), 150, 503
Psychedelics, altered consciousness and, 98. *See also* Drugs
Psychiatry. *See* Psychotherapy (psychiatry)
Psychic energy, 114–23. *See also* Energy; Psychic healing; Psychic phenomena; specific kinds, uses
Psychic healing (spiritual healing), 115–23, 324–25, 326, 362–64, 383, 385. *See also* specific therapies
Psychic phenomena, 51 (*see also* Mysticism; Parapsychology; Psychic energy; Psychic healing; specific kinds, uses); Silva Mind Control and, 240, 246 ff., 263; yoga and (*see* Yoga)
Psychoanalysis, xvi, xvii, 3–4, 5, 6, 7–9, 11, 21, 26, 29–30, 36, 43, 48–50, 65 ff., 84–85, 97, 102, 112–13, 122, 133, 156, 237, 446–47 (*see also* Psychotherapy; specific aspects, concepts, developments, individuals, problems); and alternative therapies compared and evaluated, 307–8, 417–68, 475–501 (*see also* specific aspects, therapies); bioenergetics and, 178–91; choice of analysis and, 424 ff., 494–95; *est* and, 227, 229, 233; and gestaltism evaluated and compared, 475–501; Reich and, 183–84; Rolfing and, 160–63; Silva Mind Control and, 257–60
Psychobabble (Rosen), 137
Psychological problems. *See* Health; Neurosis; Personality; Psychosis; specific aspects, concepts, individuals, kinds, problems, therapies
Psychology, 5, 6, 21, 36, 67–68, 78, 113, 122, 134, 150 (*see also* Psychoanalysis; Psychotherapy; specific aspects, concepts, individuals, kinds, problems); clinical, 5, 6, 21, 36, 67–68, 71, 124, 308, 423 ff., 453–54; humanistic (*see* Humanism); new therapies and, 412 ff. (*see also* specific aspects, therapies); yoga and, 268, 275
Psychosexual stages, gestaltism and, 488
Psychosis (psychotics), 22, 59, 60–61, 160, 209–10, 233, 498. *See also* specific kinds, therapies
Psychosomatic diseases, 85, 340. *See also* specific aspects, kinds
Psychosynthesis, 11, 25–28, 279
Psychotherapy (psychiatry), x, 5, 6, 8, 12, 16, 29–30, 33–34, 36, 47–48, 49, 52–53, 66 ff., 93–94, 113, 155 ff., 317, 318, 422 ff., 474 (*see also* Psychoanalysis; specific aspects, concepts, kinds, therapies); Alexander technique and, 172, 173, 175, 176–77; bioenergetics and, 178–91; and cancer, 309, 334–35, 336, 344, 359–60, 369–70; "conventional" vs. human potential therapies and, 48–53, 475–501 (*see also* specific therapies); evaluation of new therapies and, 418–68, 475–501; and gestalt therapy evaluated and compared, 433, 475–501; orthomolecular, 403–4; Rolfing and, 155, 159–62; TM and, 303–4; yoga and, 281–88
Pulse rates, primal therapy and, 19
Punishment or reward, behavior modification and, 30
Pyramidology, 261

Rama, Swami, 125–26, 127

Ram Dass, 38, 53–54, 55–75, 230, 267, 464
Rank, Otto, 21
Reality, new therapies and, 81, 82–83, 343, 345, 349, 420, 468 (*see also* specific aspects, therapies); *est* and, 208, 213, 229; yoga and, 279, 280
Reductionism, 51, 71–72, 319
Referrals (recommendations), choice of new therapies and, 456–57
Reflexology, 378
Reich, Wilhelm, 62, 105, 114, 115, 179, 183–85, 186
Reincarnation, 51, 80, 86, 95, 101, 281, 325
Reinforcement, behavior changes and: *est* and, 202, 224; reward or punishment and, 30
Relationships, interpersonal, 87, 243 (*see also* specific aspects, kinds, problems); authenticity in, 436–37; and cancer, 339–40, 348–50; *est* and, 211, 232–33; evaluation of new therapies and, 312–13, 322, 423, 431–33, 436–37, 468, 488, 489; role playing and (*see* Roles); therapist-patient, 431–33, 436–37, 493–94
Relaxation: and cancer, 341, 365; TM and, 290, 292, 293–304; yoga and, 271, 278
Relaxation response, Benson's, 293–94, 299
Religions, 421. *See also* God; Jesus Christ; specific religions
Repression(s), 468 (*see also* Feelings); feeling therapy and, 24; therapy and overcoming of, 434
Resistance, gestalt therapy and, 460, 482–84, 492; "going with," 483–84
Responsibility, personal. *See* Self-responsibility
Reward or punishment, behavior modification and, 30
Rheumatoid arthritis, 91–92. *See also* Arthritis
Rhine, J. B., xiii
Rice. *See* Brown rice
Riesman, David, 45
Robertson, Cliff, 23, 24
Rodale, Robert, 322
Rogers, Carl, ix–x, xiii
Roles (role playing), 31, 44, 279, 287; and disease and new medicine, 340, 348–50, 361; *est* and, 218, 219
Rolf, Ida, 158–59, 172
Rolfing (structural integration), xvi, xxi, 41, 70, 118, 141, 148; evaluation of, 159–68 *passim;* structural patterning and, 160–68; technique and theory of, 153–59, 366, 449, 457
Rosen, R. D., 137
Rosenberg, Jack, 197. *See also* Erhard, Werner
Rubenfeld, Ilana, 169–72

Sachs, Hanns, 147
Salk, Jonas, 86
Samadhi, 271
Sargent, Joseph, 133
Sarvangasana (hatha-yoga exercise), 269–71
Satir, Virginia, xiii
Schafer, Roy, 478
Schizoidness, 63
Schizophrenia, 403–4
Schmale, A. H., 339–40, 507
Schultz, Johannes, 129
Schur, Edwin, 137
Schutz, Will, xiii, xiv, 78–79, 81, 82, 83–86, 89, 95, 99, 100, 503
Schwarz, Jack, 126–27, 131
Science of Creative Intelligence, 289. *See also* Transcendental Meditation
Screaming. *See* Primal scream
Self, the (*see also* Ego, the): psychosynthesis and, 27–28
Self-actualization, TM and, 298
Self-help (*see also* specific problems, therapies): 50, 51, 498; Silva Mind Control and, 243, 244 ff., 263; TM and, 304; visualization

and meditation in cancer and (*see under* Visualization)
Self-Help Education program, 351
Selfishness, 81–82, 138–39
Self-reflection (self-analysis). *See* Introspection
Self-responsibility, decision making and, xxi, 46, 64, 79, 83, 84–86, 138–40, 280, 449 ff., 464, 465–68; alternative medicine and therapies and, 312–13, 340 ff., 354, 360, 363, 366, 391 (*see also* specific aspects, problems, therapies); and cancer, 340 ff., 354, 360, 363, 366, 391; choice and (*see* Choice); control and (*see* Control); *est* and, 206–7, 221, 229, 234, 235; gestalt therapy and, 495
Seligson, Marcia, 227
Selye, Hans, 323, 341
Sensory deprivation. *See* Stimulus deprivation experiences
Seventh-Day Adventists, 376
Sex (sexuality, sexual activity), xii, 57, 59, 105–6, 446, 459; bioenergetics and, 179–80, 184, 185, 189; body attitudes and, 147, 152; *est* and, 211; gestalt therapy and, 488; libido (energy) and, 179–80, 185, 284–85 (*see also* Libido); and orgasm (*see* Orgasm); and power, 105–6
Sexual Revolution, The (Reich), 105
Shame, feelings of, 69. *See also* Blame; Guilt feelings
Shaw, Artie, 57
Shaw, George Bernard, 170, 230
Shealy, C. Norman, 329–30, 406, 506
Shectman, Fred, vi
Shiatsu massage, 117, 118
Shri Swami Rama, 267–68
"Sick" ("well"), 47–48
Sickness. *See* Disease; Healing; Health; specific aspects, kinds, problems, therapies
Silence, 476; yoga and, 276–77, 282
Silva, José, 238, 240, 241–44, 253–54, 262. *See also* Silva Mind Control
Silva Mind Control, xvii, 118, 238–64, 451, 462; and *est* compared, 239–41; graduate seminars, 260–64; and healing, 245, 246 ff.; and leadership, 240; and problem solving, 241–42, 244–45 ff.; and "processes" (exercises), 240, 244 ff.; and psychic phenomena, 240, 246 ff.
Silverman, Beverly, 153–57, 159, 171
Silverman, Loyd, 293, 505
Simonton, O. Carl, 279, 280, 295, 335–38, 340–62, 363–64, 365–66, 368, 369, 370, 371, 383, 388, 390–92
Simonton, Stephanie Matthews, 279, 280, 295, 335, 336–38, 340–62, 363–64, 365–66, 368, 369, 370, 371, 383, 388, 390–92
Skinner, B. F., ix, xiii
Sleep (*see also* Insomnia): Alexander technique and, 169; deprivation experience, 98; TM and, 290, 295, 297
Smith, Adam (Jerry Goodman), xvii–xix, 293–94
Smith, Brewster, 105
Smith, Sydney, vi
Smoking (nicotine), 328, 341, 395, 409, 413 (*see also* Pot smoking); stopping, 31, 244
Social problems (social action), human potential movement and, 45–47, 137–41; *est* and, 205; Silva Mind Control and, 241–42
Social roles. *See* Roles
Sonopuncture, 117
"Space," *est* and, 196, 207, 209, 215, 223, 225
Speizer, Frank, 395–96
Spencer Foundation, 4
Spirit doctors, 363
Spiritual healing. *See* Psychic healing
Splitting (split thinking), 48–49. *See also* Dualisms; specific kinds, e.g., Body-mind split

Sports, 47
Stair, Nadine, 142
Stare, Frederick J., 389, 403
Starr, Larry, 91
Stevenson, Adlai E., III, 289–90
Stimulus-deprivation experiences, 97–98, 282; feeling therapy and, 24; primal therapy and, 18, 22
Stomach cancer, 375, 376
Stone, Donald, 233–34, 504
Stone, Harold, 121–22, 366–71; "From Cure to Transformation" by, 368–69
Stress (tension), 322 (*see also* Anxiety; specific kinds, problems, therapies); cancer and, 335, 339, 341, 365, 370, 397; and disease, alternative medicine and, 322, 323, 328–29, 335, 341
Structural integration. *See* Rolfing
Structural patterning, 160–68
Students International Meditation Society, 289
Sublimation, 72, 285
Success: *est* and, 199; Silva Mind Control and, 238–64; as a value, 70, 75
Suffering. *See* Pain; Traumas; specific aspects, kinds, problems, therapies
Sugar, refined, 378, 379–80, 381, 386, 389, 400, 401, 403, 405–6, 409, 413, 414
Sugar Blues (Dufty), 379–80, 396, 405–6
Suggestion (self-suggestion), 365, 425–27 (*see also* Hypnosis); alternative medicine and, 359, 411, 425–27; *est* and, 230, 233; placebo influence and, 425–26
Suicide, 498; cancer as a form of, 340, 373
Sullivan, Harry S., 424, 494
Superconscious, the, 26
Superego, the, 451
"Surveillance theory," cancer and, 340–41
Suzuki, Shunryu, 464, 509
Swanson, Gloria, 379
Swimming, 11, 41; nude, 41, 151–52
Symbols (symbolism), 19, 113, 213, 214, 478, 484
Symptoms, bodily. *See* Bodily symptoms; specific aspects, kinds, problems, therapies
"Symptom substitution," 34

Talent, therapy and therapists and, 430–31
Tale of Two Cities, A (Dickens), 73–74
Tantra yoga, 286
Taoist medicine, 326
Tears. *See* Crying
Technology (civilization, consumption, machines, production), xxi, 56–59; body attitudes and, 147, 151; cancer and, 353–54; health care and, 319
Telepathy, 62
Television, 24
Temperature, body, primal therapy and, 19
Tests (testing), psychological, 453–54
"Therapy," use of term in human potential movement, 47
Thinking (*see also* Brain; Consciousness; Mind; specific aspects, concepts, kinds, developments, therapies): diagnostic, 452–54; linear (rational), 60; primary-process, 60; split, 48–49 (*see also* Dualisms; specific kinds)
"Third ear" ("third eye"). *See* "Listening with the third ear"
Thomas, C. B., 339, 507
Time, gestaltists and psychotherapists and, 490–91
Tinbergen, Nikolas, 169–70
Titus-Maxfield, Meredith, vi
TM. *See* Transcendental Meditation
Tobacco use. *See* Smoking
Todd, Malcolm, 319
Tomkins, Calvin, xi
Torture, and altered consciousness, 98
Touching, Alexander mode of, 176

Toxins, diet and, 89–90, 377 ff.
Trace-element metabolism, 407–8
Tranquilizers, use of, 462–63
Transcendental, the, 105; altered states of consciousness and (*see* Altered states of consciousness) higher consciousness and (*see* Higher consciousness)
Transcendental Meditation (TM), xvii, 289–304; and higher consciousness, 290; and mantras, 291–94; meditation in, 290, 292, 293–304; psychotherapy and, 313–14; and relaxation and, 290, 292, 293–304; World Plan Executive Council, 290
Transference, therapy and, 439–40, 461–62, 491, 493–94
"Transformation," Leonard on, 57, 78, 92
Transformation, The (Leonard), 78
Transpersonal sense, psychosynthesis and, 28
Traumas, 68 (*see also* Pain; specific kinds, problems, therapies); Alexander technique and, 174–75; bioenergetics and, 179–80; birth, 19, 21–22; primal therapy and, 19
Travis, John, 328–29
Trouble with Cinderella, The (Shaw), 57
Truth (honesty), 81, 82 (*see also* Lies; Reality); *est* and, 218; and evaluation of new therapies, 419, 424; yoga and psychoanalysis and, 287
Tulsa (Okla.) Psychiatric Center, 185–86
Turning On (Gustaitis), xvii–xviii
2001: *A Space Odyssey*, 55

UCLA, 22, 25–26, 27, 119; Brain Research Institute of, ix; Movement Behavior Laboratory, 160
Ulcers, 340
Ulene, Arthur, 322–23
Ultimate Athlete, The (Leonard), 78
Unconscious, the (unconscious mind, unconscious motivation, unconscious processes), 131, 175, 183–84, 263, 281, 287, 380, 413, 478 (*see also* specific aspects, concepts, developments, individuals, problems, therapies); and cancer, 361–62; evaluation of new therapies and, 428, 434–35, 437–38, 442, 443 ff., 478, 494; new therapies and, 131, 175, 183–84, 263, 281, 287, 380, 413, 428, 434–35, 437–38, 442, 443 ff., 478 (*see also* specific aspects, problems, therapies)
Up to Your Ass in Aphorisms (Erhard), 195

Values, human potential movement and, 44–47, 64, 69, 70, 75, 77, 105–6; alternative medicine and healing and, 313, 315, 317, 318, 319, 327, 402; *est* and, 203; humanistic (*see* Humanism); Silva Mind Control and, 241–42; success and, 70, 75
Vegetarianism, 376 ff.
Vietnam War, xii, 45, 46, 104
Visualization, 134, 313, 426 (*see also* Guided imagery; Imagining); cancer and, 335, 337, 341 ff., 363, 364–65, 373 (*see also under* Cancer); *est* and, 236; Silva Mind Control and, 244–45, 247–56
Vitamins and minerals, use of, 39, 387, 403–5, 409; A, 375, 404; B complex, 404; C (ascorbic acid), 375, 403, 404; E, 408; megavitamins, 403–4
Voice, the: Alexander technique and, 157, 173; bioenergetics and, 180–81, 189; Rolfing and, 157

Wallace, Robert Keith, 297
Walters, Dale, 125
Washington, University of, ix
Watergate, xii
Watts, Alan, xiii, 80, 230
Weight, body, 413; behavior modification and, 31, 32

Wellness Resource Center, 328–29; Health Hazard Appraisal, 329
Western Behavioral Sciences Institute (La Jolla, Calif.), ix–x
Wheeler, J. I., 340, 507
Wheelis, Allen, 406, 478
Wilde, Oscar, 230
Will (will power), 86, 365, 478, 489; choice and (*see* Choice, freedom of); psychosynthesis and, 28
Will to live (will to die), 344 ff.; cancer and, 334 ff., 370
Will to Live, The (Hutschneker), 344
Wing, Heather, 163–64
Wolpe, Joseph, 30
Woollcott, Phillip, vi
"Working through," therapy and, 438–40
Workshops (meetings), human potential movement and, 76–109. *See also* specific groups, kinds, movements, places
Worry. *See* Anxiety; Stress

Yoga (yogis), 125–26, 128, 132, 139, 148, 243, 267–88, 341, 364–65, 426, 447, 451, 452, 468; asanas, 269; "encounter workshops," 275; exercises, 269 ff.; and higher consciousness, 271–72, 273, 277, 279, 288; human potential movement and, 278 ff.; meditation and, 268, 269, 272 ff., 282, 283; and psychoanalysis, 276–77, 279, 281–88
Yogi, Maharishi Mahesh, 291, 295
Yontef, Gary, 11–12, 13
Youmans, Randy, 241, 242